Genealogy of Batdorf, Wert, Peters, Row, Welker, Swartz, Schupp, Frantz, Steiner, Messerschmidt, Faber, Wertz, Rudy(3), Gieseman, Weiss, Jury, Schrot, Miller(2), Garman, Traut, Shirk, Gruber et al

Thompson Family History v. 2 of Baden-Wurttemberg, Hesse, & Rhineland-Palatinate, Germany; Berne, Switzerland; and Berks, Dauphin, Lancaster, Lebanon, Mifflin, Northumberland & Union Counties, PA

MARC D. THOMPSON

Family histories require constant revision. As this century moves along, more and more information becomes digitally or electronically disposable. If we do not save this information, it may be lost forever. Please contact author with any corrections or additions, marc@VirtuFit.net.

ISBN: 978-0-9883440-1-3

Photography by Marc D. Thompson

MARC D. THOMPSON - VIRTUFIT.NET®
www.VirtuFit.net - marc@VirtuFit.net
Skype: VirtuFit
Ideafit: www.ideafit.com/profile/marc-d-thompson

Also by Author

Genealogy of Thompson, Hensel, Goodman, Updegrove…, © 2013, 978-0-9883440-4-4

Virtual Personal Training Manual, © 2013, 978-0-9883440-9-9, https://www.createspace.com/4428594

Poems...Of Eternal Moments, © 2012, 978-0-9883440-8-2, https://www.createspace.com/3905443

The Fitness Book of Lists, © 2012, 978-0-6156563-0-4, https://www.createspace.com/4007866

Genealogy of Romano, Disimone, Vitale, Viviano..., © 2012, 978-0-9883440-6-8, https://www.createspace.com/4011878

Fitness Quotes of Humorous Inspiration, © 2011, 978-0-9883440-8-2, https://www.createspace.com/4052242,

Genealogy of Wittle, Acri, Stewart, Barbuscio..., © 2011, 978-0-988-3440-5-1, https://www.createspace.com/4040063

Genealogy of Mazo, Curry, Thompson, Mason..., © 2010, 978-0-988-3440-7-5, https://www.createspace.com/4005580

Thompson Family History, © 2005, 978-0-9883440-4-4

Dedication

This book is fondly dedicated to

my father, Gerald G. Thompson.

Foreword

I, like Marc D. Thompson, am a direct descendent of our Valentine Welker born about January 11, 1755 in Frankenthal, the son of John Theobald Welker and wife Johanna Margarethe Schaffer. According to IGA Records Valentine came to America on the ship Crawford, arriving in Philadelphia October 16, 1772, and gave his oath of allegiance December 29, 1772 in Philadelphia.

According to Early Pa Marriages, Valentine met and married Susannah Jory, the daughter of Abraham Shora and his wife Catherine Guerne, in Lykens Valley in 1783. They had ten children. My ancestor's second son Johannes Wilhem, and wife Susannah Schoffstall, had seven children, my 3Great-Grandfather Jonas Welker being the oldest.

My interest in my family history began when my father Bill Eugene Welker's mother Hazel Cook Welker passed. In going through her photos I found a photo from 1938 taken in Table Rock, Adams County, PA. I found out my grandfather Clarence Lungrin Welker was born and christened in Wiconisco, Dauphin County, PA and was one of seventeen children! It was then I began an exciting adventure of discovery.

I began contacting cousins I had never met gathering family stories and their branches of our family tree. Many decades and many counties later, I now have my own personal library of over 100 books and copies of books from which I help others looking for information on their own ancestors.

In my years of researching, I have met the most nicest and helpful unrelated and related people. The motto of a family historian is always keep researching for we are all related somehow and we are all family. Marc was one of my first contacts over fifteen years ago when I began my journey. We are lucky to have someone with Marc's credentials and expertise compile and publishing this information.

--Cynthia Welker-Maloney

Preface

Our 30 years journey of knowledge has led to a plethora of information. We have learned much. We have discovered our roots, good and bad. It has molded us. We have found we are related to some famous and infamous folks and there are some areas of the country that are named for our distant families.

We are direct-line descendants of King Philip of France and the Royal families Cleves. We are descended from Civil War servicemen Elijah Anderson, Thomas E. Batdorf, Andrew G. Hensel, Daniel Updegrove, John H. Wert, Louis L. Stewart and Jacob Wittle, War of 1812 servicemen Adam Frantz and Andrew Hensel, and Revolutionary War servicemen William Anderson, John Daniel Angst, Philip Jacob Bordner, Peter Brown (British), John Faber, Casper Hensel, John George Herrold, Jacob Lehman, Michael Leymon, Andrew Messerschmidt, John Miller, John Balthaser Romberger, Jonas Rudy, John George Schupp, John Peter Shaffer, John George Felten and Gottleib Zink. Our ties also include European Mayors John Guerne and John Emmerich, religious leaders John Peter Batdorf, John Batdorf, John George Bager Jr., John George Bager Sr., John Heilferich Lotz , George Gaukel and Entrepreneur Alexander Thompson.

We are direct-line descendants of the some famous homesteads and locations, including the George Bager Homestead, Abbottstown, PA, the Chris Miller Homestead, North Lebanon Township, PA, the George Mennig (Minnich) Homestead, PA,the Thomas Benfield homestead, Berks Co., PA, the Livesey Homestead, Philadelphia, PA, and the Wirth Homestead, Lykens Valley Golf Course, Dauphin Co., PA (demolished 1989). Additionally, our ancestor's names were immortalized at these locations: Bordnersville, Kelly crossroads, Livesey Street, Herrold's

Island, Keefer's Station, Deibler's Gap, Deibler's Dam, Shoemakertown, all in Pennsylvania. Finally, our ancestors had surnames named after the Jura Mountains of Switzerland and Acri, Italy, among other locations.

We are collateral descendants of Presidents Dwight D. Eisenhower and William McKinley and Pennsylvania politicians Samuel Pennypacker, John Morton and Jonas Row. Civil War Brigadier General Galushia Pennypacker, Entertainers Marlon Brando, Les Brown and Ray W Brown, Religious leaders Conrad Weiser and Michael Enderline, Melba Dodge, Jesse Runkle, Enrico Caruso and Galla Curci are all cousins. Lastly, Taylor Wittel lists relations to James Madison, Zachary Taylor, Jefferson Davis and Gene Autry

This volume will serve to honor us with the researched and documented information of our background. Our ancestry was derived from this data, the Thompson Family History (TFH) genealogy, that includes:

7,426	Relatives in TFH
2,047	Marriages in TFH
1,264	Places in TFH
1,227	Sources (over 5,000 Sources not producing information) for TFH
1,164	Surnames in TFH
332	Media in TFH
20	Generations (12 Generations in format) in TFH
95	Age of oldest ancestor at death, Sarah E Wirt & Mrs. M. Curcio
89	Ancestors named John or Albert
85	Ancestors named same male name, John, Johannes, Jean, etc
82	Ancestors names Sophia (4) or Maria (78)
74	Ancestors named same female name, Mary, Maria, Mary Ann, etc.
51	Ancestors named Dolores or Ann
50	Most variations for single surname, Batdorf, Bodorff, Buderff, Pottorf, etc.
38	Ancestors named Mary or Frances
34	Ancestors named Shirley or Mary

27	Number of letters of longest female ancestor's name, Amelia Dorothy Elizabeth Bager
24	Number of letters of longest male ancestor's name, Howard Andrew Carson Hensel
22	Age of youngest ancestor at death, Andrew Morton & Henry Rudin
21	Ancestors named Connor (1) or Adam (20)
17	Ancestors named Andrew (16) or Roman (1)
16	Youngest age when first child born, Myrtle A. Thompson & Fortune Marsico
13	Ancestors named Mary Ann
11	Number of countries ancestors born, DEU, ITA, IRL, SCO, ENG, FIN, SWE, CHE, FRA, HOL, PRT
7	Most different ancestral lines with same surname, Miller, Mueller, etc.
6	Number of states ancestors born in, PA, NY, DE, GA, SC, VA
5	Ancestors named Tyler (1) or Anthony (4)
5	Ancestors named Tiffany (1) or Rachel (4)
4	Ancestors named Paul or Paolo
4	Ancestors named Ed or Edward
3	Ancestors who died at sea, N. Benesch, G. Rieth & G. Shoemaker
2	Ancestors named Ashley (1) or Renae (1)
1	Ancestors named Gerald or Gilbert
49%	relatives born in Pennsylvania
19%	relatives born in Germany
16%	relatives born in Scotland
9%	relatives born in Italy
5%	relatives born in Georgia
5%	relatives born in South Carolina
5%	relatives born in Ireland
2%	relatives born in New York
1%	relatives born in Switzerland
<1%	relatives born in Virginia, Florida & West Indies

Acknowledgments

Thanks to my parents without whom I wouldn't exist, and hence their parents, ad infinitum. Thanks to my sisters, for being there for me and showing interest in our history. Thanks to Joe who tutored me as a teen at the Pennsylvania State Library Genealogy room. Thanks to my hundreds of cousins, close and distant, that have selflessly donated their hard–worked family history to me. Thanks to every clerk and registrar, cemetery manager and LDS employee, who has taken their time to assist me discover our roots. This book is truly the love of thousands, both literally, my family, and figuratively, everyone else who selflessly helped.

Table Of Contents

Introduction

Genealogy was created in order for people to know the history of their lineage; to discover their origins; to prove bloodlines and royalty. Responding to their deep desire to understand and discover their past, this volume was compiled. It shall stand as part of the legacy of their ancestry.

Our mission is to document and record all that is available for our direct line and reap the enjoyment that this discovery brings. The first goal of the Thompson Family History (TFH) was to amass photographs of as many ancestors as possible. As a face can tell a thousand tales, so much can be learned from them. The second goal of the TFH was to document the medical background of our ancestors, so our children can lead a healthier life. The third goal of the TFH is to amass documentation of our ancestors in order to extend the lineage and to lead to information about the personality (biography) of our forefathers. Our ancestors are not a mere name. They have tales to tell, journeys to documents. They have accomplishments and set-backs. They have remembrances. They have goals, glories, and personalitics. The Irish Kings would orally pass down their regal history. They would recite a list of names, their kin, noting outstanding events associated with the forbearers. The ancient Scottish bards similarly memorized their royal family, reciting the pedigrees of the Old Scot's Kings, regardless of the complexity.

Genealogy is a duty. The day we bear children, we took the responsibility of passing along our history. We are responsible for the knowledge of their grandparents and all the wisdom that comes with this knowledge. Our duty, then, includes our children's heritage, the names and faces of their forefathers and mothers. The medical history and genetic backgrounds of their blood lines; the Princes and the paupers; the photographs and historical areas and properties; the tragedies and joys. This TFH is our heritage and with this information we can be proud of ourselves, our past and aim toward a bright future and better lives. If our duty is neglected, as each generation passes, so will our family history.

Most genealogies tend to trace a descendancy or the paternal line (single ascendancy). Our purpose was to trace all ancestors with equal perseverance. This is a monumental, if not impossible, task. We have compiled a pedigree, beginning with our children and using an ahnentafel format. Our children are generation 1, their parents are generation 2, their grandparents are generation 3, etc. There is a family group sheet for each pair of parents along the pedigree. The emphasis at present is on generations 1 through 10, although we have researched as far back as generation 20. Additional collateral ancestors have begun to be added as of 2005. In most cases, the Anglicized first an middle name were used throughout the TFH. For example, Johann Heinrich is John Henry and Orsala Francesca is Ursula Frances. The most commonly found surname was used, whether Anglicized or not. The majority of the collateral information was derived from the US census records. To preserve privacy, all information on living persons has been removed or privatized.

As genealogists will agree, no family history is 100% accurate. We have made errors as others have before us. As this century moves along, more and more information becomes digitally or electronically disposable. If we do not save this information, it may be lost forever. The TFH is a guide for future generations who may use this information for their own goals, whatever they maybe. We have given our children a foundation. Take it, improve it, embrace it.

The continued excellence of this genealogy will be improved by the following plan.

A. Correct errors and complete Source Citations.

B. Collect photographs and medical history of ancestors.

D. Document more personal information of ancestors leading to a more biographical history of family.

E. Expound on current family group sheets and extend parentage.

F. Begin a written biographical volumes (Narratives)

I have a desire and I have a bond. I have a desire to know from whence we came. I want to know our history, our origins. I want to know what our ancestors did, how they persevered and how the spark of life made it way from Geoffrey Livesay born 1410 in England to Sophia born 2004 in Florida. I feel a bond. I have a strong connection to the late 19th century.
If I were given the opportunity to live in any era, I most certainly would pick the 1860-1880's. The time was simple and the people were honest. People worked hard and took pride in their family, their home and their reputation. When I look into the eyes of our ancestors from this time period, I feel a link. I would have fit nicely in their time. Read and enjoy.

Marc D. Thompson

Chapter One

Our family's pedigree and history.

Our ancestors and their family history, with details of life and times of all of our relatives, including cited sources.

Pedigree Chart

Myrtle Adeline Batdorf

b: January 05, 1918 in Big Run, Dauphin Co, PA
m: June 15, 1935 in St. Johns (Hill) Lutheran, Lykens, Dauphin Co, PA
d: May 08, 1983 in Polyclinic Hospital, Harrisburg, Dauphin Co, PA; Cardiorespiratory arrest w/ASHD w/pacemaker

James "Edward" Batdorf

b: February 15, 1885 in Loyalton, Dauphin Co, PA
m: February 08, 1908 in Oakdale Church, Dauphin Co, PA
d: August 19, 1954 in Home, Lykens, Dauphin Co, PA; Coronary occlusion w/hypertension w/diabetes mellitus

Beulah Irene Wert

b: December 31, 1889 in Elizabethville, Dauphin Co, PA
d: June 10, 1983 in Dr. Convalescence Center, Selinsgrove, Snyder Co, PA; Acute congestive cardiac failure w/poss. brain stem CVA & ASCVD

Thomas Edward Batdorf

b: July 02, 1851 in Big Run, Dauphin Co, PA
m: December 06, 1874 in Rev. W.G. Engle, Dauphin Co, PA
d: August 13, 1916 in Elizabethville, Dauphin Co, PA; Mitral insufficiency & Bright's disease (ie. Chronic inflammation) of kidneys w/

Mary Louisa Peters

b: March 31, 1858 in Dauphin Co, PA
d: August 03, 1924 in Home, Elizabethville, Dauphin Co, PA; Cerebral hemorrhage

John Henry Wert

b: December 23, 1855 in Northumberland Co, PA
m: Abt. 1878 in Dauphin Co, PA
d: October 30, 1924 in Harrisburg Hospital, Harrisburg, Dauphin Co, PA; Hemorrhage & shock from fractured ribs & other abd. injuries...rolling timber

Adeline Row

b: January 02, 1860 in Dauphin Co, PA
d: March 06, 1921 in Harrisburg, Dauphin Co, PA; Sero-fibrinous pleurisy w/myocarditis

Peter Batdorf

b: January 20, 1814 in Dauphin Co, PA
m: Abt. 1831 in Dauphin Co, PA
d: December 05, 1880 in Lykens, Dauphin Co, PA

Elizabeth Welker

b: November 23, 1812 in Dauphin Co?, PA
d: July 07, 1868 in Dauphin Co, PA

Samuel Peters

b: 1821 in Union Co, PA
m: Abt. 1840 in Union Co, PA
d: Bet. 1860–1870 in Perry Co, PA

Mary Ann Swartz

b: January 05, 1820 in Juniata, Perry Co, PA
d: August 09, 1897 in Washington, Dauphin Co, PA; Heart disease

David M Wert

b: April 01, 1829 in Powells Valley, Dauphin Co, PA
m: Abt. 1849 in Dauphin Co, PA
d: December 09, 1900 in Dayton, Dauphin Co, PA; Congestion of Lungs

Catherine Shoop

b: February 24, 1830 in Northumberland Co, PA
d: June 08, 1872 in Dauphin Co, PA

Daniel Row

b: July 10, 1813 in Dauphin Co, PA
m: Abt. 1840 in Dauphin Co, PA
d: July 31, 1871 in Dauphin Co, PA; Bright's disease (ie. Chronic inflammation of kidneys)

Susan Frantz

b: March 23, 1819 in Dauphin Co, PA
d: October 17, 1861 in Berrysburg, Dauphin Co, PA

Descendant Report

1 Myrtle Adeline Batdorf b: January 05, 1918 in Big Run, Dauphin Co, PA, d: May 08, 1983 in Polyclinic Hospital, Harrisburg, Dauphin Co, PA; Cardiorespiratory arrest w/ASHD w/pacemaker

... + Harper Bruce Thompson b: September 28, 1907 in Sheridan, Schuylkill Co, PA, m: June 15, 1935 in St. Johns (Hill) Lutheran, Lykens, Dauphin Co, PA, d: July 23, 1981 in Polyclinic Hospital, Harrisburg, Dauphin Co, PA; Cardiorespiratory arrest w/subdural hematoma

......2 Living Thompson

...... + Living Duncan

.........3 M Thompson

.... + Living Curry

.... + Living Romano

.... + Living Wittle

.........3 Living St. Thompson

.... + Living Shannon

.........3 Living Thompson

.... + Living

......2 Eugene Robert Thompson b: August 07, 1937 in PA, d: March 21, 2007 in Harrisburg, Dauphin Co, PA

...... + Margaret "Peggy" Evans b: 1935, d: July 31, 2005

.........3 Living Thompson

.... + Living Potteiger

.... + Stephanie Hockley

......2 Living Thompson

...... + Nancy Tutto b: 1938, d: 1988

.........3 Living Thompson

.... + Living Sikora U

...... + Living Cleary

.........3 Living Thompson

.... + Mark McCracken

.........3 Living Thompson

.... + Living Greene

.........3 Living Thompson

.... + Living Landis

...... + Living

Generation 1

1. **Myrtle Adeline Batdorf** (daughter of James "Edward" Batdorf and Beulah Irene Wert) was born on January 05, 1918 in Big Run, Dauphin Co, PA[1, 2]. She died on May 08, 1983 in Polyclinic Hospital, Harrisburg, Dauphin Co, PA (Cardiorespiratory arrest w/ASHD w/pacemaker[3, 4]). She married **Harper Bruce Thompson** (son of Abel Robert Thompson and Augusta "Gussie" Mae Hensel) on June 15, 1935 in St. Johns (Hill) Lutheran, Lykens, Dauphin Co, PA[2, 5]. He was born on September 28, 1907 in Sheridan, Schuylkill Co, PA[6, 7, 8]. He died on July 23, 1981 in Polyclinic Hospital, Harrisburg, Dauphin Co, PA (Cardiorespiratory arrest w/subdural hematoma[7, 8]).

More About Myrtle Adeline Batdorf:
Baptism: October 11, 1918 in Evangelical Lutheran Circuit, Lykens, Dauphin Co, PA[5]
Burial: May 11, 1983 in Woodlawn Memorial Gardens, Harrisburg, Dauphin Co, PA
Census: 1920 in Washington, Dauphin Co, PA[9]
Census: 1930 in Lykens, Dauphin Co, PA[10]
Census: 1940 in Tower City, Schuylkill Co, PA[11]
Education: 1930 ; School[12]
Funeral: 1983 in Jesse H Geigle, 2100 Linglestown Rd.,Harrisburg, Dauphin Co, PA[13]
Height: ; 5 ft. 9 in.
Medical Condition: ; cardiac arrest due to arteriosclerosis, arthritis, cataracts, diabetes, heart disease, hypertension, obesity
Occupation: 1983 ; Housewife[3]
Political Party: Democrat
Probate: Bet. May 10-19 1983 in Harrisburg, Dauphin Co, PA[14]
Religion: 1983 ; Lakeside Lutheran Church[4, 15]
Residence: 1983 in Beaufort Farms, Camp Curtain, Estherton, Fort Hunter, Harrisburg, Hecktown, Lucknow, Rockville, Uptown, Windsor farms, all Dauphin Co, PA[16]
Residence: 1983 in 2660A Green St., Harrisburg, Dauphin Co, PA[3, 4]
Social Security Number: 1983 ; 165-26-7303[3, 16]
Will: March 30, 1979 in Harrisburg, Dauphin Co, PA[14]

Notes for Myrtle Adeline Batdorf:
Myrtle was named for her grandmother Adeline Row [author,1990]

Born 1917 [Myrtle A Thompson, #3455802, Department of Vital records, New Castle, PA.
Democrat, [Gerald G. Thompson]

My mother Myrtle was 5'9" tall and had brown hair and hazel eyes. She was a housewife but I don't know who Myrtle was named after. She didn't drive or own a car but owned a dog named Domino. She was Lutheran and a Democrat who didn't graduate high school. She taught all 3 of us boys to cook and bake. We took turns doing the dishes. She made sure that we cleaned, dressed for school, etc. She was an outspoken, sometimes loud in correcting our errs. She was the "mother hen," She and dad made sure we children had all the necessities, for they did not have a lot. Bur love and praise took care of the rest. Not knowing the exact date we got our first TV set, maybe 1952. This was part of our education that she wanted us to have --Myrtle A. Batdorf Thompson as told to Marc D. Thompson by Gerald G Thompson, March 1995

Thank you very very much for your informative letter. The news about your mother shocked me. We extend our sincere sympathy to all you boys. We liked Harper and Myrtle very much. At one time, Harper lived with us when he worked in Allentown for the Bell Telephone Co Then the depression came and he was laid off. I met you twice. Once when you were about 2 years old, your mother, father and you visited us on S. 18th St. Your mother wouldn't let you do something and you banged your head against the wall. It scared me but you were not hurt. The second time I saw you was 2 years ago at your father's funeral. Dorothy & Roy Strohecker and Jim & I went to the funeral, the cemetery and back to the church for refreshments. That was the last time I saw Myrtle. At one time we had relatives allover Tower City. Now we have no one; and that is the reason I wrote to your mother to find out if my sister Gussie's house was sold and who bought it. Thanks for giving me the latest news. I have not been in touch with Abel for many years. Thanks for the addresses; I copied them all in my address book. I'm sorry we could not get to Lydia's funeral but we were told the weather was bad up that way. Jim does not drive any more because he had bad operations on his eyes at Wills Eye Hospital. I do the driving but do not take long trips anymore. I am just glad I am able to do the errands and shopping around

Allentown, and trips to the doctor, dentist, etc. It keeps me busy. My sister, Myrtie Hensel Sterner, lives in Manheim and we hope to get a trip over that way very soon with Dorothy & Hay. Myrtie will be 90 years old in October. I want to see her soon. For your information, Dorothy is a cousin of Harper's; her mother was Lilly Hensel Yohe. She & Roy live here in Allentown. The Hensel family was a big relation and I am proud to be one of them. It is impossible to keep track of' everybody. Thank you, Gerald, for your informative letter. Best wishes to you. Your great-aunt Edna P.S. Excuse the typing. I hurt my right hand some time ago and now have arthritis in it; and being a secretary for many years, typing is so much easier for me. --Myrtle Batdorf Thompson Letter to Gerald G Thompson by Aunt Edna Hensel, Allentown, PA, June 1983

Myrtle Thompson's death came as a big surprise to me. I'm sure that was true for many of you--especially her family. I was called by Vaughn Miller on Monday morning. The family had asked if I would take care of the funeral services. I said I would and asked who died. 'Myrtle Thompson', he said. The name didn't ring a bell. I thought for a while. 'You took care of her husband's funeral.' Thompson. Harper. Myrtle. I was stunned. I sat down. I had visited her Friday and she was fine. We had a good talk. She had been thinking a lot about her mom, her sons and Harper, with .Mother's Day coming up and all. She shared some stories--and told me her doctor said she was fine but she wanted to lose some weight. She hugged me when I left with the bags she had kept for the Food Pantry. Then on Sunday, I saw Myrtle in church. I was stunned on Monday morning. I liked Myrtle. I will miss her. So will you. A sad Mother's Day for you--Beulah, Gerry, Gene and Bob--for your families, for friends. A sad day--period. We begin to think of the 'what ifs' or the 'might have beens. I know I do. I think: I might have visited Myrtle more often, to talk. She worried a lot. I might have helped. You probably do the same. Perhaps you are somewhat angry--with yourself; with God for taking her; with Myrtle for leaving so suddenly" --and on Mother's Day, no less. Martha was angry with Jesus when Lazarus died. They had called him when their brother became ill. But he had delayed, taken too long. Lazarus died. His friend Jesus--the healer and wonder-worker--had failed him. And Jesus wept. But Martha was angry. Listen to their dialog with some different tones: 'Jesus, where've you been? If you wouldn't have taken so long, Lazarus wouldn't have died. So, why don't you ask God to do something now.' Jesus replied, 'Martha, you know Lazarus will rise again.' 'Of course I know that--on the last day.' But I'm talking about now! Perhaps not. Perhaps Martha was soft and pious in her sorrow. She went out to meet him though. She was aggressive. Perhaps seeking. I suspect angry. And Jesus accepted the confrontation with care and comfort and strength: 'I am the resurrection and the life; whoever believes in me will live and never die.' Yet Myrtle is dead. We know that. The story of her life for us has come to a sudden close. All we have left are the memories. Yet, a sudden unexpected death was just like Myrtle. I mean, it fits the story. The time I've known Myrtle she's been loving, but tough. Caring but straight forward and painfully honest. She said what she thought and meant it. I always knew where I stood with Myrtle. And she told me stories of how she handled I her boys and how she always told Harper, "You let people use you too much." "I won't put up with that!" Fiercely independent and self-assertive. Even abrupt. But caring--sort of the 'thundering, velvet hand' of Dan Fogleberg's song. Myrtle loved her family deeply. And you loved her and remember her. So, we come together wondering, perhaps, 'where were you Lord?' Sad, angry, hurt. Yet, we recognize that all of us will die, all of our stories, our biographies will end. Lazarus died. But Jesus called him back 'that you may come to believe', he told his disciples. Jesus added a few chapters. And changed the message. Like the disciples, we look at death as the last reality, the lost fight-of-life, the end. Even when we think in terms of the dead person's soul going to heaven, we have to face the reality that Myrtle is no longer with us--no more talking, or laughing or yelling or threats or love will come from Myrtle. We see death as the end of the story. But the story of Lazarus is a sign for us that the story is not over--'whoever believes in me will never die! That's the promise of Jesus--the one who died and who now lives. Lazarus would die again. Jesus is risen and returned to the Father--forever. I am the way, the truth and the life. No one comes to the Father except by me'. Risen. To give us hope--for life, for living. Yes, Myrtle is dead. But we are not. We remember her life, and we will tell stories about her, and we will live with hope that new chapters will yet be added by our Lord who brings life from death. We are alive--to go from here back to our world--home, school, work, play. Having faced death we can laugh--the laughter of hope and faith in the Lord of life. The laughter of the living. And I remember well that Myrtle really knew how to laugh. I am the resurrection and the life. Whoever believes in me will never die. Amen. Funeral for Myrtle Thompson, Pastor Gregory Harbaugh, John 11:1-43, May 1983

More About Harper Bruce Thompson:
Burial: 1981 in Woodlawn Memorial Gardens, Harrisburg, Dauphin Co, PA[7]
Census: 1910 in Porter, Schuylkill Co, PA[17]
Census: 1920 in Porter, Schuylkill Co, PA[18, 19]
Census: 1930 in Emmaus, Lehigh Co, PA (Uncle James Knittle)[20]
Census: 1940 in Tower City, Schuylkill Co, PA[11]
Education: 1920 ; School[21]
Funeral: 1981 in Jesse H Geigle, 2100 Linglestown Rd.,Harrisburg, Dauphin Co, PA[7]
Medical Condition: ; cardiac arrest due to clot in brain, cataracts, heart disease, hernia
Occupation: Abt. 1929 ; Boxer
Occupation: 1930 ; Lineman (Telephone Co)[20]
Occupation: 1935 ; Laborer
Occupation: 1981 ; Retired mail handler (Harrisburg Post Office)[7]
Occupation: ; Lineman (Bell Telephone Co)[11]
Political Party: Republican
Religion: 1981 ; Lakeside Lutheran Church[7]
Residence: 1930 in 914 ? St., Emmaus, Lehigh Co, PA[20]
Residence: 1972 in Harrisburg, Dauphin Co, PA[22]
Residence: 1981 in Beaufort Farms, Camp Curtain, Estherton, Fort Hunter, Harrisburg, Hecktown, Lucknow, Rockville, Uptown, Windsor farms, all Dauphin Co, PA[23]
Residence: 1981 in 2600 Green St., Harrisburg, Dauphin Co, PA[8]
Social Security Number: 1981 ; 205-05-3254[23]

Notes for Harper Bruce Thompson:
Harper was named for his grandfather, Robert Bruce Thompson [author,1990] Born Tower City, PA [Gerald Gilbert Thompson birth record, #1170270-1935, 09-23-1935, Dauphin Co, PA, Department of Vital Records, New Castle, PA]

I must tell you a story that I hadn't thought about in years. When I was a little girl we used to watch the Santa Claus Truck first down at Grandmas (Carole's now) and then back to the corner at my uncles. Then we would walk along with the truck up North Street until it got to our house besides the [Batdorf's], your family! My Mom would run and turn on the lights before the Truck got there. And the people would all be hollering "run Vera!" There were always a lot of people on Batdorf's porch and [your grandfather] Harper used to come down the steps to the sidewalk and give Wanda and I a candy cane! Ask your daddy if he remembers that. I hadn't thought about it in years but in the mail last night we got your gift cert and the Upper Dauphin Sentinel. Here was a whole page about our Santa Truck! I guess in my mind it made me remember about the candy canes. I don't remember if he did it every year or one year BUT he did do it at least one year. So, Marc, 55 years ago your grandfather gave me a candy cane and now you gave us [a present] again for Christmas! What a family legacy! I am sooooo glad that I remembered and could share it with you . --Jeanne Romberger, June 1997, Email to Marc D. Thompson

Harper Thompson, 73, died Thursday at Polyclinic Hospital. He was a member of Lakeside Lutheran Church. A former Postal Service employee, Mr. Thompson is survived by his wife Myrtle, and 3 sons Eugene, Gerald and Robert, and 10 grandchildren and 2 great grandchildren. Services will be held...and so on reads the obituary. And that's all it says. But what about the man, the husband, the father, the brother, grandfather and friend? That's the person you and I have known. A tall, rugged-looking man who sometimes cried at movies, who was sensitive to others, and friendly. I only knew Harper for two years, but I won't forget him. Every Sunday when he and Myrtle were in church, I could depend on hearing Harper's deep baritone, 'Hi ya Gregg!' as the tall man walked by and shook my hand. I remember, too, the man in the hospital who got. teary-eyed talking about his sons - 'good sons' he would say; who nearly beamed when Myrtle was near. And who cried when he received communion. You have memories, too. Some fonder than others, I suspect. Some of joy and fun. Others, perhaps, of father angry with erring boys. Of a husband maybe working too hard or worried about bills. Others of Harper's broad smile and great laugh. Of dad playing with his 'boys. You remember, too. That's Harper. For him we grieve. For him we weep. Because we loved him and will miss him. Like Jesus and Lazarus. A good friend. Dead. So he mourned. But the question came "Could not the one who opened the eyes of the blind kept this man from dying?" That's our question too, I think, if we really face up to our grief. “Why couldn't God keep Harper alive and well?" Though death comes to each of us, the timing could usually do better. So we not only weep but we are somewhat angry as well: with hospitals, doctors and a God who didn't seem to help. Yet in the midst of our grief and anger comes a word, a story, of life and hope that overcome death and sorrow.“I am the resurrection and the life - unbind him and let him go." Lazarus was raised - a sign to John's church that resurrection is not only for the end-time but happens now - in the midst of life and death, joy and sorrow - new life, restored life comes into our world. As we may loosen and let go of the bonds of death and the past. Harper, unlike Lazarus, will not rise and walk among us. Lazarus was for John's church and for us a sign that life overcomes death. We have the sign. Yet not only that. For Jesus' own death and resurrection stand before us - cross and empty tomb - not only as sign but as gift and power. For we, like Harper, who are baptized have taken part in that death and resurrection - washed in it, enlivened through it, "I am the resurrection and the life" said Jesus. Yet he wept and grieved as we do. But death and grief are not final. God has the last word and the last laugh. We are resurrection and life in the midst of Sorrow and death. For God is with us, inseparable from us and Harper. We remember him. And we untie him, to let him go. For us there is life now. There is more to give and to receive. There is time for joy and laughter.We remember Harper. But we also hope - as the communion of saints and in the resurrection of the dead - for nothing, not even death, can separate him or us from God's love in Christ Jesus. I am the resurrection and the life.Funeral of Harper Thompson, Pastor Gregory Harbaugh, John 11:17-44, July 1981

Generation 2

2. **James "Edward" Batdorf** (son of Thomas Edward Batdorf and Mary Louisa Peters) was born on February 15, 1885 in Loyalton, Dauphin Co, PA[24, 25, 26, 27]. He died on August 19, 1954 in Home, Lykens, Dauphin Co, PA (Coronary occlusion w/hypertension w/diabetes mellitus[24]). He married **Beulah Irene Wert** (daughter of John Henry Wert and Adeline Row) on February 08, 1908 in Oakdale Church, Dauphin Co, PA[5, 28].

3. **Beulah Irene Wert** (daughter of John Henry Wert and Adeline Row) was born on December 31, 1889 in Elizabethville, Dauphin Co, PA[29]. She died on June 10, 1983 in Dr. Convalescence Center, Selinsgrove, Snyder Co, PA (Acute congestive cardiac failure w/poss. brain stem CVA & ASCVD[29, 30, 31]).

More About James "Edward" Batdorf:
Baptism: June 06, 1886 in Oakdale Church Circuit, Dauphin Co, PA[5, 32]

Burial: August 23, 1954 in Calvary United Methodist, Wiconisco, Dauphin Co, PA[24, 33]
Census: 1900 in Washington, Dauphin Co, PA[34]
Census: 1910 in Washington, Dauphin Co, PA[35]
Census: 1920 in Washington, , PA[9]
Census: 1930 in Lykens, Dauphin Co, PA[36]
Census: 1940 in Lykens, Dauphin Co, PA[37]
Funeral: 1954 in Reiff? Helt?, 523 W. Main St., Lykens, Dauphin Co, PA[33, 38]
Funeral: 1954 in John R. Shultz Funeral Home, 406 Market St., Lykens, Dauphin Co, PA[39]
Height: ; 5 ft. 6 in.
Medical Condition: ; Short height, Medium build, Brown eyes, ? gray hair [1917] Gray eyes, Brown hair, Light complexion, Height 5'6", Weight 143# [1942][40, 41]
Occupation: 1900 ; Day laborer[34]
Occupation: 1908 ; Miner[28]
Occupation: 1910 ; Miner (coal miner)[42]
Occupation: 1918 ; Miner (Susquehanna Colliery Co)[40]
Occupation: 1920 ; Miner (Coal mine)[43]
Occupation: Abt. 1925 ; Miner (Lykens Coal Co)[44]
Occupation: 1930 ; Laborer (Coal washery)[10]
Occupation: 1935 ; Laborer[2]
Occupation: 1942 ; WPA (Harrisburg, Dauphin Co, PA)[40]
Occupation: 1954 ; Labor (Lykens Borough)[24]
Occupation: ; Laborer (Road construction)
Probate: 1954
Property: 1930 in $4500[12]
Religion: 1954 ; Loyalton EUB Church[33]
Residence: 1918 in Loyalton, Dauphin Co, PA[40]
Residence: 1918 in Loyalton, Dauphin Co, PA[40]
Residence: 1920 in State Road 199, Washington Tp., Dauphin Co, PA[43]
Residence: 1930 in 480 North St., Lykens, Dauphin Co, PA[12]
Residence: 1942 in 542 North Street, Lykens, Dauphin Co, PA[40]
Residence: 1954 in 542 North St., Lykens, Dauphin Co, PA[24, 33]
Social Security Number: 1954 ; 205-09-5145[24]
Weight: ; 143 lb. 0 oz.

Notes for James "Edward" Batdorf:
James was name for and nicknamed Edward after his father, Thomas

Edward Batdorf [author,1995]

Batdorf: German: habitational name from an unidentified place, perhaps one called Betdorf.

More About Beulah Irene Wert:
Baptism: May 18, 1890 in St. Johns (Hill) Lutheran, Berrysburg, Dauphin Co, PA[5]
Burial: June 14, 1983 in Calvary United Methodist, Wiconisco, Dauphin Co, PA[29]
Census: 1900 in Washington, Dauphin Co, PA[45]
Census: 1910 in Washington, Dauphin Co, PA
Census: 1920 in Washington, Dauphin Co, PA
Census: 1930 in Lykens, Dauphin Co, PA
Census: 1940 in Lykens, Dauphin Co, PA[37]
Education: 1900 ; School[45]
Funeral: 1983 in Schultz Funeral Home, 406 Market St., Lykens, Dauphin Co, PA[29, 31]
Occupation: 1920 ; Dressmaker (at home)[43]
Occupation: 1935 ; Housewife[2]
Occupation: Abt. 1950 ; Wallpaperer
Occupation: 1983 ; Seamstress (Clothing)[29]
Religion: 1983 ; St. Christopher Evangelical Lutheran Church[31]
Residence: 1956 in Harrisburg, Dauphin Co, PA[46]
Residence: 1983 in Dauphin Co, PA
Residence: 1983 in 800 Broad St., Selinsgrove, Snyder Co, PA 17870[29]
Residence: 1983 in Big Run, Coaldale, Erdman, Germantown, Loyalton, Lykens, Specktown, all Dauphin Co, PA[30]
Social Security Number: 1983 ; 162-22-1417[29, 30]

Notes for Beulah Irene Wert:
Have photograph.

Beulah Irene Wert and James "Edward" Batdorf had the following children:

i. Alvin Leroy Batdorf (son of James "Edward" Batdorf and Beulah Irene Wert) was born in 1908 in PA. He died in 1972[47]. He married Margaret Elizabeth Marlow. She was born in 1908 in PA. She died in 2004 in PA[48].

ii. Margaret Irene Batdorf (daughter of James "Edward" Batdorf and Beulah Irene Wert) was born on December 05, 1909 in PA. She died in December 1990 in Wiconisco, Dauphin Co, PA. She married Albert Forrest Kohler. He was born in 1908. He died in 1991[47].

iii. Mildred Catherine Batdorf (daughter of James "Edward" Batdorf and Beulah Irene Wert) was born in 1912 in PA. She died in June 2010 in Herndon, Dauphin Co., PA. She married Thomas Randall Moon. He died in 1960.

Notes for Mildred Catherine Batdorf:
Mildred Batdorf Moon
by Marc D. Thompson
as told by Mildred Moon, January 1999
Mildred was born Mildred Catherine Batdorf on January 29, 1911 the daughter of Beulah Wert and James “Edward” Batdorf. She was the sister of my grandmother Myrtle, Alvin, Margaret, Harry, Ruth and Romaine. Mildred and Myrtle were born and raised in Big Run, Pennsylvania. Their mother Beulah was the daughter of John and Adaline Wert of Big Run. The Wert family farmed and "were hard-working people." James Edward was the son of Thomas and Mary Batdorf, also of Big Run. Their "grandmother Batdorf was a housewife and grandfather Batdorf was a farmer and worked in the mines." Myrtle and Mildred "lived in a two-story house and ate in the kitchen." Their home was heated by coal and they did not have a fireplace. The family did not always have electricity, as candles, kerosene and coal were used. The home had a cellar and water was retrieved from a well. Mail was delivered by rural route and they "had a cat named Blacky." Mildred was the fourth child born and Myrtle was the youngest of the seven children. As a child, their major chore, among others, was doing the dishes. Their mother did the cooking and ironing and she taught them to sew, crochet, knit and embroider. Mildred learned to drive a car from a neighborhood boy and her husband Randall Moon taught her to cook. Mildred and Myrtle's father, Edward Batdorf, was a miner and Mildred worked to help contribute to the family income. She was fourteen years old when she

secured her first job. The family had a garden and they "dug the ground and got it ready to plant. They grew potatoes, lettuce, celery, onions, tomatoes, peppers, cabbage and a lot more." They had cherry and peach trees. Their mother did canning and raised chickens and the family often ate beef, pork and chicken. Her parents and siblings did all the work, hiring no one to help with the house, garden or animals. "Saturday was the day that you got a rest for the weekend and Sunday we got ready for church." The family attended a little church in Loyalton. For Christmas they would wake up early to see the tree and they received clothes as gifts. On July Fourth, "my brother had a birthday and we had games that we played." In general, however, sibling's birthdays were just another day. For her birthday, Mildred received clothes made by her mother. The family did not entertain often but they did go to family picnics. She kept in touch with distant family and visited relatives often. In the summer, "we sat under a nice shade tree to keep cool" and in the winter kept warm with long johns. Mildred recalls one extreme winter storm when the snow reached up over the fences. For recreation, the children played jump rope, ball and cards. Mildred's best friend was Hilda Buffington and they often played games for fun. Mildred did not learn to swim and the family never went on vacation. Growing up, there was no place to shop so the family ordered items from "men who came around and the next day he came with it." They never went to the city to shop but there was a small country store. Lykens was the largest town nearby and Mildred used to take the train to visit her grandmother in Elizabethville. My father "got a car when I was ten years old. It was a Ford model T." Mildred attended a little red one-room schoolhouse in Big Run. It was only two houses away and she usually walked to school alone. Mildred was closest to her mother and she admired her father most. When young, Mildred "hoped to be a good housekeeper." Her family supported and encouraged her and they influenced her and helped her develop skills. When asked if she would choose the same career path, she said, "No. I would choose for a better life." "I met my husband in Lykens. I was engaged on Easter and married on October 1, 1926." Mildred was married in Hagerstown to her husband, a dentist, and her children were born in…(remainder missing)

iv. Harry Franklin Batdorf (son of James "Edward" Batdorf and Beulah Irene Wert) was born on July 21, 1912 in PA. He died in August 1977 in Lykens, Dauphin Co, PA[47]. He married Grace Naomi Hoy. She was born in 1915. She died in 1962[47].

1. v. Myrtle Adeline Batdorf (daughter of James "Edward" Batdorf and Beulah Irene Wert) was born on January 05, 1918 in Big Run, Dauphin Co, PA[1, 2]. She died on May 08, 1983 in Polyclinic Hospital, Harrisburg, Dauphin Co, PA (Cardiorespiratory arrest w/ASHD w/pacemaker[3, 4]). She married Harper Bruce Thompson (son of Abel Robert Thompson and Augusta "Gussie" Mae Hensel) on June 15, 1935 in St. Johns (Hill) Lutheran, Lykens, Dauphin Co, PA[2, 5]. He was born on September 28, 1907 in Sheridan, Schuylkill Co, PA[6, 7, 8]. He died on July 23, 1981 in Polyclinic Hospital, Harrisburg, Dauphin Co, PA (Cardiorespiratory arrest w/subdural hematoma[7, 8]).

vi. Ruth E Batdorf (daughter of James "Edward" Batdorf and Beulah Irene Wert) was born on April 29, 1923 in PA. She died on August 16, 2006 in Ridgeway, Elk Co, PA. She married Claude M Reed. He was born in 1921. He died in 1986[47].

vii. Romaine Batdorf (daughter of James "Edward" Batdorf and Beulah Irene Wert) was born on May 24, 1925 in PA. She died in July 1981 in Lykens, Dauphin Co, PA. She married Clarence "Bess" D Messner. He was born in 1925. He died in 2005.

Generation 3

4. **Thomas Edward Batdorf** (son of Peter Batdorf and Elizabeth Welker) was born on July 02, 1851 in Big Run, Dauphin Co, PA[49, 50]. He died on August 13, 1916 in Elizabethville, Dauphin Co, PA (Mitral insufficiency & Bright's disease (ie, Chronic inflammation) of kidneys w/[50]). He married **Mary Louisa Peters** (daughter of Samuel Peters and Mary Ann Swartz) on December 06, 1874 in Rev. W.G. Engle, Dauphin Co, PA[5].

5. **Mary Louisa Peters** (daughter of Samuel Peters and Mary Ann

Swartz) was born on March 31, 1858 in Dauphin Co, PA[49, 51]. She died on August 03, 1924 in Home, Elizabethville, Dauphin Co, PA (Cerebral hemorrhage[5, 49]).

More About Thomas Edward Batdorf:
Baptism: October 12, 1851 in St. Peters (Hoffmans) Church, Lykens, Dauphin Co, PA[5]
Burial: August 16, 1916 in St. Johns (Oakdale) Cemetery, Loyalton, Dauphin Co, PA[50]
Census: 1860 in Lykens, Dauphin Co, PA[52]
Census: 1870 in Berrysburg, Dauphin Co, PA (Wise)[53]
Census: 1880 in Washington, Dauphin Co, PA[54]
Census: 1900 in Washington, Dauphin Co, PA[34]
Census: 1910 in Elizabethville, Dauphin Co, PA[55]
Education: 1860 ; School[52]
Funeral: 1916 in Buffington Funeral Home, Elizabethville, Dauphin Co, PA[50]
Height: ; 6 ft. 0 in.
Military Service: Bet. 1861-1865 ; Civil War
Occupation: 1870 ; Apprentice to Blacksmith[53]
Occupation: 1880 ; Laborer[54]
Occupation: 1900 ; Coal miner[34]
Occupation: 1910 ; Retired laborer[55]
Occupation: 1916 ; Laborer[50]
Residence: 1910 in W. Main St., Elizabethville, Dauphin Co, PA[56]

Notes for Thomas Edward Batdorf:
Have photograph.

Thomas was named after his uncle, Thomas Batdorf [author, 2010]

More About Mary Louisa Peters:
Burial: August 06, 1924 in St. Johns (Oakdale) Cemetery, Loyalton, Dauphin Co, PA[51]
Census: 1860 in Mifflin, Dauphin Co, PA[57]
Census: 1870
Census: 1880 in Washington, Dauphin Co, PA
Census: 1900 in Washington, Dauphin Co, PA
Census: 1910 in Elizabethville, Dauphin Co, PA

Census: 1920 in Elizabethville, Dauphin Co, PA[58]
Funeral: 1924 in Buffington Funeral Home, Elizabethville, Dauphin Co, PA[51]
Height: ; 4 ft. 12 in.
Occupation: 1880 ; Keeping house[54]
Occupation: 1924 ; Housekeeper[51]
Religion: ; Evangelical Church[44]
Residence: 1920 in Main St., Elizabethville, Dauphin Co, PA[59]

Notes for Mary Louisa Peters:
Have photograph.

Mary was named for her mother Mary [author, 2005]

Mary Louisa Peters and Thomas Edward Batdorf had the following children:

i. George Batdorf (son of Thomas Edward Batdorf and Mary Louisa Peters) was born in 1875 in PA. He died in 1881.

ii. Kirby Batdorf (son of Thomas Edward Batdorf and Mary Louisa Peters) was born in 1877 in PA. He died in 1881.

iii. John Batdorf (son of Thomas Edward Batdorf and Mary Louisa Peters) was born on September 07, 1878 in PA. He died in January 1968 in Annville, Lebanon Co, PA.

iv. William Batdorf (son of Thomas Edward Batdorf and Mary Louisa Peters) was born in 1880 in PA. He married <No name>. She was born in 1874 in PA.

v. Mary Ellen Batdorf (daughter of Thomas Edward Batdorf and Mary Louisa Peters) was born in 1881 in PA. She died in 1963.

vi. Adam Scorvella Batdorf (son of Thomas Edward Batdorf and Mary Louisa Peters) was born in 1882 in PA. He died in 1952. He married Caroline "Carrie" May Boyer. She was born in 1884 in PA. She died in 1973[47].

2. vii. James "Edward" Batdorf (son of Thomas Edward Batdorf and Mary Louisa Peters) was born on February 15, 1885 in Loyalton, Dauphin Co, PA[24, 25, 26, 27]. He died on August 19,

1954 in Home, Lykens, Dauphin Co, PA (Coronary occlusion w/hypertension w/diabetes mellitus[24]). He married Beulah Irene Wert (daughter of John Henry Wert and Adeline Row) on February 08, 1908 in Oakdale Church, Dauphin Co, PA[5, 28]. She was born on December 31, 1889 in Elizabethville, Dauphin Co, PA[29]. She died on June 10, 1983 in Dr. Convalescence Center, Selinsgrove, Snyder Co, PA (Acute congestive cardiac failure w/poss. brain stem CVA & ASCVD[29, 30, 31]).

viii. Oscar Newton Batdorf (son of Thomas Edward Batdorf and Mary Louisa Peters) was born on August 15, 1886 in Loyalton, Dauphin Co, PA. He died in August 1981 in Sarasota, Sarasota Co, FL. He married Mabel Susan Elizabeth Motter. She was born in 1887 in PA.

ix. Frances I Batdorf (daughter of Thomas Edward Batdorf and Mary Louisa Peters) was born in 1887 in PA. She married Samuel W Lentz. He was born in 1886. He died in 1940[47].

x. Joseph Warren Batdorf (son of Thomas Edward Batdorf and Mary Louisa Peters) was born in 1888 in Elizabethtown, Dauphin Co, PA. He died in 1928[47].

xi. Harvey Clarence Batdorf (son of Thomas Edward Batdorf and Mary Louisa Peters) was born in 1891 in Loyalton, Dauphin Co, PA. He died in 1949[47]. He married Living Bahney.

xii. Cora Annette Batdorf (daughter of Thomas Edward Batdorf and Mary Louisa Peters) was born on April 18, 1892 in PA. She died in May 1981 in Harrisburg, Dauphin Co, PA[47]. She married Herbert Eugene Buffington. He was born in 1888. He died in 1959[47].

xiii. Stella Louisa Batdorf (daughter of Thomas Edward Batdorf and Mary Louisa Peters) was born in 1893 in PA. She died in 1981. She married Paul. She married Lafayette DeWees. He was born in 1883. He died in 1981[47].

xiv Verna A Batdorf (daughter of Thomas Edward Batdorf and Mary Louisa Peters) was born on June 02, 1899 in PA.

She died in December 1992 in Sherman Oaks, Los Angeles Co, CA. She married Leon Washington Shultz. He was born in 1890.

xv. Living Batdorf (daughter of Thomas Edward Batdorf and Mary Louisa Peters).

xvi. Norman Batdorf (son of Thomas Edward Batdorf and Mary Louisa Peters) was born in 1896 in PA. He died in 1896.

xvii. Alvin Thomas Batdorf (son of Thomas Edward Batdorf and Mary Louisa Peters) was born in 1898 in PA. He died in 1898.

6. **John Henry Wert** (son of David M Wert and Catherine Shoop) was born on December 23, 1855 in Northumberland Co, PA[60]. He died on October 30, 1924 in Harrisburg Hospital, Harrisburg, Dauphin Co, PA (Hemorrhage & shock from fractured ribs & other abd. injuries...rolling timber.[60]). He married **Adeline Row** (daughter of Daniel Row and Susan Frantz) about Abt. 1878 in Dauphin Co, PA.

7. **Adeline Row** (daughter of Daniel Row and Susan Frantz) was born on January 02, 1860 in Dauphin Co, PA[61, 62, 63]. She died on March 06, 1921 in Harrisburg, Dauphin Co, PA (Sero-fibrinous pleurisy w/myocarditis[62]).

More About John Henry Wert:
Baptism: December 23, 1855 in Northumberland Co?, PA
Burial: November 02, 1924 in St. Johns (Hill) Lutheran, Berrysburg, Dauphin Co, PA[60, 64]
Census: 1860 in Lower Mahanoy, Northumberland Co, PA[65]
Census: 1870 in Lykens, Dauphin Co, PA[66]
Census: 1880 in Washington, Dauphin Co, PA[67]
Census: 1900 in Washington, Dauphin Co, PA[45]
Census: 1910 in Washington, Dauphin Co, PA (enumerated twice)[68]
Census: 1920 in Washington, Dauphin Co, PA[69]
Funeral: 1924 in Buffington Funeral Home, Elizabethville, Dauphin Co, PA[60]
Height: ; 6 ft. 0 in.
Occupation: 1880 ; Blacksmith[67]
Occupation: 1900 ; Day laborer[45]

Occupation: 1910 ; Laborer (?)[68]
Occupation: 1920 ; Laborer (Coal mine)[70]
Occupation: 1924 ; Timber laborer (Susquehanna Colliery)[60]
Probate: Bet. November 19, 1924-1938 in Washington Tp, Dauphin Co, PA (listed in index only)[71]
Residence: 1920 in State Road 199, Washington, Dauphin Co, PA[70]

Notes for John Henry Wert:
Have photograph.

John was named for his uncle John Henry Wert and his grandfather John Shoop [author, 1995, 2010]

More About Adeline Row:
Baptism: March 11, 1860 in St. Johns (Hill) Lutheran, Berrysburg, Dauphin Co, PA[61]
Burial: March 10, 1921 in St. Johns (Hill) Lutheran, Berrysburg, Dauphin Co, PA[62]
Census: 1860 in Washington, Dauphin Co, PA[72]
Census: 1870 in Wiconisco, Dauphin Co, PA[73]
Census: 1880 in Washington, Dauphin Co, PA
Census: 1900 in Washington, Dauphin Co, PA
Census: 1910 in Washington, Dauphin Co, PA
Census: 1920 in Washington, Dauphin Co, PA
Education: 1870 ; School[73]
Funeral: 1921 in Buffington Funeral Home, Elizabethville, Dauphin Co, PA[62]
Height: ; 5 ft. 5 in.
Occupation: 1880 ; Keeping house[67]
Occupation: Abt. 1900 ; Owned farm[44]
Occupation: 1921 ; Housewife[62]
Religion: ; Lutheran[44]
Residence: 1921 in Lykens, Dauphin Co, PA[62]

Notes for Adeline Row:
Have photograph.

Adeline Row and John Henry Wert had the following children:

i. Caroline "Carrie" Catherine Wert (daughter of John Henry Wert and Adeline Row) was born in 1880 in PA.

ii. "Hattie" May Wert (daughter of John Henry Wert and Adeline Row) was born in 1881 in PA. She married Daniel George Romberger. He was born in 1879 in PA. He died in 1959[74].

iii. Florence Stella Wert (daughter of John Henry Wert and Adeline Row) was born on March 06, 1886 in PA. She died in November 1972 in Elizabethville, Dauphin Co, PA. She married John Adam Kocher. He was born in 1872 in PA.

3. iv. Beulah Irene Wert (daughter of John Henry Wert and Adeline Row) was born on December 31, 1889 in Elizabethville, Dauphin Co, PA[29]. She died on June 10, 1983 in Dr. Convalescence Center, Selinsgrove, Snyder Co, PA (Acute congestive cardiac failure w/poss. brain stem CVA & ASCVD[29, 30, 31]). She married James "Edward" Batdorf (son of Thomas Edward Batdorf and Mary Louisa Peters) on February 08, 1908 in Oakdale Church, Dauphin Co, PA[5, 28]. He was born on February 15, 1885 in Loyalton, Dauphin Co, PA[24, 25, 26, 27]. He died on August 19, 1954 in Home, Lykens, Dauphin Co, PA (Coronary occlusion w/hypertension w/diabetes mellitus[24]).

v. Living Wert (daughter of John Henry Wert and Adeline Row). She married Living Naughton.

vi. U Wert (child of John Henry Wert and Adeline Row) was born about Abt. 1883 in PA (U).

Generation 4

8. **Peter Batdorf** (son of Jacob Peter Batdorf and Maria Catherine Steiner) was born on January 20, 1814 in Dauphin Co, PA[49, 75, 76, 77, 78]. He died on December 05, 1880 in Lykens, Dauphin Co, PA[49, 75, 76, 77, 78, 79, 80]. He married **Elizabeth Welker** (daughter of John Welker and Maria Elizabeth Messerschmidt) about Abt. 1831 in Dauphin Co, PA.

9. **Elizabeth Welker** (daughter of John Welker and Maria Elizabeth Messerschmidt) was born on November 23, 1812 in Dauphin Co?, PA[49, 75, 76]. She died on July 07, 1868 in Dauphin Co, PA[49, 75, 76, 81].

More About Peter Batdorf:
Baptism: February 27, 1814 in St. Peters (Hoffman) Reformed, Loyalton, Dauphin Co, PA[49]
Burial: 1880 in St. Peters (Hoffman) Reformed, Loyalton, Dauphin Co, PA[49, 75, 76, 77]
Census: 1820 in father; Lykens, Dauphin Co, PA w[82]
Census: 1830 in mother; Lykens, Dauphin Co, PA w[83]
Census: 1840 in Lykens, Dauphin Co, PA[84, 85]
Census: 1850 in Lykens, Dauphin Co, PA[86]
Census: 1860 in Lykens, Dauphin Co, PA[52]
Census: 1870 in Lykens, Dauphin Co, PA[87]
Census: 1880 in Lykens, Dauphin Co, PA[88]
Occupation: Abt. 1840 ; Yeoman
Occupation: Bet. 1850-1870 ; Carpenter[86]
Occupation: 1880 ; Farmer[88]
Probate: January 04, 1881 in Dauphin Co, PA[79]
Property: 1850 in $500[86]
Property: 1860 in $900 + $250[52]
Property: 1870 in $1000 + $400[89]

Notes for Peter Batdorf:
Peter was named after his father Jacob Peter Batdorf [author, 2010]

More About Elizabeth Welker:
Burial: 1868 in St. Peters (Hoffman) Reformed, Loyalton, Dauphin Co, PA[76]
Census: 1820 in father; Lykens, Dauphin Co, PA w[90]
Census: 1830 in father; Lykens, Dauphin Co, PA w[91]
Census: 1840 in husband; Lykens, Dauphin Co, PA w
Census: 1850 in Lykens, Dauphin Co, PA
Census: 1860 in Lykens, Dauphin Co, PA
Occupation: Abt. 1840 ; Homemaker

Notes for Elizabeth Welker:
Elizabeth was named after her mother Maria Elizabeth Messerschmidt [author, 2010]

Elizabeth was not mentioned in father's will [Welker family, Gratz History, p 450-455]

Elizabeth Welker and Peter Batdorf had the following children:

i. Esther Batdorf (daughter of Peter Batdorf and Elizabeth Welker) was born in 1836 in PA.

ii. Jonas Batdorf (son of Peter Batdorf and Elizabeth Welker) was born in 1837 in PA. He married Lucetta Rickert. She was born in 1840. She died in 1867[48].

iii. Elizabeth Batdorf (daughter of Peter Batdorf and Elizabeth Welker) was born in 1839 in PA. She married Joseph Russell. He was born in 1836. He died in 1901[48].

iv. Susan Batdorf (daughter of Peter Batdorf and Elizabeth Welker) was born in 1842 in PA. She married Miller.

v. John Batdorf (son of Peter Batdorf and Elizabeth Welker) was born in 1844 in PA. He married Sarah Miller. She was born in 1842 in PA.

vi. Sarah Batdorf (daughter of Peter Batdorf and Elizabeth Welker) was born in 1845 in PA. She married James H Smith. He was born in 1845. He died in 1904[48].

vii. Peter S Batdorf (son of Peter Batdorf and Elizabeth Welker) was born in 1848 in PA. He married Mary Elizabeth Sierer. She was born in 1853 in PA.

viii. Anna Batdorf (daughter of Peter Batdorf and Elizabeth Welker) was born about Abt. 1850 in PA.

ix. Rebecca Batdorf (daughter of Peter Batdorf and Elizabeth Welker) was born about Abt. 1850 in PA.

4. x. Thomas Edward Batdorf (son of Peter Batdorf and Elizabeth Welker) was born on July 02, 1851 in Big Run, Dauphin Co, PA[49, 50]. He died on August 13, 1916 in Elizabethville, Dauphin Co, PA (Mitral insufficiency & Bright's disease (ie, Chronic inflammation) of kidneys w/[50]). He married Mary Louisa Peters (daughter of Samuel Peters and Mary Ann Swartz) on December 06, 1874 in Rev. W.G. Engle, Dauphin Co, PA[5]. She was born on March 31, 1858 in Dauphin Co, PA[49, 51]. She died on August 03, 1924 in Home, Elizabethville, Dauphin Co, PA

(Cerebral hemorrhage[5, 49]).

xi. Louisa Batdorf (daughter of Peter Batdorf and Elizabeth Welker) was born in 1854 in PA. She married William Frantz. He was born about Abt. 1850.

10. **Samuel Peters** (son of John Peters and Anna Maria) was born in 1821 in Union Co, PA. He died between 1860-1870 in Perry Co, PA. He married **Mary Ann Swartz** (daughter of John Swartz and <No name>) about Abt. 1840 in Union Co, PA.

11. **Mary Ann Swartz** (daughter of John Swartz and <No name>) was born on January 05, 1820 in Juniata, Perry Co, PA[92]. She died on August 09, 1897 in Washington, Dauphin Co, PA (Heart disease[93, 94]).

More About Samuel Peters:
Burial: Bet. 1860-1870 in Perry Co, PA
Census: 1830 in Buffalo, Union Co, PA[95]
Census: 1840 in mother; w
Census: 1850 in Union, Union Co, PA[96, 97]
Census: 1860 in Mifflin, Dauphin Co, PA[57]
Occupation: 1850 ; Laborer[96, 97]
Occupation: 1860 ; Laborer[57]
Property: 1860 in $150[57]

More About Mary Ann Swartz:
Burial: August 12, 1897 in St. Johns (Oakdale) Cemetery, Loyalton, Dauphin Co, PA[93, 98]
Census: 1830 in Juniata, Perry Co, PA; w/parents[99]
Census: 1840 in Juniata, Perry Co, PA; w/parents[100]
Census: 1850 in Union, Union Co, PA
Census: 1860 in Mifflin, Dauphin Co, PA
Census: 1870 in Lykens, Dauphin Co, PA[101]
Census: 1880 in Washington, Dauphin Co, PA (Row)[102]
Occupation: 1870 ; Keeping house[101]
Occupation: 1880 ; Retired house keeper[102]
Property: 1870 in $100[101]

Notes for Mary Ann Swartz:
Birth could be Juniata Tp or Juniata Co, PA [Mary Peters death cert,

Bk C, #945, 1897, Dauphin County Register of Wills, Harrisburg, PA]

Mary Ann Swartz and Samuel Peters had the following children:

i. John Peters (son of Samuel Peters and Mary Ann Swartz) was born in 1844 in PA. He married Mary. She was born in 1848 in PA.

ii. Emma C Peters (daughter of Samuel Peters and Mary Ann Swartz) was born in 1846 in PA.

iii. Jonathan Peters (son of Samuel Peters and Mary Ann Swartz) was born in 1848 in PA. He married Elizabeth. She was born in 1854 in PA.

iv. Matthew Peters (son of Samuel Peters and Mary Ann Swartz) was born in 1849 in PA.

v. Matilda "Tillie" Peters (daughter of Samuel Peters and Mary Ann Swartz) was born in 1852 in PA.

5. vi. Mary Louisa Peters (daughter of Samuel Peters and Mary Ann Swartz) was born on March 31, 1858 in Dauphin Co, PA[49, 51]. She died on August 03, 1924 in Home, Elizabethville, Dauphin Co, PA (Cerebral hemorrhage[5, 49]). She married Thomas Edward Batdorf (son of Peter Batdorf and Elizabeth Welker) on December 06, 1874 in Rev. W.G. Engle, Dauphin Co, PA[5]. He was born on July 02, 1851 in Big Run, Dauphin Co, PA[49, 50]. He died on August 13, 1916 in Elizabethville, Dauphin Co, PA (Mitral insufficiency & Bright's disease (ie, Chronic inflammation) of kidneys w/[50]).

vii. Jane R Peters (daughter of Samuel Peters and Mary Ann Swartz) was born on March 31, 1858 in PA. She married Alfred C Row. He was born in 1855 in PA.

12. **David M Wert** (son of Jacob Wert and Sarah Elizabeth Faber) was born on April 01, 1829 in Powells Valley, Dauphin Co, PA[64, 103, 104, 105]. He died on December 09, 1900 in Dayton, Dauphin Co, PA (Congestion of Lungs[103, 104, 105, 106]). He married **Catherine Shoop** (daughter of John Shoop and Sarah Wertz) about Abt. 1849 in Dauphin Co, PA.

13. **Catherine Shoop**[66] (daughter of John Shoop and Sarah Wertz) was born on February 24, 1830 in Northumberland Co, PA[64, 104, 105, 107, 108].

She died on June 08, 1872 in Dauphin Co, PA[64, 104, 105, 107].

More About David M Wert:
Burial: December 12, 1900 in Calvary United Methodist (aka Union), Wiconisco, Dauphin Co, PA[103, 106, 109, 110, 111]
Census: 1830 in father; Halifax, Dauphin Co, PA w[112]
Census: 1840 in parents; w[113]
Census: 1850 in Upper Paxton, Dauphin Co, PA[114]
Census: 1860 in Lower Mahanoy Northumberland Co, PA[65]
Census: 1870 in Lykens, Dauphin Co, PA[66, 107]
Census: 1880
Census: 1900 in Washington, Dauphin Co, PA (West)
Occupation: 1850 ; Laborer[115]
Occupation: 1870 ; Laborer[66, 107]
Occupation: 1900 ; Laborer[103, 106]
Property: 1850 in $100[114]
Property: 1870 in $1000 + $400[66]

Notes for David M Wert:
Have photograph.

More About Catherine Shoop:
Baptism: March 06, 1830 in Zion (Stone Valley) Lutheran, Dalmatia, Northumberland Co, PA[108]
Burial: 1872 in St. Peters (Hoffman) Reformed, Loyalton, Dauphin Co, PA[64, 104, 107]
Census: 1830 in father; Lower Mahanoy, Northumberland Co, PA w
Census: 1840 in father; Lower Mahanoy, Northumberland Co, PA w[116]
Census: 1850 in Upper Paxtang, Dauphin Co, PA[114]
Census: 1850 in Lower Mahanoy, Northumberland Co, PA[117]
Census: 1860 in Lower Mahanoy Northumberland Co, PA
Census: 1870 in Lykens, Dauphin Co, PA
Occupation: 1870 ; Keeping house
Probate: June 23, 1880 in Dauphin Co, PA (listed in index only)[118]

Notes for Catherine Shoop:
Check 1850 census, Catherine is both her parent's and husband's

household.

Catherine Shoop and David M Wert had the following children:

i. Elizabeth Jane Wert (daughter of David M Wert and Catherine Shoop) was born in 1853 in PA. She married Jacob Asbury Troxell.

ii. Anna Elizabeth Wert (daughter of David M Wert and Catherine Shoop) was born in 1855 in PA. She married Adam Diller Row. He was born in 1851 in PA. He died in 1929.

6. iii. John Henry Wert (son of David M Wert and Catherine Shoop) was born on December 23, 1855 in Northumberland Co, PA[60]. He died on October 30, 1924 in Harrisburg Hospital, Harrisburg, Dauphin Co, PA (Hemorrhage & shock from fractured ribs & other abd. injuries...rolling timber.[60]). He married Adeline Row (daughter of Daniel Row and Susan Frantz) about Abt. 1878 in Dauphin Co, PA. She was born on January 02, 1860 in Dauphin Co, PA[61, 62, 63]. She died on March 06, 1921 in Harrisburg, Dauphin Co, PA (Sero-fibrinous pleurisy w/myocarditis[62]).

iv. Mary Ellen Wert (daughter of David M Wert and Catherine Shoop) was born in 1859 in PA. She married John Edward Troxell.

v. Melinda "Polly" Wert (daughter of David M Wert and Catherine Shoop) was born in 1861 in PA. She died in 1864.

vi. Martha "Mattie" Valery Wert (daughter of David M Wert and Catherine Shoop) was born in 1864 in PA. She died in 1945. She married Henry Brown. He was born in 1860.

vii. Catherine "Kate" Ann Wert (daughter of David M Wert and Catherine Shoop) was born in 1866 in PA. She married John Copp. He was born in 1860.

viii. Amelia Ida Wert (daughter of David M Wert and Catherine Shoop) was born in 1868 in PA. She married Isaac Smith. He was born in 1860.

ix. Daniel Monroe Wert (son of David M Wert and Catherine Shoop) was born in 1870 in PA. He married Emma. She was born in 1870 in PA. He married Susan. She was born in 1880.

x. Isaac Franklin Wert (son of David M Wert and Catherine Shoop) was born in 1871 in PA. He married Catherine "Kate" M Carl. She was born in 1873 in PA.

14. **Daniel Row** (son of John William Rowe and Barbara Rudy) was born on July 10, 1813 in Dauphin Co, PA[62, 119, 120, 121]. He died on July 31, 1871 in Dauphin Co, PA (Bright's disease (ie, Chronic inflammation of kidneys)[120, 121]). He married **Susan Frantz** (daughter of Adam Frantz and Susan Gieseman) about Abt. 1840 in Dauphin Co, PA.

15. **Susan Frantz** (daughter of Adam Frantz and Susan Gieseman) was born on March 23, 1819 in Dauphin Co, PA[62, 120, 122]. She died on October 17, 1861 in Berrysburg, Dauphin Co, PA[120, 122].

More About Daniel Row:
Baptism: August 14, 1813 in St. Johns (Hill) Lutheran, Berrysburg, Dauphin Co, PA[119, 120]
Burial: July 1871 in St. Johns (Hill) Lutheran, Berrysburg, Dauphin Co, PA[121]
Census: 1820 in father; Mifflin, Dauphin Co, PA w[123]
Census: 1830 in father; Halifax, Dauphin Co, PA w[124]
Census: 1840 in Wiconisco, Dauphin Co, PA[125, 126]
Census: 1850 in Washington, Dauphin Co, PA[127]
Census: 1860 in Washington, Dauphin Co, PA[72, 128]
Census: 1870 in Wiconisco, Dauphin Co, PA[129]
Occupation: Bet. 1850-1870 ; Laborer[72, 127, 128, 129]
Probate: August 28, 1871 in Dauphin Co, PA (listed in index only)[130]
Property: 1850 in $240[127]
Property: 1860 in $9450 + $200[128]

More About Susan Frantz:
Burial: 1861 in St. Johns (Hill) Lutheran, Berrysburg, Dauphin Co, PA[131]
Census: 1820 in father; Mifflin, Dauphin Co, PA w[132]
Census: 1830 in parents; w

Census: 1840 in husband; Wiconisco, Dauphin Co, PA w
Census: 1850 in Washington, Dauphin Co, PA
Census: 1860 in Washington, Dauphin Co, PA
Occupation: ; Homemaker

Notes for Susan Frantz:
Susan was named after her mother, Susan Gieseman [author, 2010]

Susan Frantz and Daniel Row had the following children:

i. Sarah Ann Row (daughter of Daniel Row and Susan Frantz) was born in 1841 in PA. She died in 1859[74].

ii. Angelina Row (daughter of Daniel Row and Susan Frantz) was born in 1843 in PA. She died in 1936[74]. She married Jacob Zerby. He was born in 1840 in PA. He died in 1913[74].

iii. Adam Diller Row (son of Daniel Row and Susan Frantz) was born in 1851 in PA. He died in 1929. He married Anna Elizabeth Wert. She was born in 1855 in PA.

iv. Susan Row (daughter of Daniel Row and Susan Frantz) was born in 1852 in PA. She died in 1933. She married William Henry Keiper. He was born in 1851 in PA. He died in 1913[74].

v. Amelia Row (daughter of Daniel Row and Susan Frantz) was born in 1854 in PA. She married Isaac F Chubb. He was born in 1849 in PA.

vi. Leah Jane Row (daughter of Daniel Row and Susan Frantz) was born in 1857 in PA. She married Michael.

7. vii. Adeline Row (daughter of Daniel Row and Susan Frantz) was born on January 02, 1860 in Dauphin Co, PA[61, 62, 63]. She died on March 06, 1921 in Harrisburg, Dauphin Co, PA (Sero-fibrinous pleurisy w/myocarditis[62]). She married John Henry Wert (son of David M Wert and Catherine Shoop) about Abt. 1878 in Dauphin Co, PA. He was born on December 23, 1855 in Northumberland Co, PA[60]. He died on October 30, 1924 in Harrisburg Hospital, Harrisburg, Dauphin Co, PA (Hemorrhage & shock from

fractured ribs & other abd. injuries...rolling timber.[60]).

Generation 5

16. **Jacob Peter Batdorf** (son of George Peter Batdorf and Barbara Weiss) was born about Abt. 1793 in PA. He died in 1829 in Dauphin Co, PA[76]. He married **Maria Catherine Steiner** (daughter of Jacob? Steiner and Elizabeth) on February 20, 1813 in Christ Lutheran, Stouchsburg, Berks Co, PA.

17. **Maria Catherine Steiner** (daughter of Jacob? Steiner and Elizabeth) was born about Abt. 1790 in Berks Co, PA[133]. She died about Abt. 1840 in Dauphin Co, PA.

More About Jacob Peter Batdorf:
Burial: 1829 in Loyalton, Dauphin Co, PA
Census: 1800 in father; Heidelberg, Dauphin Co, PA w[134]
Census: 1810 in parents; w
Census: 1820 in Lykens, Dauphin Co, PA[135, 136]
Occupation: Abt. 1820 ; Farmer
Probate: 1829 in Dauphin Co, PA (listed in index only)[137]
Residence: Bet. 1815-1828 in Berrysburg, Dauphin Co, PA[138]

Notes for Jacob Peter Batdorf:
More research needs done here. Many inconsistencies. It seems at this point most probable that this Peter and wife Catherine have been confused with his parents, Peter and Catherine. It seems there may have been a skipped generation in most data I have seen.

Also Berdolph

More About Maria Catherine Steiner:
Census: 1820 in husband; Lykens, Dauphin Co, PA w[139]
Census: 1830 in Lykens, Dauphin Co, PA[139, 140, 141]
Residence: Bet. 1832-1833 in Dauphin Co, PA[76]

Maria Catherine Steiner and Jacob Peter Batdorf had the following children:

8. i. Peter Batdorf (son of Jacob Peter Batdorf and Maria Catherine Steiner) was born on January 20, 1814 in Dauphin Co, PA[49, 75, 76, 77, 78]. He died on December 05,

1880 in Lykens, Dauphin Co, PA[49, 75, 76, 77, 78, 79, 80]. He married Elizabeth Welker (daughter of John Welker and Maria Elizabeth Messerschmidt) about Abt. 1831 in Dauphin Co, PA. She was born on November 23, 1812 in Dauphin Co?, PA[49, 75, 76]. She died on July 07, 1868 in Dauphin Co, PA[49, 75, 76, 81]. He married Magdalena "Mollie" Lettich. She was born in 1829. She died in 1891[48].

ii. Sarah Batdorf (daughter of Jacob Peter Batdorf and Maria Catherine Steiner) was born in 1815 in PA.

iii. John Batdorf (son of Jacob Peter Batdorf and Maria Catherine Steiner) was born in 1817 in PA.

iv. Catherine Batdorf (daughter of Jacob Peter Batdorf and Maria Catherine Steiner) was born in 1818 in PA.

v. Thomas Batdorf (son of Jacob Peter Batdorf and Maria Catherine Steiner) was born in 1820 in PA. He married <No name>. She was born in 1823 in PA.

vi. Jonathan Batdorf (son of Jacob Peter Batdorf and Maria Catherine Steiner) was born in 1822 in PA.

vii. Daniel Batdorf (son of Jacob Peter Batdorf and Maria Catherine Steiner) was born in 1824 in PA. He married Christina Zimmerman. She was born in 1826 in PA.

viii. Jacob Batdorf (son of Jacob Peter Batdorf and Maria Catherine Steiner) was born in 1826 in PA. He married Rosanna. She was born in 1828 in PA.

ix. Elizabeth Batdorf (daughter of Jacob Peter Batdorf and Maria Catherine Steiner) was born in 1828 in PA.

18. **John Welker** (son of Valentine Welker and Susan Jury) was born on August 10, 1783 in Millersburg, Lancaster (Dauphin) Co, PA[142, 143]. He died on November 11, 1854 in Dauphin Co, PA (Influenza[75, 144]). He married **Maria Elizabeth Messerschmidt** (daughter of Andrew Messerschmidt and Eva Schrot) about Abt. 1806 in Dauphin Co, PA.

19. **Maria Elizabeth Messerschmidt** (daughter of Andrew Messerschmidt and Eva Schrot) was born in 1784 in Elizabethville, Lancaster (Dauphin) Co, PA[145, 146]. She died in 1850 in Gratz,

Dauphin Co, PA[146].

More About John Welker:
Baptism: September 22, 1783 in Old Salem (Werts) Lutheran, Millersburg, Lancaster (Dauphin) Co, PA[142]
Burial: 1854 in Simeon Union Cemetery, Gratz, Dauphin Co, PA[75, 145, 147]
Census: 1790 in father; Dauphin Co, PA w[148]
Census: 1800 in father age 16; Upper Paxton, Dauphin Co, PA w[149]
Census: 1810 in Northern Dauphin Co, PA[150]
Census: 1820 in Lykens, Dauphin Co, PA[90, 151]
Census: 1830 in Lykens, Dauphin Co, PA[91, 152]
Census: 1840 in Lykens, Dauphin Co, PA[153, 154]
Census: 1850 in Lykens, Dauphin Co, PA[155]
Occupation: 1820 ; Manufacturing[90]
Occupation: 1843 ; Weaver[145, 147]
Occupation: 1850 ; Laborer[155]
Probate: 1854 in Dauphin Co, PA (listed in index only)[156]
Property: 1850 in $200[155]

Notes for John Welker:
Born 1784, Pats family, Pat Scott, pat.scott@@comcast.net, awt.ancestry.com, Welkers in the USA & Nulls from PA, Greg Welker, gwelker@@chesapeake.net, awt.ancestry.com & Welker Family, Gratz History, p 450-455.

More About Maria Elizabeth Messerschmidt:
Burial: 1850
Census: 1790 in parents; w
Census: 1800 in father; Upper Paxton, Dauphin Co, PA w[157]
Census: 1810 in husband; Northern Dauphin Co, PA w
Census: 1820 in husband; Lykens, Dauphin Co, PA w
Census: 1830 in husband; Lykens, Dauphin Co, PA w
Census: 1840 in husband; Lykens, Dauphin Co, PA w
Census: 1850 in Lykens, Dauphin Co, PA

Maria Elizabeth Messerschmidt and John Welker had the following children:

i. George Welker (son of John Welker and Maria Elizabeth Messerschmidt) was born in 1807 in Dauphin Co, PA. He died in 1889. He married Catherine. She was born in 1805 in PA.

ii. Rachel Welker (daughter of John Welker and Maria Elizabeth Messerschmidt) was born in 1809 in Dauphin Co, PA. She married Jacob Martz. He was born in 1800.

iii. Welker (daughter of John Welker and Maria Elizabeth Messerschmidt) was born about Abt. 1811 in PA.

9. iv. Elizabeth Welker (daughter of John Welker and Maria Elizabeth Messerschmidt) was born on November 23, 1812 in Dauphin Co?, PA[49, 75, 76]. She died on July 07, 1868 in Dauphin Co, PA[49, 75, 76, 81]. She married Peter Batdorf (son of Jacob Peter Batdorf and Maria Catherine Steiner) about Abt. 1831 in Dauphin Co, PA. He was born on January 20, 1814 in Dauphin Co, PA[49, 75, 76, 77, 78]. He died on December 05, 1880 in Lykens, Dauphin Co, PA[49, 75, 76, 77, 78, 79, 80].

v. William Henry Welker (son of John Welker and Maria Elizabeth Messerschmidt) was born in 1814 in PA. He married Anna. She was born in 1810 in PA.

vi. David Welker (son of John Welker and Maria Elizabeth Messerschmidt) was born in 1815 in Dauphin Co, PA.

vii. Living Welker (daughter of John Welker and Maria Elizabeth Messerschmidt).

viii. Sarah Welker (daughter of John Welker and Maria Elizabeth Messerschmidt) was born in 1818 in Dauphin Co, PA.

ix. Joseph Welker (son of John Welker and Maria Elizabeth Messerschmidt) was born in 1820 in Dauphin Co, PA. He married Susan. She was born in 1823 in PA.

20. **John Peters** (son of Peters) was born about Abt. 1785 in NJ[158]. He died about Abt. 1846 in Buffalo, Union Co, PA[158]. He married **Anna Maria** about Abt. 1815 in Union Co, PA[158].

21. **Anna Maria** was born about Abt. 1792 in PA[158, 159]. She died on October 22, 1852 in East Buffalo, Union Co, PA[160].

More About John Peters:
Census: 1790 in parents; w
Census: 1800 in parents; w
Census: 1810[161]
Census: 1820 in Buffalo, Union Co, PA[162]
Census: 1830 in Buffalo, Union Co, PA[95]
Census: 1840 in Buffalo, Union Co, PA
Probate: Bet. April 13-27 1846 in East Buffalo Tp, Union Co, PA[163]
Residence: Abt. 1830 in East Buffalo, Union Co, PA[164]

Notes for John Peters:
also b PA

More About Anna Maria:
Census: 1850 in East Buffalo, Union Co, PA[159]

Notes for Anna Maria:
also b Germany

Anna Maria and John Peters had the following children:

10. i. Samuel Peters (son of John Peters and Anna Maria) was born in 1821 in Union Co, PA. He died between 1860-1870 in Perry Co, PA. He married Mary Ann Swartz (daughter of John Swartz and <No name>) about Abt. 1840 in Union Co, PA. She was born on January 05, 1820 in Juniata, Perry Co, PA[92]. She died on August 09, 1897 in Washington, Dauphin Co, PA (Heart disease[93, 94]).

ii. Andrew J Peters (son of John Peters and Anna Maria) was born about Abt. 1822 in PA. He married Sarah Bird?. She was born about Abt. 1825 in PA.

iii. Jonathan Peters (son of John Peters and Anna Maria) was born about Abt. 1825 in PA.

iv. Elias Peters (son of John Peters and Anna Maria) was born in April 1829 in PA. He married Angelina. She was born in March 1835 in PA.

v. Matilda Peters (daughter of John Peters and Anna Maria) was born about Abt. 1837 in PA.

22. **John Swartz** (son of Peter Swartz) was born about Abt. 1794 in PA. He died between 1840-1850 in PA?. He married **<No name>** about Abt. 1815.

23. **<No name>** was born about Abt. 1800 in PA.

More About John Swartz:
Census: 1800 in parents; Greenwood, Mifflin, PA w
Census: 1810 in parents; Greenwood, Mifflin, PA w
Census: 1820 in Juniata, Perry Co, PA[165]
Census: 1830 in Juniata, Perry Co, PA
Census: 1840 ; Juniata, Perry Co, PA

<No name> and John Swartz had the following children:

11. i. Mary Ann Swartz (daughter of John Swartz and <No name>) was born on January 05, 1820 in Juniata, Perry Co, PA[92]. She died on August 09, 1897 in Washington, Dauphin Co, PA (Heart disease[93, 94]). She married Samuel Peters (son of John Peters and Anna Maria) about Abt. 1840 in Union Co, PA. He was born in 1821 in Union Co, PA. He died between 1860-1870 in Perry Co, PA.

ii. Living Swartz (son of John Swartz and <No name>).

24. **Jacob Wert** (son of John Jacob Wirth and Anna Sophia Miller) was born on July 20, 1804 in Lykens, Dauphin Co, PA[64, 105]. He died in 1890 in Halifax, Dauphin Co, PA[105, 166, 167]. He married **Sarah Elizabeth Faber** (daughter of John Faber and Maria "Mollie" Magdalena Rudy) about Abt. 1828 in Dauphin Co, PA[64].

25. **Sarah Elizabeth Faber** (daughter of John Faber and Maria "Mollie" Magdalena Rudy) was born on May 25, 1807 in Lancaster (Lebanon) Co, PA[64, 105]. She died on April 05, 1902 in Dauphin Co, PA[64, 168].

More About Jacob Wert:
Burial: 1890 in St. Peters (Fetterhoff) Union, Halifax, Dauphin Co, PA[64]
Burial: St. Pauls (Bowermans) Lutheran, Enterline, Dauphin Co, PA[169]

Census: 1810 in father; Upper Paxton, Dauphin Co, PA w[170]
Census: 1820 in father; Upper Paxton, Dauphin Co, PA w[171]
Census: 1830 in Halifax, Dauphin Co, PA[172, 173]
Census: 1840[113]
Census: 1850 in Jackson, Dauphin Co, PA[114]
Census: 1860 in Halifax, Dauphin Co, PA (Wist)[174]
Census: 1870 in Slatington, Lehigh Co, PA[175]
Census: 1880
Occupation: 1850 ; Farmer[114]
Occupation: 1860 ; Laborer[174]
Occupation: 1870 ; Works on RR[176]
Property: 1860 in $500 + $100[174]
Property: 1870 in $100[176]

More About Sarah Elizabeth Faber:
Burial: 1902 in St. Pauls (Bowermans) Lutheran, Enterline, Dauphin Co, PA[167, 168, 177]
Burial: 1902 in St. Peters (Fetterhoff) Union, Halifax, Dauphin Co, PA[178]
Census: 1810 in father; Upper Paxton, Dauphin Co, PA w[179]
Census: 1820 in father; Upper Paxton, Dauphin Co, PA w[180]
Census: 1830 in Halifax, Dauphin Co, PA
Census: 1840 in husband; w
Census: 1850 in Jackson, Dauphin Co, PA
Census: 1860 in Halifax, Dauphin Co, PA
Census: 1870 in Upper Paxton, Dauphin Co, PA[181]
Census: 1880
Census: 1900
Occupation: 1870 ; Domestic[182]
Occupation: 1870 ; Keeping house[176]

Sarah Elizabeth Faber and Jacob Wert had the following children:

12. i. David M Wert (son of Jacob Wert and Sarah Elizabeth Faber) was born on April 01, 1829 in Powells Valley, Dauphin Co, PA[64, 103, 104, 105]. He died on December 09, 1900 in Dayton, Dauphin Co, PA (Congestion of Lungs[103, 104, 105, 106]). He married Catherine Shoop (daughter of John Shoop and Sarah Wertz) about Abt. 1849 in Dauphin Co, PA. She was born on February 24, 1830 in Northumberland Co, PA[64, 104, 105, 107, 108]. She died on June 08, 1872 in Dauphin Co, PA[64, 104, 105, 107]. He married

Elizabeth Bellis. She was born in 1843 in PA.

ii. Living Wert (daughter of Jacob Wert and Sarah Elizabeth Faber).

iii. Living Wert (daughter of Jacob Wert and Sarah Elizabeth Faber).

iv. Catherine Wert (daughter of Jacob Wert and Sarah Elizabeth Faber) was born in 1835 in PA.

v. John Henry Wert (son of Jacob Wert and Sarah Elizabeth Faber) was born in 1837 in PA. He married Mary Margaret Pinkerton. She was born in 1841 in PA.

vi. Adam Washington Wert (son of Jacob Wert and Sarah Elizabeth Faber) was born in 1841 in PA. He married Sarah Elizabeth Faber. She was born in 1846 in PA.

vii. Peter Martin Wert (son of Jacob Wert and Sarah Elizabeth Faber) was born in 1843 in Dauphin Co, PA.

viii. Matthew Wert (son of Jacob Wert and Sarah Elizabeth Faber) was born in 1847 in PA.

ix. Martha Wert (daughter of Jacob Wert and Sarah Elizabeth Faber) was born in 1848 in PA.

26. **John Shoop** (son of John George Schupp and Anna Margaret Miller) was born on August 01, 1805 in Dauphin Co?, PA[109, 183, 184]. He died on December 13, 1858 in Lower Mahanoy, Northumberland Co, PA[109, 184, 185]. He married **Sarah Wertz** (daughter of John Wertz and Joanna Catherine Garman) about Abt. 1826 in Northumberland Co, PA.

27. **Sarah Wertz** (daughter of John Wertz and Joanna Catherine Garman) was born about Abt. 1811 in Northumberland Co, PA[107, 109]. She died about Abt. 1842 in Lower Mahanoy, Northumberland Co, PA.

More About John Shoop:
Baptism: August 08, 1805 in St. Davids (Salem) Reformed, Millersburg, Dauphin Co, PA

Burial: 1858 in Zion (Stone Valley) Lutheran, Dalmatia, Northumberland Co, PA
Census: 1810 in father; Upper Paxton, Dauphin Co, PA w[186]
Census: 1820 in father; Upper Paxton, Dauphin Co, PA w[187]
Census: 1830 in Lower Mahanoy, Northumberland Co, PA[188]
Census: 1840 in Lower Mahanoy, Northumberland Co, PA
Census: 1850 in Lower Mahanoy, Northmuberland, PA (Joyn)[189]
Occupation: 1850 ; Farmer[189]
Probate: December 23, 1858 in Lower Mahanoy, Northumberland Co, PA[190]
Property: 1850 in $800[189]

More About Sarah Wertz:
Burial: Abt. 1842 in Zion (Stone Valley) Lutheran, Dalmatia, Northumberland Co, PA
Census: 1820 in father; Lower Mahanoy, Northumberland Co, PA w[191]
Census: 1830 in husband; Lower Mahanoy, Northumberland Co, PA w
Census: 1840 in husband; Lower Mahanoy, Northumberland Co, PA w
Occupation: Abt. 1835 ; Homemaker

Sarah Wertz and John Shoop had the following children:

13. i. Catherine Shoop[66] (daughter of John Shoop and Sarah Wertz) was born on February 24, 1830 in Northumberland Co, PA[64, 104, 105, 107, 108]. She died on June 08, 1872 in Dauphin Co, PA[64, 104, 105, 107]. She married David M Wert (son of Jacob Wert and Sarah Elizabeth Faber) about Abt. 1849 in Dauphin Co, PA. He was born on April 01, 1829 in Powells Valley, Dauphin Co, PA[64, 103, 104, 105]. He died on December 09, 1900 in Dayton, Dauphin Co, PA (Congestion of Lungs[103, 104, 105, 106]).

ii. Elizabeth Shoop (daughter of John Shoop and Sarah Wertz) was born in 1833 in Dauphin Co, PA. She married William Henry Welker. He was born in 1835.

iii. Salome "Sarah" Shoop (daughter of John Shoop and Sarah Wertz) was born in 1841 in PA. She married Simon Tschopp. He was born in 1833.

iv. Living Shoop (daughter of John Shoop and Sarah Wertz). She married Jeremiah Crawford. He was born in 1833.

v. Living Shoop (daughter of John Shoop and Sarah Wertz).

28. **John William Rowe** (son of Francis "Frank" Rowe and Maria Catherine Traut) was born in June 1785 in Strasburg, Lancaster Co, PA[192, 193, 194, 195]. He died in 1877 in Berrysburg, Dauphin Co, PA[192, 194]. He married **Barbara Rudy** (daughter of Jacob Rudy and Susan Jungblut) in 1810 in Strasburg, Lancaster Co, PA[120, 194].

29. **Barbara Rudy** (daughter of Jacob Rudy and Susan Jungblut) was born on April 11, 1796 in Strasburg, Lancaster Co, PA[193, 196]. She died on December 15, 1881 in Berrysburg, Dauphin Co, PA[120, 193, 196].

More About John William Rowe:
Burial: 1877 in St. Johns (Hill) Lutheran, Berrysburg, Dauphin Co, PA[120, 196, 197]
Census: 1790 in father; Strasburg, Lancaster Co, PA w[198]
Census: 1800 in father age 16; Strasburg, Lancaster Co, PA w[199]
Census: 1810
Census: 1820 in Mifflin, Dauphin Co, PA (Rosie)[200, 201]
Census: 1830 in Halifax, Dauphin Co, PA[202, 203]
Census: 1840 in Wiconisco, Dauphin Co, PA[204]
Census: 1850 in Wiconisco, Dauphin Co, PA[205]
Census: 1860 in Wiconisco, Dauphin Co, PA[128]
Census: 1870 in Washington, Dauphin Co, PA[206]
Occupation: 1820 ; Agriculture[207]
Occupation: Abt. 1840 ; Carpenter
Occupation: Bet. 1850-1870 ; Laborer[128, 206, 208]
Property: 1850 in $150[208]
Property: 1860 in $100[128]
Religion: Bet. 1812-1820 ; St. Johns (Hill) Lutheran, Lykens, Dauphin Co, PA[209]
Residence: Bet. 1812-1820 in Berrysburg, Dauphin Co, PA[142]
Will: April 03, 1873 in Dauphin Co, PA (listed in index)[210]

Notes for John William Rowe:
Ancestor of Jonas Row farmer and justice of the peace, was born in Mifflin township, now Washington Township, Dauphin county, Pa.,

May 11, 1839. He owned, improved and worked a farm of ninety acres in Washington township in connection with which he carried on a butchering business, also a store at Matterstown. Mr. Row first held Democratic views in politics, but changed for a time to the Republican party, and finally returned to the Democratic party. He has served as supervisor of roads, tax collector, and in other offices. He died in Schuylkill County at the age of eighty-two. Mr. Row was well known and highly respected. He was comfortably cared for in his declining years by his faithful son, Jonas. He was a member of the old school Lutheran church, in which he was deacon and trustee, also Sunday-school superintendent and teacher. Jonas Row attended the schools of Washington Township in the winter, and worked with his father in the various departments of his business until he was twenty-one years of age. On reaching his majority he was employed by his father on wages. He worked two years on the homestead farm, at Matterstown, and two years in Lykens Valley, at butchering, etc. In 1863 Mr. Row enlisted, at Harrisburg, in the One Hundred and Twenty-seventh regiment, Pennsylvania volunteers, under Colonel Jennings and Captain Bell. He participated in the battle of Gettysburg, and was wounded in the knee, the result of which was to lame him fur life. He was discharged at the end of three months' service, but re-enlisted in the fall of 1863, in company F, Sixteenth Pennsylvania cavalry, under Colonel Robinson and Capt. J. H. Ressler. He was at Petersburg five days, and on account of bravery in action was promoted to the rank of orderly to General Gregg. Mr. Row was at the surrender of General Lee, and was mustered out of service in 1865. He returned home and engaged in trading in Lykens Valley for two years, after which he bought thirty-three acres of land and added twenty-two acres more, in Washington Township. This farm he improved at an expense of $5,000. But Mr. Row became security for a friend, through which he sustained a loss of $4000, and was forced to sell his farm which brought only $5,000. In 1890 he removed to Jefferson Township and purchased eighty acres, the buildings on which he remodeled and enlarged, and fitted the place for farming and stock raising. [Dauphin County, Pennsylvania Genealogy Transcription Project, http://maley.net/transcription/]

Have photograph.

Born England, Rowe family information, Jean Row Romberger, Allentown, PA, jmrrrer@@juno.com.

More About Barbara Rudy:
Burial: 1881 in St. Johns (Hill) Lutheran, Berrysburg, Dauphin Co, PA[120, 211]
Census: 1800 in father; Lancaster Co, PA w[212]
Census: 1810 in husband; w
Census: 1820 in husband; Mifflin, Dauphin Co, PA w
Census: 1830 in husband; Halifax, Dauphin Co, PA w
Census: 1840 in husband; Wiconisco, Dauphin Co, PA w
Census: 1850 in Wiconisco, Dauphin Co, PA
Census: 1860 in Wiconisco, Dauphin Co, PA
Census: 1870 in Washington, Dauphin Co, PA[206]
Census: 1880 in son Jacob; Washington, Dauphin Co, PA w[213]
Occupation: 1870 ; Keeping house[206]
Occupation: 1880 ; Lady[213]

Notes for Barbara Rudy:
Have photograph.

Barbara Rudy and John William Rowe had the following children:

i. Wendel Row (son of John William Rowe and Barbara Rudy) was born in 1811 in PA. He married Rachel. She was born in 1813 in PA.

ii. Jacob Row (son of John William Rowe and Barbara Rudy) was born in 1812 in Dauphin Co, PA. He married Susan Matter. She was born in 1820 in PA.

14. iii. Daniel Row (son of John William Rowe and Barbara Rudy) was born on July 10, 1813 in Dauphin Co, PA[62, 119, 120, 121]. He died on July 31, 1871 in Dauphin Co, PA (Bright's disease (ie, Chronic inflammation of kidneys)[120, 121]). He married Susan Frantz (daughter of Adam Frantz and Susan Gieseman) about Abt. 1840 in Dauphin Co, PA. She was born on March 23, 1819 in Dauphin Co, PA[62, 120, 122]. She died on October 17, 1861 in Berrysburg, Dauphin Co, PA[120, 122].

iv. Susan Row (daughter of John William Rowe and Barbara Rudy) was born in 1815 in PA.

v. John Row (son of John William Rowe and Barbara Rudy) was born in 1817 in PA. He married Matilda. She was born in 1821 in PA.

vi. Elizabeth Row (daughter of John William Rowe and Barbara Rudy) was born in 1819 in PA.

vii. Sarah Row (daughter of John William Rowe and Barbara Rudy) was born in 1820 in PA.

viii. Joseph Row (son of John William Rowe and Barbara Rudy) was born in 1828 in PA. He married Catherine. She was born in 1833 in PA.

30. **Adam Frantz** (son of John William Frantz and Anna Margaret Gieseman Shirk) was born in 1780 in Lykens, Lancaster (Dauphin) Co, PA[214, 215]. He died between 1825-1830 in Dauphin Co, PA. He married **Susan Gieseman** (daughter of John William Gieseman and Anna Margaret Gruber) on October 06, 1811 in Upper Paxton, Dauphin Co, PA[216, 217, 218].

31. **Susan Gieseman** (daughter of John William Gieseman and Anna Margaret Gruber) was born on November 10, 1787 in Tulpehocken, Berks Co, PA[216, 219]. She died on February 15, 1826 in Mifflin, Dauphin Co, PA (Pilger Fieber u. Kindes Nothen (ie, Pilgrim fever)[216, 219, 220]).

More About Adam Frantz:
Baptism: Abt. 1785 in St. Johns (Hill) Lutheran, Berrysburg, Dauphin Co, PA
Census: 1790 in father; Strasburg, Lancaster Co, PA w[221]
Census: 1800 in father; Upper Paxton, Dauphin Co, PA w[222]
Census: 1810
Census: 1820 in Mifflin, Dauphin Co, PA[223]
Military Service: Bet. September 02, 1814-March 05, 1815 ; War of 1812, Private, 2nd Reg PA Militia (Ritschers), 1st Brig (York, Capt. Philip Fetterhoff)[224]
Occupation: 1820 ; Manufacturing[225]
Religion: Bet. 1812-1824 ; St.John (Hill) Church, Lykens, Upper Paxton, PA[226]
Religion: Bet. 1816-1819 ; St. Peters (Hoffmans) Church, Lykens, Dauphin Co, PA[227]

More About Susan Gieseman:
Baptism: May 30, 1788 in PA[220]
Burial: February 17, 1826 in St. Johns (Hill) Lutheran, Berrysburg, Dauphin Co, PA[219, 220]
Census: 1790 in father; Tulpehocken, Berks Co, PA w[228]
Census: 1800 in father; Tulpehocken, Berks Co, PA w[229]
Census: 1810 in father; Upper Paxton, Dauphin Co, PA w[230]
Census: 1820 in husband; Mifflin, Dauphin Co, PA w
Residence: Bet. 1816-1824 in Dauphin County, PA[231]

Notes for Susan Gieseman:
Baptism is prior to birth.

Susan Gieseman and Adam Frantz had the following children:

i. Adam Frantz (son of Adam Frantz and Susan Gieseman) was born in 1811 in PA.

ii. William Frantz (son of Adam Frantz and Susan Gieseman) was born in 1812 in PA. He married Elizabeth. She was born in 1812 in PA.

iii. Jacob Frantz (son of Adam Frantz and Susan Gieseman) was born in 1814 in PA.

iv. John Frantz (son of Adam Frantz and Susan Gieseman) was born about Abt. 1815 in PA.

v. Catherine Frantz (daughter of Adam Frantz and Susan Gieseman) was born about Abt. 1815 in PA.

vi. Christina Frantz (daughter of Adam Frantz and Susan Gieseman) was born in 1818 in PA.

15. vii. Susan Frantz (daughter of Adam Frantz and Susan Gieseman) was born on March 23, 1819 in Dauphin Co, PA[62, 120, 122]. She died on October 17, 1861 in Berrysburg, Dauphin Co, PA[120, 122]. She married Daniel Row (son of John William Rowe and Barbara Rudy) about Abt. 1840 in Dauphin Co, PA. He was born on July 10, 1813 in Dauphin Co, PA[62, 119, 120, 121]. He died on July 31, 1871 in Dauphin Co, PA (Bright's disease (ie, Chronic inflammation of kidneys)[120, 121]).

viii. Sarah Frantz (daughter of Adam Frantz and Susan Gieseman) was born in 1821 in PA.

ix. Samuel Frantz (son of Adam Frantz and Susan Gieseman) was born in 1824 in PA.

Generation 6

32. **George Peter Batdorf** (son of Martin Batdorf and Barbara Elizabeth Saltzegber) was born on February 11, 1768 in Lancaster Co, PA[232, 233, 234]. He died between 1830-1840 in OH (PA[133]). He married **Barbara Weiss** (daughter of John Weiss) about Abt. 1792 in Dauphin?, PA.

33. **Barbara Weiss** (daughter of John Weiss) was born about Abt. 1772 in PA. She died after Aft. 1830 in OH (PA).

More About George Peter Batdorf:
d: Aft. 1854[234]
Baptism: February 14, 1768[234]
Census: 1790
Census: 1800 in Heidelberg, Dauphin Co, PA[134]
Census: 1810 in Heidelberg, Dauphin Co, PA[235]
Census: 1820 in Lykens, Dauphin Co, PA[236]
Census: 1830 in Lykens, Dauphin Co, PA[83, 139]
Census: 1840
Residence: Abt. 1854 in Forreston, IN[234]

Notes for George Peter Batdorf:
I believe Peter Batdorf married two Catherine (Brine & LNU), one Catherine was mother to issue born 1794-1805 & the other was mother to issue 1813-1820. There were two Johns, Peters & Catherines born; one Peter born circa 1790 and another Peter 1813. Peter Daniel born 1813 is confused with Peter born 1814.

More About Barbara Weiss:
Census: 1820 in husband; Lykens, Dauphin Co, PA w[237]
Census: 1830 in husband; Lykens, Dauphin Co, PA w[139]
Census: 1840

Barbara Weiss and George Peter Batdorf had the following children:

16. i. Jacob Peter Batdorf (son of George Peter Batdorf and Barbara Weiss) was born about Abt. 1793 in PA. He died in 1829 in Dauphin Co, PA[76]. He married Maria Catherine Steiner (daughter of Jacob? Steiner and Elizabeth) on February 20, 1813 in Christ Lutheran, Stouchsburg, Berks Co, PA. She was born about Abt. 1790 in Berks Co, PA[133]. She died about Abt. 1840 in Dauphin Co, PA.

ii. John Batdorf (son of George Peter Batdorf and Barbara Weiss) was born in 1794 in PA. He married Catherine Daniels. She was born in 1795.

iii. Catherine Batdorf (daughter of George Peter Batdorf and Barbara Weiss) was born in 1796 in PA.

iv. Christina Batdorf (daughter of George Peter Batdorf and Barbara Weiss) was born in 1799 in PA.

v. Eva Batdorf (daughter of George Peter Batdorf and Barbara Weiss) was born in 1802 in PA.

vi. Christian Batdorf (son of George Peter Batdorf and Barbara Weiss) was born in 1803 in PA. He married Sarah. She was born in 1805 in PA.

vii. John Jacob Batdorf (son of George Peter Batdorf and Barbara Weiss) was born in 1805 in PA. He married Christina Bush.

34. **Jacob? Steiner** was born about Abt. 1760. He died after Aft. 1790. He married **Elizabeth** about Abt. 1785.

35. **Elizabeth** was born about Abt. 1760. She died after Aft. 1790.

More About Elizabeth:
Census: 1790
Census: 1800

Elizabeth and Jacob? Steiner had the following children:

i. George Steiner (son of Jacob? Steiner and Elizabeth) was born about Abt. 1787.

17. ii. Maria Catherine Steiner (daughter of Jacob? Steiner and

Elizabeth) was born about Abt. 1790 in Berks Co, PA[133]. She died about Abt. 1840 in Dauphin Co, PA. She married Jacob Peter Batdorf (son of George Peter Batdorf and Barbara Weiss) on February 20, 1813 in Christ Lutheran, Stouchsburg, Berks Co, PA. He was born about Abt. 1793 in PA. He died in 1829 in Dauphin Co, PA[76].

36. **Valentine Welker** (son of Valentine Welker and Anna Elizabeth Schaffer?) was born on January 11, 1755 in Schwandorf, Germany[238]. He died in 1831 in Carsonville, Dauphin Co, PA[75, 146, 239]. He married **Susan Jury** (daughter of Abraham Joray and Catherine Guerne) in 1783 in Northumberland Co, PA[240].

37. **Susan Jury** (daughter of Abraham Joray and Catherine Guerne) was born in 1755 in Upper Paxton, Lancaster (Dauphin) Co, PA[146, 239]. She died about Abt. 1801 in Upper Paxtang, Dauphin Co, PA.

More About Valentine Welker:
b: January 11, 1755 in Frankenthal, Rhineland-Palatinate, Germany[75, 143, 241]
Baptism: January 14, 1755 in Germany[239]
Burial: 1831
Census: 1790 in Dauphin Co, PA
Census: 1800 in Upper Paxton, Dauphin Co, PA[145]
Census: 1810 in Mifflin, Dauphin Co, PA[242]
Census: 1820 in Millersburg, Dauphin Co, PA[90, 151]
Census: 1830 in Millersburg, Dauphin Co, PA[91, 152]
Immigration: October 16, 1772 in Germany to USA (ship Crawford)[143, 239, 243]
Military Service: 1778 ; American Revolution, Private 4th PA Reg, 4th Co, 5th class, (Lancaster, Capt. Jonathan McClure)[244]
Naturalization: December 28, 1772[239]
Probate: 1831 in Upper Paxtang Tp, Dauphin Co, PA[245]
Religion: 1812 ; St. Davids (Salem) Reformed, Millersburg, Dauphin Co, PA[145, 240]
Residence: 1772 in Philadelphia, PA[246]
Residence: 1779 in Middletown, Lancaster (Dauphin) Co, PA[247]
Residence: Bet. 1784-1801 in Killinger, Dauphin Co, PA[142]
Will: 1831 in Upper Paxtang Tp, Dauphin Co, PA[248]

More About Susan Jury:

Baptism: 1759 in Salem Lutheran, Millersburg, Lancaster (Dauphin) Co, PA[249]
Census: 1790 in husband; Dauphin Co, PA w
Census: 1800 in husband; Upper Paxton, Dauphin Co, PA w
Confirmation: July 17, 1777 in St. Davids (Salem) Reformed, Millersburg, Lancaster (Dauphin) Co, PA[250]

Susan Jury and Valentine Welker had the following children:

18. i. John Welker (son of Valentine Welker and Susan Jury) was born on August 10, 1783 in Millersburg, Lancaster (Dauphin) Co, PA[142, 143]. He died on November 11, 1854 in Dauphin Co, PA (Influenza[75, 144]). He married Maria Elizabeth Messerschmidt (daughter of Andrew Messerschmidt and Eva Schrot) about Abt. 1806 in Dauphin Co, PA. She was born in 1784 in Elizabethville, Lancaster (Dauphin) Co, PA[145, 146]. She died in 1850 in Gratz, Dauphin Co, PA[146].

ii. Elizabeth Welker (daughter of Valentine Welker and Susan Jury) was born in 1784 in PA.

iii. John William Welker (son of Valentine Welker and Susan Jury) was born in 1786 in Dauphin Co, PA. He married Susan Schoffstall. She was born in 1791 in PA.

iv. Elizabeth Welker (daughter of Valentine Welker and Susan Jury) was born in 1787 in PA.

v. Salome "Sarah" Welker (daughter of Valentine Welker and Susan Jury) was born in 1788 in Dauphin Co, PA.

vi. Peter Welker (son of Valentine Welker and Susan Jury) was born in 1788 in PA. He married Susan.

vii. Catherine Welker (daughter of Valentine Welker and Susan Jury) was born in 1796 in Dauphin Co, PA. She married Jacob Meck.

viii. Jacob Welker (son of Valentine Welker and Susan Jury) was born in 1798 in Dauphin Co, PA. He married Elizabeth Siegel. She was born in 1798 in PA.

ix. Daniel Welker (son of Valentine Welker and Susan Jury) was born in 1801 in PA.

38. **Andrew Messerschmidt** (son of Andrew Messerschmidt and Susan Groetzinge) was born about Abt. 1751 in Lancaster Co, PA[75]. He died in 1801 in Upper Paxton, Dauphin Co, PA[75]. He married **Eva Schrot** (daughter of John Schrot and <No name>) on September 26, 1779 in Christ Lutheran, Stouchsburg, Berks Co, PA[251].

39. **Eva Schrot** (daughter of John Schrot and <No name>) was born about Abt. 1753 in PA[142]. She died after Aft. 1810 in Lancaster Co, PA.

More About Andrew Messerschmidt:
Burial: 1801
Census: 1790
Census: 1800 in Upper Paxton, Dauphin Co, PA
Military Service: 1776 ; American Revolution, Private 1st PA Reg, Rifle (Lancaster, Capt. Peter Grubb)[252]
Occupation: Abt. 1785 ; Farmer
Probate: 1801 in Dauphin Co, PA (listed in index only)[253]
Religion: Bet. 1787-1792 ; Zion Lutheran, Harrisburg, Dauphin Co, PA[254]

More About Eva Schrot:
Census: 1790 in husband; w
Census: 1800 in husband; Upper Paxton, Dauphin Co, PA w
Census: 1810 in Lancaster, Lancaster Co, PA (widow)[255]

Eva Schrot and Andrew Messerschmidt had the following children:

19. i. Maria Elizabeth Messerschmidt (daughter of Andrew Messerschmidt and Eva Schrot) was born in 1784 in Elizabethville, Lancaster (Dauphin) Co, PA[145, 146]. She died in 1850 in Gratz, Dauphin Co, PA[146]. She married John Welker (son of Valentine Welker and Susan Jury) about Abt. 1806 in Dauphin Co, PA. He was born on August 10, 1783 in Millersburg, Lancaster (Dauphin) Co, PA[142, 143]. He died on November 11, 1854 in Dauphin Co, PA (Influenza[75, 144]).

ii. Julia Messerschmidt (daughter of Andrew Messerschmidt and Eva Schrot) was born in PA.

iii. Catherine Messerschmidt (daughter of Andrew

Messerschmidt and Eva Schrot) was born in PA.

iv. Andrew Messerschmidt (son of Andrew Messerschmidt and Eva Schrot) was born in PA.

v. Louis Messerschmidt (son of Andrew Messerschmidt and Eva Schrot) was born in 1787 in PA.

vi. George Messerschmidt (son of Andrew Messerschmidt and Eva Schrot) was born in 1790 in PA.

vii. Henry Messerschmidt (son of Andrew Messerschmidt and Eva Schrot) was born in 1790 in PA.

viii. Jacob Messerschmidt (son of Andrew Messerschmidt and Eva Schrot) was born in 1792 in PA.

ix. Messerschmidt (daughter of Andrew Messerschmidt and Eva Schrot) was born in PA.

40. **Peters** (son of <No name> and <No name>) was born about Abt. 1760.

Peters had the following children:

i. William Peters (son of Peters) was born about Abt. 1781.

20. ii. John Peters (son of Peters) was born about Abt. 1785 in NJ[158]. He died about Abt. 1846 in Buffalo, Union Co, PA[158]. He married Anna Maria about Abt. 1815 in Union Co, PA[158]. She was born about Abt. 1792 in PA[158, 159]. She died on October 22, 1852 in East Buffalo, Union Co, PA[160].

iii. Peters (daughter of Peters) was born about Abt. 1787.

iv. Leonard Peters (son of Peters) was born in 1789.

44. **Peter Swartz** was born about Abt. 1770 in PA. He died between 1810-1820 in PA?.

Peter Swartz had the following children:

22. i. John Swartz (son of Peter Swartz) was born about Abt. 1794 in PA. He died between 1840-1850 in PA?. He married <No name> about Abt. 1815. She was born about Abt. 1800 in PA.

ii. Peter Swartz (son of Peter Swartz) was born about Abt. 1795.

iii. David Swartz (son of Peter Swartz) was born about Abt. 1795.

iv. Matthew Swartz (son of Peter Swartz) was born about Abt. 1800.

48. **John Jacob Wirth** (son of John Adam Wirth and Eva Elizabeth Schnug) was born in February 1763 in Lebanon, Lancaster (Lebanon) Co, PA[167, 256]. He died on January 01, 1833 in Millersburg, Dauphin Co, PA[64, 257, 258]. He married **Anna Sophia Miller** (daughter of John Miller and Frances Kerstetter) about Abt. 1794 in Dauphin Co, PA[257].

49. **Anna Sophia Miller** (daughter of John Miller and Frances Kerstetter) was born on August 02, 1776 in Millersburg, Lancaster (Dauphin) Co, PA[64, 105, 257, 259]. She died on October 22, 1842 in Lykens, Dauphin Co, PA[64, 257, 259, 260].

More About John Jacob Wirth:
Baptism: March 25, 1763 in PA[167, 256]
Burial: January 03, 1833 in Old Salem (Werts) Lutheran, Millersburg, Dauphin Co, PA[64, 167, 257]
Census: 1790 in father; Dauphin Co, PA w[261, 262]
Census: 1800 in Upper Paxton, Dauphin Co, PA
Census: 1810 in Upper Paxton, Dauphin Co, PA[263]
Census: 1820 in Upper Paxton, Dauphin Co, PA[264]
Census: 1830 in Upper Paxton, Dauphin Co, PA[265, 266]
Occupation: 1820 ; Agriculture[264]
Probate: January 16, 1833 in Dauphin Co, PA (listed in index only)[267]

Notes for John Jacob Wirth:
Died 1833 Wert Tree, K. Shuey, kshuey208@@hotmail.com, www.ancestry.com.
Born 1753, Monn & Related families, Danni Monn Hopkins, clueless@@clnk.com, www.ancestry.com.
Mar 21, 1764, Jacob Wirth, Wirth's Evangelical Lutheran Church Cemetery, Dauphin Co, PA, www.USGenweb.com, Jonathan Wert.

More About Anna Sophia Miller:
Baptism: Abt. 1776 in Old Salem (Werts) Lutheran, Millersburg, Lancaster (Dauphin) Co, PA
Burial: 1842 in Old Salem (Werts) Lutheran, Millersburg, Dauphin Co, PA[64, 257]
Census: 1790 in father; Upper Paxton, Dauphin Co, PA w
Census: 1800 in husband; Upper Paxton, Dauphin Co, PA w
Census: 1810 in husband; Paxton, Dauphin Co, PA w
Census: 1820 in husband; Upper Paxton, Dauphin Co, PA w
Census: 1830 in husband; Upper Paxton, Dauphin Co, PA w
Census: 1840

Notes for Anna Sophia Miller:
Aka Sophia Susan, Wert Tree, K Shuey, kshuey208@@hotmail.com, www.ancestry.com.

Anna Sophia Miller and John Jacob Wirth had the following children:

i. Eva Elizabeth Wert (daughter of John Jacob Wirth and Anna Sophia Miller) was born in 1795 in Dauphin Co, PA.

ii. John Wert (son of John Jacob Wirth and Anna Sophia Miller) was born in 1796 in Dauphin Co, PA.

iii. Daniel Wert (son of John Jacob Wirth and Anna Sophia Miller) was born in 1796 in Dauphin Co, PA. He married Susan Schupp. She was born in 1797 in Dauphin Co, PA.

More About Daniel Wert:
b: 1796

iv. Anna Maria Wert (daughter of John Jacob Wirth and Anna Sophia Miller) was born in 1799 in Dauphin Co, PA. She died in 1859.

v. John Wert (son of John Jacob Wirth and Anna Sophia Miller) was born in 1804 in Dauphin Co, PA. He died in 1829 in OH.

24. vi. Jacob Wert (son of John Jacob Wirth and Anna Sophia Miller) was born on July 20, 1804 in Lykens, Dauphin Co, PA[64, 105]. He died in 1890 in Halifax, Dauphin Co, PA[105, 166,

[167]. He married Sarah Elizabeth Faber (daughter of John Faber and Maria "Mollie" Magdalena Rudy) about Abt. 1828 in Dauphin Co, PA[64]. She was born on May 25, 1807 in Lancaster (Lebanon) Co, PA[64, 105]. She died on April 05, 1902 in Dauphin Co, PA[64, 168].

vii. Sarah Wert (daughter of John Jacob Wirth and Anna Sophia Miller) was born in 1805 in Dauphin Co, PA.

viii. Isaac Wert (son of John Jacob Wirth and Anna Sophia Miller) was born in 1808 in Dauphin Co, PA. He died in 1863. He married Elizabeth. She was born in 1806 in PA.

ix. Henry Wert (son of John Jacob Wirth and Anna Sophia Miller) was born in 1810 in Dauphin Co, PA. He died in 1880. He married Elizabeth. She was born in 1813 in PA.

x. Living Wert (daughter of John Jacob Wirth and Anna Sophia Miller).

xi. Magdalena Wert (daughter of John Jacob Wirth and Anna Sophia Miller) was born in 1813 in PA.

50. **John Faber** (son of John Faber and Margaret Rudy) was born on March 30, 1777 in Lancaster (Lebanon) Co, PA[105, 268, 269, 270, 271, 272, 273]. He died on July 15, 1828 in Halifax Tp, Dauphin Co, PA[272, 273, 274, 275, 276]. He married **Maria "Mollie" Magdalena Rudy** (daughter of Jonas Rudy and Anna Barbara Overcash) in 1805 in Lancaster (Lebanon) Co, PA[105, 269, 270, 272, 273, 274].

51. **Maria "Mollie" Magdalena Rudy** (daughter of Jonas Rudy and Anna Barbara Overcash) was born on April 14, 1784 in Bethel, Lancaster (Lebanon) Co, PA[269, 270, 272, 273, 274, 276]. She died on July 16, 1845 in Jefferson Tp, Dauphin Co, PA[167, 272, 273, 277].

More About John Faber:
Baptism: April 21, 1777 in Swatara Reformed, Fredericksburg, Lancaster (Lebanon) Co, PA[274]
Burial: 1828 in Hill Cemetery, Halifax, Dauphin Co, PA[105, 274]
Census: 1790 in father; Dauphin Co, PA w
Census: 1800 in father; Not listed w
Census: 1810 in Upper Paxton, Dauphin Co, PA age 45[278]

Census: 1820 in Upper Paxton, Dauphin Co, PA
Probate: Bet. August 08-13 1828 in Dauphin Co, PA (listed in index only)[274, 279]
Religion: Bet. 1819-1825 ; Evangelical Reformed Church, Lykens, Upper Paxton, Dauphin Co, PA[280]

Notes for John Faber:
Died 1826, Monn & Related Families, Danni Monn Hopkins, clueless@@clnk.com, www.ancestry.com.
Burial records at St. Peters (Fetterhoff) Union, Halifax, Dauphin Co, PA & St. Davids Reformed Church, Killinger, Dauphin Co, PA.

More About Maria "Mollie" Magdalena Rudy:
d: January 16, 1845 in Dauphin Co, PA[105, 274, 276, 281]
Baptism: November 14, 1784 in St. Johns Union, Fredericksburg, Lancaster (Lebanon) Co, PA[167, 274, 276]
Burial: 1845 in St. Pauls (Bowermans) Lutheran, Enterline, Dauphin Co, PA[105, 274, 276]
Census: 1790 in father; Dauphin Co, PA w
Census: 1800 in father; Bethel, Dauphin (Lebanon) Co, PA w
Census: 1810 in husband; Upper Paxton, Dauphin Co, PA w
Census: 1820 in husband; Upper Paxton, Dauphin Co, PA w
Census: 1830 in Halifax, Dauphin Co, PA[282]
Census: 1840
Probate: August 01, 1845 in Jefferson Tp, Dauphin Co, PA[283]
Will: July 10, 1845 in Jefferson Tp, Dauphin Co, PA[283]

Notes for Maria "Mollie" Magdalena Rudy:
Surname aka Ruthy, Kuthy [DAR, Application of Mary I Bowerman Dininni, Harrisburg, PA, Natl #596079, May 1981]

Born April 6 [Monn & related Families, Danni Monn Hopkins, clueless@@clnk.com, www.ancestry.com]

Burial [St. Pauls (Bowermans) Enterline, Dauphin Co, PA, Evelyn S Hartman, deanh@@voicenet.com]

Maria "Mollie" Magdalena Rudy and John Faber had the following children:

25. i. Sarah Elizabeth Faber (daughter of John Faber and Maria "Mollie" Magdalena Rudy) was born on May 25, 1807 in Lancaster (Lebanon) Co, PA[64, 105]. She died on April 05, 1902 in Dauphin Co, PA[64, 168]. She married Jacob Wert (son of John Jacob Wirth and Anna Sophia Miller) about Abt. 1828 in Dauphin Co, PA[64]. He was born on July 20, 1804 in Lykens, Dauphin Co, PA[64, 105]. He died in 1890 in Halifax, Dauphin Co, PA[105, 166, 167].

ii. Michael Faber (son of John Faber and Maria "Mollie" Magdalena Rudy) was born in 1808 in PA. He married Elizabeth. She was born in 1806 in PA.

iii. John Faber (son of John Faber and Maria "Mollie" Magdalena Rudy) was born in 1809 in PA. He married Elizabeth. She was born in 1816 in PA.

iv. Catherine Faber (daughter of John Faber and Maria "Mollie" Magdalena Rudy) was born on January 14, 1810 in Lebanon Co, PA[273]. She married John Baker. He was born on May 19, 1804 in PA[272, 273].

v. Adam Faber (son of John Faber and Maria "Mollie" Magdalena Rudy) was born in 1814 in PA. He married Anna. She was born in 1815 in PA.

vi. George Faber (son of John Faber and Maria "Mollie" Magdalena Rudy) was born in 1815 in PA.

vii. Susan L Faber (daughter of John Faber and Maria "Mollie" Magdalena Rudy) was born about Abt. 1817.

viii. Faber (son of John Faber and Maria "Mollie" Magdalena Rudy) was born about Abt. 1817.

ix. Flora Lou Faber (daughter of John Faber and Maria "Mollie" Magdalena Rudy) was born in 1818.

x. Jacob Faber (son of John Faber and Maria "Mollie" Magdalena Rudy) was born in 1819 in PA. He married Catherine. She was born in 1831 in PA.

xi. Magdalena Faber (daughter of John Faber and Maria "Mollie" Magdalena Rudy) was born in 1822 in Dauphin

Co, PA.

xii. Lucy Ann Faber (daughter of John Faber and Maria "Mollie" Magdalena Rudy) was born in 1825 in Dauphin Co, PA.

52. **John George Schupp** (son of John George Schupp and Anna Maria Elizabeth Deibler) was born in May 1780 in Upper Paxton, Lancaster (Dauphin) Co, PA[75, 284, 285, 286]. He died on January 20, 1854 in Dauphin Co, PA[286, 287, 288]. He married **Anna Margaret Miller** (daughter of John Miller and Frances Kerstetter) about Abt. 1801 in Dauphin Co, PA.

53. **Anna Margaret Miller** (daughter of John Miller and Frances Kerstetter) was born on February 12, 1784 in Lancaster (Dauphin) Co, PA[289, 290, 291]. She died on July 24, 1857 in Dauphin Co, PA[284, 285, 291].

More About John George Schupp:
Baptism: May 24, 1780 in St. Davids (Salem) Reformed, Millersburg, Lancaster (Dauphin) Co, PA
Burial: 1854 in Zion (Stone Valley) Lutheran, Dalmatia, Northumberland Co, PA
Census: 1790 in father; Dauphin Co, PA w
Census: 1800 in father; Upper Paxton, Dauphin Co, PA w[292]
Census: 1810 in Upper Paxton, Dauphin Co, PA[186]
Census: 1820 in Upper Paxton, Dauphin Co, PA[187]
Census: 1830 in Upper Paxton, Dauphin Co, PA[292]
Census: 1840 in Upper Paxton, Dauphin Co, PA[293]
Census: 1850 in Mifflin, Dauphin Co, PA[189, 284]
Occupation: 1820 ; Agriculture[187]
Property: 1850 in $1100[189]
Residence: Abt. 1852 in Alleghenyville, Berks Co, PA[284]

Notes for John George Schupp:
Died 1851

More About Anna Margaret Miller:
Baptism: April 18, 1784 in Dalmatia, Northumberland Co, PA[289]

Burial: 1857 in Zion (Stone Valley) Lutheran, Dalmatia, Northumberland Co, PA[285, 291]
Census: 1790 in father; Upper Paxton, Dauphin Co, PA w
Census: 1800 in father age 15; Upper Paxton, Dauphin Co, PA w
Census: 1810 in husband; Upper Paxton, Dauphin Co, PA w
Census: 1820 in husband; Upper Paxton, Dauphin Co, PA w
Census: 1830 in husband; Upper Paxton, Dauphin Co, PA w
Census: 1840 in husband; Upper Paxton, Dauphin Co, PA w
Census: 1850 in Mifflin, Dauphin Co, PA

Notes for Anna Margaret Miller:
Born 4/12/1784, Ancestors of Richard Alan Lebo, The Schupp/Shoop Line, Richard A. Lebo, aqua.dev.uga.edu/~lebo.

Anna Margaret Miller and John George Schupp had the following children:

26. i. John Shoop (son of John George Schupp and Anna Margaret Miller) was born on August 01, 1805 in Dauphin Co?, PA[109, 183, 184]. He died on December 13, 1858 in Lower Mahanoy, Northumberland Co, PA[109, 184, 185]. He married Sarah Wertz (daughter of John Wertz and Joanna Catherine Garman) about Abt. 1826 in Northumberland Co, PA. She was born about Abt. 1811 in Northumberland Co, PA[107, 109]. She died about Abt. 1842 in Lower Mahanoy, Northumberland Co, PA. He married Catherine Lenker. She was born in 1821.

ii. Michael Shoop (son of John George Schupp and Anna Margaret Miller) was born in 1806 in PA. He died in 1873. He married Elizabeth Knarr. She was born in 1810 in PA.

iii. Anna Maria Shoop (daughter of John George Schupp and Anna Margaret Miller) was born about Abt. 1808 in PA.

iv. Anna Catherine Shoop (daughter of John George Schupp and Anna Margaret Miller) was born in 1810.

v. Living Shoop (son of John George Schupp and Anna Margaret Miller).

vi. Elizabeth Shoop (daughter of John George Schupp and Anna Margaret Miller) was born about Abt. 1808 in PA.

vii. Joseph Shoop (son of John George Schupp and Anna Margaret Miller) was born about Abt. 1808 in PA.

viii. Magdalena Shoop (daughter of John George Schupp and Anna Margaret Miller) was born about Abt. 1808 in PA.

ix. Jacob Shoop (son of John George Schupp and Anna Margaret Miller) was born about Abt. 1808 in PA.

54. **John Wertz** (son of John Deitrich Wertz and Mary Miller) was born on May 05, 1783 in Northumberland (Union) Co, PA[108, 294]. He died on May 13, 1861 in Lower Mahanoy, Northumberland Co, PA[108]. He married **Joanna Catherine Garman** (daughter of Michael Garman and Susan Sheets) about Abt. 1809 in Northumberland Co, PA.

55. **Joanna Catherine Garman** (daughter of Michael Garman and Susan Sheets) was born on August 02, 1791 in PA[108]. She died on September 23, 1864 in Northumberland Co, PA[108].

More About John Wertz:
Baptism: May 15, 1783 in PA
Burial: 1861 in Zion (Stone Valley) Lutheran, Dalmatia, Northumberland Co, PA[107, 108]
Census: 1790 in father; Northumberland Co, PA w
Census: 1800 in father; White Deer, Northumberland (Union) Co, PA w
Census: 1810 in Mahanoy, Northumberland Co, PA[295]
Census: 1820 in Lower Mahanoy, Northumberland Co, PA[191]
Census: 1830 in Lower Mahanoy, Northumberland Co, PA (Wert)[296]
Census: 1840 in Lower Mahanoy, Northumberland Co, PA (Wertz)[297]
Census: 1850 in Lower Mahanoy, Northumberland Co, PA (Mertz)[108, 298]
Census: 1860 in Lower Mahanoy, Northumberland Co, PA (Wartzs)[299]
Occupation: 1810 ; Far (Farm)[295]
Occupation: 1820 ; Agriculture[191]
Occupation: 1850 ; Farmer[298]
Occupation: 1860 ; Retired farmer[299]
Probate: June 03, 1861 in Northumberland Co, PA[300]
Property: 1850 in $1000[298]
Property: 1860 in $2000 + $214[299]

More About Joanna Catherine Garman:
Burial: 1864 in Zion (Stone Valley) Lutheran, Dalmatia, Northumberland Co, PA[107, 301]
Census: 1800 in father; Heidelberg, Dauphin (Lebanon) Co, PA w
Census: 1810 in husband; Mahanoy, Northumberland Co, PA w
Census: 1820 in husband; Lower Mahanoy, Northumberland Co, PA w
Census: 1830 in husband; Lower Mahanoy, Northumberland Co, PA w
Census: 1840 in husband; Lower Mahanoy, Northumberland Co, PA w
Census: 1850 in Lower Mahanoy, Northumberland Co, PA
Census: 1860 in Lower Mahanoy, Northumberland Co, PA
Probate: October 1864

Joanna Catherine Garman and John Wertz had the following children:

27. i. Sarah Wertz (daughter of John Wertz and Joanna Catherine Garman) was born about Abt. 1811 in Northumberland Co, PA[107, 109]. She died about Abt. 1842 in Lower Mahanoy, Northumberland Co, PA. She married John Shoop (son of John George Schupp and Anna Margaret Miller) about Abt. 1826 in Northumberland Co, PA. He was born on August 01, 1805 in Dauphin Co?, PA[109, 183, 184]. He died on December 13, 1858 in Lower Mahanoy, Northumberland Co, PA[109, 184, 185].

ii. Jacob Wertz (son of John Wertz and Joanna Catherine Garman) was born in 1816 in PA. He married Anna Maria Tschopp. She was born in 1819 in PA.

iii. Samuel Wertz (son of John Wertz and Joanna Catherine Garman) was born in 1821 in PA. He married Anna Mary Tschopp. She was born in 1831 in PA.

iv. John George Wertz (son of John Wertz and Joanna Catherine Garman) was born in 1828 in PA. He married Anna Shaffer. She was born in 1832.

v. John Wertz (son of John Wertz and Joanna Catherine Garman) was born in 1829 in PA.

vi. Catherine Wertz (daughter of John Wertz and Joanna

Catherine Garman) was born in 1831 in PA. She married John William Riegel. He was born in 1829.

56. **Francis "Frank" Rowe** was born about Abt. 1745 in Strasburg, Lancaster Co, PA[193, 302, 303]. He died between January 08-13 1806 in Lancaster Co, PA[192, 303, 304, 305, 306]. He married **Maria Catherine Traut** (daughter of John Wendel George Traut and Maria Magdalena Walter) on January 24, 1764 in Trinity Lutheran, New Holland, Lancaster Co, PA[302, 303].

57. **Maria Catherine Traut** (daughter of John Wendel George Traut and Maria Magdalena Walter) was born on January 24, 1748 in Paradise, Lancaster, PA[302, 307, 308]. She died in 1813 in Lancaster Co, PA[303].

More About Francis "Frank" Rowe:
Burial: 1806 in Lancaster Co, PA[120, 309]
Census: 1790 in Strasburg, Lancaster Co, PA
Census: 1800 in Strasburg, Lancaster Co, PA (Rough)[310]
Military Service: Abt. 1778 ; American Revolution, Private 1st PA Reg (Lancaster, Capt. Alexander White)[303, 304]
Military Service: Abt. 1778 ; American Revolution, Private 1st PA Reg (Lancaster, Capt. James Brown)[303]
Occupation: 1806 ; Wagon maker[305]
Probate: January 13, 1806 in Lancaster Co, PA[307, 311, 312]
Religion: 1791 ; St. Michaels Lutheran Church, Strasburg, PA[313]
Will: January 08, 1806 in Strasburg, Lancaster Co, PA[305]

Notes for Francis "Frank" Rowe:
Unrecorded deed, Lancaster County, PA, Janet Welty, JNWelty@@aol.com.
Died 1813, Frank Rowe, FHL, Pedigree chart, www.familysearch.org & Frank Row, St. John Evangelical Lutheran Church, Berrysburg, PA, Sara S. Neagley, Elizabethville, PA.

More About Maria Catherine Traut:
Burial: 1813 in Lancaster Co, PA[120, 314]
Census: 1790 in husband; Strasburg, Lancaster Co, PA w
Census: 1800 in husband; Strasburg, Lancaster Co, PA w
Census: 1810

Probate: 1813 in Lancaster Co, PA

Maria Catherine Traut and Francis "Frank" Rowe had the following children:

i. John Rowe (son of Francis "Frank" Rowe and Maria Catherine Traut) was born about Abt. 1765 in PA. He married Maria.

ii. Margaret Rowe (daughter of Francis "Frank" Rowe and Maria Catherine Traut) was born about Abt. 1767 in PA. She married Frederick Crum.

iii. Adam Rowe (son of Francis "Frank" Rowe and Maria Catherine Traut) was born on September 21, 1770 in Lancaster Co, PA[303]. He died on September 05, 1830 in Harrisburg, Dauphin Co, PA[303]. He married Christina Diller. She was born in 1772. She died in 1823. He married Mary Ward. She was born about Abt. 1780.

iv. John George Rowe (son of Francis "Frank" Rowe and Maria Catherine Traut) was born in 1772 in PA. He died in 1841. He married Catherine Elizabeth. She was born in 1777. She died in 1848[315].

v. Wendel Rowe (son of Francis "Frank" Rowe and Maria Catherine Traut) was born on August 07, 1777 in PA[303]. He died in 1843. He married Isabelle Harper. She was born about Abt. 1770.

vi. Francis Rowe (son of Francis "Frank" Rowe and Maria Catherine Traut) was born about Abt. 1778 in PA. He married Elizabeth Hertzog.

vii. Catherine Rowe (daughter of Francis "Frank" Rowe and Maria Catherine Traut) was born in 1779 in Lancaster Co, PA. She married Henry Rudy. He was born about Abt. 1770.

viii. Anna M Rowe (daughter of Francis "Frank" Rowe and Maria Catherine Traut) was born about Abt. 1780 in PA. She married Lawrence Shomper.

28. ix. John William Rowe (son of Francis "Frank" Rowe and

Maria Catherine Traut) was born in June 1785 in Strasburg, Lancaster Co, PA[192, 193, 194, 195]. He died in 1877 in Berrysburg, Dauphin Co, PA[192, 194]. He married Barbara Rudy (daughter of Jacob Rudy and Susan Jungblut) in 1810 in Strasburg, Lancaster Co, PA[120, 194]. She was born on April 11, 1796 in Strasburg, Lancaster Co, PA[193, 196]. She died on December 15, 1881 in Berrysburg, Dauphin Co, PA[120, 193, 196].

x. Sarah Rowe (daughter of Francis "Frank" Rowe and Maria Catherine Traut) was born in 1791 in PA. She married William Hegans. He was born about Abt. 1790.

58. **Jacob Rudy** (son of Rudy and <No name>) was born about Abt. 1765 in Lancaster Co, PA. He died in 1813 in Lancaster Co, PA. He married **Susan Jungblut** about Abt. 1785 in PA.

59. **Susan Jungblut** was born about Abt. 1770 in Lancaster Co, PA. She died about Abt. 1830 in PA.

More About Jacob Rudy:
Burial: 1813 in Greensburg Cemetery, Lancaster, Lancaster Co, PA[120, 316]
Census: 1790 in Donegal, Lancaster Co, PA
Census: 1800 in Donegal, Lancaster Co, PA
Census: 1810 in Donegal, Lancaster Co, PA[317]
Military Service: 1782 ; American Revolution, Private 3rd PA Reg, 8th Co, 7th class (Lancaster)[318]

More About Susan Jungblut:
Burial: 1833 in St. Peters (Hoffman) Reformed, Loyalton, Dauphin Co, PA[120, 319]
Census: 1790 in Warwick, Lancaster Co, PA
Census: 1800 in Brecknock, Lancaster Co, PA
Census: 1810 in Donegal, Lancaster Co, PA
Census: 1820 in Mifflin, Dauphin Co, PA[200]
Census: 1830 in Halifax, Dauphin Co, PA

Susan Jungblut and Jacob Rudy had the following children:

29. i. Barbara Rudy (daughter of Jacob Rudy and Susan Jungblut) was born on April 11, 1796 in Strasburg,

Lancaster Co, PA[193, 196]. She died on December 15, 1881 in Berrysburg, Dauphin Co, PA[120, 193, 196]. She married John William Rowe (son of Francis "Frank" Rowe and Maria Catherine Traut) in 1810 in Strasburg, Lancaster Co, PA[120, 194]. He was born in June 1785 in Strasburg, Lancaster Co, PA[192, 193, 194, 195]. He died in 1877 in Berrysburg, Dauphin Co, PA[192, 194].

ii. Rudy (son of Jacob Rudy and Susan Jungblut).

iii. Rudy (son of Jacob Rudy and Susan Jungblut).

iv. Rudy (daughter of Jacob Rudy and Susan Jungblut).

v. Rudy (daughter of Jacob Rudy and Susan Jungblut).

vi. Rudy (daughter of Jacob Rudy and Susan Jungblut).

vii. Rudy (daughter of Jacob Rudy and Susan Jungblut).

viii. Rudy (daughter of Jacob Rudy and Susan Jungblut).

60. **John William Frantz** (son of Daniel Frantz and Barbara) was born about Abt. 1750. He died in 1804 in Upper Paxton, Dauphin Co, PA[320]. He married **Anna Margaret Gieseman Shirk** about Abt. 1773.

61. **Anna Margaret Gieseman Shirk** was born between 1756-1759. She died after Aft. 1805 in Dauphin Co, PA.

More About John William Frantz:
Burial: 1804
Census: 1790 in Strasburg, Lancaster Co, PA (France)
Census: 1800 in Upper Paxton, Dauphin Co, PA[321]
Probate: February 11, 1805 in Dauphin Co, PA[322]
Religion: Bet. 1774-1785 ; St. Peters (Hoffmans) Church, Lykens, Dauphin Co, PA[323]

Notes for John William Frantz:
Frantz, Franz German: older spelling of Franz. German: from the personal name Franz, a vernacular form of Latin Franciscus (see Francis).

More About Anna Margaret Gieseman Shirk:
Census: 1790 in husband; Strasburg, Lancaster Co, PA w
Census: 1800 in husband; Upper Paxton, Dauphin Co, PA w

Notes for Anna Margaret Gieseman Shirk:
Poss. related to Ulrich Schroerk (Shirk)

Anna Margaret Gieseman Shirk and John William Frantz had the following children:

30. i. Adam Frantz (son of John William Frantz and Anna Margaret Gieseman Shirk) was born in 1780 in Lykens, Lancaster (Dauphin) Co, PA[214, 215]. He died between 1825-1830 in Dauphin Co, PA. He married Susan Gieseman (daughter of John William Gieseman and Anna Margaret Gruber) on October 06, 1811 in Upper Paxton, Dauphin Co, PA[216, 217, 218]. She was born on November 10, 1787 in Tulpehocken, Berks Co, PA[216, 219]. She died on February 15, 1826 in Mifflin, Dauphin Co, PA (Pilger Fieber u. Kindes Nothen (ie, Pilgrim fever)[216, 219, 220]).

ii. Henry Frantz (son of John William Frantz and Anna Margaret Gieseman Shirk). He married Magdelene Margaret.

iii. Living Frantz (son of John William Frantz and Anna Margaret Gieseman Shirk).

iv. Living Frantz (daughter of John William Frantz and Anna Margaret Gieseman Shirk).

v. Elizabeth Frantz (daughter of John William Frantz and Anna Margaret Gieseman Shirk).

vi. Living Frantz (daughter of John William Frantz and Anna Margaret Gieseman Shirk).

vii. John Frantz (son of John William Frantz and Anna Margaret Gieseman Shirk) was born in 1783 in PA.

viii. William Frantz (son of John William Frantz and Anna Margaret Gieseman Shirk) was born in 1785 in PA.

ix. Isaac Frantz (son of John William Frantz and Anna Margaret Gieseman Shirk).

62. **John William Gieseman** (son of George William Gieseman and Anna Catherine Heck) was born on March 23, 1761 in Lebanon, Lancaster (Lebanon) Co, PA[324]. He died on August 26, 1843 in Dauphin Co, PA[324]. He married **Anna Margaret Gruber** (daughter of Christian Gruber and Anna Gunigunda Stupp) on February 19, 1782 in Christ (Little Tulpehocken) Lutheran, Bernville, Berks Co, PA[325].

63. **Anna Margaret Gruber** (daughter of Christian Gruber and Anna Gunigunda Stupp) was born on August 02, 1759 in Berks Co, PA[326]. She died on June 12, 1837 in Dauphin Co, PA.

More About John William Gieseman:
Baptism: May 03, 1761 in PA[142]
Burial: August 1843 in St. Johns (Hill) Lutheran, Berrysburg, Dauphin Co, PA[142, 324]
Census: 1790 in Tulpehocken, Berks Co, PA[327]
Census: 1800 in Tulpehocken, Berks Co, PA
Census: 1810 in Upper Paxton, Dauphin Co, PA[230]
Census: 1820 in Mifflin, Dauphin Co, PA[328]
Census: 1830 in Mifflin, Dauphin Co, PA[329]
Census: 1840 in Mifflin, Dauphin Co, PA[330]
Occupation: Abt. 1830 ; Elder
Probate: October 02, 1843 in Mifflin Tp, Dauphin Co, PA[331]
Will: June 23, 1841 in Mifflin Tp, Dauphin Co, PA[331]

Notes for John William Gieseman:
Married 1788, PA & Other Assorted Data, R Howard, rmhoward45@@aol.com, www.ancestry.com.

More About Anna Margaret Gruber:
Baptism: April 16, 1759 in Old Northkill, Berks Co, PA[332]
Burial: 1837 in St. Johns (Hill) Lutheran, Berrysburg, Dauphin Co, PA
Census: 1790 in husband; Tulpehocken, Berks Co, PA w
Census: 1800 in husband; Tulpehocken, Berks Co, PA w
Census: 1810 in husband; Upper Paxton, Dauphin Co, PA w
Census: 1820 in husband; Mifflin, Dauphin Co, PA w

Census: 1830 in husband; Mifflin, Dauphin Co, PA w

Anna Margaret Gruber and John William Gieseman had the following children:

31. i. Susan Gieseman (daughter of John William Gieseman and Anna Margaret Gruber) was born on November 10, 1787 in Tulpehocken, Berks Co, PA[216, 219]. She died on February 15, 1826 in Mifflin, Dauphin Co, PA (Pilger Fieber u. Kindes Nothen (ie, Pilgrim fever)[216, 219, 220]). She married Adam Frantz (son of John William Frantz and Anna Margaret Gieseman Shirk) on October 06, 1811 in Upper Paxton, Dauphin Co, PA[216, 217, 218]. He was born in 1780 in Lykens, Lancaster (Dauphin) Co, PA[214, 215]. He died between 1825-1830 in Dauphin Co, PA.

ii. Catherine Gieseman (daughter of John William Gieseman and Anna Margaret Gruber) was born in 1791 in PA. She married John Schweinfort. She married Frederick Merriman.

iii. Magdalena Gieseman (daughter of John William Gieseman and Anna Margaret Gruber) was born in 1798 in PA. She married Balthaser Matter. He was born about Abt. 1800.

iv. Anna Maria Gieseman (daughter of John William Gieseman and Anna Margaret Gruber) was born in 1800 in PA. She married William Snodgrass.

v. Christina Gieseman (daughter of John William Gieseman and Anna Margaret Gruber) was born in PA. She married Michael Metz.

vi. John Gieseman (son of John William Gieseman and Anna Margaret Gruber) was born in PA.

vii. Margaret Elizabeth Gieseman (daughter of John William Gieseman and Anna Margaret Gruber) was born in PA. She married Christian Mertz.

viii. George Gieseman (son of John William Gieseman and Anna Margaret Gruber) was born in PA.

Generation 7

64. **Martin Batdorf** was born in 1726 in Chester Co, PA[233]. He married **Barbara Elizabeth Saltzegber** about Abt. 1756 in Lancaster?, PA.

65. **Barbara Elizabeth Saltzegber** was born in 1738 in Berks Co., PA[233].

More About Martin Batdorf:
Census: 1790
Census: 1800

Notes for Martin Batdorf:
s/o Johann Martin Batdorf b 1695 Darmstadt, Hesse, Germany & Maria Elizabeth Walborn
s/o Johann Jacob Batdorf Darmstadt, Hesse, Germany & Anna Maria Herber of Wold, Switzerland
d/o Johann Adam Walborn b c1668 Wiesbaden, Hesse, Gemrany & Anna Elizabeh Feg
s/o Johannes Batdorf 1630 Germany & ?
d/o Johann Heinrich Herber 1659 Germany & Anna Maria Seeman
s/o Jaochim Waldbrunn b 1629 Germany & Anna Maria ?
d/o Johann Peter Feg 1646 US & Anna Maria Risch

More About Barbara Elizabeth Saltzegber:
Census: 1790

Notes for Barbara Elizabeth Saltzegber:
d/o Andrew Saltzgeber & Anna Maria Zeller
s/o Johann Fernidnand Saltzgeber b1672 Baden-Wuerttemberg, Germany & Barbara Ringer
d/o Johann Heinrich Zeller 1684 Paris, France & Anna Maria Perigal
s/o Johann Saltzgaber 1640 Germany & Anna Maria Schweitzer
d/o Ludwig Ringer b Switzerland & Anna Habersaat
s/o Jacques DeSellaire 1660 Switzerland & Clothilde DeValois 1660 France
d/o James Briegal 1664 Netherlands

Barbara Elizabeth Saltzegber and Martin Batdorf had the following children:

i. Eva Batdorf (daughter of Martin Batdorf and Barbara Elizabeth Saltzegber) was born in 1757. She married Peter

Kister.

ii. John Michael Batdorf (son of Martin Batdorf and Barbara Elizabeth Saltzegber) was born in 1758. He married Catherine Emmerich.

iii. Maria Elizabeth Batdorf (daughter of Martin Batdorf and Barbara Elizabeth Saltzegber) was born in 1760.

iv. John Adam Batdorf (son of Martin Batdorf and Barbara Elizabeth Saltzegber) was born in 1762. He married Susan Merkey.

v. Martin Batdorf (son of Martin Batdorf and Barbara Elizabeth Saltzegber) was born in 1763. He married Wendelina Ebrecht.

vi. Maria Barbara Batdorf (daughter of Martin Batdorf and Barbara Elizabeth Saltzegber) was born in 1766.

32. vii. George Peter Batdorf (son of Martin Batdorf and Barbara Elizabeth Saltzegber) was born on February 11, 1768 in Lancaster Co, PA[232, 233, 234]. He died between 1830-1840 in OH (PA[133]). He married Barbara Weiss (daughter of John Weiss) about Abt. 1792 in Dauphin?, PA. She was born about Abt. 1772 in PA. She died after Aft. 1830 in OH (PA).

66. **John Weiss**.

John Weiss had the following child:

33. i. Barbara Weiss (daughter of John Weiss) was born about Abt. 1772 in PA. She died after Aft. 1830 in OH (PA). She married George Peter Batdorf (son of Martin Batdorf and Barbara Elizabeth Saltzegber) about Abt. 1792 in Dauphin?, PA. He was born on February 11, 1768 in Lancaster Co, PA[232, 233, 234]. He died between 1830-1840 in OH (PA[133]).

72. **Valentine Welker** was born about Abt. 1730 in Rhineland-Palatinate, Germany. He died in 1782 in Donegal, Lancaster Co, PA[333]. He married **Anna Elizabeth Schaffer?** about Abt. 1748 in Germany.

73. **Anna Elizabeth Schaffer?** was born about Abt. 1730 in Germany.

She died in 1782 in Lancaster Co, PA.

More About Valentine Welker:
Burial: 1782
Immigration: October 16, 1772[143, 240, 334]
Probate: October 22, 1782 in Lancaster Co, PA[335, 336, 337]
Residence: Bet. 1772-1779 in Donegal, Lancaster Co, PA
Will: January 06, 1778 in Donegal Tp, Lancaster Co, PA[337]

Notes for Valentine Welker:
Messerschmidt: German: occupational name for a cutler, from Middle High German mezzer 'knife' + smit 'smith'. See also Messer 1.

More About Anna Elizabeth Schaffer?:
Burial: 1782
Immigration: Abt. 1750

Anna Elizabeth Schaffer? and Valentine Welker had the following children:

i. Anna Christina Welker (daughter of Valentine Welker and Anna Elizabeth Schaffer?) was born on February 06, 1750.

ii. John William Welker (son of Valentine Welker and Anna Elizabeth Schaffer?) was born in 1752. He married Veronica Leim.

iii. Peter Welker (son of Valentine Welker and Anna Elizabeth Schaffer?) was born about Abt. 1753. He married Elizabeth.

36. iv. Valentine Welker (son of Valentine Welker and Anna Elizabeth Schaffer?) was born on January 11, 1755 in Schwandorf, Germany[238]. He died in 1831 in Carsonville, Dauphin Co, PA[75, 146, 239]. He married Susan Jury (daughter of Abraham Joray and Catherine Guerne) in 1783 in Northumberland Co, PA[240]. She was born in 1755 in Upper Paxton, Lancaster (Dauphin) Co, PA[146, 239]. She died about Abt. 1801 in Upper Paxtang, Dauphin Co, PA. He married Catherine Waring Guerne. She was born about Abt. 1760.

v. John Welker (son of Valentine Welker and Anna Elizabeth Schaffer?) was born about Abt. 1756.

74. **Abraham Joray** was born on March 19, 1718 in Belphrahon, Berne, Switzerland[338, 339]. He died in December 1785 in Upper Paxton, Dauphin Co, PA[239]. He married **Catherine Guerne** on August 06, 1743 in Moutier, Berne, Switzerland[338, 339, 340].

75. **Catherine Guerne** was born on December 25, 1720 in Eschert, Berne, Switzerland[239, 338]. She died before Bef. February 15, 1785 in Upper Paxton, Dauphin Co, PA.

More About Abraham Joray:
Baptism: March 20, 1718 in Moutier, Berne, Switzerland[339]
Burial: 1785 in St. Davids (Salem) Reformed, Millersburg, Dauphin Co, PA[339]
Immigration: September 14, 1754 in Switzerland to USA (ship Nancy)[341, 342, 343]
Naturalization: September 14, 1754[341, 344]
Occupation: 1779 ; Overseer of Poor[339]
Occupation: 1784 ; Constable[339]
Occupation: 1785 ; Yeoman[345]
Religion: ; St. Davids (Salem) Reformed, Millersburg, Dauphin Co, PA[342]
Residence: 1754 in Philadelphia, PA[346]
Residence: Abt. 1755 in Dauphin Co, PA[347]
Residence: 1771 in Upper Paxton, Lancaster (Dauphin) Co, PA[339]
Residence: Bet. 1778-1782 in Wiconisco, Lancaster (Dauphin) Co, PA[339]
Will: September 22, 1785 in Upper Paxton, Dauphin Co, PA[339, 345, 348]

Notes for Abraham Joray:
s/o Isaac Jury b1687 Moutier, Bern, Switzerland & Margaret Belat
s/o John Joray b1666 Moutier, Bern, Switzerland & Catherine Joray
d/o Abraham Belat
s/o Isaac Joray b1640/5 Moutier, Bern, Switzerland & Margaret ?
d/o Isaac Joray of b1640/5 Moutier, Bern, Switzerland & Maria ?
s/o Leonard Joray b1619 & Anne ?
s/o Leonard Joray b1619 & Anne ?

The Jura Mountains are a small mountain range located north of the Alps, separating the Rhine and Rhone rivers and forming part of the watershed of each. The mountain range is located in France, Switzerland, and Germany.

Wirth & Jury were two of the first five families to settle Lykens Valley, Wert History, Jonathan Wert.
French Hugeonaut descent, Renee Waring, reneelwaring@@aol.com.
Died August 1785, Abraham Joray, FHL, Pedigree chart, www.familysearch.org.
Rev War service, Private, Reg ?, 2nd class, Capt.Martin Weaver, Comprehensive Hostory of the town of Gratz, PA, p784, Elsie Eaves, EKEaves@@cox.net

More About Catherine Guerne:
Burial: 1785 in St. Davids (Salem) Reformed, Millersburg, Dauphin Co, PA[339]
Immigration: 1754 in Switzerland to USA (ship Nancy)

Notes for Catherine Guerne:
Guerne, Guerren: French and the Coat of Arms contains a blue shield with three gold pierced stars, and a red demi- lion rampant on a gold chief. The family motto is Stemmata rutilent auro. Spelling variations include: Guerrin, Guerren, Guerin, Guerinne, Guerrein, Guereon, Gueron, Gerin, Garin, Le Guerin, Guerenne, Le Guerinne, De Guerin, De Guerrin, Du Guerin and many more. First found in Normandy where they were anciently seated at Gueron and were the seigneurie of that area, in the department of Calvados in the arrondissement of Bayou. Some of the first settlers of this name or some of its variants were: Guillaume Guerin who settled in Quebec in 1704 from Normandy; Bertrand Guerin settled in Quebec in 1739 also from Normandy; Jacques Benjamin Guerin from Brittany settled in Quebec in 1759.

Catherine Guerne and Abraham Joray had the following children:

i. Maria Elizabeth Jury (daughter of Abraham Joray and Catherine Guerne) was born in 1744 in Switzerland. She married John George Etzweiler. He was born about Abt. 1740.

ii. Isaac Jury (son of Abraham Joray and Catherine Guerne) was born in 1745 in Switzerland.

iii. Maria Magdalena Jury (daughter of Abraham Joray and Catherine Guerne) was born in 1747 in Switzerland. She married John Peter Wieulle. He was born in 1744.

iv. Maria Margaret Jury (daughter of Abraham Joray and Catherine Guerne) was born in 1749 in Switzerland. She married Andrew Spangler. He was born about Abt. 1740.

v. Samuel Frederick Jury (son of Abraham Joray and Catherine Guerne) was born in 1751 in Switzerland. He married Joanna.

vi. Salome Jury (daughter of Abraham Joray and Catherine Guerne) was born in 1752 in Switzerland.

vii. Abraham Jury (son of Abraham Joray and Catherine Guerne) was born in 1753 in Switzerland. He married Anna Margaret Ulsh. She was born about Abt. 1756. He married Elizabeth Bretz.

37. viii. Susan Jury (daughter of Abraham Joray and Catherine Guerne) was born in 1755 in Upper Paxton, Lancaster (Dauphin) Co, PA[146, 239]. She died about Abt. 1801 in Upper Paxtang, Dauphin Co, PA. She married Valentine Welker (son of Valentine Welker and Anna Elizabeth Schaffer?) in 1783 in Northumberland Co, PA[240]. He was born on January 11, 1755 in Schwandorf, Germany[238]. He died in 1831 in Carsonville, Dauphin Co, PA[75, 146, 239].

ix. Catherine Jury (daughter of Abraham Joray and Catherine Guerne) was born in 1755 in PA. She married John Scheisly. He was born about Abt. 1750.

x. Salome "Sarah" Jury (daughter of Abraham Joray and Catherine Guerne) was born in 1761 in PA. She married Adam King. He was born about Abt. 1760.

76. **Andrew Messerschmidt** was born on October 02, 1708 in Ofterdingen, Baden-Wurttemberg, Germany. He died about Abt. 1776 in Lancaster Co, PA. He married **Susan Groetzinge** about Abt. 1750

in PA (Germany).

77. **Susan Groetzinge** was born about Abt. 1730. She died after Aft. 1759 in Lancaster Co, PA.

More About Andrew Messerschmidt:
Burial: Abt. 1776 in Zion Lutheran, Manheim, Lancaster Co, PA
Immigration: September 16, 1751 in Germany to USA (ship Nancy)[349, 350]
Occupation: Abt. 1750 ; Tinsmith
Residence: 1751 in Philadelphia, PA[351]
Residence: 1765 in Lancaster (Lebanon) Co, PA
Residence: Bet. 1770-1772 in Warwick, Lancaster Co, PA

Susan Groetzinge and Andrew Messerschmidt had the following children:

38. i. Andrew Messerschmidt (son of Andrew Messerschmidt and Susan Groetzinge) was born about Abt. 1751 in Lancaster Co, PA[75]. He died in 1801 in Upper Paxton, Dauphin Co, PA[75]. He married Eva Schrot (daughter of John Schrot and <No name>) on September 26, 1779 in Christ Lutheran, Stouchsburg, Berks Co, PA[251]. She was born about Abt. 1753 in PA[142]. She died after Aft. 1810 in Lancaster Co, PA.

ii. Catherine Messerschmidt (daughter of Andrew Messerschmidt and Susan Groetzinge).

iii. George? Messerschmidt (son of Andrew Messerschmidt and Susan Groetzinge).

iv. Jacob? Messerschmidt (son of Andrew Messerschmidt and Susan Groetzinge).

78. **John Schrot** was born about Abt. 1730. He died about Abt. 1800 in Lancaster Co, PA. He married **<No name>** about Abt. 1750.

79. **<No name>** was born about Abt. 1730. She died between 1790-1800.

More About John Schrot:
Census: 1790 in Little Britian, Lancaster Co, PA (Sproat)[352]

Census: 1800 in Little Britain, Lancaster Co, PA
Religion: 1750 ; Tabor Reformed, Lebanon, Lebanon,PA[353]

Notes for John Schrot:
aka Schroth

More About <No name>:
Census: 1790 in Little Britian, Lancaster Co, PA (Sproat)[354]

<No name> and John Schrot had the following children:

i. Augustina Schrot (daughter of John Schrot and <No name>) was born in 1750.

39. ii. Eva Schrot (daughter of John Schrot and <No name>) was born about Abt. 1753 in PA[142]. She died after Aft. 1810 in Lancaster Co, PA. She married Andrew Messerschmidt (son of Andrew Messerschmidt and Susan Groetzinge) on September 26, 1779 in Christ Lutheran, Stouchsburg, Berks Co, PA[251]. He was born about Abt. 1751 in Lancaster Co, PA[75]. He died in 1801 in Upper Paxton, Dauphin Co, PA[75].

iii. Schrot (son of John Schrot and <No name>).

iv. Samuel? Schrot (son of John Schrot and <No name>).

80. **<No name>**. He married **<No name>**.

81. **<No name>**.

<No name> and <No name> had the following child:

40. i. Peters (son of <No name> and <No name>) was born about Abt. 1760.

96. **John Adam Wirth** was born on August 23, 1727 in Borod, Rhineland-Palatinate, Germany[64, 260, 355]. He died on August 25, 1806 in Upper Paxton, Dauphin Co, PA[64, 260, 355]. He married **Eva Elizabeth Schnug** on August 03, 1755 in Rev. Stoever, Bindagles Lutheran, Palmyra, Lancaster (Lebanon) Co, PA[64, 356].

97. **Eva Elizabeth Schnug** was born in 1730 in Baden-Wurttemberg, Germany[357, 358, 359]. She died in 1800 in Upper Paxton, Dauphin Co, PA[167, 260, 359].

More About John Adam Wirth:
Baptism: August 28, 1727 in Germany
Burial: 1806 in Old Salem (Werts) Lutheran, Millersburg, Dauphin Co, PA[64]
Census: 1790 in Dauphin Co, PA (Wertz)
Census: 1800
Immigration: September 28, 1753 in Germany to USA (ship Two Brothers)[64, 355, 357]
Naturalization: September 28, 1753 in Philadelphia, PA[360]
Occupation: Abt. 1780 ; Church Treasurer
Occupation: Farmer; Weaver[357]
Probate: 1807 in Harrisburg, Dauphin Co, PA[357]
Religion: ; Lutheran[361]
Residence: 1753 in Philadelphia, PA[362]
Residence: Abt. 1754 in Montgomery Co, PA[361]
Residence: 1755 in Lebanon, PA[356]
Residence: Bet. 1755-1763 in Derry, Lancaster (Lebanon) Co, PA[361, 363]
Residence: Abt. 1755 in Tulpehocken, Berks Co, PA[361]
Residence: Abt. 1765 in Lykens Valley, Lancaster (Dauphin) Co, PA[355]
Residence: 1774 in Millersburg, Lancaster (Dauphin) Co, PA[64]

Notes for John Adam Wirth:
s/o John Jacob Wirth c1697 Hochstenbach, Rhineland-Palatinate, Germany & Maria Eva Sohn b1701
s/o Henry Wirth b1670 Winkelbach, Rhineland-Palatinate, Germany & Anna Gertrude Miller
d/o John Peter Sohn & Freuen Margaret ?
d/o Adam Moller 1631 & Anna Elizabeth Linde
s/o Johann Theiss Sohn b1650 Germany & Catherine ?
s/o John Matthew Sohn & Catherine ?

Wirth Homestead (John Adam), Hbg N Golf Course, Killinger, Dauphin, PA

Wirth & Jury were two of the first five families to settle Lykens Valley, Wert History, Jonathan Wert.

Johann Adam Wirth was born on August 30, 1727 in Berod, Westerwald, Germany. Johan Adam Wirth emigrated to America on the Ship Two Brothers, Thomas Arnot, Commander, qualifying on September 28, 1753 at the Court House in Philadelphia, Pa. He was the son of Johann Jacob Wirth b. February 11, 1697 in Hochstenbach, Westerwald, Germany; died 1734 or 1735, and Maria Eva Sohn b. July 1, 1704 in Berod, Westerwald, Germany; died March 13, 1784. Maria was the daughter of Johann Peter Sohn who died on November 9, 1749 in Berod, Westerwald, Germany. The name of Johann Adam Wirth is spelled that way on the ship passenger list. The name of his mother's brother, Johann Peter Sohn (b.18Janl725) appears next to Johann Adam's on the ship list. There are emigration records specifying that Johann Adam Wirth left Berod where he was born and came to America on the Ship Two Brothers in 1753. (see more Palatine Families, Henry Jones, Jr., 1991 p. 506) His birth date was found in the Parish Records at Hochstenbach, Westerwald Region of Germany. This date corresponds to Johann Adam's birth, death date, and age given on his tombstone and found in the Old Wirth Evangelical Lutheran Church records at Killinger, PA. John Adam Wirth married on August 3, 1755 by Rev. John Caspar Stoever at Bindnagels Evangelical Lutheran Church in Lebanon, P A to Eva Elizabeth Schnug 1730-1800, daughter of J. Matthias Schnug 1711-1795 and Elizabeth Schall. The Schnug's, like the Wirth's, were also from Berod, Westerwald, Germany, and they came to America in 1740. One of Eva's brothers, Christian Schnug was born at sea in 1740; d. in 1783, and he resided in the Berrysburg, PA area of Dauphin County, PA not far from where his sister resided. Records on the Schnug's can be found in the Parish of Hochstenbach, Westerwald, Germany. Johann Adam Wirth may have first settled in Montgomery County, Pa., then removed to the Tulpehocken Settlement, and on to the Lebanon area, then finally to Clover Hill in Lykens Valley, Upper Paxton Township, Dauphin County. This area was then still part of Lancaster County. Records indicate that Johann Adam traveled from Lebanon on several occasions between 1763-1768 to claim and clear land in Lykens Valley. He was one of the first five families settling in Lykens Valley, others being Andrew and Jane Lykens, Ludwig Shott, John Rewalt, and Abraham Shora (Jury). Buffington's, Hoffman's, Umholtz's and Woodside's were also early settlers of Lykens Valley. [Records of Dr. Jonathan Wert, Port Royal, PA, jwert@@mdi-wert.com]

More About Eva Elizabeth Schnug:
Burial: Abt. 1800 in Old Salem (Werts) Lutheran, Millersburg, Dauphin Co, PA[167]
Census: 1790 in husband; Dauphin Co, PA w
Immigration: 1740 in Germany to USA (ship Samuel Elizabeth)[364]
Residence: 1755 in Lebanon, PA[356]

Notes for Eva Elizabeth Schnug:
d/o John Michael Schnug & Anna Catherine Heylmon
s/o Adam Schnug b1684 Welkenbach, Rhineland-Palatinate, Germany & Elizabeth Gertrude ?
s/o Henry Schnug b1660 Borod, Rhineland-Palatinate, or Hesse, Germany & Johannetta ?

also s/o John Matthias Schnug 1711 Germany & Elizabeth Schall

Born Upper Paxton, Dauphin Co, PA, Wert Tree, K Shuey, kshuey208@@hotmail.com, awt.ancestry.com.

Eva Elizabeth Schnug and John Adam Wirth had the following children:

i. John Adam Wirth (son of John Adam Wirth and Eva Elizabeth Schnug) was born in 1756 in Lancaster Co, PA. He married Mary Elizabeth Nye Preiss. She was born about Abt. 1760.

ii. John Wirth (son of John Adam Wirth and Eva Elizabeth Schnug) was born in 1758 in Lancaster (Lebanon) Co, PA. He died in 1805. He married Anna Maria Miller. She was born about Abt. 1760.

iii. John Christian Wirth (son of John Adam Wirth and Eva Elizabeth Schnug) was born in 1760 in Lancaster (Lebanon) Co, PA. He married Catherine Bretz.

iv. Anna Catherine Wirth (daughter of John Adam Wirth and Eva Elizabeth Schnug) was born in 1762 in Lancaster (Lebanon) Co, PA. She married Sebastian Metz. He was born about Abt. 1760.

48. v. John Jacob Wirth (son of John Adam Wirth and Eva Elizabeth Schnug) was born in February 1763 in Lebanon,

Lancaster (Lebanon) Co, PA[167, 256]. He died on January 01, 1833 in Millersburg, Dauphin Co, PA[64, 257, 258]. He married Anna Sophia Miller (daughter of John Miller and Frances Kerstetter) about Abt. 1794 in Dauphin Co, PA[257]. She was born on August 02, 1776 in Millersburg, Lancaster (Dauphin) Co, PA[64, 105, 257, 259]. She died on October 22, 1842 in Lykens, Dauphin Co, PA[64, 257, 259, 260].

vi. John Peter Wirth (son of John Adam Wirth and Eva Elizabeth Schnug) was born in 1766 in Lancaster (Dauphin) Co, PA. He died in 1844. He married Elizabeth Sheesley. She was born about Abt. 1770.

vii. John Henry Wirth (son of John Adam Wirth and Eva Elizabeth Schnug) was born in 1769 in Lancaster (Dauphin) Co, PA. He died in 1846. He married Elizabeth Enderline. She was born about Abt. 1770.

viii. John George Wirth (son of John Adam Wirth and Eva Elizabeth Schnug) was born in 1770 in Lancaster (Dauphin) Co, PA. He married Anna Catherine Miller. She was born in 1775 in PA. She died in 1842.

More About John George Wirth:
b: Abt. 1770

ix. Anna Margaret Wirth (daughter of John Adam Wirth and Eva Elizabeth Schnug) was born in 1771 in Lancaster (Dauphin) Co, PA. She married George Michael Radel.

x. John Philip Wirth (son of John Adam Wirth and Eva Elizabeth Schnug) was born in 1773 in Lancaster (Dauphin) Co, PA. He married Elizabeth Loos.

xi. John Joseph Wirth (son of John Adam Wirth and Eva Elizabeth Schnug) was born in 1775 in Lancaster (Dauphin) Co, PA. He married Barbara Kitch.

98. **John Miller** was born in 1751 in Lebanon, Lancaster (Lebanon) Co, PA[287, 365]. He died in 1812 in Upper Paxton, Dauphin Co, PA[287, 365]. He married **Frances Kerstetter** on January 01, 1774 in Lebanon Tp, Lancaster (Lebanon) Co, PA[287, 365].

99. **Frances Kerstetter** was born on April 09, 1752 in Cleona, Lancaster (Lebanon) Co, PA[365]. She died in 1818 in Northumberland Co, PA[365].

More About John Miller:
Burial: 1812 in Zion (Stone Valley) Lutheran, Dalmatia, Northumberland Co, PA[287, 366]
Census: 1790 in Dauphin Co, PA[367]
Census: 1800 in Upper Paxton, Dauphin Co, PA
Census: 1810 in Upper Paxton, Dauphin Co, PA[368]
Military Service: Bet. 1778-1781 ; American Revolution, Private 4th PA Reg, 6th Co, 2nd class (Lancaster, Capt. Martin Weaver)[365]
Occupation: Abt. 1785 ; Farmer
Probate: April 29, 1812 in Dauphin Co, PA (listed in index only)[369]

Notes for John Miller:
d/o Christopher Miller of Baden-Wurttemberg, Germany & Margaret Barbara Zuppinger
d/o Conrad Schuppinger

Miller Homestead (Christopher), North area, Lebanon, PA

Miller: English and Scottish: occupational name for a miller. The standard modern vocabulary word represents the northern Middle English term, an agent derivative of mille 'mill', reinforced by Old Norse mylnari (see Milner). In southern, western, and central England Millward (literally, 'mill keeper') was the usual term. The American surname has absorbed many cognate surnames from other European languages, for example French Meunier, Dumoulin, Demoulins, and Moulin; German Mueller; Dutch Molenaar; Italian Molinaro; Spanish Molinero; Hungarian Molnár; Slavic Mlinar, etc.

More About Frances Kerstetter:
Baptism: April 12, 1752 in St John Hill (Quittaphilla) Lutheran, Cleona, Lancaster (Lebanon) Co, PA[370]
Burial: 1818 in Zion (Stone Valley) Lutheran, Dalmatia, Northumberland Co, PA[287]
Census: 1790 in husband; Dauphin Co, PA w
Census: 1800 in husband; Upper Paxton, Dauphin Co, PA w
Census: 1810 in husband; Not listed w

Notes for Frances Kerstetter:
d/o Sebastian Kerstetter b1727 Cleona, Lancaster (Lebanon) Co, PA, PA & Magdelena Deibler
s/o John Martin Kerstetter b1697 Obergimpern, Baden-Wurttemberg, Germany & Maria Dorothy Frey
s/o John Leonard Kerstetter b1668 Obergimpern, Baden-Wurttemberg, Germany & Anna Ursula ?
d/o John Martin Frey b1672 Bonfeld, Baden-Wurttemberg, Germany & Anna Apollonia Junker
s/o Wolf Kirstatter b1618 Obergimpern, Baden-Wurttemberg, Germany & Magdelene ?
s/o John Jacob Frey b1640 Germany & Elizabeth ?
d/o George Melchios Jungert 1640 Germany & Margaret Mann
s/o Wolflein Kurstetter bc1595 Germany & ?
s/o Martin Jungert 1619 Germany & ?
d/o Johannes Mann 1600 & maria Geiger
s/o Wolf Kurstetter bc1575 7 Anna ?

Kerstetter: Altered form of German Kirchstetter, habitational name for someone from a place called Kirchstätt in Upper Bavaria, or from Kirchstetten.

Frances Kerstetter and John Miller had the following children:

i. Anna Magdalena Miller (daughter of John Miller and Frances Kerstetter) was born in 1774 in PA. She died in 1850.

ii. Anna Catherine Miller (daughter of John Miller and Frances Kerstetter) was born in 1775 in PA. She died in 1842. She married John George Wirth. He was born in 1770 in Lancaster (Dauphin) Co, PA.

More About John George Wirth:
b: Abt. 1770

49. iii. Anna Sophia Miller (daughter of John Miller and Frances Kerstetter) was born on August 02, 1776 in Millersburg, Lancaster (Dauphin) Co, PA[64, 105, 257, 259]. She died on

October 22, 1842 in Lykens, Dauphin Co, PA[64, 257, 259, 260]. She married John Jacob Wirth (son of John Adam Wirth and Eva Elizabeth Schnug) about Abt. 1794 in Dauphin Co, PA[257]. He was born in February 1763 in Lebanon, Lancaster (Lebanon) Co, PA[167, 256]. He died on January 01, 1833 in Millersburg, Dauphin Co, PA[64, 257, 258].

iv. John Miller (son of John Miller and Frances Kerstetter) was born in 1777 in PA. He died in 1861. He married Anna Catherine Seiler. She was born about Abt. 1780.

v. John Peter Miller (son of John Miller and Frances Kerstetter) was born on May 17, 1780 in Upper Paxton, Dauphin Co, PA[365]. He died in 1842. He married Maria Magdalena Weaver. She was born in 1777.

vi. John Jacob Miller (son of John Miller and Frances Kerstetter) was born in 1782 in PA. He died in 1860. He married Elizabeth Heckert. She was born in 1793.

vii. Christina Miller (daughter of John Miller and Frances Kerstetter) was born in 1782 in PA. She died in 1860. She married Michael Heckert. He was born about Abt. 1780.

53. viii. Anna Margaret Miller (daughter of John Miller and Frances Kerstetter) was born on February 12, 1784 in Lancaster (Dauphin) Co, PA[289, 290, 291]. She died on July 24, 1857 in Dauphin Co, PA[284, 285, 291]. She married John George Schupp (son of John George Schupp and Anna Maria Elizabeth Deibler) about Abt. 1801 in Dauphin Co, PA. He was born in May 1780 in Upper Paxton, Lancaster (Dauphin) Co, PA[75, 284, 285, 286]. He died on January 20, 1854 in Dauphin Co, PA[286, 287, 288].

ix. Elizabeth Miller (daughter of John Miller and Frances Kerstetter) was born in 1787 in PA. She died in 1844. She married Jeremiah Shawbell. He was born about Abt. 1780.

x. Daniel Miller (son of John Miller and Frances Kerstetter) was born in 1792 in PA. He died in 1859. He married Mary Ann Heckert. She was born in 1800.

100. **John Faber** was born on February 07, 1750 in Swatara, Lancaster (Lebanon) Co, PA[269, 272, 371]. He died in 1804 in Bethel, Dauphin

(Lebanon) Co, PA[272]. He married **Margaret Rudy** on February 02, 1774 in Zion Lutheran, Jonestown, Lancaster (Lebanon) Co, PA[271, 372].

101. **Margaret Rudy** was born on December 18, 1753 in Swatara, Lancaster (Lebanon) Co, PA[269, 271, 371, 372]. She died on October 04, 1825 in Bethel, Lebanon Co, PA[269, 271, 371, 372].

More About John Faber:
Baptism: March 18, 1750 in Lancaster (Lebanon) Co?, PA[271, 373]
Burial: 1804 in Bethel Moravian Cemetery, Lebanon, Dauphin (Lebanon) Co, PA[269]
Census: 1790 in Dauphin Co, PA (Fawper)[374]
Census: 1800 in Heidelberg, Dauphin (Lebanon) Co, PA (Faler)
Military Service: 1782 ; American Revolution, Private 2nd PA Reg, 8th Co, 4th class (Lancaster, Capt. Mathias Henning)[271, 375]

Notes for John Faber:
s/o Frederick Adam Faber b1717 Daxhandten, Baden-Wurttemberg, Germany & Anna Maria Hautsch

Possible relation to Johann Faber (1478 - 1541) was a Catholic theologian. He was born in Leutkirch, Swabia and studied theology and canon law at Tübingen and Freiburg in the Breisgau region and was made doctor of sacred theology in Freiburg. He subsequently became, (in succession) Minister of Lindau, Leutkirch Vicar-General of Constance (1518), Chaplain and confessor to King Ferdinand I of Austria (1524), Bishop of Vienna (1530) . Like others of his time Faber was at first friendly with the Reformers, Melanchthon, Zwingli, and Oecolampadius, sympathizing with their efforts at reform and opposing certain abuses himself; but when he realized that neither dogma nor the Church itself was spared by the Reformers, he broke with them and became their most consistent opponent. Faber wrote his first polemic against Martin Luther, "Opus adversus nova quaedam dogmata Martini Lutheri" in 1552. This was soon followed by his "Malleus Haereticorum, sex libris ad Hadrianum VI summum Pontificem" published in Cologne, in 1524, and Rome in 1569. [http://en.wikipedia.org/wiki/Johann_Faber]

Faber: Occupational name for a smith or ironworker, from Latin faber 'craftsman'. This was in use as a surname in England, Scotland, and elsewhere in the Middle Ages and is also found as a personal name. At the time of the Reformation, it was much used as a humanistic name, a translation into Latin of vernacular surnames such as German Schmidt and Dutch Smit.

More About Margaret Rudy:
Burial: 1825 in St John Hill (Quittaphilla) Lutheran, Cleona, Lebanon Co, PA[269]
Census: 1790 in husband; Dauphin Co, PA w
Census: 1800 in Bethel, Dauphin Co, PA (listed as head of house)[376]
Census: 1810
Census: 1820
Confirmation: 1774 in Zion Lutheran, Jonestown, Lancaster (Lebanon) Co, PA[372]
Probate: October 25, 1825 in Bethel, Lebanon Co, PA[377, 378, 379]
Will: October 01, 1825 in Bethel, Lebanon Co, PA[379]

Notes for Margaret Rudy:

SIL's Peter & John Rudy, probably relatives, Probate files, 1825, No F-9, 15, Lebanon County Reg of Wills & Clerk of Orphans Court, Lebaonn, PA, Dawn L Resanovich, Register, Dec 2008

Buried Jonestown, Zion Evangelical Lutheran Church, Marriages & Burials, 1768-1858, bk 1, p 392, Lebanon County Historical Society

Margaret Rudy and John Faber had the following children:

i. Magdalena Faber (daughter of John Faber and Margaret Rudy) was born on November 26, 1775 in Lancaster Co, PA[272]. She married Jacob Sattazahn. He was born about Abt. 1770.

50. ii. John Faber (son of John Faber and Margaret Rudy) was born on March 30, 1777 in Lancaster (Lebanon) Co, PA[105, 268, 269, 270, 271, 272, 273]. He died on July 15, 1828 in Halifax Tp, Dauphin Co, PA[272, 273, 274, 275, 276]. He married Maria "Mollie" Magdalena Rudy (daughter of Jonas Rudy and Anna Barbara Overcash) in 1805 in Lancaster (Lebanon) Co, PA[105, 269, 270, 272, 273, 274]. She was born on April 14, 1784 in Bethel, Lancaster (Lebanon) Co, PA[269, 270, 272, 273, 274, 276].

She died on July 16, 1845 in Jefferson Tp, Dauphin Co, PA[167, 272, 273, 277].

iii. Elizabeth Faber (daughter of John Faber and Margaret Rudy) was born on April 10, 1784 in Lancaster Co, PA[272]. She married Henry Bucher. He was born about Abt. 1780.

iv. Barbara Faber (daughter of John Faber and Margaret Rudy) was born in 1786 in Dauphin Co, PA. She married John Rudy. He was born about Abt. 1780.

v. Catherine Faber (daughter of John Faber and Margaret Rudy) was born about Abt. 1788 in Dauphin Co., PA. She married George Binner.

vi. Philip Faber (son of John Faber and Margaret Rudy) was born in 1790 in Dauphin Co, PA. He died in 1841. He married Anna Lentz. She was born about Abt. 1790.

vii. Margaret Faber (daughter of John Faber and Margaret Rudy) was born in 1792 in Dauphin Co., PA. She died in 1858. She married Peter Rudy. He was born in 1785 in Dauphin Co, PA. He died in 1863.

More About Peter Rudy:
b: 1785

viii. George Faber (son of John Faber and Margaret Rudy) was born in 1793 in Dauphin Co, PA. He died in 1870. He married Elizabeth Reinel. She was born in 1800.

102. **Jonas Rudy** was born on December 16, 1751 in Bethel, Lancaster (Lebanon) Co, PA[269, 270, 273, 380, 381, 382]. He died on December 20, 1810 in Bethel, Dauphin (Lebanon) Co, PA[269, 270, 383]. He married **Anna Barbara Overcash** about Abt. 1773 in Lancaster (Lebanon) Co, PA[273, 276].

103. **Anna Barbara Overcash** was born on September 28, 1751 in Bethel, Lancaster (Lebanon) Co, PA[273, 276]. She died on April 08, 1836 in Bethel, Lebanon Co, PA[273, 276].

More About Jonas Rudy:
Baptism: December 16, 1751 in Bethel, Lancaster (Lebanon) Co, PA[380]
Burial: 1810 in St. Johns Union Cemetery, Fredericksburg, Dauphin (Lebanon) Co, PA[269, 270, 276]
Census: 1790 in Dauphin Co, PA[384]
Census: 1800 in Bethel, Dauphin (Lebanon) Co, PA (Jones)[385]
Census: 1810 in Hanover, Dauphin (Lebanon) Co, PA[386]
Military Service: 1781 ; American Revolution, Private 2nd PA Reg, 3rd Co, 8th class (Lancaster, Capt. Casper Stoever)[273, 380, 387, 388]
Probate: Bet. February 04-November 29, 1811 in Bethel Tp, Dauphin (Lebanon) Co, PA[389]
Will: October 15, 1810 in Bethel Tp, Dauphin (Lebanon) Co, PA

Notes for Jonas Rudy:
s/o Frederick Rudin b1716 Bubendorf, Basel, Switzerland & Elizabeth Schaublin
s/o Jerome Rudin b1693 Bubendorf, Basel, Switzerland & Catherine Salathe
d/o Martin Schaublin b1676 Bubendorf, Basel, Switzerland & Frances Weisner b1674
s/o Jerome Rudin b1665 Bubendorf, Basel, Switzerland & Barbara Stohler
d/o Martin Salathe of Liestal, Basel, Switzerland & Anna Haring
s/o Imbert Schaublin b1638 Bubendorf, Basel, Switzerland & Catherine Stohler
d/o Adam Weisner b1650 Bubendorf, Basel, Switzerland & Elizabeth "Elsie" Stohler
s/o Henry Rudin b1627 Bubendorf, Basel, Switzerland & Magdelene Tschudy
d/o Werlin Stohler & Margaret Rudin
s/o Johannes Wilhelm Schaublin 1584 Germany & Anna Meyer
d/o Johann Jacob Stohler & Catherine Ludin
d/o Matthew Weisner & Elsa Buser
s/o Jacob Rudin b1601 Bubendorf, Basel, Switzerland & Barbara Bratteler
s/o Nicholas Rudin b1574 Basel, Switzerland & Elizabeth Ludin
d/o Hans Bratteler of Switzerland & Adelheit Stohler

Died 12/30/1810, House of Rudy, Jonas Rudy, Chapter III, p 80-81

More About Anna Barbara Overcash:
Burial: 1836 in St. Johns Union Cemetery, Fredericksburg, Dauphin (Lebanon) Co, PA[276]
Census: 1790 in husband; Dauphin Co, PA w
Census: 1800 in husband; Bethel, Dauphin (Lebanon) Co, PA w
Census: 1810 in husband; Dauphin (Lebanon) Co, PA w
Census: 1820
Census: 1830 in Bethel, Lebanon Co, PA[390]

Notes for Anna Barbara Overcash:
d/o Michael Overkirsh b1728 Germany & Anna Barbara ?
s/o Casper Overkirsch Germany & Susan ? Germany

Overcash: Americanized form of South German Oberkirch, a habitational name meaning 'upper church' from a place so named in Baden (or possibly from places called Oberkirchen, in Westphalia and Saar district).

Anna Barbara Overcash and Jonas Rudy had the following children:

i. Jacob Rudy (son of Jonas Rudy and Anna Barbara Overcash) was born in 1774 in Lancaster (Dauphin) Co, PA.

ii. Frederick Rudy (son of Jonas Rudy and Anna Barbara Overcash) was born in 1776 in Lancaster (Dauphin) Co, PA. He married Elizabeth Layman.

iii. Jonas Rudy (son of Jonas Rudy and Anna Barbara Overcash) was born in 1778 in Lancaster (Dauphin) Co, PA. He married Eva Cook.

iv. Elizabeth Rudy (daughter of Jonas Rudy and Anna Barbara Overcash) was born in 1779 in Lancaster (Dauphin) Co, PA. She married Samuel Hooker.

v. John Rudy (son of Jonas Rudy and Anna Barbara Overcash) was born in 1780 in Lancaster (Dauphin) Co, PA.

vi. Christina Barbara Rudy (daughter of Jonas Rudy and Anna

Barbara Overcash) was born in 1782 in Lancaster (Dauphin) Co, PA. She married Jacob Bixler.

51. vii. Maria "Mollie" Magdalena Rudy (daughter of Jonas Rudy and Anna Barbara Overcash) was born on April 14, 1784 in Bethel, Lancaster (Lebanon) Co, PA[269, 270, 272, 273, 274, 276]. She died on July 16, 1845 in Jefferson Tp, Dauphin Co, PA[167, 272, 273, 277]. She married John Faber (son of John Faber and Margaret Rudy) in 1805 in Lancaster (Lebanon) Co, PA[105, 269, 270, 272, 273, 274]. He was born on March 30, 1777 in Lancaster (Lebanon) Co, PA[105, 268, 269, 270, 271, 272, 273]. He died on July 15, 1828 in Halifax Tp, Dauphin Co, PA[272, 273, 274, 275, 276].

viii. Peter Rudy (son of Jonas Rudy and Anna Barbara Overcash) was born in 1785 in Dauphin Co, PA. He died in 1863. He married Margaret Faber. She was born in 1792 in Dauphin Co., PA. She died in 1858.

More About Peter Rudy:
b: 1785

ix. John Joseph Rudy (son of Jonas Rudy and Anna Barbara Overcash) was born about Abt. 1787.

x. Michael Rudy (son of Jonas Rudy and Anna Barbara Overcash) was born on May 16, 1789 in Dauphin Co, PA[388]. He died in 1842. He married Catherine Elizabeth.

xi. Mildred Rudy (daughter of Jonas Rudy and Anna Barbara Overcash) was born about Abt. 1790.

104. **John George Schupp** was born on August 04, 1759 in Upper Paxton, Lancaster (Dauphin) Co, PA[284, 287, 391]. He died on August 27, 1839 in Millersburg, Dauphin Co, PA[75, 284, 285, 391]. He married **Anna Maria Elizabeth Deibler** in 1779 in Lancaster (Dauphin) Co, PA[285].

105. **Anna Maria Elizabeth Deibler** was born on January 10, 1760 in Millersburg, Lancaster (Dauphin) Co, PA[75, 284, 285, 287, 392, 393]. She died on April 18, 1840 in Millersburg, Dauphin Co, PA[75, 287, 392, 393].

More About John George Schupp:
Baptism: September 01, 1759 in Trinity Lutheran, New Holland, Lancaster Co, PA[284, 285]
Burial: 1839 in Old Salem (Werts) Lutheran, Millersburg, Dauphin Co, PA[284, 287, 392]
Census: 1790 in Dauphin Co, PA (Soop)[394]
Census: 1800 in Upper Paxton, Dauphin Co, PA[395]
Census: 1810 in Upper Paxton, Dauphin Co, PA[186]
Census: 1820 in Upper Paxton, Dauphin Co, PA[187]
Census: 1830 in Upper Paxton, Dauphin Co, PA[396]
Military Service: Bet. 1775-1781 ; American Revolution, Private 4th PA Reg, ? Co, 4th class (Lancaster, Capt. Martin Weaver)
Residence: Abt. 1770 in Earl, Lancaster Co, PA[284]
Residence: Bet. 1780-1802 in Killinger, Dauphin Co, PA[142]

Notes for John George Schupp:
s/o John George Schupp b1728 Alteckendorf, Rhineland-Palatinate, Germany & Anna Catherine Matter
s/o John George Schupp b1705 Merzweiler, Rhineland-Palatinate, Germany & Barbara Schaffner
d/o John Michael Matter of Germany & Anna Christina Keiser
s/o John Sebastian Schupp b1678 Merzweiler, Rhineland-Palatinate, Germany & Barbara Brand
s/o Diebold Matter b1648 Eckendorf, Bas Rhine, France & Magaret Kueffer
d/o Jacob Keiser of France & Maria Veit
s/o John Schupp b1647 Merzweiler, Rhineland-Palatinate, Germany & Elizabeth Catherine Hengen
s/o John Matter b1614 Alsace, Bas Rhine, France & Catherine ?
d/o Christman Kueffer b1632 Altdorf, Bas Rhine, France & Catherine Gautzberger
s/o John Keiser of France & Barbara ?
d/o Jacob Veit of France & Maria Soachler
s/o Daniel Schupp b1610 Merzweiler, Rhineland-Palatinate, Germany & Maria Klein
s/o Christman Kueffer b1606 Eckendorf, Rhineland-Palatinate, Germany & Margaret ?

Little Cemetery, Ancestors of Richard Alan Lebo, The Schupp/Shoop Line, Richard A. Lebo, aqua.dev.uga.edu/~lebo.
Born New Holland, Lancaster Co, PA, Jonathan Wert & Welkers in

the USA & Nuls from PA, Greg Welker, gwelker@@chesapeake.net, awt.ancestry.com.

More About Anna Maria Elizabeth Deibler:
Burial: 1840 in Old Salem (Werts) Lutheran, Millersburg, Dauphin Co, PA[284, 392]
Census: 1790 in husband; Dauphin Co, PA w
Census: 1800 in husband; Upper Paxton, Dauphin Co, PA w
Census: 1810 in husband; Upper Paxton, Dauphin Co, PA w
Census: 1820 in husband; Upper Paxton, Dauphin Co, PA w
Census: 1830 in husband; Upper Paxton, Dauphin Co, PA w

Notes for Anna Maria Elizabeth Deibler:
d/o Michael Deibler b1733 Dauphin Co, PA & Anna Maria Helt
s/o Matthew Deibler b1707 PA
d/o Henry Helt & Elizabeth ?

Died April 8, 1840, Ancestors of Richard Alan Lebo, The Schupp/Shoop Line, Richard A. Lebo, aqua.dev.uga.edu/~lebo & untitled, Jonathan Wert.
Born Earl, Lancaster Co, PA, Jonathan Wert.

Deibler: German occupational name for a dove keeper, from an agent derivative of Middle High German tube 'dove' (see Taube).

Anna Maria Elizabeth Deibler and John George Schupp had the following children:

52. i. John George Schupp (son of John George Schupp and Anna Maria Elizabeth Deibler) was born in May 1780 in Upper Paxton, Lancaster (Dauphin) Co, PA[75, 284, 285, 286]. He died on January 20, 1854 in Dauphin Co, PA[286, 287, 288]. He married Anna Margaret Miller (daughter of John Miller and Frances Kerstetter) about Abt. 1801 in Dauphin Co, PA. She was born on February 12, 1784 in Lancaster (Dauphin) Co, PA[289, 290, 291]. She died on July 24, 1857 in Dauphin Co, PA[284, 285, 291].

ii. John Schupp (son of John George Schupp and Anna Maria Elizabeth Deibler) was born in 1782 in Dauphin Co, PA. He married Anna Maria Yeager. She was born in 1787.

iii. Daniel Schupp (son of John George Schupp and Anna Maria Elizabeth Deibler) was born in 1783 in Dauphin Co, PA. He married Margaret. He married Susan Bresel.

iv. John Michael Schupp (son of John George Schupp and Anna Maria Elizabeth Deibler) was born in 1786 in Dauphin Co, PA. He married Anna Margaret Weiss.

v. Christopher Schupp (son of John George Schupp and Anna Maria Elizabeth Deibler) was born in 1788 in Dauphin Co, PA.

vi. Joseph Schupp (son of John George Schupp and Anna Maria Elizabeth Deibler) was born in 1790 in Dauphin Co, PA. He married Elizabeth Kemmerer. She was born in 1798.

vii. Eva Catherine Schupp (daughter of John George Schupp and Anna Maria Elizabeth Deibler) was born in 1792 in Dauphin Co, PA. She married John Daniel Jury. He was born in 1790.

viii. Maria Elizabeth Schupp (daughter of John George Schupp and Anna Maria Elizabeth Deibler) was born in 1794 in Dauphin Co, PA.

ix. Susan Schupp (daughter of John George Schupp and Anna Maria Elizabeth Deibler) was born in 1797 in Dauphin Co, PA. She married Daniel Wert. He was born in 1796 in Dauphin Co, PA.

More About Daniel Wert:
b: 1796

x. Schupp (daughter of John George Schupp and Anna Maria Elizabeth Deibler) was born about Abt. 1800 in PA.

xi. John Henry Schupp (son of John George Schupp and Anna Maria Elizabeth Deibler) was born in 1802 in Dauphin Co, PA.

106. **John Miller** was born in 1751 in Lebanon, Lancaster (Lebanon) Co, PA[287, 365]. He died in 1812 in Upper Paxton, Dauphin Co, PA[287, 365]. He married **Frances Kerstetter** on January 01, 1774 in Lebanon Tp, Lancaster (Lebanon) Co, PA[287, 365].

107. **Frances Kerstetter** was born on April 09, 1752 in Cleona, Lancaster (Lebanon) Co, PA[365]. She died in 1818 in Northumberland Co, PA[365].

More About John Miller:
Burial: 1812 in Zion (Stone Valley) Lutheran, Dalmatia, Northumberland Co, PA[287, 366]
Census: 1790 in Dauphin Co, PA[367]
Census: 1800 in Upper Paxton, Dauphin Co, PA
Census: 1810 in Upper Paxton, Dauphin Co, PA[368]
Military Service: Bet. 1778-1781 ; American Revolution, Private 4th PA Reg, 6th Co, 2nd class (Lancaster, Capt. Martin Weaver)[365]
Occupation: Abt. 1785 ; Farmer
Probate: April 29, 1812 in Dauphin Co, PA (listed in index only)[369]

Notes for John Miller:
d/o Christopher Miller of Baden-Wurttemberg, Germany & Margaret Barbara Zuppinger
d/o Conrad Schuppinger

Miller Homestead (Christopher), North area, Lebanon, PA

Miller: English and Scottish: occupational name for a miller. The standard modern vocabulary word represents the northern Middle English term, an agent derivative of mille 'mill', reinforced by Old Norse mylnari (see Milner). In southern, western, and central England Millward (literally, 'mill keeper') was the usual term. The American surname has absorbed many cognate surnames from other European languages, for example French Meunier, Dumoulin, Demoulins, and Moulin; German Mueller; Dutch Molenaar; Italian Molinaro; Spanish Molinero; Hungarian Molnár; Slavic Mlinar, etc.

More About Frances Kerstetter:
Baptism: April 12, 1752 in St John Hill (Quittaphilla) Lutheran, Cleona,

Lancaster (Lebanon) Co, PA[370]
Burial: 1818 in Zion (Stone Valley) Lutheran, Dalmatia, Northumberland Co, PA[287]
Census: 1790 in husband; Dauphin Co, PA w
Census: 1800 in husband; Upper Paxton, Dauphin Co, PA w
Census: 1810 in husband; Not listed w

Notes for Frances Kerstetter:
d/o Sebastian Kerstetter b1727 Cleona, Lancaster (Lebanon) Co, PA, PA & Magdelena Deibler
s/o John Martin Kerstetter b1697 Obergimpern, Baden-Wurttemberg, Germany & Maria Dorothy Frey
s/o John Leonard Kerstetter b1668 Obergimpern, Baden-Wurttemberg, Germany & Anna Ursula ?
d/o John Martin Frey b1672 Bonfeld, Baden-Wurttemberg, Germany & Anna Apollonia Junker
s/o Wolf Kirstatter b1618 Obergimpern, Baden-Wurttemberg, Germany & Magdelene ?
s/o John Jacob Frey b1640 Germany & Elizabeth ?
d/o George Melchios Jungert 1640 Germany & Margaret Mann
s/o Wolflein Kurstetter bc1595 Germany & ?
s/o Martin Jungert 1619 Germany & ?
d/o Johannes Mann 1600 & maria Geiger
s/o Wolf Kurstetter bc1575 7 Anna ?

Kerstetter: Altered form of German Kirchstetter, habitational name for someone from a place called Kirchstätt in Upper Bavaria, or from Kirchstetten.

Frances Kerstetter and John Miller had the following children:

i. Anna Magdalena Miller (daughter of John Miller and Frances Kerstetter) was born in 1774 in PA. She died in 1850.

ii. Anna Catherine Miller (daughter of John Miller and Frances Kerstetter) was born in 1775 in PA. She died in 1842. She married John George Wirth. He was born in 1770 in Lancaster (Dauphin) Co, PA.

More About John George Wirth:

b: Abt. 1770

49. iii. Anna Sophia Miller (daughter of John Miller and Frances Kerstetter) was born on August 02, 1776 in Millersburg, Lancaster (Dauphin) Co, PA[64, 105, 257, 259]. She died on October 22, 1842 in Lykens, Dauphin Co, PA[64, 257, 259, 260]. She married John Jacob Wirth (son of John Adam Wirth and Eva Elizabeth Schnug) about Abt. 1794 in Dauphin Co, PA[257]. He was born in February 1763 in Lebanon, Lancaster (Lebanon) Co, PA[167, 256]. He died on January 01, 1833 in Millersburg, Dauphin Co, PA[64, 257, 258].

iv. John Miller (son of John Miller and Frances Kerstetter) was born in 1777 in PA. He died in 1861. He married Anna Catherine Seiler. She was born about Abt. 1780.

v. John Peter Miller (son of John Miller and Frances Kerstetter) was born on May 17, 1780 in Upper Paxton, Dauphin Co, PA[365]. He died in 1842. He married Maria Magdalena Weaver. She was born in 1777.

vi. John Jacob Miller (son of John Miller and Frances Kerstetter) was born in 1782 in PA. He died in 1860. He married Elizabeth Heckert. She was born in 1793.

vii. Christina Miller (daughter of John Miller and Frances Kerstetter) was born in 1782 in PA. She died in 1860. She married Michael Heckert. He was born about Abt. 1780.

53. viii. Anna Margaret Miller (daughter of John Miller and Frances Kerstetter) was born on February 12, 1784 in Lancaster (Dauphin) Co, PA[289, 290, 291]. She died on July 24, 1857 in Dauphin Co, PA[284, 285, 291]. She married John George Schupp (son of John George Schupp and Anna Maria Elizabeth Deibler) about Abt. 1801 in Dauphin Co, PA. He was born in May 1780 in Upper Paxton, Lancaster (Dauphin) Co, PA[75, 284, 285, 286]. He died on January 20, 1854 in Dauphin Co, PA[286, 287, 288].

ix. Elizabeth Miller (daughter of John Miller and Frances Kerstetter) was born in 1787 in PA. She died in 1844. She married Jeremiah Shawbell. He was born about Abt. 1780.

x. Daniel Miller (son of John Miller and Frances Kerstetter) was born in 1792 in PA. He died in 1859. He married Mary Ann Heckert. She was born in 1800.

108. **John Deitrich Wertz** was born on June 24, 1740 in Schwaigern, Baden-Wurttemberg, Germany[107, 397]. He died on October 16, 1804 in White Deer, Northumberland (Union) Co, PA[397, 398, 399, 400]. He married **Mary Miller** about Abt. 1770 in Northumberland?, PA[397].

109. **Mary Miller** was born in 1742 in Germany[401]. She died in 1804 in White Deer, Northumberland (Union) Co, PA[397, 400].

More About John Deitrich Wertz:
Burial: 1804 in Northumberland Co, PA[397]
Census: 1790 in Northumberland Co, PA (Teterie Vertz)[397]
Census: 1800 in White Deer, Northumberland (Union) Co, PA[107]
Immigration: 1750
Probate: January 30, 1805 in Estate recorded[402]
Residence: 1767 in Heidelberg, Berks Co, PA[403]
Residence: 1775 in White Deer, Northumberland (Union) Co, PA[397, 404]
Will: Bet. May 08, 1803-1804 in White Deer, Northumberland (Union), PA[405, 406]

Notes for John Deitrich Wertz:
s/o John Wertz 1719 Schwaigern, Baden-Wurttemberg, Germany & Maria Eva Bickel
s/o John Casper Wertz bc1693 Schwaigern, Baden-Wurttemberg, Germany & Anna Barbara ?
d/o John George Bikel b1652 Massenbach, Baden-Wurttemberg, Germany & Catherine Anna Margaret Musser
s/o John Pauli Bickel b1618 Massenbach, Baden-Wurttemberg, Germany & Anna Barbara ?

More About Mary Miller:
Burial: 1804 in PA
Census: 1790 in Northumberland Co, PA
Census: 1800 in White Deer, Northumberland (Union) Co, PA

Mary Miller and John Deitrich Wertz had the following children:

i. John Jacob Wertz (son of John Deitrich Wertz and Mary Miller) was born in 1776 in Northumberland Co, PA. He died in 1836.

ii. Elizabeth Wertz (daughter of John Deitrich Wertz and Mary Miller) was born in 1778 in Northumberland Co, PA. She married Goodlander.

iii. John Adam Wertz (son of John Deitrich Wertz and Mary Miller) was born in 1780 in Northumberland Co, PA. He died in 1825.

iv. Casper Wertz (son of John Deitrich Wertz and Mary Miller) was born in 1782 in Northumberland (Union) Co, PA. He died in 1831. He married Martha.

54. v. John Wertz (son of John Deitrich Wertz and Mary Miller) was born on May 05, 1783 in Northumberland (Union) Co, PA[108, 294]. He died on May 13, 1861 in Lower Mahanoy, Northumberland Co, PA[108]. He married Joanna Catherine Garman (daughter of Michael Garman and Susan Sheets) about Abt. 1809 in Northumberland Co, PA. She was born on August 02, 1791 in PA[108]. She died on September 23, 1864 in Northumberland Co, PA[108].

vi. Wertz (child of John Deitrich Wertz and Mary Miller) was born about Abt. 1785 in PA (U).

vii. Magdelena Wertz (daughter of John Deitrich Wertz and Mary Miller) was born about Abt. 1785 in PA. She married John Ranck.

110. **Michael Garman** was born in 1747 in York Co, PA[407, 408, 409]. He died on January 08, 1800 in IL (PAIllness[407, 409]). He married **Susan Sheets** (daughter of John George Sheetz and Anna Margaret Wolfkill) in 1785 in Dauphin Co, PA[407, 409].

111. **Susan Sheets** (daughter of John George Sheetz and Anna Margaret Wolfkill) was born on August 16, 1768 in Lancaster Co, PA[407, 409, 410]. She died on March 23, 1854 in Ogle, IL[407, 411].

More About Michael Garman:
Burial: 1800
Census: 1790 in Dauphin Co, PA[412]
Census: 1800 in Heidelberg, Dauphin (Lebanon) Co, PA[413]
Military Service: Bet. March 01-July 31, 1776 ; American Revolution, Private 3rd PA Reg (Capt. Thomas Moore)[414]
Military Service: Bet. March 03-November 25, 1776 ; American Revolution, Private 2nd PA Reg (Capt. Samuel Watson)[414]
Military Service: Abt. 1781 ; American Revolution, Private 4th PA Reg 3rd Co (Lancaster, Capt. George Gantze)[414]
Military Service: Abt. 1782 ; American Revolution, Sergeant[301, 407, 408, 414, 415]
Occupation: ; Blacksmith[410]

Notes for Michael Garman:
POW (NY), Battle of Brandwine [The Biographical Record of Ogle Co,IL, Published by S.J. Clarke, 1899, Original from the New York Public Library, Digitized Feb 28, 2008, 492 pages]

Manager of blacksmith operation during American Revolution [DAR, Application of Kris E Garman, Crystal Lake, IL, Comp #5-065 IL, Aug 2000]

Garman, German: German: variant of German. German: from the saint's name German(us). See also Germann.

More About Susan Sheets:
Burial: 1854 in West Grove Cemetery, Lincoln, Ogle, IL[407]
Census: 1790 in husband; Dauphin Co, PA w
Census: 1800 in husband; Heidelberg, Dauphin (Lebanon) Co, PA w
Census: 1810 in Mahanoy, Northumberland Co, PA[416]
Census: 1820
Census: 1830
Census: 1840
Census: 1850 in Brookville, Ogle, IL[417]

Susan Sheets and Michael Garman had the following children:

i. Martin "Marty" Garman (son of Michael Garman and Susan Sheets) was born in 1790 in Northumberland Co, PA. He married Elizabeth Michael. She was born in 1794.

55. ii. Joanna Catherine Garman (daughter of Michael Garman and Susan Sheets) was born on August 02, 1791 in PA[108]. She died on September 23, 1864 in Northumberland Co, PA[108]. She married John Wertz (son of John Deitrich Wertz and Mary Miller) about Abt. 1809 in Northumberland Co, PA. He was born on May 05, 1783 in Northumberland (Union) Co, PA[108, 294]. He died on May 13, 1861 in Lower Mahanoy, Northumberland Co, PA[108].

iii. Jacob Garman (son of Michael Garman and Susan Sheets) was born on March 07, 1792 in PA[409]. He died in 1864. He married Sarah Kneis. She was born in 1800.

iv. Benjamin Garman (son of Michael Garman and Susan Sheets) was born in 1794 in PA. He died about Abt. 1795.

v. George Garman (son of Michael Garman and Susan Sheets) was born in 1796 in PA.

vi. Michael Garman (son of Michael Garman and Susan Sheets) was born in 1798 in Northumberland Co, PA. He died in 1870. He married Rebecca Mace. She was born in 1800.

vii. Garman (daughter of Michael Garman and Susan Sheets) was born about Abt. 1800 in PA.

114. **John Wendel George Traut** was born in 1689 in Kleinfischlingen, Rhineland-Palatinate, Germany[308, 418, 419]. He died between February-March 1761 in Paradise, Lancaster Co, PA[418, 419]. He married **Maria Magdalena Walter** on January 23, 1739 in Rev. Stoever, Trinity Lutheran, New Holland, Lancaster Co, PA[420, 421].

115. **Maria Magdalena Walter** was born in January 1717 in Strasburg, Chester (Lancaster) Co, PA[418, 419, 421, 422]. She died in February 1761 in Paradise, Lancaster Co, PA[418, 423].

More About John Wendel George Traut:
Burial: 1761 in Cedar Hill (Trout) Cemetery, Strasburg, Lancaster Co, PA
Immigration: August 27, 1738 in Germany to USA (ship Winter Gallery)

Residence: 1739 in Lebanon area, PA[420]
Will: February 19, 1760 in Strasburg, Lancaster Co, PA[424, 425]

Notes for John Wendel George Traut:
s/o John Velten Traut b1645 Impflingen, Rhineland-Palatinate, Germany & Margaret Mock of Germany
s/o John Leonard Traut b1620 Impflingen, Pfalz, Germany & Agnes ?
d/o Wendel Mock of Rhineland-Palatinate, Germany
s/o Balthaser Traut b1570 of Rhineland-Palatinate, Germany & Appollonia ?
s/o Balthaser Traut

Died Strasburg, PA, Hutchinson & Allied Families from East TN, Terry L Hutchinson, tlhutch_kr@@yahoo.com, awt.ancestry.com.

Also m. St. Michaels Church, Strasburg, Lancaster Co, PA, Trout Family Descendancy, Descendants of Balthasar Troutc1750750, www.jaknouse.athens.oh.us/genealogy/trout1.html.

More About Maria Magdalena Walter:
Burial: February 1761 in Cedar Hill (Trout) Cemetery, Strasburg, Lancaster Co, PA[419]
Immigration: Bet. 1717-1738
Probate: 1761 in Lancaster Co, PA[426]
Residence: 1739 in Strassburg, PA[420]

Notes for Maria Magdalena Walter:
Died 1794, Trout Family descendancy, Descendants of Balthasar Trout born 1750, www.jaknouse.athens.oh.us/genealogy/trout1.html.

Born Palatinate, Craig H Trout, www.rootsweb.com, CraigTrout@@aol.com

Maria Magdalena Walter and John Wendel George Traut had the following children:

i. John Paul Traut (son of John Wendel George Traut and Maria Magdalena Walter) was born in 1739 in Lancaster Co, PA.

ii. John Henry Traut (son of John Wendel George Traut and Maria Magdalena Walter) was born in 1742 in Lancaster Co, PA.

iii. Anna Magdalena Traut (daughter of John Wendel George Traut and Maria Magdalena Walter) was born in 1743 in Lancaster Co, PA.

iv. Wendel Traut (son of John Wendel George Traut and Maria Magdalena Walter) was born in 1743 in Lancaster Co, PA. He married Elizabeth Druckenbrod. She was born in 1743.

v. Maria Barbara Traut (daughter of John Wendel George Traut and Maria Magdalena Walter) was born in 1745 in Lancaster Co, PA.

57. vi. Maria Catherine Traut (daughter of John Wendel George Traut and Maria Magdalena Walter) was born on January 24, 1748 in Paradise, Lancaster, PA[302, 307, 308]. She died in 1813 in Lancaster Co, PA[303]. She married Francis "Frank" Rowe on January 24, 1764 in Trinity Lutheran, New Holland, Lancaster Co, PA[302, 303]. He was born about Abt. 1745 in Strasburg, Lancaster Co, PA[193, 302, 303]. He died between January 08-13 1806 in Lancaster Co, PA[192, 303, 304, 305, 306].

116. **Rudy**. He married **<No name>**.

117. **<No name>**.

<No name> and Rudy had the following children:

58. i. Jacob Rudy (son of Rudy and <No name>) was born about Abt. 1765 in Lancaster Co, PA. He died in 1813 in Lancaster Co, PA. He married Susan Jungblut about Abt. 1785 in PA. She was born about Abt. 1770 in Lancaster Co, PA. She died about Abt. 1830 in PA.

ii. Henry Rudy (son of Rudy and <No name>).

iii. Charles "Carl" Rudy (son of Rudy and <No name>).

iv. Christopher Rudy (son of Rudy and <No name>).

v. Peter Rudy (son of Rudy and <No name>).

120. **Daniel Frantz** (son of Frantz) was born about Abt. 1718. He died about Abt. 1780. He married **Barbara** about Abt. 1740.

121. **Barbara** was born about Abt. 1720. She died after Aft. 1760.

Barbara and Daniel Frantz had the following children:

60. i. John William Frantz (son of Daniel Frantz and Barbara) was born about Abt. 1750. He died in 1804 in Upper Paxton, Dauphin Co, PA[320]. He married Anna Margaret Gieseman Shirk about Abt. 1773. She was born between 1756-1759. She died after Aft. 1805 in Dauphin Co, PA.

ii. Jacob Frantz (son of Daniel Frantz and Barbara) was born about Abt. 1752.

iii. George Frantz (son of Daniel Frantz and Barbara) was born about Abt. 1755.

iv. Henry Frantz (son of Daniel Frantz and Barbara) was born about Abt. 1760.

v. Nicholas Frantz (son of Daniel Frantz and Barbara).

vi. Johannes Frantz (son of Daniel Frantz and Barbara).

124. **George William Gieseman** was born on March 03, 1718 in Darmstadt, Hesse, Germany[325]. He died in 1761 in Berks Co, PA[427]. He married **Anna Catherine Heck** on December 12, 1749 in Christ (Little Tulpehocken) Lutheran, Bernville, Lancaster (Berks) Co, PA[427].

125. **Anna Catherine Heck** was born in 1723 in Tulpehocken, Chester (Berks) Co, PA[427, 428]. She died after Aft. 1767 in Berks Co, PA.

More About George William Gieseman:
Burial: 1761
Confirmation: 1731 in Freidens (Old Northkill) Lutheran Cemetery, Bernville, Lancaster (Berks) Co, PA
Immigration: October 26, 1741 in Germany to USA (ship Snow Mollie)[429, 430]
Occupation: ; Blacksmith[431]
Religion: ; Evangelical Lutheran Church, Northkill, Berks Co, PA[325]
Residence: 1741 in Philadelphia, PA[432]

Will: May 1761 in Tulpehocken, Berks Co, PA[430, 433]

Notes for George William Gieseman:
s/o Clements Gieseman & Anna Maria Stapfer
d/o Michael Stapfer of Germany & Anna Catherine Roth
d/o Conrad Roth

Gussman, Geiseman: German (Güssmann): from the personal name Goswin, composed of the elements goss 'Gaut' (name of a tribe) + wine 'friend'.

More About Anna Catherine Heck:
Immigration: September 28, 1733 in parents); Germany to USA (ship Richard & Elizabeth w[434]
Religion: 1767 ; Tulpehocken, Berks Co, PA[435]

Notes for Anna Catherine Heck:
d/o John Joseph Heck b c1698 & Eva Maria ? b c1698

Heck: German: topographic name from Middle High German hecke, hegge 'hedge'. This name is common in southern Germany and the Rhineland. Shortened form of the Dutch surname van (den) Hecke, a habitational name from any of several places called ten Hekke in the Belgian provinces of East and West Flanders.

Anna Catherine Heck and George William Gieseman had the following children:

i. Anna Margaret Gieseman (daughter of George William Gieseman and Anna Catherine Heck) was born in 1749 in PA.

ii. John Gieseman (son of George William Gieseman and Anna Catherine Heck) was born about Abt. 1750 in PA.

iii. John George Gieseman (son of George William Gieseman and Anna Catherine Heck) was born in 1754 in Berks Co, PA. He died in 1810. He married Catherine Wagner. She was born in 1758. She died in 1818.

iv. Anna Barbara Gieseman (daughter of George William

Gieseman and Anna Catherine Heck) was born in 1760 in PA. She married Bernard Souers.

62. v. John William Gieseman (son of George William Gieseman and Anna Catherine Heck) was born on March 23, 1761 in Lebanon, Lancaster (Lebanon) Co, PA[324]. He died on August 26, 1843 in Dauphin Co, PA[324]. He married Anna Margaret Gruber (daughter of Christian Gruber and Anna Gunigunda Stupp) on February 19, 1782 in Christ (Little Tulpehocken) Lutheran, Bernville, Berks Co, PA[325]. She was born on August 02, 1759 in Berks Co, PA[326]. She died on June 12, 1837 in Dauphin Co, PA.

126. **Christian Gruber** was born on October 18, 1712 in Sinzeim, Baden-Wurttemberg, Germany[436, 437, 438]. He died on November 14, 1781 in Bernville, Tulpehocken, Berks Co, PA[326, 436, 438, 439]. He married **Anna Gunigunda Stupp** on January 26, 1742 in Rev. Stoever, Christ (Little Tulpehocken) Lutheran, Bernville, Lancaster (Berks) Co, PA[436, 440, 441, 442].

127. **Anna Gunigunda Stupp**[438] was born on December 21, 1721 in Schoharie Valley, Schoharie, NY[326, 443, 444]. She died on May 30, 1799 in Bernville, Tulpehocken, Berks Co, PA[436, 439, 445].

More About Christian Gruber:
Burial: 1781 in Christ (Little Tulpehocken) Lutheran, Old Graveyard, Bernville, Berks Co, PA[438, 446]
Immigration: September 30, 1732 in Germany to USA (ship Dragon)[447, 448, 449]
Naturalization: April 10, 1760[446]
Occupation: 1781 ; Yeoman[450]
Probate: Bet. December 04-14 1781 in Reading, Berks Co, PA[450]
Probate: Bet. July 23, 1784-October 31, 1795 in Bern Tp, Berks Co, PA[450]
Probate: May 24, 1800 in Reading, Berks Co, PA[450]
Residence: Bet. 1743-1759 in Northkill, PA[451]
Residence: Now Jefferson Tp, Berks Co, PA[446]
Will: July 07, 1780 in Tulpehocken, Berks Co, PA[450, 452]

Notes for Christian Gruber:
s/o Henry Gruber b1671 Steinsfurt, Baden-Wurttemberg, Germany &

Elizabeth Huber
s/o Bartolomus Gruber b1645 Germany & Anna Maria Reittenbach
d/o Jacob Huber bc1640 Steinsfurt, Baden-Wurttemberg, Germany & Barbara Kuss
s/o Hans Gruber b 1628 Steinsfurt, Shinsheim, Baden, Germany & Anna ?
d/o Matthew Reittenbach bc1625

Gruber: German (Grüber) topographic name for someone who lived in a depression or hollow, from (respectively) Middle High German gruobe, German Grube 'pit', 'hollow' + the suffix -er denoting an inhabitant.

More About Anna Gunigunda Stupp:
Burial: 1799 in Christ (Little Tulpehocken) Lutheran, Old Graveyard, Bernville, Berks Co, PA[438, 446]
Census: 1790
Probate: Bet. June 04-14 1799 in Tulpehocken, Berks Co, PA[445, 453]
Residence: 1742 in Tulpehocken, PA[440]
Will: November 09, 1796 in Tulpehocken, Berks Co, PA[445]

Notes for Anna Gunigunda Stupp:
s/o Martin Stupp b1683 Adelshofen, Baden-Wurttemberg, Germany & Anna Catherine Schultheis
s/o Martin Stupp & Anne Catherine ?
d/o John George Schultheiss of Germany & Anna Elizabeth Weidman/Walborn
d/o Henry Weidman or John Adam Waldorn b1666 Germany

Born 12/21/1712 Christian Gruber, Old Graveyard & Two Cemeteries, Bernville, Berks Co, PA, www.interment.net.

Anna Gunigunda Stupp and Christian Gruber had the following children:

i. John George Gruber (son of Christian Gruber and Anna Gunigunda Stupp) was born in 1743 in PA. He died in 1792. He married Elizabeth Emerich. She was born about Abt. 1750.

ii. Christina Elizabeth Gruber (daughter of Christian Gruber and Anna Gunigunda Stupp) was born in 1745 in PA.

iii. Christian Gruber (son of Christian Gruber and Anna Gunigunda Stupp) was born in 1745 in PA. He died in 1822. He married Susan Sliger. She was born about Abt. 1750.

iv. Susan Gruber (daughter of Christian Gruber and Anna Gunigunda Stupp) was born in 1746 in PA. She died about Abt. 1805. She married Matthew Schmidt.

v. Maria Catherine Gruber (daughter of Christian Gruber and Anna Gunigunda Stupp) was born in 1749 in PA. She married Zuber. He was born about Abt. 1740.

vi. Henry Gruber (son of Christian Gruber and Anna Gunigunda Stupp) was born about Abt. 1750 in PA.

vii. John Adam Gruber (son of Christian Gruber and Anna Gunigunda Stupp) was born in 1752 in PA.

viii. John Albright Gruber (son of Christian Gruber and Anna Gunigunda Stupp) was born in 1754 in PA. He married Susan Vilbina Knapp. She was born about Abt. 1760.

63. ix. Anna Margaret Gruber (daughter of Christian Gruber and Anna Gunigunda Stupp) was born on August 02, 1759 in Berks Co, PA[326]. She died on June 12, 1837 in Dauphin Co, PA. She married John William Gieseman (son of George William Gieseman and Anna Catherine Heck) on February 19, 1782 in Christ (Little Tulpehocken) Lutheran, Bernville, Berks Co, PA[325]. He was born on March 23, 1761 in Lebanon, Lancaster (Lebanon) Co, PA[324]. He died on August 26, 1843 in Dauphin Co, PA[324].

Generation 8

222. **John George Sheetz** (son of George Shuetz and Elizabeth Kibler) was born in 1746 in PA[454]. He died about Abt. 1791 in Dauphin Co, PA. He married **Anna Margaret Wolfkill** (daughter of John Henry Wolfskiel and Maria Magdalena Mahr) on June 30, 1767 in Lebanon, PA (Rev. Casper Stoever, Dauphin[455]).

223. **Anna Margaret Wolfkill** (daughter of John Henry Wolfskiel and Maria

Magdalena Mahr) was born on July 16, 1732 in Neider-Hilbersheim, Rhineland-Palatinate, Germany[454, 455]. She died between 1790-1800 in Dauphin Co, PA.

More About John George Sheetz:
Census: 1790 in Dauphin Co, PA[456]
Military Service: Abt. 1775 ; American Revolution, Private 4th PA Reg, ? Co, Paxtang Volunteers (Lancaster, Capt. John Rutherford)[457]
Residence: 1767 in Paxton, Lancaster (Dauphin) Co, PA[458]

More About Anna Margaret Wolfkill:
Census: 1790 in husband; Dauphin Co, PA w
Immigration: 1760 in with father
Residence: 1767 in Earltown, PA[458]

Anna Margaret Wolfkill and John George Sheetz had the following children:

111. i. Susan Sheets (daughter of John George Sheetz and Anna Margaret Wolfkill) was born on August 16, 1768 in Lancaster Co, PA[407, 409, 410]. She died on March 23, 1854 in Ogle, IL[407, 411]. She married Andrew Keck. He was born about Abt. 1760. She married Michael Garman in 1785 in Dauphin Co, PA[407, 409]. He was born in 1747 in York Co, PA[407, 408, 409]. He died on January 08, 1800 in IL (PAIllness[407, 409]).

ii. John George Sheets (son of John George Sheetz and Anna Margaret Wolfkill) was born between 1773-1774 in Paxtang, Lancaster (Dauphin) Co, PA[454, 459]. He died in 1822 in Dauphin Co, PA[454]. He married Mary "Polly" Forman (daughter of <No name> and <No name>) about Abt. 1798 in Dauphin Co, PA. She was born on January 05, 1778 in PA[454, 460]. She died on June 03, 1848 in Dauphin Co, PA[454, 460].

More About John George Sheets:
Burial: 1822
Census: 1790 in father; Dauphin Co, PA w
Census: 1800 in Upper Paxton, Dauphin Co, PA[461]
Census: 1810 in Swatara, Dauphin Co, PA (Shits)[462]

Census: 1820 in Susquehanna, Dauphin Co, PA[463]
Religion: Bet. 1799-1814 ; Salem Reformed Church, Harrisburg, Dauphin Co, PA[464]
Will: Abt. 1822 in Dauphin Co, PA

Notes for John George Sheets:
1. Rob Sheetz, Robsheetz32@@wmconnect.com.

More About Mary "Polly" Forman:
Burial: 1848
Census: 1790 in parents; w
Census: 1800 in husband; w
Census: 1810 in husband; Swatara, Dauphin Co, PA w
Census: 1820 in husband; Susquehanna, Dauphin Co, PA w[463]
Census: 1830
Census: 1840 in Jackson, Dauphin Co, PA

Notes for Mary "Polly" Forman:
Forman: English: occupational name for a keeper of swine, Middle English foreman, from Old English for 'hog', 'pig' + mann 'man'. English: status name for a leader or spokesman for a group, from Old English fore 'before', 'in front' + mann 'man'. The word is attested in this sense from the 15th century, but is not used specifically for the leader of a gang of workers before the late 16th century. Czech occupational name for a carter, Czech forman, a loanword from German.

iii. Michael Sheets (son of John George Sheetz and Anna Margaret Wolfkill) was born in PA.

iv. Jacob Sheets (son of John George Sheetz and Anna Margaret Wolfkill) was born about Abt. 1769 in PA.

v. Catherine Sheets (daughter of John George Sheetz and Anna Margaret Wolfkill) was born about Abt. 1775 in PA.

vi. Elizabeth Sheets (daughter of John George Sheetz and Anna Margaret Wolfkill) was born about Abt. 1777 in PA.

vii. Mary Sheets (daughter of John George Sheetz and Anna Margaret Wolfkill) was born about Abt. 1779.

viii. Leonard Sheets (son of John George Sheetz and Anna Margaret Wolfkill) was born about Abt. 1781 in PA.

240. **Frantz**.

Frantz had the following children:

120. i. Daniel Frantz (son of Frantz) was born about Abt. 1718. He died about Abt. 1780. He married Barbara about Abt. 1740. She was born about Abt. 1720. She died after Aft. 1760.

ii. George Adam Frantz (son of Frantz) was born about Abt. 1722.

iii. Johannes Frantz (son of Frantz) was born about Abt. 1725.

Generation 9

444. **George Shuetz** was born in 1716 in Germany[465]. He died about Abt. 1768 in Lancaster (Dauphin) Co, PA[466]. He married **Elizabeth Kibler** about Abt. 1740 in Lancaster?, PA.

445. **Elizabeth Kibler** was born in 1720 in Germany?[465]. She died after Aft. 1769 in Lancaster (Dauphin) Co, PA.

More About George Shuetz:
Burial: Abt. 1769
Immigration: Abt. 1737 in Germany to USA (ship Philadelphia)[467]
Residence: Bet. 1749-1751 in Paxtang, Lancaster (Dauphin) Co, PA[468, 469]
Residence: 1749 in Swatara, PA[470]
Will: October 11, 1768 in Lancaster Co, PA[471]

Notes for Elizabeth Kibler:
Widow Sheets, living alone, 1790 United States Census, Dauphin Co, PA, ancestry.com & Microfilm, PA State Library, Hbg, PA

Kibler: Austrian, Swiss, and South German: variant of Kuebler.

Elizabeth Kibler and George Shuetz had the following children:

222. i. John George Sheetz (son of George Shuetz and Elizabeth Kibler) was born in 1746 in PA[454]. He died about Abt. 1791 in Dauphin Co, PA. He married Anna Margaret Wolfkill (daughter of John Henry Wolfskiel and Maria Magdalena Mahr) on June 30, 1767 in Lebanon, PA (Rev. Casper Stoever, Dauphin[455]). She was born on July 16, 1732 in Neider-Hilbersheim, Rhineland-Palatinate, Germany[454, 455]. She died between 1790-1800 in Dauphin Co, PA.

ii. Jacob Sheets (son of George Shuetz and Elizabeth Kibler) was born in PA.

iii. Susan Sheets (daughter of George Shuetz and Elizabeth Kibler) was born in PA. She married Conrad Renninger.

iv. Catherine Sheets (daughter of George Shuetz and Elizabeth Kibler) was born in PA. She married Martin Gross.

v. Elizabeth Sheets (daughter of George Shuetz and Elizabeth Kibler) was born in PA. She married George Segar.

vi. Mary Sheets (daughter of George Shuetz and Elizabeth Kibler) was born in PA.

vii. John Leonard Sheets (son of George Shuetz and Elizabeth Kibler) was born in 1749 in PA.

446. **John Henry Wolfskiel** was born on November 03, 1706 in Neider-Hilbersheim, Rhineland-Palatinate, Germany[455]. He died on June 17, 1787 in Earl, Lancaster Co, PA[455]. He married **Maria Magdalena Mahr** about Abt. 1730 in Germany.

447. **Maria Magdalena Mahr** was born about Abt. 1712 in Germany?[472]. She died in January 1767 in Lancaster Co, PA.

More About John Henry Wolfskiel:
Burial: 1787
Immigration: 1760[473]

Naturalization: September 21, 1760 in Lancaster Co, PA[474]
Occupation: June 12, 1787 ; Yeoman[475]
Probate: July 08, 1788 in Earl Tp, Lancaster Co, PA[475, 476, 477]
Residence: 1742 in Philadelphia, PA[478]
Will: June 12, 1787 in Earl Tp, Lancaster Co, PA[475]

Notes for John Henry Wolfskiel:
s/o John Wolfskehl b1661 Neider-Hilbersheim, Rhineland-Palatinate, Germany & Angelica Otter
s/o John Wolfskehl b1635 & Elizabeth Winck
s/o Killian Wolfskiehl b 1600

Born November 13, 1705, Johann Heinrich Wolfkiehl, Millennium File, myfamily.com, Heritage Consulting, www.ancestry.com

More About Maria Magdalena Mahr:
Burial: January 25, 1767 in Cocalico Reformed Church, Lancaster Co, PA[455, 472]

Maria Magdalena Mahr and John Henry Wolfskiel had the following children:

223. i. Anna Margaret Wolfkill (daughter of John Henry Wolfskiel and Maria Magdalena Mahr) was born on July 16, 1732 in Neider-Hilbersheim, Rhineland-Palatinate, Germany[454, 455]. She died between 1790-1800 in Dauphin Co, PA. She married John George Sheetz (son of George Shuetz and Elizabeth Kibler) on June 30, 1767 in Lebanon, PA (Rev. Casper Stoever, Dauphin[455]). He was born in 1746 in PA[454]. He died about Abt. 1791 in Dauphin Co, PA.

ii. Killian Wolfkill (son of John Henry Wolfskiel and Maria Magdalena Mahr) was born in 1734 in Germany. He married Maria Magdalena Wenhert. She was born about Abt. 1740.

iii. Philip Wolfkill (son of John Henry Wolfskiel and Maria Magdalena Mahr) was born in 1736 in Germany. He married Wendelina. She was born about Abt. 1740.

iv. Conrad Wolfkill (son of John Henry Wolfskiel and Maria Magdalena Mahr) was born in 1738 in Germany. He died in 1813. He married Anna Maria Sprenger. She was born about Abt. 1740.

v. Anna Maria Wolfkill (daughter of John Henry Wolfskiel and Maria Magdalena Mahr) was born in 1740 in Germany. She married Herman Waltman. He was born about Abt. 1730.

vi. Magdalena Wolfkill (daughter of John Henry Wolfskiel and Maria Magdalena Mahr) was born in 1743 in Germany.

vii. Dorothy Wolfkill (daughter of John Henry Wolfskiel and Maria Magdalena Mahr) was born in 1745 in Germany. She married George Dietrich. He was born about Abt. 1740.

Sources

1 Myrtle A. Batdorf birth certificate, January 1918, Department of Vital records, New Castle, PA.
2 Thompson-Batdorf marriage record, Register of Wills, Clerk of Orphans Court, Dauphin Co, PA, 1935.
3 Myrtle A Thompson death certificate, #3455802, Department of Vital records, New Castle, PA.
4 Myrtle Thompson, Obituary, Harrisburg Patriot newspaper, 1983.
5 Samuel Peters, Descendants of John Peters, Evelyn S. Hartman.
6 Harper Bruce Thompson birth record, #344701, #122649-07, September 1907, Schuylkill Co, PA, Department of Vital Records, New Castle, PA.
7 Harper B Thompson, Obituary, Harrisburg Patriot Newspaper, July 1981.
8 Harper B Thompson death certificate, #2501265, Department of Vital Records, New Castle, PA.
9 Batdorf household, 1920 United States Census, Dauphin Co, PA, Roll T625 1559, p 3A, ED 148, Image 1081, ancestry.com & Microfilm, PA State Library, Hbg, PA.
10 Batdorf household, 1930 United States Census, Dauphin Co, PA, Roll T626 2027, p 19A, ED 76, Image 0959, ancestry.com & Microfilm, PA State Library, Hbg, PA.
11 Thompson household, 1940 US Federal census, Bruce Thompson, Snyder, PA, www.ancestry.com.

Sources (con't)

12 Batdorf household, 1930 United States Census, Dauphin Co, PA, Roll T626 2027, p 19A, ED 76, Image 0959, ancestry.com & Microfilm, PA State Library, Hbg, PA.

13 Myrtle A Thompson, Obituary, Harrisburg Patriot newspaper, 1983.

14 Myrtle A Thompson, Probate files, 1983, File 424-1983, Dauphin County Courthouse, Reg of Wills, Deborah Hershey, Elizabethtown, PA, Mar 2008.

15 Myrtle Thompson, Gerald G Thompson.

16 Myrtle Thompson, May 1983, PA, Social Security Death Index, www.familysearch.org.

17 Thompson household, 1910 United States Census, Schuylkill Co, PA, www.ancestry.com and 1910 United States Census, Schuylkill Co, PA, ED 62, Sheet 32A, PA State Library.

18 Thompson household, 1920 United States Census, Schuylkill Co, PA, PA State library, microfilm image.

19 Thompson household, 1920 United States Census, Schuylkill Co, PA, Roll T625 1651, ED 84, Image 0280, ancestry.com & Microfilm, PA State Library, Hbg, PA.

20 Knittle household, 1930 United States Census, Lehigh Co, PA, ancestry.com & Microfilm, PA State Library, Hbg, PA.

21 Thompson household, 1920 United States Census, Schuylkill Co, PA, Roll T625 1651, ED 84, Image 0280, www.ancestry.com and 1920 United States Census, Schuylkill Co, PA, PA State library, microfilm image.

22 Harper B Thompson, Social Seurity numident record, application for SS-5, SSA, Nov 2006, Baltimore, MD.

23 Harper Thompson, July 1981, PA, Social Security Death Index, www.familysearch,org.

24 James Edward Batdorf death certificate, #0506183, #66234-39, August 1954, Department of Vital Records, New Castle, PA.

25 James Edward Batdorf, Church record, Rev. O.S. Moyer, Angie Eddy, Maple Grove Cemetery, Eluzabethville, PA, p 29.

26 James Edward Batdorf, United States WW II Draft Reg. Cards, 1942 Record, 2243624, www.ancestry.com.

27 James Edward Batdorf, Social Seurity numident record, application for SS-5, SSA, Nov 2006, Baltimore, MD.

28 Batdorf-Wert marriage record, Church record, Rev. O.S. Moyer, Angie Eddy, Maple Grove Cemetery, Elizabethville, PA, p 16.

Sources (con't)

29 Beulah I Batdorf death certificate, #0506188, #057537, June 1983, Department of Vital records, New Castle, PA.
30 Beulah Batdorf, June 1983, PA, Social Security Death Index, www.familysearch.org.
31 Beulah I Batdorf, Obituary, Harrisburg Patriot News, 1983.
32 James Edward Batdorf, Church record, Rev. O.S. Moyer, Angie Eddy, Maple Grove Cemetery, Eluzabethville, PA, p 16.
33 James E Batdorf, Obituary, Harrisburg Patriot news, 1954.
34 Bordorf household, 1900 United States Census, Dauphin Co, PA, T623 1401, p 76, ED 39, sheet 10B, ancestry.com & Microfilm, PA State Library, Hbg, PA.
35 Batdorf household, 1900 United States Census, Dauphin Co, PA, ancestry.com & Microfilm, PA State Library, Hbg, PA.
36 Batdorf household, 1930 United States Census, , PA, Roll T626 2027, p 19A, ED 76, Image 0959, ancestry.com & Microfilm, PA State Library, Hbg, PA.
37 Batdorf household, 1940 US Federal census, James E Batdorf, Snyder, PA, www.ancestry.com.
38 James Edward Batdorf, #0506183, #66234-39, August 1954, Department of Vital Records, New Castle, PA.
39 James Edward Batdorf, Funeral record copy, John R. Shultz Funeral Home, Lykens, Dauphin Co, PA, 2006, John Shultz, Director.
40 James Edward Batdorf, World War I Draft Registration Cards, 1917-1918 Record, United States WW II Draft Reg. Cards, 1942 Record, 2243624, www.ancestry.com.
41 James Edward Batdorf, U.S. World War II Draft Registration Cards, 1942, www.ancestry.com.
42 Batdorf household, 1900 United States Census, Dauphin Co, PA, ancestry.com & Microfilm, PA State Library, Hbg, PA.
43 Batdorf household, 1920 United States Census, Dauphin Co, PA, Roll T625 1559, p 3A, ED 148, Image 1081, ancestry.com & Microfilm, PA State Library, Hbg, PA.
44 Batdorf Family information, Mildred Moon, Herndon, PA.
45 Wert household, 1900 United States Census, Dauphin Co, PA, www.ancestry.com and 1900 United States Census, Dauphin Co, PA, Pa State Library microfilm image.
46 Beulah I Batdorf, Social Seurity numident record, application for SS-5, SSA, Nov 2006, Baltimore, MD.

Sources (con't)

47 John Peters, Peters family information, Evelyn S Hartman, deanh@@voicenet.com.
48 Peter Batdorf, Descendants of Peter Batdorf, Evelyn S Hartman, deanh@@voicenet.com.
49 Batdorf Family information, Virginia Faust.
50 Thomas Batdorf, #0102590, #81400-17, 1916, Department of Vital records, New Castle, PA.
51 Mary L Batdorf, #0042526, #7?-23, 1924, Department of Vital records, New Castle, PA.
52 Bodorff household, 1860 United States Census, Dauphin Co, PA, ancestry.com & Microfilm, PA State Library, Hbg, PA.
53 Baddorf household, 1870 United States Census, Dauphin Co, PA, ancestry.com & Microfilm, PA State Library, Hbg, PA.
54 Baddorf household, 1880 United States Census, Dauphin Co, PA, FHL 1255124, Film T9-1124, p 246A, www.familysearch.org.
55 Batdorf household, 1910 United States Census, Dauphin Co, PA, ED 120, Sheet 6, ancestry.com & Microfilm, PA State Library, Hbg, PA.
56 Batdorf household, 1910 United States Census, Dauphin Co, PA, ED 120, Sheet 6, ancestry.com & Microfilm, PA State Library, Hbg, PA.
57 Peters household, 1860 United States Census, Dauphin Co, PA, Series M653, Roll 1103, p 568, ancestry.com & Microfilm, PA State Library, Hbg, PA.
58 Batdorf household, 1920 United States Census, Dauphin Co, PA, T625 1557, p 10a, ED 53, Image 0812, ancestry.com & Microfilm, PA State Library, Hbg, PA.
59 Batdorf household, 1920 United States Census, Dauphin Co, PA, T625 1557, p 10a, ED 53, Image 0812, ancestry.com & Microfilm, PA State Library, Hbg, PA.
60 John Wert, #0042527, #95868-1303, 1924, Department of Vital records, New Castle, PA.
61 Adeline Row, St. John Evangelical Lutheran Church, Berrysburg, PA, Sara S. Neagley, Elizabethville, PA.
62 Mrs. Adeline Wert death certificate, #26162, #3457526, March 1921, Department of Vital Records, New Castle, PA.
63 Descendants of Frederick Adam Faber, Evelyn S Hartman, deanh@@voicenet.com.
64 Wert Family, Jonathan Wert.

65 Wert, Sr. household, 1860 United States Census, Northumberland Co, PA, ancestry.com & Microfilm, PA State Library, Hbg, PA.
66 Wert household, 1870 United States Census, Dauphin Co, PA, PA State library microfilm.
67 Wert household, 1880 United States Census, Dauphin Co, PA, FHL 1255124, Film T9-1124, p 251D, www.familysearch.org.
68 Wert household, 1910 United States Census, Dauphin Co, PA, ancestry.com & Microfilm, PA State Library, Hbg, PA.
69 Wert household, 1920 United States Census, Dauphin Co, PA, PA State Library, microfilm image and 1920 United States Census, Dauphin Co, PA, ancestry.com & Microfilm, PA State Library, Hbg, PA.
70 Wert household, 1920 United States Census, Dauphin Co, PA, PA State Library, microfilm image and 1920 United States Census, Dauphin Co, PA, www.ancestry.com.
71 John Henry Wert, Probate files, 1938, #988, Letter of Admin, A 213 21/329, Inv 23 N-512, Dauphin County Courthouse, Reg of Wills, Deborah Hershey, Elizabethtown, PA, Mar 2008.
72 Row household, 1860 United States Census, Dauphin Co, PA, PA State library microfilm.
73 Ely household, 1870 United States Census, Dauphin Co, PA, ancestry.com & Microfilm, PA State Library, Hbg, PA.
74 Michael Goodman, Descendants of Michael Goodman, Evelyn S Hartman, deanh@@voicenet.com.
75 Welkers in the USA & Nulls from PA, Greg Welker, gwelker@@chesapeake.net, awt.ancestry.com.
76 Baddorf Family, Gratz History, p 193.
77 Peter Batdorf, St. Peters (Hoffmans) Union Church, Burials.
78 Peter Botdorf, St. Peter's (Hoffman's) Union Church, Lykens, Dauphin Co, PA, Gert Mysliwski, gert@@foothill.net.
79 Peter Batdorf, Probate files, 1881, Affidavit Rep #5, Dauphin County Courthouse, Reg of Wills, Deborah Hershey, Elizabethtown, PA, Mar 2008.
80 Peter Batdorf, Hoffmans Reformed Church, Lykens Valley, Dauphin Co, PA, Historical & Genealogical, pp 227-8.
81 Elizabeth Batdorf, Hoffmans Reformed Church, Lykens Valley, Dauphin Co, PA, Historical & Genealogical, pp 227-8.
82 Batdorf household, 1820 United States Census, Dauphin Co, PA, ancestry.com & Microfilm, PA State Library, Hbg, PA.

83 Batdorf household, 1830 United States Census, Dauphin Co, PA, ancestry.com & Microfilm, PA State Library, Hbg, PA.
84 Batdorf household, 1840 United States Census, Dauphin Co, PA, ancestry.com & Microfilm, PA State Library, Hbg, PA.
85 Batdorf household, 1840 United States Census, Dauphin Co, PA, PA State library microfilm.
86 Bottorff household, 1850 United States Census, Dauphin Co, PA, Roll M432-775, [age 399, Image 363, ancestry.com & Microfilm, PA State Library, Hbg, PA.
87 Baddorf household, 1870 United States Census, Dauphin Co, PA, PA State library microfilm.
88 Batdorf household, 1880 United States Census, Dauphin Co, PA, Roll T9-1124, p 57A, ED 106, Image 0924, ancestry.com & Microfilm, PA State Library, Hbg, PA.
89 Baddorf household, 1870 United States Census, Dauphin Co, PA, PA State library microfilm.
90 Welker household, 1820 United States Census, Dauphin Co, PA, ancestry.com & Microfilm, PA State Library, Hbg, PA.
91 Welker household, 1830 United States Census, Dauphin Co, PA, ancestry.com & Microfilm, PA State Library, Hbg, PA.
92 Mary Peters death certificate, bk C, #945, 1897, Dauphin County Register of Wills, Harrisburg, PA.
93 Mary Peters death certificate, Dauphin County Register of Wills, bk C, #945, 1897, Harrisburg, PA. Source 140, bk C, #945, 1897, Perry County Historians.
94 Mary Peters death certificate, Dauphin County Register of Wills, bk C, #945, 1897, Harrisburg, PA.
95 Peters household, 1830 United States Census, Union Co, PA, ancestry.com & Microfilm, PA State Library, Hbg, PA.
96 Peters household, 1850 United States Census, Dauphin Co, PA, Pam Patton, poohie@@penn.com.
97 Peters household, 1850 United States Census, Dauphin Co, PA, FTM CD305, Disk 10, film 831.
98 Mary Peters death certificate, Mary Peters death record, bk C, #945, 1897, Dauphin County Register of Wills, Harrisburg, PA.
99 Swartz household, 1830 United States Census, Perry Co, PA, ancestry.com & Microfilm, PA State Library, Hbg, PA.
100 Swartz household, 1840 United States Census, Perry Co, PA, ancestry.com & Microfilm, PA State Library, Hbg, PA.

Sources (con't)

101 Peters household, 1870 United States Census, Dauphin Co, PA, Series M593, Roll 1335 p 538, ancestry.com & Microfilm, PA State Library, Hbg, PA.
102 Row household, 1880 United States Census, Dauphin Co, PA, FHLF 1255124, NA film T9-1124, p 245c, ancestry.com & Microfilm, PA State Library, Hbg, PA.
103 David Wert death certificate, Dauphin County Register of Wills, bk E, #852, December 20, 1900, , Harrisburg, PA.
104 Shoop family information, Are you my cousin, Howard Ward, haroldw1@@juno.com, awt.ancestry.com.
105 Monn & Related Families, Danni Monn Hopkins, clueless@@clnk.com, awt.ancestry.com.
106 David Wert (West) death record, Extract from County Death records, 1893-1906.
107 Wertz family information, Bob Messerschmidt, Laurel, MD, SusanM4383@@aol.com.
108 Wertz family information, Cindi Grimm, Grimm@@ruralife.net.
109 Shoop family information, Are you my cousin, Harold Ward, haroldw1@@juno.com, awt.ancestry.com.
110 David Wert, Wiconisco Calvary Cemetery.
111 David Wert, Dauphin County Register of Wills, bk E, #852, December 20, 1900, , Harrisburg, PA.
112 Wert household, 1830 United States Census, Dauphin Co, PA, ancestry.com & Microfilm, PA State Library, Hbg, PA.
113 Wert household, 1840 United States Census, Dauphin Co, PA, ancestry.com & Microfilm, PA State Library, Hbg, PA.
114 Wert household, 1850 United States Census, Dauphin Co, PA, PA State library microfilm.
115 Schamper?/Buffington household, 1850 United States Census, Dauphin Co, PA, PA State library microfilm.
116 Shoop household, 1840 United States Census, Northumberland Co, PA, ancestry.com & Microfilm, PA State Library, Hbg, PA.
117 Shoop household, 1850 United States Census, Northumberland Co, PA, ancestry.com & Microfilm, PA State Library, Hbg, PA.
118 Catherine Wert, Probate files, 1880, A-3, Dauphin County Courthouse, Reg of Wills, Deborah Hershey, Elizabethtown, PA, Mar 2008.
119 Daniel Row, Baptismal record, St. John Evangelical Lutheran Church, Dauphin Co, PA, p 64.
120 Rowe family information, Howard E Row, Dover, DE.

Sources (con't)

121 Daniel Rowe, St. John Evangelical Lutheran Church, Berrysburg, PA, Sara S. Neagley, Elizabethville, PA, 424 6M 24D.

122 Susanna Rowe, St. John Evangelical Lutheran Church, Berrysburg, PA, Sara S. Neagley, Elizabethville, PA.

123 Row household, 1820 United States Census, Dauphin Co, PA, ancestry.com & Microfilm, PA State Library, Hbg, PA.

124 Row household, 1830 United States Census, Dauphin Co, PA, ancestry.com & Microfilm, PA State Library, Hbg, PA.

125 Rowe household, 1840 United States Census, Dauphin Co, PA, ancestry.com & Microfilm, PA State Library, Hbg, PA.

126 Rowe household, 1840 United States Census, Dauphin Co, PA, PA State library microfilm.

127 Row household, 1850 United States Census, Dauphin Co, PA, PA State library microfilm.

128 Row household, 1860 United States Census, Dauphin Co, PA, ancestry.com & Microfilm, PA State Library, Hbg, PA.

129 Zerber household, 1870 United States Census, Dauphin Co, PA, PA State library microfilm.

130 Daniel Row, Probate files, 1871, Letter of Admin, Dauphin County Courthouse, Reg of Wills, Deborah Hershey, Elizabethtown, PA, Mar 2008.

131 Susanna Rowe, St. John Evangelical Lutheran Church, Berrysburg, PA, Sara S. Neagley, Elizabethville, PA, 424 6M 24D.

132 Frantz household, 1820 United States Census, Dauphin Co, PA, ancestry.com & Microfilm, PA State Library, Hbg, PA.

133 Peter Batdorf, Descendants of Peter Batdorf, Evelyn S. Hartman.

134 Pottorff household, 1800 United States Federal Census, Dauphin Co, PA, ancestry.com & Microfilm, PA State Library, Hbg, PA.

135 Badorf Jr household, 1820 United States Census, Dauphin Co, PA, ancestry.com & Microfilm, PA State Library, Hbg, PA.

136 Badorf Jr household, 1820 United States Census, Dauphin Co, PA, PA State Library microfilm.

137 Peter Batdorf, Probate files, 1829, Letter of Admin, P248 A, Dauphin County Courthouse, Reg of Wills, Deborah Hershey, Elizabethtown, PA, Mar 2008.

138 Dauphin County Names, Data p, www://genealogy.lv/howard/.

139 Baddorf household, 1830 United States Census, Dauphin Co, PA, PA State library microfilm.

140 Baddorf household, 1830 United States Census, Dauphin Co, PA, ancestry.com & Microfilm, PA State Library, Hbg, PA.

141 Batrdorf household, 1830 United States Census, Dauphin Co, PA, ancestry.com & Microfilm, PA State Library, Hbg, PA.
142 Dauphin County Names, Data p, Robert M Howard, www://genealogy.lv/howard/.
143 Valentine Welker, Direct Descendants of Valentine (Welcher) Welker, Evelyn S. Hartman.
144 Welker family information, Roger Cramer, rogercubs@@aol.com.
145 Welker Family, Gratz History, p 450-455.
146 Pats Family, Pat Scott, pat.scott@@comcast.net, awt.ancestry.com.
147 John Welker, Barbara Brady O'Keefe, 2120 SW 127 Avenue, Miami, FL & Cindy Maloney, cynwelker8@@rurelated.com.
148 Welker household, 1790 United States Census, Dauphin Co, PA, ancestry.com & Microfilm, PA State Library, Hbg, PA.
149 Welker household, 1800 United States Census, Dauphin Co, PA, ancestry.com & Microfilm, PA State Library, Hbg, PA.
150 Welker household, 1821 United States Census, Dauphin Co, PA, Roll M252 54m p 538, Image 123, ancestry.com & Microfilm, PA State Library, Hbg, PA.
151 Welker household, 1820 United States Census, Dauphin Co, PA, PA State library microfilm.
152 Welker household, 1830 United States Census, Dauphin Co, PA, PA State library microfilm.
153 Welker household, 1840 United States Census, Dauphin Co, PA, ancestry.com & Microfilm, PA State Library, Hbg, PA.
154 Welker household, 1840 United States Census, Dauphin Co, PA, PA State library microfilm.
155 Welker household, 1850 United States Census, Dauphin Co, PA, ancestry.com & Microfilm, PA State Library, Hbg, PA.
156 John Welker, Probate files, 1854, F-413-4, Dauphin County Courthouse, Reg of Wills, Deborah Hershey, Elizabethtown, PA, Mar 2008.
157 Messerschmidt household, 1800 United States Census, Dauphin Co, PA, ancestry.com & Microfilm, PA State Library, Hbg, PA.
158 Peters Research, Michael McCormick, Enduring Legacy, Gardners, PA, Feb 2009.
159 Peters household, 1850 United States Federal Census, Union, PA, 288, ancestry.com & Microfilm, PA State Library, Hbg, PA.

Sources (con't)

160 Maria Peters, Death notice, Lewisburg Chronicle, Oct. 1852 c/o Union County Historical Society, Maggie Miller, hstorici@@ptd.net.
161 Peters household, 1810 United States Census, Northumberland Co, PA, ancestry.com & Microfilm, PA State Library, Hbg, PA.
162 Peters household, 1820 United States Census, Union Co, PA, ancestry.com & Microfilm, PA State Library, Hbg, PA.
163 John Peters, Probate files, 1846, Union County Courthouse, Reg of Wills, Union Co, PA, 2008.
164 Maria Peters, Death notice, Lewisburg Chronicle, octo. 1852 c/o Union County Historical Society, Maggie Miller, hstorici@@ptd.net.
165 Swartz household, 1820 US Federal Census, Juniata, Perry Co, PA, www.ancestry.com.
166 Jacob Wert, Wert family, Onetree, ancestry.com.
167 Wert Family History, complied genealogy, Jonathan Wert, www.mdi-wert.com, jwert@@mdi-wert.com.
168 Elizabeth Wert death record, Extract from County Death records, 1893-1906.
169 Jacob Wert, HSMUP, Mbg, PA 17061, via mail, not dated or cited.
170 Wert household, 1810 United States Census, Dauphin Co, PA, ancestry.com & Microfilm, PA State Library, Hbg, PA.
171 Wert household, 1820 United States Census, Dauphin Co, PA, ancestry.com & Microfilm, PA State Library, Hbg, PA.
172 Wert household, 1830 United States Census, Dauphin Co, PA ancestry.com & Microfilm, PA State Library, Hbg, PA.
173 Wert household, 1830 United States Census, Dauphin Co, PA, PA State library microfilm.
174 Wirt household, 1860 United States Census, Dauphin Co, PA, PA State library microfilm.
175 Wert household, 1870 United States Census, Lehigh Co, PA, ancestry.com.
176 Wert household, 1870 United States Census, Lehigh Co, PA, ancestry.com.
177 Wert Family.
178 Sarah Elizabeth Faber Wert, HSMUP, Mbg, PA 17061, via mail, not dated or cited.
179 Faber household, 1810 United States Census, Dauphin Co, PA, ancestry.com & Microfilm, PA State Library, Hbg, PA.

Sources (con't)

180 Faber household, 1820 United States Census, Dauphin Co, PA, ancestry.com & Microfilm, PA State Library, Hbg, PA.

181 Wert, Sr. household, 1870 United States Census, Roll M593 1335, p 649, Image 420, ancestry.com & Microfilm, PA State Library, Hbg, PA.

182 Harman household, 1870 United States Census, Roll M593 1335, p 649, Image 420, ancestry.com & Microfilm, PA State Library, Hbg, PA.

183 Shoop family information, Northumberland Co County, PA 1777-1865, Stone Valley Lutheran, www.ancestry.com.

184 Johannes Schup, Stone Valley Cemetery, Robert Straub, Dalmatia, PA, Section A, Row 16, Grave 30.

185 Wert Family, Jonathan Wert, www.mdi-wert.com.

186 Shoop household, 1810 United States Census, Dauphin Co, PA, ancestry.com & Microfilm, PA State Library, Hbg, PA.

187 Shoop household, 1820 United States Census, Dauphin Co, PA, ancestry.com & Microfilm, PA State Library, Hbg, PA.

188 Shoop household, 1830 United States Census, Northumberland Co, PA, ancestry.com & Microfilm, PA State Library, Hbg, PA.

189 Shoop household, 1850 United States Census, Dauphin Co, PA, ancestry.com & Microfilm, PA State Library, Hbg, PA.

190 John Shoop, Probate files, 1862, Northumberland County Courthouse, Reg of Wills, Sunbury, Bk B, p629, PA, Robyn Jackson, genealogylover@@msn.com, 2008.

191 Wertz household, 1820 United States Census, Northumberland Co, PA, ancestry.com & Microfilm, PA State Library, Hbg, PA.

192 The Lunnys, William Lunny, rlunny@@msn.com, awt.ancestry.com.

193 Frank Rowe, FHL, Pedigree chart, www.familysearch.org.

194 William Rowe, Family Data Collection, Individual Records, www.ancestry.com, Edmund West, comp.

195 William Rowe, Rowe family, Onetree, ancestry.com.

196 William Rowe, Descendants of Frank (Rau) Rowe, Evelyn S. Hartman.

197 William Rowe, St. John Evangelical Lutheran Church, Berrysburg, PA, Sara S. Neagley, Elizabethville, PA, 424 6M 24D.

198 Rowe household, 1790 United States Census, Lancaster Co, PA, ancestry.com & Microfilm, PA State Library, Hbg, PA.

199 Rowe household, 1800 United States Census, Lancaster Co, PA, ancestry.com & Microfilm, PA State Library, Hbg, PA.

200 Rowe household, 1820 United States Census, Dauphin Co, PA, ancestry.com & Microfilm, PA State Library, Hbg, PA.
201 Rowe household, 1820 United States Census, Dauphin Co, PA, PA State library microfilm.
202 Rowe household, 1830 United States Census, Dauphin Co, PA, ancestry.com & Microfilm, PA State Library, Hbg, PA.
203 Rowe household, 1830 United States Census, Dauphin Co, PA, PA State library microfilm.
204 Row household, 1840 United States Census, Dauphin Co, PA, ancestry.com & Microfilm, PA State Library, Hbg, PA.
205 Row household, 1850 United States Census, Dauphin Co, PA, ancestry.com & Microfilm, PA State Library, Hbg, PA.
206 Row household, 1870 United States Census, Dauphin Co, PA, Roll M593-1335, p 710, Image 542, ancestry.com & Microfilm, PA State Library, Hbg, PA.
207 Rosie household, 1820 United States Census, Dauphin Co, PA, ancestry.com & Microfilm, PA State Library, Hbg, PA.
208 Row household, 1850 United States Census, Dauphin Co, PA, ancestry.com & Microfilm, PA State Library, Hbg, PA.
209 Rau/Row, PA Births, Dauphin County, J. Humphrey.
210 William Row, Probate files, 1873, Letter of Admin, Dauphin County Courthouse, Reg of Wills, Deborah Hershey, Elizabethtown, PA, Mar 2008.
211 Barbara Rowe, St. John Evangelical Lutheran Church, Berrysburg, PA, Sara S. Neagley, Elizabethville, PA, 424 6M 24D.
212 Rudy household, 1800 United States Census, Lancaster Co, PA, ancestry.com & Microfilm, PA State Library, Hbg, PA.
213 Row household, 1880 United States Census, Dauphin Co, PA, FHL 1255124, Film T9-1124, p 244A, www.familysearch.org.
214 Johann Wilhelm Frantz, Descendants of Johann Wilhelm Frantz, Evelyn S. Hartman.
215 Adam Frantz, Frantz family, Onetree, ancestry.com.
216 Gieseman family information, Mary Smith.
217 Franz-Gieseman marriage record, October 1811, source unknown.
218 Susanna Franz, St. John's Congr., 17 feb 1826, Mifflin, Dauphin Co, PA, Gert, gert@@foothill.net.
219 Franz-Gieseman marriage record, October 1811, Lykens Valley lower church (David's Reformed) Millersburg, Upper Paxton, Dauphin Co, 1774-1844.

Sources (con't)

220 Susanna Franz, St. John's Congr., 17 feb 1826, Mifflin, Dauphin Co, PA, Gert Mysliwski, gert@@foothill.net.
221 Frantz household, 1790 United States Census, Lancaster Co, PA, ancestry.com & Microfilm, PA State Library, Hbg, PA.
222 Frantz household, 1800 United States Census, Dauphin Co, PA, ancestry.com & Microfilm, PA State Library, Hbg, PA.
223 Frontz household, 1820 United States Census, Dauphin Co, PA, ancestry.com & Microfilm, PA State Library, Hbg, PA.
224 Adam Frantz, War of 1812 Records, DDC, 1999-, www.ancestry.com.
225 Frontz household, 1820 United States Census, Dauphin Co, PA, ancestry.com & Microfilm, PA State Library, Hbg, PA.
226 Frantz, PA Births, Dauphin County, J. Humphrey.
227 Adam Frantz, Dauphin County, Pennnsylavnia, 1800-55, St. Peters (Hoffmans) Church, Lykens, Dauphin Co, PA, www.ancestry.com.
228 Gieseman household, 1790 United States Census, Berks Co, PA, ancestry.com & Microfilm, PA State Library, Hbg, PA.
229 Gieseman household, 1800 United States Census, Berks Co, PA, ancestry.com & Microfilm, PA State Library, Hbg, PA.
230 Geseman household, 1810 United States Census, Dauphin Co, PA, ancestry.com & Microfilm, PA State Library, Hbg, PA.
231 Susanna Frantz, Dauphin County, Pennnsylavnia, 1800-55, St. Peters (Hoffmans) Church, Lykens, Dauphin Co, PA, www.ancestry.com.
232 A Potrait of Our Ancestors.
233 Batdorf data, Ancestor Chart for John Batdorf 1812 Vet, Early record sof Batdorf Family, Arthur Batdorf & Associ., YCHS verticle files.
234 The Batdorf Family History, Virgina Faust Batdorf, Mennonite Family History, 1990, Elverson, PA.
235 Baddorf household, 1810 United States Federal Census, Dauphin Co, PA, ancestry.com & Microfilm, PA State Library, Hbg, PA.
236 Badorf Sr household, 1820 United States Census, Dauphin Co, PA, ancestry.com & Microfilm, PA State Library, Hbg, PA.
237 Baddorf household, 1820 United States Census, Dauphin Co, PA, PA State library microfilm.
238 Welcker Data, Roger Cramer, rogercubs@@aol.com.
239 Schneider-Cornelius (7/2000), Lynn Schneider, JLynnAS@@aol.com, awt.ancestry.com.

240 Valentine Welker, Greg Welker, gwelker@@chesapeake.net.
241 Pats Family, Pat Scott, pat.scott@@comcast.net, awt.anecstry.com.
242 Welker household, 1810 United States Census, Dauphin Co, PA, ancestry.com & Microfilm, PA State Library, Hbg, PA.
243 Valentin Welcker, Immigrants into Pennsylvania, vol 1, ancestry.com.
244 Felty Welker, Revolutionary War Military Abstract Card File, PA State Archives, www.digitalarchives.state.pu.us/archive.
245 Valentine Welker, Probate files, 1831, W-4, Roll 43, E-85-4, Dauphin County Courthouse, Reg of Wills, Deborah Hershey, Elizabethtown, PA, Mar 2008.
246 Valentin Welcker, PA Census,1772-1890 Record, Ronald V Jackson, AIS, ancestry.com.
247 Felty Welker, Greg Welker, gwelker@@chesapeake.net, Dauphin County PA Early Assessment Lists.
248 Valentin Welcker, Probate files, 1831, W-4, Roll 43, E-85-4, Dauphin County Courthouse, Reg of Wills, Deborah Hershey, Elizabethtown, PA, Mar 2008.
249 Susanna Jury (Schorah), 1759, Salem Lutheran Church, Millersburg, Dauphin Co, PA, www.genealogy.com.
250 Jury Family, A Genealogical Record, 1754-1973, James W. Jury, Wiconisco, PA, rev. 1986.
251 Andreas Messerschmidt, Direct Descendants of Andreas Messerschmidt, Evelyn S. Hartman.
252 Andreas Messersmith, Revolutionary War Military Abstract Card File, PA State Archives, www.digitalarchives.state.pu.us/archive.
253 Andrew Messerschmidt, Probate files, 1801, Dauphin County Courthouse, Reg of Wills, Deborah Hershey, Elizabethtown, PA, Mar 2008.
254 Messerschmidt, PA Births, Dauphin County, J. Humphrey.
255 Messersmith household, 1810 United States Census, Lancaster Co, PA, ancestry.com & Microfilm, PA State Library, Hbg, PA.
256 John Jacob Wirth, Adam Wirth (Derry), Baptismal records of Rev. John Casper Stoever, PAGenWeb Lebanon County, PA, Church Records, c/o Mildred Smith.
257 PA & Other Assorted Data, R Howard, rmhoward45@@aol.com, awt.ancestry.com.
258 Jacob Wirth, Wirth's Evangelical Lutheran Church Cemetery, Dauphin Co, PA, www.USGenweb.com, Jonathan Wert.

259 Sophia Miller Wirth, Wirth's Evangelical Lutheran Church Cemetery, Dauphin Co, PA, www.USGenweb.com, Jonathan Wert.
260 Wert Tree, K Shuey, kshuey208@@hotmail.com, awt.ancestry.com.
261 Wirth household, 1790 United States Census, Northumberland Co, PA, ancestry.com & Microfilm, PA State Library, Hbg, PA.
262 Wert household, 1790 United States Census, Northumberland Co, PA, Roll M637-9, p 183, Image 0257, ancestry.com & Microfilm, PA State Library, Hbg, PA.
263 Wirt household, 1810 United States Census, Dauphin Co, PA, ancestry.com & Microfilm, PA State Library, Hbg, PA.
264 Wirt household, 1820 United States Census, Dauphin Co, PA, Roll M33 102, p 276, Image 114, ancestry.com & Microfilm, PA State Library, Hbg, PA.
265 Wert, Sr. household, 1820 United States Census, Dauphin Co, PA ancestry.com & Microfilm, PA State Library, Hbg, PA.
266 Wert Sr household, 1830 United States Census, Dauphin Co, PA, PA State library microfilm.
267 Jacob Wirt, Probate files, 1833, Letter of Admin, A 7/6, Dauphin County Courthouse, Reg of Wills, Deborah Hershey, Elizabethtown, PA, Mar 2008.
268 John Faber, 1777, PA Births, Lebanon County 1714-1800, J.T. Humphreys, 1996, Washington DC.
269 Hoover/McHenry family, Dave Van Doren, dvanore@@neo.rr.com, awt.ancestry.com.
270 Weller Family Search for Roots, Brenda Weller, bfw512@@cognigenmail.com, awt.ancestry.com.
271 Dininni Book, The Faber/Fauber/Fawber/Fawver/Farver Family, Chapter XII.
272 Johannes (John) Faber, DAR, Application of Mary I Bowerman Dininni, Harrisburg, PA, Natl #596079, May 1981.
273 Jonas Rudy, NSSAR, Application of Kimber D Smith, Allentown, PA, Natl #109281, State #8159, Apr 2004.
274 Dininni Book, The Faber/Fauber/Fawber/Fawver/Farver Family, Chapter XII.
275 Hoover/McHenry family, Dave Van Doren, dvanore@@neo.rr.com, awt.ancestry.com & Dinini Book.
276 The Rudys of Gods House & Related Families, Jonas Rudy, Chapter III, p 80-81.

277 Magdalene Faver, Probate files, 1845, microfilm file 3, roll 17, Dauphin County Courthouse, Reg of Wills, Deborah Hershey, Elizabethtown, PA, Mar 2008.
278 Faver household, 1810 United States Census, Dauphin Co, PA, ancestry.com & Microfilm, PA State Library, Hbg, PA.
279 John Faber, Probate files, 1828, Letter of Admin., p70, Dauphin County Courthouse, Reg of Wills, Deborah Hershey, Elizabethtown, PA, Mar 2008.
280 Faber, PA Births, Dauphin County, J. Humphrey.
281 Dininni Book, July 10, 1845, August 1, 1845, Dauphin Co, PA, Book E, p 430, The Faber/Fauber/Fawber/Fawver/Farver Family, Chapter XII.
282 Fawver household, 1830 United States Census, Northumberland Co, PA, ancestry.com & Microfilm, PA State Library, Hbg, PA.
283 Magdalene Faver, Probate files, 1845, Bk E, p430, microfilm file 3, roll 17, Dauphin County Courthouse, Reg of Wills, Deborah Hershey, Elizabethtown, PA, Mar 2008.
284 Ancestors of Richard Alan Lebo, The Schupp/Shoop Line, Richard A. Lebo, aqua.dev.uga.edu/~lebo.
285 Schupp family information, untitled, Jonathan Wert.
286 George Schupp, Stone Valley Cemetery, Robert Straub, Dalmatia, PA, Section A, Row 15, Grave 15.
287 Miller family information, Jim Miller, Halifax, PA.
288 Welkers in the USA & Nulls from PA, Greg Welker, gwelker@@chesapeake.net, awt.ancestry.com.
289 Anna Margaretha Miller, April 18, 1784, Northumberland Co County, PA 1777-1854, Stone Valley Lutheran, www.ancestry.com.
290 Wert family information, Dr. Jonathan Wert.
291 Margaret Shoop, Stone Valley Cemetery, Robert Straub, Dalmatia, PA, Section A, Row 16, Grave 14.
292 Shoop household, 1800 United States Census, Dauphin Co, PA, ancestry.com & Microfilm, PA State Library, Hbg, PA.
293 Shoop household, 1840 United States Census, Dauphin Co, PA, 344, ancestry.com & Microfilm, PA State Library, Hbg, PA.
294 Wertz family information, Northumberland Co County, PA 1777-1865, Stone Valley Lutheran, www.ancestry.com.
295 Wertz household, 1810 United States Census, Northumberland Co, PA, ancestry.com & Microfilm, PA State Library, Hbg, PA.

Sources (con't)

296 Wert, Sr. household, 1830 United States Census, Northumberland Co, PA, ancestry.com & Microfilm, PA State Library, Hbg, PA.
297 Wertz household, 1840 United States Census, Northumberland Co, PA, ancestry.com & Microfilm, PA State Library, Hbg, PA.
298 Mertz household, 1850 United States Census, Northumberland Co, PA, ancestry.com & Microfilm, PA State Library, Hbg, PA.
299 Wartzs household, 1860 United States Census, Northumberland Co, PA, ancestry.com & Microfilm, PA State Library, Hbg, PA.
300 John Mertz (Wertz), Probate files, 1862, Northumberland County Courthouse, Reg of Wills, Sunbury, Bk 5, p122, PA, Robyn Jackson, genealogylover@@msn.com, 2008.
301 Descendants of Michael Garman, Evelyn S Hartman, deanh@@voicenet.com.
302 April's Ancestors, April Moss, Moss.bunch@@verizon.net, awt.ancestry.com.
303 Francis Rowe, DAR, Application of Janet O N Welty, Wooster, OH, Natl #720047, Aug 2001.
304 Francis Rowe, DAR patriot index, www.dar.org.
305 Francis Rou, Probate files, Bk I, vol 1, p403, Lancaster County Archives Division, Lancaster Co Courthouse, Lancaster, PA, Deborah Hershey, Elizabethtown, PA, Mar 2008.
306 Rowe family information, Janet Welty, JNWelty@@aol.com.
307 Rowe family information, Jean Row Romberger, Allentown, PA, jmrrrer@@juno.com.
308 Traut family information, Craig H. Trout, Family Research Site, January 3, 2004, CraigTrout@@aol.com.
309 Frank Rowe, St. John Evangelical Lutheran Church, Berrysburg, PA, Sara S. Neagley, Elizabethville, PA, 424 6M 24D.
310 Rough household, 1800 United States Census, Lancaster Co, PA, ancestry.com & Microfilm, PA State Library, Hbg, PA.
311 Francis Row, 1806, Lancaster County, PA Wills, bk I 1-403, Lancaster Co, PA.
312 Francis Row, Will I-1-403, Estate Inventory 1806, b117, f3, Marge Bardeen, 2006, Lancaster County Historical Society, Lancaster, PA.
313 Rowe family information, St. Michaels Lutheran Church, Strasburg, PA, 1753-1816, Lancaster County Historical Society.
314 Mary Rowe, St. John Evangelical Lutheran Church, Berrysburg, PA, Sara S. Neagley, Elizabethville, PA, 424 6M 24D.

315 Rowe family information, St. Michaels Lutheran Churchyard, Lancaster Co, PA, Lancaster County Historical Society.
316 Jacob Rudy, St. John Evangelical Lutheran Church, Berrysburg, PA, Sara S. Neagley, Elizabethville, PA, 424 6M 24D.
317 Roote household, 1810 United States Census, Lancaster Co, PA, ancestry.com & Microfilm, PA State Library, Hbg, PA.
318 Jacob Rudy, Revolutionary War Military Abstract Card File, PA State Archives, www.digitalarchives.state.pu.us/archive.
319 Jacob Rudy wife, St. John Evangelical Lutheran Church, Berrysburg, PA, Sara S. Neagley, Elizabethville, PA, 424 6M 24D.
320 Johann Wilhelm Frantz, Descendants of JohAnnaWilhelm Frantz, Evelyn S. Hartman.
321 Franz household, 1800 United States Census, Dauphin Co, PA, Roll M32 40, p 174, Image 7, ancestry.com & Microfilm, PA State Library, Hbg, PA.
322 William Frantz, July 28, 1804, February 11, 1805, Will Abstracts, Dauphin County, PA p 254.
323 William Frantz, Hoffman's Church, Dauphin County records, Nancy Hendricks, NJHendricks@@earthlink.net.
324 PA & Other Assorted Data, R Howard, rmhoward45@@aol.com, awt.anecstry.com.
325 Gieseman family information, Geeseman Cousins Newlsetter, Bernadine N. Geesaman, Quincy, PA.
326 Fidler, Rick Hostetter, PaInfantry@@aol.com, awt.ancestry.com.
327 Geeseman household, 1790 United States Census, Berks Co, PA, Roll M637-8, p 8-0145, Image 0145, ancestry.com & Microfilm, PA State Library, Hbg, PA.
328 Geeseman household, 1820 United States Census, Dauphin Co, PA, ancestry.com & Microfilm, PA State Library, Hbg, PA.
329 Geeseman household, 1830 United States Census, Dauphin Co, PA, ancestry.com & Microfilm, PA State Library, Hbg, PA.
330 Gusman household, 1840 United States Census, Dauphin Co, PA, ancestry.com & Microfilm, PA State Library, Hbg, PA.
331 William Gieseman, Probate files, 1843, Bk E, p380, file 3, microfilmG-3 (4427), roll 20, Dauphin County Courthouse, Reg of Wills, Deborah Hershey, Elizabethtown, PA, Mar 2008.
332 Anna Margaretha Gruber, Old Northkill records, c/o Rene, rene@@hurstlandscaping.com.
333 Valentine Welker, Brenda Wallace, February 10, 1997, wallace@@ccia.com.

Sources (con't)

334 Valentin Welcker, Passenger and Immigration Lists Index, 1500-1900, myfamily.com, P. William Filby, ancestry.com.
335 Valentine Welcker, Index of Wills and Estates records of Lancaster Co, PA, 1729-1850, 1782, bk D, p 261, Sue suestu@@chartner.net.
336 Valentine Welker, Will D-1-261, Estate Inventory 1782, bv148, f5, Marge Bardeen, 2006, Lancaster County Historical Society, Lancaster, PA.
337 Phalatien Welcker, Probate files, 1, Bk D, vol 1, p261, Lancaster County Archives Division, Lancaster Co Courthouse, Lancaster, PA, Deborah Hershey, Elizabethtown, PA, Mar 2008.
338 Abraham Joray, FHL, Pedigree chart, www.familysearch.org.
339 A Potrait of Our Ancestors, Jury, vol I, I.P. Baker, 1983, rev. 1986, Selby Publishing, Kokomo, IN, 46902.
340 Abraham Jury, Renee Waring, reneelwaring@@aol.com.
341 Abraham Zora, Renee Waring, reneelwaring@@aol.com.
342 The Jury Family, Gratz History, p 151.
343 Abraham Joray, Passenger and Immigration Lists Index, 1500-1900, myfamily.com, P. William Filby, ancestry.com.
344 A Potrait of Our Ancestors, Names of Foreigners Who Took the Oath of Allegiance, 1727-1755, Jury, vol I, I.P. Baker, 1983, rev. 1986, Selby Publishing, Kokomo, IN, 46902.
345 Abraham Shorah, Probate files, 1785, Bk B, p297, file 3, Dauphin County Courthouse, Reg of Wills, Deborah Hershey, Elizabethtown, PA, Mar 2008.
346 Abram Joray, PA Census, 1772-1890, Philadelphia, PA, www.ancestry.com.
347 Abram Joray, Comprehensive Hostory of the town of Gratz, PA, p50, Elsie Eaves, EKEaves@@cox.net.
348 Abraham Shora, February 15, 1785, September 22, 1785, Will Abstracts, Dauphin Co, PA, p 22.
349 Andreas Messerschmidt, Immigrants to Pennsylvania, vol 1, ancestry.com.
350 Andreas Messerschmidt, Passenger and Immigration Lists Index, 1500-1900, myfamily.com, P. William Filby, ancestry.com.
351 Andreas Messerschmidt, PA Census, 1772-1890, Philadelphia, PA, www.ancestry.com.
352 Sproat household, 1790 United States Census, Lancaster Co, PA, Roll M637-8, p 139, Image 0761, ancestry.com.
353 Shrott, PA Births, Lebanon County, J. Humphrey.

354 Sproat household, 1790 United States Census, Lancaster Co, PA, Roll M637-8, p 139, Image 0761, ancestry.com.
355 Johann Adam Wirth, Wirth's Evangelical Lutheran Church Cemetery, Dauphin Co, PA, www.USGenweb.com, Jonathan Wert.
356 Johan Adam Wirth, Marriage Records of Rev. John Casper Stoever, http://www.chm.davidson.edu/PAGenWeb/records/StoeverMarriages.txt.
357 Wirth family information, WFT 10, Tree 728, genealogy.com.
358 Wert Family History, Jonathan Wert.
359 Eva Elizabeth Schnug Wirth, Wirth's Evangelical Lutheran Church Cemetery, Dauphin Co, PA, www.USGenweb.com, Jonathan Wert.
360 Johan Adam Wirth, Immigrants to Pennsylvania, vol 1, ancestry.com.
361 Johann Adam Wirth, Lykens Valley, Dauphin Co, PA, Wertz Book, Ch 9, pp 221-237, Newsletter 2,3,6,7, Kathleen Odom, knko2@@mci2000.com.
362 Johan Adam Wirth, PA Census, 1772-1890, Philadelphia, PA, www.ancestry.com.
363 Adam Wirth, Baptismal records of Rev. John Casper Stoever, PAGenWeb Lebanon County, PA, Church Records, c/o Mildred Smith.
364 Eva Elisabeth Schnug, Passenger and Immigration Lists Index, 1500-1900, myfamily.com, P. William Filby, ancestry.com.
365 John Miller, NSSAR, Application of Robert T Coleman, Summerdale, PA, Natl #122061, State #8984, Apr 1996.
366 J.M, Stone Valley Cemetery, Robert Straub, Dalmatia, PA, Section A, Row 3, Grave 2.
367 Miller household, 1790 United States Census, Dauphin Co, PA ancestry.com & Microfilm, PA State Library, Hbg, PA.
368 Miller household, 1810 United States Census, Dauphin Co, PA, ancestry.com & Microfilm, PA State Library, Hbg, PA.
369 John Miller, Probate files, 1812, Letter of Admin, p97, Dauphin County Courthouse, Reg of Wills, Deborah Hershey, Elizabethtown, PA, Mar 2008.
370 Veronica Kirstetter, PA Births, Lebanon County, J. Humphrey.
371 John Faber, FHL, Pedigree chart, www.familysearch.org.

372 Mother Faber, Zion Evangelical Lutheran Church, Marriages & Burials, 1768-1858, bk 1, p 392, Lebanon County Historical Society.
373 Adam Faber, Baptismal records of Rev. John Casper Stoever, PAGenWeb Lebanon County, PA, Church Records, c/o Mildred Smith.
374 Fawper household, 1790 United States Census, Dauphin Co, PA, Roll M637 8, p 88, Image 0352, ancestry.com & Microfilm, PA State Library, Hbg, PA.
375 John Faber, Revolutionary War Military Abstract Card File, PA State Archives, www.digitalarchives.state.pu.us/archive.
376 Faber household, 1800 United States Census, Dauphin, PA, ancestry.com & Microfilm, PA State Library, Hbg, PA.
377 Margaret Faber, October 1, 1825, October 25, 1825, Lebanon County Will abstracts, Lebanon County, PA, bk A, p 448.
378 Dininni Book, October 1, 1825, October 25, 1825, Lebanon County Will Book, bk A, p 448, The Faber/Fauber/Fawber/Fawver/Farver Family, Chapter XII.
379 Margaret Faber, Probate files, 1825, No F-9, 15, Lebanon County Reg of Wills & Clerk of Orphans Court, Lebaonn, PA, Dawn L Resanovich, Register, Dec 2008.
380 The Rudys of Gods House & Related Families, Jonas Rudy, Chapter III, p 66.
381 Jonas Rudy, Rudy family, Onetree, ancestry.com.
382 Jonas Rudy, DAR patriot index, www.dar.org.
383 Jonas Rudy, October 15, 1810, February 4, 1811, Abstracts of Wills, Bethel, PA, p 179.
384 Rudy household, 1790 United States Census, Dauphin Co, PA, Roll M637 8, p 88, Image 0352, ancestry.com & Microfilm, PA State Library, Hbg, PA.
385 Rudy household, 1800 United States Census, Dauphin Co, PA, Roll M32 40, p 266, Image 54, ancestry.com & Microfilm, PA State Library, Hbg, PA.
386 Rudy household, 1810 United States Census, Dauphin Co, PA, ancestry.com & Microfilm, PA State Library, Hbg, PA.
387 Jonas Rudy, Revolutionary War Military Abstract Card File, PA State Archives, www.digitalarchives.state.pu.us/archive.
388 Jonas Rudy Sr, DAR, Application of Jeanne R Miller, New Harmony, IN, Comp #4-035 IN, Jan 1982.

Sources (con't)

389 Jonas Rudy, Probate files, Bk R-1, roll 37, Lancaster County Archives Division, Lancaster Co Courthouse, Lancaster, PA, Deborah Hershey, Elizabethtown, PA, Mar 2008.
390 Rudy household, 1830 United States Census, Lebanon Co, PA, Roll M19 154, p 12, Image 27, ancestry.com & Microfilm, PA State Library, Hbg, PA.
391 George Schup, Wirth's Evangelical Lutheran Church Cemetery, Dauphin Co, PA, www.USGenweb.com, Jonathan Wert.
392 Deibler family information, Sonny Deibler, sdeibler@@gte.net.
393 Maria Elizabeth Deibler Schup, Wirth's Evangelical Lutheran Church Cemetery, Dauphin Co, PA, www.USGenweb.com, Jonathan Wert.
394 Soop household, 1790 United States Census, Dauphin Co, PA, M637-8, p 92, lamge 0373, ancestry.com & Microfilm, PA State Library, Hbg, PA.
395 Shup household, 1800 United States Census, Dauphin Co, PA, ancestry.com & Microfilm, PA State Library, Hbg, PA.
396 Shoop household, 1830 United States Census, Dauphin Co, PA, ancestry.com & Microfilm, PA State Library, Hbg, PA.
397 Wertz family information, Carolyn C. Choppin, Puyallup, WA.
398 Werts (Wertz, Wirtz) Notes, Northumberland Co County Historical Society, pp 1-6.
399 Johann Dietrich Wuerz, Wuerz family, Onetree, ancestry.com.
400 Johann Dietrich Wertz, One tree, from WFT collection, trees.ancestry.com/owt, www.ancestry.com.
401 Johann Dietrich Wuerz, Bucher family, Onetree, ancestry.com.
402 Johann Dietrich Wertz, Recorded, M503, Northumberland Co, PA, c/o K Poorman, kporrman@@verizon.net.
403 Dieter Wurtz, 1767 Pennsylvania Tax Lists, http://freepages.genealogy.rootsweb.com/~genbel/sept/patowshp 1767.htm.
404 Wurtz/Werts/Wertz Family, Our Keystone Families, S.C. Brossman, Rehrersburg, PA.
405 Johann Dietrich Wertz, Property Deed, M503, Northumberland Co, PA, c/o K Poorman, kporrman@@verizon.net.
406 Deterick Wertz, Northumberland Co County Will Index, 1772-1859, http://ftp.rootsweb.com/pub/usgenweb/pa/Northumberland Co/wills/willindx.txt.

Sources (con't)

407 Descendants of Michael Garman, Roger Cramer, rogercubs@@aol.com, www.rootsweb.com.

408 Michael Garman, The Biographical Record of Ogle Co,IL, Published by S.J. Clarke, 1899, Original from the New York Public Library, Digitized Feb 28, 2008, 492 pages.

409 Michael Garman, DAR, Application of Kris E Garman, Crystal Lake, IL, Comp #5-065 IL, Aug 2000.

410 Michael Garman, Potrait & Biographical Album of Ogle County, IL, pub 1886, pp220-221, Cindi Grimm, ggrimm48@@comcast.net.

411 Michael Garman, Garman family, Onetree, ancestry.com.

412 Garmon household, 1790 United States Census, Dauphin Co, PA, ancestry.com & Microfilm, PA State Library, Hbg, PA.

413 Garmon household, 1800 United States Census, Northumberland Co, PA, ancestry.com & Microfilm, PA State Library, Hbg, PA.

414 Michael Garman, DAR, Application of Emma G Krape, A044052, 265635, Nov 1930.

415 Michael Garman, DAR patriot index, www.dar.org.

416 German household, 1810 United States Census, Northumberland Co, PA, ancestry.com & Microfilm, PA State Library, Hbg, PA.

417 Garman household, 1850 United States Census, Ogle, IL, p 49, Roll M432-123, ancestry.com.

418 Trout Family Descendancy, Descendants of Balthasar Troutc1750750, www.jaknouse.athens.oh.us/genealogy/trout1.html.

419 Hutchinson & Allied Families from East TN, Terry L Hutchinson, tlhutch_kr@@yahoo.com, awt.ancestry.com.

420 Wendel Traut, Marriage Records of Rev. John Casper Stoever, http://www.chm.davidson.edu/PAGenWeb/records/StoeverMarriages.txt.

421 Johann Wendel Traut, The Trout Family Hsitorian, Craig Trout, 2006, familytreemaker.genealogy.com/users/t/r/o/Craig-Trout/FILE/0011page.html.

422 Maria Magdalena Walter, Family Data Collection, Individual records, ancestry.com.

423 Maria Magdelena Walter, Family Data Collection, Individual Records, www.ancestry.com.

424 Wendle Trout, Wills: Index to Abstracts, 1721-1819, Lancaster County, PA, http://ftp.rootsweb.com/pub/usgenweb/pa/lancaster/wills/willabsurndxr-z.txt.
425 Wendell Trout, Estate Inventory 1760, b124, f8, Marge Bardeen, 2006, Lancaster County Historical Society, Lancaster, PA.
426 Magdalene Trout, Estate Inventory b124, f6, Marge Bardeen, 2006, Lancaster County Historical Society, Lancaster, PA.
427 Gieseman family information, Geeseaan Cousins Newlsetter, Bernadine N. Geesaman, Quincy, PA.
428 Anna Catherine Heck, Family Data Collection, Individual Records, www.ancestry.com.
429 Johan George Wilhelm Gussemann, Passenger and Immigration Lists Index, 1500-1900, myfamily.com, P. William Filby, ancestry.com.
430 Barr Genealogy & Related Families, The Gieseman Family, pp 29-67, Rev Ed, Ira R. Barr.
431 Gieseman family information, Barr Genealogy & related Families: Johns, Gieseman, Replogle, reitz/Wrights and Van Hook, Rev. Ed., Ira R. barr, Abstract, p 29, c/o Mary Ann Booher, LBOOHER6@@woh.rr.com.
432 Yerigh William Geeseman, PA Census, 1772-1890, Philadelphia, PA, www.ancestry.com.
433 William Giessman, April 23, 1761, May 26, 1761, Abstracts of Berks Co, PA Wills, 1752-1785.
434 GUESMAN-L, Geeseman Cousins vol 1, No 3, the Geesman Genealogy, sprocket62@@aol.com,1999.
435 Cather Gissemenen, 1767 Pennsylvania Tax Lists, http://freepages.genealogy.rootsweb.com/~genbel/sept/patowshp1767.htm.
436 Gruber family information, Christina, c_aller@@geocities.com and Gwen, GGDGEN@@aol.com.
437 Gruber family information, Harry C. Adams Co, Box E, Bedminster, PA 18910.
438 Christian Gruber, Old Graveyard & Two Cemeteries, Bernville, Berks Co, PA, www.interment.net.
439 Descendants of Henry Gruber, WFT 16, Tree 482, www.genealogy.com.

Sources (con't)

440 Christian Gruber, Marriage Records of Rev. John Casper Stoever, http://www.chm.davidson.edu/PAGenWeb/records/StoeverMarriages.txt.

441 Gruber-Stulp marriage record, 1742, Marriage Records of Rev. John Casper Stoever, pa-roots.com.

442 Anna Kinugonda Stupp, A Forest of family Trees, www.siteservers.net/family/default.aspx.

443 Gruber family information, Christina, GGDGEN@@aol.com.

444 Descedants of Martin Stupp, 4 generations, Roger Cramer.

445 Anna Guniunda Gubern, Probate file, 1799, unnumbered original papers, 9pp, Berks Co Courthouse, Berks, PA, Norman Nicol, Apr 2008.

446 Christian Gruber, Biographies from Historical & Biographical Annals, Morton Montgomery, p392, Line of Christian Gruber, www.roostweb.com/~paberks/books/montgomery/g16.html.

447 Christian Gruber, 1732, 18th Century Emigrants from German-speaking Lands to North America, A. Kunselman, Birdsboro, PA, Volume 1, 1983, p 461, www.genealogy.com.

448 Christian Gruber, Passenger and Immigration Lists Index, 1500-1900, myfamily.com, P. William Filby, ancestry.com.

449 Descendants of Christian Gruber, WFT 10, Tree 1010, genealogy.com.

450 Christian Gruber, Probate file, 1781, unnumbered original papers, 30pp, Berks Co Courthouse, Berks, PA, Norman Nicol, Apr 2008.

451 Christian Gruber, Baptismal records of Rev. John Casper Stoever, PAGenWeb Lebanon County, PA, Church Records, c/o Mildred Smith.

452 Christian Gruber, Berks County Register of Wills, http://www.berksregofwills.com/Berks_estate_1_search.asp.

453 Cuniganda Gruber, November 9, 1796, June 4, 1799, Abstracts of Berks Co, PA Wills, 1785-1800.

454 Sheetz family information, Rob Sheetz, Robsheetz32@@wmconnect.com.

455 Clay/Klees, Nesbit, etc, Mike Milliken, MillikenM@@aol.com, rootsweb.com.

456 Sheets household, 1790 United States Census, Dauphin Co, PA, ancestry.com & Microfilm, PA State Library, Hbg, PA.

457 George Sheets, Paxtang Volunteers, Troops sent to Bedford to protect the inhabitants, www.pa-roots.org/data/read.php?51.239165 c/o Sherul Kelso.

458 John Geo. Schuetz, Marriage Records of Rev. John Casper Stoever, http://www.chm.davidson.edu/PAGenWeb/records/StoeverMarriages.txt.
459 George Sheets Jr, FHL, Individual record, www.familysearch.org.
460 Maria Sheetz, St. Paul/Bauerman Lutheran & Reformed Church, Enterline, PA, The Perry Historians.
461 Shetz household, 1800 United States Census, Dauphin Co, PA, ancestry.com & Microfilm, PA State Library, Hbg, PA.
462 Sheetz household, 1810 United States Census, Dauphin Co, PA, Series M252, Roll 54, Part 1, p 99, ancestry.com & Microfilm, PA State Library, Hbg, PA.
463 Shetz household, 1820 United States Census, Dauphin Co, PA, ancestry.com & Microfilm, PA State Library, Hbg, PA.
464 Schitz family information, PA Births, Dauphin County, J. Humphrey.
465 George Shitz, Rob Sheetz, Robsheetz32@@wmconnect.com.
466 Sheetz family information, Connie Sheets, clsheets1@@prodigy.net.
467 George Shutz, Passenger and Immigration Lists Index, 1500-1900, myfamily.com, P. William Filby, ancestry.com.
468 George Sheets, 1749-1750 Assessment of the Taxables of The South End of Paxtang Township, Lancaster County Taken From Middletown on the Swatara, A. Boyd Hamilton, Harrisburg, PA p 38 Online Transcription by Nancy Piper, http://genealogytrails.com/penn/Dauphin/Census/paxt.
469 George Sheets, Early Assessment List, South End of Paxtang, 1751, http://maley.net/transcription.
470 George Schuetz, Baptismal records of Rev. John Casper Stoever, PAGenWeb Lebanon County, PA, Church Records, c/o Mildred Smith.
471 George Shitz, Wills: Index to Abstracts, 1721-1819, Lancaster County, PA, http://ftp.rootsweb.com/pub/usgenweb/pa/lancaster/wills/willabsurndxr-z.txt.
472 Magdalene Wolffshiel, Lancaster County, PA, Church Records of the 18th Century, vol 1, FE Wright, p 41, Marge Bardeen, 2006, Lancaster County Historical Society, Lancaster, PA.
473 Henry Woolfkull, Passenger and Immigration Lists Index, 1500-1900, myfamily.com, P. William Filby, ancestry.com.

474 Henry Wollfkull, Pennsylvania Naturalizations, 1740-1773, Persons naturalized in the Province of PA, ancestry.com.
475 Henry Wolffskeil, Probate files, 1, Bk F, vol 1, p32, Lancaster County Archives Division, Lancaster Co Courthouse, Lancaster, PA, Deborah Hershey, Elizabethtown, PA, Mar 2008.
476 Henry Wolffskeil, Wills: Index to Abstracts, 1721-1819, Lancaster County, PA, http://ftp.rootsweb.com/pub/usgenweb/pa/lancaster/wills/willabsurndxr-z.txt.
477 Henry Wolfsiel, Will F-1-32, Estate Inventory 1788, b128, f9, Marge Bardeen, 2006, Lancaster County Historical Society, Lancaster, PA.
478 Henrich Wolffskehl, PA Census, 1772-1890, www.ancestry.com.

Chapter Two

Our family's photos.

Some photographs of our family.
A picture is worth a thousand words.

Photos Myrtle Batdorf

Myrtle Adeline Batdorf

Birth:	January 05, 1918	Father:	James "Edward" Batdorf
Death:	May 08, 1983	Mother:	Beulah Irene Wert
Marriage:	June 15, 1935	Spouse:	Harper Bruce Thompson

8 Harper Thompson,
Myrtle Batdorf & Jill - Copy

9 Myrtle Batdorf

9 Myrtle Batdorf (2)

9 Myrtle Batdorf (3)

Photos James Batdorf

James "Edward" Batdorf

Birth:	February 15, 1885	Father:	Thomas Edward Batdorf
Death:	August 19, 1954	Mother:	Mary Louisa Peters
Marriage:	February 08, 1908	Spouse:	Beulah Irene Wert

18 James & Alvin Batdorf

18 James Batdorf

18 James Batdorf & Beulah Wert

18 James Batdorf & Beulah Wert (2)

18 James Batdorf (2)

Photos Beulah Wert

Beulah Irene Wert

Birth:	December 31, 1889	Father:	John Henry Wert
Death:	June 10, 1983	Mother:	Adeline Row
Marriage:	February 08, 1908	Spouse:	James "Edward" Batdorf

19 Beulah Wert

19 Beulah Wert (2)

19 Beulah Wert (Seated), daughter, Charles Moon, Mildred Batdorf & daughter Moon

Photos for Thomas Batdorf

Thomas Edward Batdorf

Birth:	July 02, 1851	Father:	Peter Batdorf
Death:	August 13, 1916	Mother:	Elizabeth Welker
Marriage:	December 06, 1874	Spouse:	Mary Louisa Peters

36 Thomas Batdorf

36 Thomas Batdorf & Mary Peters

Photos for Mary Peters

Mary Louisa Peters

Birth:	March 31, 1858	Father:	Samuel Peters
Death:	August 03, 1924	Mother:	Mary Ann Swartz
Marriage:	December 06, 1874	Spouse:	Thomas Edward Batdorf

37 Mary Peters

37 Mary Peters (2)

Photos for John Wert

John Henry Wert

Birth:	December 23, 1855	Father:	David M Wert
Death:	October 30, 1924	Mother:	Catherine Shoop
Marriage:	Abt. 1878	Spouse:	Adeline Row

38 John Wert

38 John Wert & Adeline Row

38 John Wert & Adeline Row (2)

Photos for Adeline Row

Adeline Row

Birth:	January 02, 1860	Father:	Daniel Row
Death:	March 06, 1921	Mother:	Susan Frantz
Marriage:	Abt. 1878	Spouse:	John Henry Wert

39 Adeline Row

39 Adeline Row (2)

Photos for Peter Batdorf

Peter Batdorf

Birth:	January 20, 1814	Father:	Jacob Peter Batdorf
Death:	December 05, 1880	Mother:	Maria Catherine Steiner
Marriage:	Abt. 1831	Spouse:	Elizabeth Welker

72 Peter Batdorf

Photos for Elizabeth Welker

Elizabeth Welker

Birth:	November 23, 1812	Father:	John Welker
Death:	July 07, 1868	Mother:	Maria Elizabeth Messerschmidt
Marriage:	Abt. 1831	Spouse:	Peter Batdorf

73 Eliz Batdorf

Photos for David Wert

David M Wert

Birth:	April 01, 1829	Father:	Jacob Wert
Death:	December 09, 1900	Mother:	Sarah Elizabeth Faber
Marriage:	Abt. 1849	Spouse:	Catherine Shoop

76 David Wert

76 David Wert (2)

Photos for Catherine Shoop

Catherine Shoop

Birth:	February 24, 1830	Father:	John Shoop
Death:	June 08, 1872	Mother:	Sarah Wertz
Marriage:	Abt. 1849	Spouse:	David M Wert

77 Catherine Shoop Wert

Photos for Daniel Row

Daniel Row

Birth:	July 10, 1813	Father:	John William Rowe
Death:	July 31, 1871	Mother:	Barbara Rudy
Marriage:	Abt. 1840	Spouse:	Susan Frantz

78 Daniel Row

Photos for Susan Frantz

Susan Frantz

Birth:	March 23, 1819	Father:	Adam Frantz
Death:	October 17, 1861	Mother:	Susan Gieseman
Marriage:	Abt. 1840	Spouse:	Daniel Row

79 Susan Frantz Row

Photos for William Rowe

John William Rowe

Birth:	June 1785	Father:	Francis "Frank" Rowe
Death:	1877	Mother:	Maria Catherine Traut
Marriage:	1810	Spouse:	Barbara Rudy

156 John William Rowe & Barbara Rudy(1)

156 John William Rowe(1)

Photos for Barbara Rudy

Barbara Rudy

Birth:	April 11, 1796	Father:	Jacob Rudy
Death:	December 15, 1881	Mother:	Susan Jungblut
Marriage:	1810	Spouse:	John William Rowe

157 Barbara Rudy(1)

Chapter Three

Our family's places.

Where we're from, born, raised, lived and roamed through and what property value our ancestors had.

$100
Rowe, John William
Propty: 1860
Swartz, Mary Ann
Propty: 1870
Wert, David M
Propty: 1850
Wert, Jacob
Propty: 1870

$1000
Wertz, John
Propty: 1850

$1000 + $400
Batdorf, Peter
Propty: 1870
Wert, David M
Propty: 1870

$1100
Schupp, John George
Propty: 1850

$150
Peters, Samuel
Propty: 1860
Rowe, John William
Propty: 1850

$200
Welker, John
Propty: 1850

$2000 + $214
Wertz, John
Propty: 1860

$240
Row, Daniel
Propty: 1850

$4500
Batdorf, James "Edward"
Propty: 1930

$500
Batdorf, Peter
Propty: 1850

$500 + $100
Wert, Jacob
Propty: 1860

$800

$800 (con't)
Shoop, John
Propty: 1850

$900 + $250
Batdorf, Peter
Propty: 1860

$9450 + $200
Row, Daniel
Propty: 1860

2600 Green St., Harrisburg, Dauphin Co, PA
Thompson, Harper Bruce
Res: 1981

2660A Green St., Harrisburg, Dauphin Co, PA
Batdorf, Myrtle Adeline
Res: 1983

480 North St., Lykens, Dauphin Co, PA
Batdorf, James "Edward"
Res: 1930

542 North St., Lykens, Dauphin Co, PA
Batdorf, James "Edward"
Res: 1954

542 North Street, Lykens, Dauphin Co, PA
Batdorf, James "Edward"
Res: 1942

800 Broad St., Selinsgrove, Snyder Co, PA 17870
Wert, Beulah Irene
Res: 1983

914 ? St., Emmaus, Lehigh Co, PA
Thompson, Harper Bruce
Res: 1930

Alleghenyville, Berks Co, PA
Schupp, John George
Res: Abt. 1852

Annville, Lebanon Co, PA
Batdorf, John
Death: January 1968

Baden-Wurttemberg, Germany
Schnug, Eva Elizabeth
Birth: 1730

Beaufort Farms, Camp Curtain, Estherton, Fort Hunter, Harrisburg, Hecktown, Lucknow, Rockville, Uptown, Windsor farms, all Dauphin Co, PA
Batdorf, Myrtle Adeline
Res: 1983
Thompson, Harper Bruce
Res: 1981

Belphrahon, Berne, Switzerland

Belphrahon, Berne, Switzerland (con't)
Joray, Abraham
Birth: March 19, 1718

Berks Co, PA
Gieseman, George William
Death: 1761
Gieseman, John George
Birth: 1754
Gruber, Anna Margaret
Birth: August 02, 1759
Heck, Anna Catherine
Death: Aft. 1767
Steiner, Maria Catherine
Birth: Abt. 1790

Berks Co., PA
Saltzegber, Barbara Elizabeth
Birth: 1738

Bern Tp, Berks Co, PA
Gruber, Christian
Prob: Bet. July 23, 1784–October 31, 1795

Bernville, Tulpehocken, Berks Co, PA
Gruber, Christian
Death: November 14, 1781
Stupp, Anna Gunigunda
Death: May 30, 1799

Berrysburg, Dauphin Co, PA
Batdorf, Jacob Peter
Res: Bet. 1815–1828
Frantz, Susan
Death: October 17, 1861
Rowe, John William
Res: Bet. 1812–1820
Death: 1877
Rudy, Barbara
Death: December 15, 1881

Berrysburg, Dauphin Co, PA (Wise)
Batdorf, Thomas Edward
Census: 1870

Bethel Moravian Cemetery, Lebanon, Dauphin (Lebanon) Co, PA
Faber, John
Burial: 1804

Bethel Tp, Dauphin (Lebanon) Co, PA
Rudy, Jonas
Prob: Bet. February 04–November 29, 1811
Will: October 15, 1810

Bethel, Dauphin (Lebanon) Co, PA
Faber, John
Death: 1804

Bethel, Dauphin (Lebanon) Co, PA (con't)

Rudy, Jonas

Death: December 20, 1810

Bethel, Dauphin (Lebanon) Co, PA (Jones)

Rudy, Jonas

Census: 1800

Bethel, Dauphin Co, PA (listed as head of house)

Rudy, Margaret

Census: 1800

Bethel, Lancaster (Lebanon) Co, PA

Overcash, Anna Barbara

Birth: September 28, 1751

Rudy, Jonas

Birth: December 16, 1751

Baptism: December 16, 1751

Rudy, Maria "Mollie" Magdalena

Birth: April 14, 1784

Bethel, Lebanon Co, PA

Overcash, Anna Barbara

Death: April 08, 1836

Census: 1830

Rudy, Margaret

Prob: October 25, 1825

Will: October 01, 1825

Death: October 04, 1825

Big Run, Coaldale, Erdman, Germantown, Loyalton, Lykens, Specktown, all Dauphin Co, PA

Wert, Beulah Irene

Res: 1983

Big Run, Dauphin Co, PA

Batdorf, Myrtle Adeline

Birth: January 05, 1918

Batdorf, Thomas Edward

Birth: July 02, 1851

Borod, Rhineland-Palatinate, Germany

Wirth, John Adam

Birth: August 23, 1727

Brecknock, Lancaster Co, PA

Jungblut, Susan

Census: 1800

Brookville, Ogle, IL

Sheets, Susan

Census: 1850

Buffalo, Union Co, PA

Peters, John

Death: Abt. 1846

Census: 1820

Census: 1830

Census: 1840

Buffalo, Union Co, PA (con't)

Peters, Samuel

Census: 1830

Buffington Funeral Home, Elizabethville, Dauphin Co, PA

Batdorf, Thomas Edward

Funrl: 1916

Peters, Mary Louisa

Funrl: 1924

Row, Adeline

Funrl: 1921

Wert, John Henry

Funrl: 1924

Calvary United Methodist (aka Union), Wiconisco, Dauphin Co, PA

Wert, David M

Burial: December 12, 1900

Calvary United Methodist, Wiconisco, Dauphin Co, PA

Batdorf, James "Edward"

Burial: August 23, 1954

Wert, Beulah Irene

Burial: June 14, 1983

Carsonville, Dauphin Co, PA

Welker, Valentine

Death: 1831

Cedar Hill (Trout) Cemetery, Strasburg, Lancaster Co, PA

Traut, John Wendel George

Burial: 1761

Walter, Maria Magdalena

Burial: February 1761

Chester Co, PA

Batdorf, Martin

Birth: 1726

Christ (Little Tulpehocken) Lutheran, Bernville, Berks Co, PA

Gieseman, John William

Marr: February 19, 1782

Gruber, Anna Margaret

Marr: February 19, 1782

Christ (Little Tulpehocken) Lutheran, Bernville, Lancaster (Berks) Co, PA

Gieseman, George William

Marr: December 12, 1749

Heck, Anna Catherine

Marr: December 12, 1749

Christ (Little Tulpehocken) Lutheran, Old Graveyard, Bernville, Berks Co, PA

Gruber, Christian

Burial: 1781

Stupp, Anna Gunigunda

Burial: 1799

Christ Lutheran, Stouchsburg, Berks Co, PA

Batdorf, Jacob Peter

Marr: February 20, 1813
Messerschmidt, Andrew
Marr: September 26, 1779
Schrot, Eva
Marr: September 26, 1779
Steiner, Maria Catherine
Marr: February 20, 1813

Cleona, Lancaster (Lebanon) Co, PA
Kerstetter, Frances
Birth: April 09, 1752

Cocalico Reformed Church, Lancaster Co, PA
Mahr, Maria Magdalena
Burial: January 25, 1767

Dalmatia, Northumberland Co, PA
Miller, Anna Margaret
Baptism: April 18, 1784

Darmstadt, Hesse, Germany
Gieseman, George William
Birth: March 03, 1718

Dauphin Co, PA
Batdorf, Jacob Peter
Death: 1829
Batdorf, Peter
Birth: January 20, 1814
Prob: January 04, 1881
Marr: Abt. 1831
Faber, Barbara
Birth: 1786
Faber, George
Birth: 1793
Faber, Lucy Ann
Birth: 1825
Faber, Magdalena
Birth: 1822
Faber, Philip
Birth: 1790
Faber, Sarah Elizabeth
Death: April 05, 1902
Marr: Abt. 1828
Forman, Mary "Polly"
Death: June 03, 1848
Marr: Abt. 1798
Frantz, Adam
Death: Bet. 1825–1830
Frantz, John William
Prob: February 11, 1805
Frantz, Susan
Birth: March 23, 1819
Marr: Abt. 1840

Dauphin Co, PA (con't)

Garman, Michael
Census: 1790
Marr: 1785

Gieseman, John William
Death: August 26, 1843

Gruber, Anna Margaret
Death: June 12, 1837

Joray, Abraham
Res: Abt. 1755

Messerschmidt, Maria Elizabeth
Marr: Abt. 1806

Miller, Anna Margaret
Death: July 24, 1857
Marr: Abt. 1801

Miller, Anna Sophia
Marr: Abt. 1794

Miller, John
Census: 1790

Peters, Mary Louisa
Birth: March 31, 1858

Row, Adeline
Birth: January 02, 1860
Marr: Abt. 1878

Row, Daniel
Birth: July 10, 1813
Death: July 31, 1871; Bright's disease (ie, Chronic inflammation of kidneys)
Marr: Abt. 1840

Row, Jacob
Birth: 1812

Rudy, Jonas
Census: 1790

Rudy, Maria "Mollie" Magdalena
Death: January 16, 1845

Rudy, Michael
Birth: May 16, 1789

Rudy, Peter
Birth: 1785

Schupp, Christopher
Birth: 1788

Schupp, Daniel
Birth: 1783

Schupp, Eva Catherine
Birth: 1792

Schupp, John
Birth: 1782

Schupp, John George
Death: January 20, 1854
Marr: Abt. 1801

Schupp, John Henry
Birth: 1802

Schupp, John Michael

Dauphin Co, PA (con't)

Birth: 1786

Schupp, Joseph

Birth: 1790

Schupp, Maria Elizabeth

Birth: 1794

Schupp, Susan

Birth: 1797

Sheets, John George

Will: Abt. 1822

Death: 1822

Marr: Abt. 1798

Sheets, Susan

Marr: 1785

Sheetz, John George

Census: 1790

Death: Abt. 1791

Shirk, Anna Margaret Gieseman

Death: Aft. 1805

Shoop, Catherine

Death: June 08, 1872

Marr: Abt. 1849

Shoop, Elizabeth

Birth: 1833

Steiner, Maria Catherine

Res: Bet. 1832–1833

Death: Abt. 1840

Welker, Catherine

Birth: 1796

Welker, David

Birth: 1815

Welker, Elizabeth

Death: July 07, 1868

Marr: Abt. 1831

Welker, George

Birth: 1807

Welker, Jacob

Birth: 1798

Welker, John

Death: November 11, 1854; Influenza

Marr: Abt. 1806

Welker, John William

Birth: 1786

Welker, Joseph

Birth: 1820

Welker, Rachel

Birth: 1809

Welker, Salome "Sarah"

Birth: 1788

Welker, Sarah

Birth: 1818

Welker, Valentine

Dauphin Co, PA (con't)

Census: 1790

Wert, Anna Maria

Birth: 1799

Wert, Beulah Irene

Res: 1983

Wert, Daniel

Birth: 1796

Wert, David M

Marr: Abt. 1849

Wert, Eva Elizabeth

Birth: 1795

Wert, Henry

Birth: 1810

Wert, Isaac

Birth: 1808

Wert, Jacob

Marr: Abt. 1828

Wert, John

Birth: 1796

Wert, John

Birth: 1804

Wert, John Henry

Marr: Abt. 1878

Wert, Peter Martin

Birth: 1843

Wert, Sarah

Birth: 1805

Wirth, John Jacob

Marr: Abt. 1794

Wolfkill, Anna Margaret

Death: Bet. 1790–1800

Dauphin Co, PA (Fawper)

Faber, John

Census: 1790

Dauphin Co, PA (listed in index only)

Batdorf, Jacob Peter

Prob: 1829

Faber, John

Prob: Bet. August 08–13 1828

Messerschmidt, Andrew

Prob: 1801

Miller, John

Prob: April 29, 1812

Row, Daniel

Prob: August 28, 1871

Shoop, Catherine

Prob: June 23, 1880

Welker, John

Prob: 1854

Wirth, John Jacob

Dauphin Co, PA (listed in index only) (con't)
Prob: January 16, 1833

Dauphin Co, PA (listed in index)
Rowe, John William
Will: April 03, 1873

Dauphin Co, PA (Soop)
Schupp, John George
Census: 1790

Dauphin Co, PA (Wertz)
Wirth, John Adam
Census: 1790

Dauphin Co., PA
Faber, Catherine
Birth: Abt. 1788
Faber, Margaret
Birth: 1792

Dauphin Co?, PA
Shoop, John
Birth: August 01, 1805
Welker, Elizabeth
Birth: November 23, 1812

Dauphin County, PA
Gieseman, Susan
Res: Bet. 1816–1824

Dauphin?, PA
Batdorf, George Peter
Marr: Abt. 1792
Weiss, Barbara
Marr: Abt. 1792

Dayton, Dauphin Co, PA
Wert, David M
Death: December 09, 1900; Congestion of Lungs

Democrat
Batdorf, Myrtle Adeline
PoliticalParty:

Derry, Lancaster (Lebanon) Co, PA
Wirth, John Adam
Res: Bet. 1755–1763

Donegal Tp, Lancaster Co, PA
Welker, Valentine
Will: January 06, 1778

Donegal, Lancaster Co, PA
Jungblut, Susan
Census: 1810
Rudy, Jacob
Census: 1790
Census: 1800

Donegal, Lancaster Co, PA (con't)

Census: 1810

Welker, Valentine

Res: Bet. 1772–1779

Death: 1782

Dr. Convalescence Center, Selinsgrove, Snyder Co, PA

Wert, Beulah Irene

Death: June 10, 1983; Acute congestive cardiac failure w/poss. brain stem CVA & ASCVD

Earl Tp, Lancaster Co, PA

Wolfskiel, John Henry

Prob: July 08, 1788

Will: June 12, 1787

Earl, Lancaster Co, PA

Schupp, John George

Res: Abt. 1770

Wolfskiel, John Henry

Death: June 17, 1787

Earltown, PA

Wolfkill, Anna Margaret

Res: 1767

East Buffalo Tp, Union Co, PA

Peters, John

Prob: Bet. April 13–27 1846

East Buffalo, Union Co, PA

Maria, Anna

Census: 1850

Death: October 22, 1852

Peters, John

Res: Abt. 1830

Elizabethtown, Dauphin Co, PA

Batdorf, Joseph Warren

Birth: 1888

Elizabethville, Dauphin Co, PA

Batdorf, Thomas Edward

Death: August 13, 1916; Mitral insufficiency & Bright's disease (ie, Chronic inflammation) of kidneys w/

Census: 1910

Peters, Mary Louisa

Census: 1910

Census: 1920

Wert, Beulah Irene

Birth: December 31, 1889

Wert, Florence Stella

Death: November 1972

Elizabethville, Lancaster (Dauphin) Co, PA

Messerschmidt, Maria Elizabeth

Birth: 1784

Emmaus, Lehigh Co, PA (Uncle James Knittle)
Thompson, Harper Bruce
Census: 1930

Eschert, Berne, Switzerland
Guerne, Catherine
Birth: December 25, 1720

Estate recorded
Wertz, John Deitrich
Prob: January 30, 1805

Evangelical Lutheran Circuit, Lykens, Dauphin Co, PA
Batdorf, Myrtle Adeline
Baptism: October 11, 1918

Farmer
Wirth, John Adam
Occu: Weaver

father
Batdorf, Jacob Peter
Census: 1800; Heidelberg, Dauphin Co, PA w
Batdorf, Peter
Census: 1820; Lykens, Dauphin Co, PA w
Faber, John
Census: 1790; Dauphin Co, PA w
Census: 1800; Not listed w
Faber, Sarah Elizabeth
Census: 1810; Upper Paxton, Dauphin Co, PA w
Census: 1820; Upper Paxton, Dauphin Co, PA w
Frantz, Adam
Census: 1790; Strasburg, Lancaster Co, PA w
Census: 1800; Upper Paxton, Dauphin Co, PA w
Frantz, Susan
Census: 1820; Mifflin, Dauphin Co, PA w
Garman, Joanna Catherine
Census: 1800; Heidelberg, Dauphin (Lebanon) Co, PA w
Gieseman, Susan
Census: 1790; Tulpehocken, Berks Co, PA w
Census: 1800; Tulpehocken, Berks Co, PA w
Census: 1810; Upper Paxton, Dauphin Co, PA w
Messerschmidt, Maria Elizabeth
Census: 1800; Upper Paxton, Dauphin Co, PA w
Miller, Anna Margaret
Census: 1790; Upper Paxton, Dauphin Co, PA w
Miller, Anna Sophia
Census: 1790; Upper Paxton, Dauphin Co, PA w
Row, Daniel
Census: 1820; Mifflin, Dauphin Co, PA w
Census: 1830; Halifax, Dauphin Co, PA w
Rowe, John William
Census: 1790; Strasburg, Lancaster Co, PA w
Rudy, Barbara
Census: 1800; Lancaster Co, PA w

father (con't)

Rudy, Maria "Mollie" Magdalena

Census: 1790; Dauphin Co, PA w

Census: 1800; Bethel, Dauphin (Lebanon) Co, PA w

Schupp, John George

Census: 1790; Dauphin Co, PA w

Census: 1800; Upper Paxton, Dauphin Co, PA w

Sheets, John George

Census: 1790; Dauphin Co, PA w

Shoop, Catherine

Census: 1830; Lower Mahanoy, Northumberland Co, PA w

Census: 1840; Lower Mahanoy, Northumberland Co, PA w

Shoop, John

Census: 1810; Upper Paxton, Dauphin Co, PA w

Census: 1820; Upper Paxton, Dauphin Co, PA w

Welker, Elizabeth

Census: 1820; Lykens, Dauphin Co, PA w

Census: 1830; Lykens, Dauphin Co, PA w

Welker, John

Census: 1790; Dauphin Co, PA w

Wert, David M

Census: 1830; Halifax, Dauphin Co, PA w

Wert, Jacob

Census: 1810; Upper Paxton, Dauphin Co, PA w

Census: 1820; Upper Paxton, Dauphin Co, PA w

Wertz, John

Census: 1790; Northumberland Co, PA w

Census: 1800; White Deer, Northumberland (Union) Co, PA w

Wertz, Sarah

Census: 1820; Lower Mahanoy, Northumberland Co, PA w

Wirth, John Jacob

Census: 1790; Dauphin Co, PA w

father age 15

Miller, Anna Margaret

Census: 1800; Upper Paxton, Dauphin Co, PA w

father age 16

Rowe, John William

Census: 1800; Strasburg, Lancaster Co, PA w

Welker, John

Census: 1800; Upper Paxton, Dauphin Co, PA w

Forreston, IN

Batdorf, George Peter

Res: Abt. 1854

Frankenthal, Rhineland-Palatinate, Germany

Welker, Valentine

Birth: January 11, 1755

Freidens (Old Northkill) Lutheran Cemetery, Bernville, Lancaster (Berks) Co, PA

Gieseman, George William

Confir: 1731

Germany

Germany (con't)

Mahr, Maria Magdalena
Marr: Abt. 1730

Miller, Mary
Birth: 1742

Schaffer?, Anna Elizabeth
Birth: Abt. 1730
Marr: Abt. 1748

Shuetz, George
Birth: 1716

Welker, Valentine
Baptism: January 14, 1755

Welker, Valentine
Marr: Abt. 1748

Wirth, John Adam
Baptism: August 28, 1727

Wolfkill, Anna Maria
Birth: 1740

Wolfkill, Conrad
Birth: 1738

Wolfkill, Dorothy
Birth: 1745

Wolfkill, Killian
Birth: 1734

Wolfkill, Magdalena
Birth: 1743

Wolfkill, Philip
Birth: 1736

Wolfskiel, John Henry
Marr: Abt. 1730

Germany to USA (ship Crawford)

Welker, Valentine
Immigr: October 16, 1772

Germany to USA (ship Dragon)

Gruber, Christian
Immigr: September 30, 1732

Germany to USA (ship Nancy)

Messerschmidt, Andrew
Immigr: September 16, 1751

Germany to USA (ship Philadelphia)

Shuetz, George
Immigr: Abt. 1737

Germany to USA (ship Samuel Elizabeth)

Schnug, Eva Elizabeth
Immigr: 1740

Germany to USA (ship Snow Mollie)

Gieseman, George William
Immigr: October 26, 1741

Germany to USA (ship Two Brothers)

Germany to USA (ship Two Brothers) (con't)

Wirth, John Adam
Immigr: September 28, 1753

Germany to USA (ship Winter Gallery)

Traut, John Wendel George
Immigr: August 27, 1738

Germany?

Kibler, Elizabeth
Birth: 1720

Mahr, Maria Magdalena
Birth: Abt. 1712

Gratz, Dauphin Co, PA

Messerschmidt, Maria Elizabeth
Death: 1850

Greensburg Cemetery, Lancaster, Lancaster Co, PA

Rudy, Jacob
Burial: 1813

Greenwood, Mifflin, PA

Swartz, Peter
Census: 1800
Census: 1810

Halifax Tp, Dauphin Co, PA

Faber, John
Death: July 15, 1828

Halifax, Dauphin Co, PA

Faber, Sarah Elizabeth
Census: 1830
Census: 1860

Jungblut, Susan
Census: 1830

Rowe, John William
Census: 1830

Rudy, Maria "Mollie" Magdalena
Census: 1830

Wert, Jacob
Death: 1890
Census: 1830

Halifax, Dauphin Co, PA (Wist)

Wert, Jacob
Census: 1860

Hanover, Dauphin (Lebanon) Co, PA

Rudy, Jonas
Census: 1810

Harrisburg Hospital, Harrisburg, Dauphin Co, PA

Wert, John Henry
Death: October 30, 1924; Hemorrhage & shock from fractured ribs & other abd. injuries...rolling timber.

Harrisburg, Dauphin Co, PA

Batdorf, Cora Annette

Death: May 1981

Batdorf, Myrtle Adeline

Will: March 30, 1979

Prob: Bet. May 10–19 1983

Row, Adeline

Death: March 06, 1921; Sero-fibrinous pleurisy w/myocarditis

Rowe, Adam

Death: September 05, 1830

Thompson, Eugene Robert

Death: March 21, 2007

Thompson, Harper Bruce

Res: 1972

Wert, Beulah Irene

Res: 1956

Wirth, John Adam

Prob: 1807

Heidelberg, Berks Co, PA

Wertz, John Deitrich

Res: 1767

Heidelberg, Dauphin (Lebanon) Co, PA

Garman, Michael

Census: 1800

Heidelberg, Dauphin (Lebanon) Co, PA (Faler)

Faber, John

Census: 1800

Heidelberg, Dauphin Co, PA

Batdorf, George Peter

Census: 1800

Census: 1810

Herndon, Dauphin Co., PA

Batdorf, Mildred Catherine

Death: June 2010

Hill Cemetery, Halifax, Dauphin Co, PA

Faber, John

Burial: 1828

Home, Elizabethville, Dauphin Co, PA

Peters, Mary Louisa

Death: August 03, 1924; Cerebral hemorrhage

Home, Lykens, Dauphin Co, PA

Batdorf, James "Edward"

Death: August 19, 1954; Coronary occlusion w/hypertension w/diabetes mellitus

husband

Deibler, Anna Maria Elizabeth

Census: 1790; Dauphin Co, PA w

Census: 1800; Upper Paxton, Dauphin Co, PA w

Census: 1810; Upper Paxton, Dauphin Co, PA w

husband (con't)

Census: 1820; Upper Paxton, Dauphin Co, PA w
Census: 1830; Upper Paxton, Dauphin Co, PA w

Faber, Sarah Elizabeth
Census: 1840; w

Forman, Mary "Polly"
Census: 1800; w
Census: 1810; Swatara, Dauphin Co, PA w
Census: 1820; Susquehanna, Dauphin Co, PA w

Frantz, Susan
Census: 1840; Wiconisco, Dauphin Co, PA w

Garman, Joanna Catherine
Census: 1810; Mahanoy, Northumberland Co, PA w
Census: 1820; Lower Mahanoy, Northumberland Co, PA w
Census: 1830; Lower Mahanoy, Northumberland Co, PA w
Census: 1840; Lower Mahanoy, Northumberland Co, PA w

Gieseman, Susan
Census: 1820; Mifflin, Dauphin Co, PA w

Gruber, Anna Margaret
Census: 1790; Tulpehocken, Berks Co, PA w
Census: 1800; Tulpehocken, Berks Co, PA w
Census: 1810; Upper Paxton, Dauphin Co, PA w
Census: 1820; Mifflin, Dauphin Co, PA w
Census: 1830; Mifflin, Dauphin Co, PA w

Jury, Susan
Census: 1790; Dauphin Co, PA w
Census: 1800; Upper Paxton, Dauphin Co, PA w

Kerstetter, Frances
Census: 1790; Dauphin Co, PA w
Census: 1800; Upper Paxton, Dauphin Co, PA w
Census: 1810; Not listed w

Messerschmidt, Maria Elizabeth
Census: 1810; Northern Dauphin Co, PA w
Census: 1820; Lykens, Dauphin Co, PA w
Census: 1830; Lykens, Dauphin Co, PA w
Census: 1840; Lykens, Dauphin Co, PA w

Miller, Anna Margaret
Census: 1810; Upper Paxton, Dauphin Co, PA w
Census: 1820; Upper Paxton, Dauphin Co, PA w
Census: 1830; Upper Paxton, Dauphin Co, PA w
Census: 1840; Upper Paxton, Dauphin Co, PA w

Miller, Anna Sophia
Census: 1800; Upper Paxton, Dauphin Co, PA w
Census: 1810; Paxton, Dauphin Co, PA w
Census: 1820; Upper Paxton, Dauphin Co, PA w
Census: 1830; Upper Paxton, Dauphin Co, PA w

Overcash, Anna Barbara
Census: 1790; Dauphin Co, PA w
Census: 1800; Bethel, Dauphin (Lebanon) Co, PA w
Census: 1810; Dauphin (Lebanon) Co, PA w

Rudy, Barbara
Census: 1810; w

husband (con't)

Census: 1820; Mifflin, Dauphin Co, PA w
Census: 1830; Halifax, Dauphin Co, PA w
Census: 1840; Wiconisco, Dauphin Co, PA w

Rudy, Margaret
Census: 1790; Dauphin Co, PA w

Rudy, Maria "Mollie" Magdalena
Census: 1810; Upper Paxton, Dauphin Co, PA w
Census: 1820; Upper Paxton, Dauphin Co, PA w

Schnug, Eva Elizabeth
Census: 1790; Dauphin Co, PA w

Schrot, Eva
Census: 1790; w
Census: 1800; Upper Paxton, Dauphin Co, PA w

Sheets, Susan
Census: 1790; Dauphin Co, PA w
Census: 1800; Heidelberg, Dauphin (Lebanon) Co, PA w

Shirk, Anna Margaret Gieseman
Census: 1790; Strasburg, Lancaster Co, PA w
Census: 1800; Upper Paxton, Dauphin Co, PA w

Steiner, Maria Catherine
Census: 1820; Lykens, Dauphin Co, PA w

Traut, Maria Catherine
Census: 1790; Strasburg, Lancaster Co, PA w
Census: 1800; Strasburg, Lancaster Co, PA w

Weiss, Barbara
Census: 1820; Lykens, Dauphin Co, PA w
Census: 1830; Lykens, Dauphin Co, PA w

Welker, Elizabeth
Census: 1840; Lykens, Dauphin Co, PA w

Wertz, Sarah
Census: 1830; Lower Mahanoy, Northumberland Co, PA w
Census: 1840; Lower Mahanoy, Northumberland Co, PA w

Wolfkill, Anna Margaret
Census: 1790; Dauphin Co, PA w

IL

Garman, Michael
Death: January 08, 1800; PAIllness

Jackson, Dauphin Co, PA

Faber, Sarah Elizabeth
Census: 1850

Forman, Mary "Polly"
Census: 1840

Wert, Jacob
Census: 1850

Jefferson Tp, Dauphin Co, PA

Rudy, Maria "Mollie" Magdalena
Prob: August 01, 1845
Will: July 10, 1845
Death: July 16, 1845

Jesse H Geigle, 2100 Linglestown Rd.,Harrisburg, Dauphin Co, PA

Batdorf, Myrtle Adeline
Funrl: 1983
Thompson, Harper Bruce
Funrl: 1981

John R. Shultz Funeral Home, 406 Market St., Lykens, Dauphin Co, PA
Batdorf, James "Edward"
Funrl: 1954

Juniata, Perry Co, PA
Swartz, John
Census: 1820
Census: 1830
Swartz, Mary Ann
Birth: January 05, 1820
Census: 1830; w/parents
Census: 1840; w/parents

Killinger, Dauphin Co, PA
Schupp, John George
Res: Bet. 1780–1802
Welker, Valentine
Res: Bet. 1784–1801

Kleinfischlingen, Rhineland-Palatinate, Germany
Traut, John Wendel George
Birth: 1689

Lancaster (Dauphin) Co, PA
Deibler, Anna Maria Elizabeth
Marr: 1779
Kibler, Elizabeth
Death: Aft. 1769
Miller, Anna Margaret
Birth: February 12, 1784
Rudy, Christina Barbara
Birth: 1782
Rudy, Elizabeth
Birth: 1779
Rudy, Frederick
Birth: 1776
Rudy, Jacob
Birth: 1774
Rudy, John
Birth: 1780
Rudy, Jonas
Birth: 1778
Schupp, John George
Marr: 1779
Shuetz, George
Death: Abt. 1768
Wirth, Anna Margaret
Birth: 1771
Wirth, John George
Birth: 1770

Lancaster (Dauphin) Co, PA (con't)

Wirth, John Henry
Birth: 1769
Wirth, John Joseph
Birth: 1775
Wirth, John Peter
Birth: 1766
Wirth, John Philip
Birth: 1773

Lancaster (Lebanon) Co, PA

Faber, John
Birth: March 30, 1777
Marr: 1805
Faber, Sarah Elizabeth
Birth: May 25, 1807
Messerschmidt, Andrew
Res: 1765
Overcash, Anna Barbara
Marr: Abt. 1773
Rudy, Jonas
Marr: Abt. 1773
Rudy, Maria "Mollie" Magdalena
Marr: 1805
Wirth, Anna Catherine
Birth: 1762
Wirth, John
Birth: 1758
Wirth, John Christian
Birth: 1760

Lancaster (Lebanon) Co?, PA

Faber, John
Baptism: March 18, 1750

Lancaster Co, PA

Batdorf, George Peter
Birth: February 11, 1768
Faber, Elizabeth
Birth: April 10, 1784
Faber, Magdalena
Birth: November 26, 1775
Groetzinge, Susan
Death: Aft. 1759
Jungblut, Susan
Birth: Abt. 1770
Mahr, Maria Magdalena
Death: January 1767
Messerschmidt, Andrew
Birth: Abt. 1751
Messerschmidt, Andrew
Death: Abt. 1776
Rowe, Adam
Birth: September 21, 1770

Lancaster Co, PA (con't)

Rowe, Catherine
Birth: 1779

Rowe, Francis "Frank"
Burial: 1806
Prob: January 13, 1806
Death: Bet. January 08–13 1806

Rudy, Jacob
Birth: Abt. 1765
Death: 1813

Schaffer?, Anna Elizabeth
Death: 1782

Schrot, Eva
Death: Aft. 1810

Schrot, John
Death: Abt. 1800

Sheets, Susan
Birth: August 16, 1768

Shuetz, George
Will: October 11, 1768

Traut, Anna Magdalena
Birth: 1743

Traut, John Henry
Birth: 1742

Traut, John Paul
Birth: 1739

Traut, Maria Barbara
Birth: 1745

Traut, Maria Catherine
Burial: 1813
Prob: 1813
Death: 1813

Traut, Wendel
Birth: 1743

Walter, Maria Magdalena
Prob: 1761

Welker, Valentine
Prob: October 22, 1782

Wirth, John Adam
Birth: 1756

Wolfskiel, John Henry
Naturl: September 21, 1760

Lancaster, Lancaster Co, PA (widow)

Schrot, Eva
Census: 1810

Lancaster?, PA

Batdorf, Martin
Marr: Abt. 1756

Kibler, Elizabeth
Marr: Abt. 1740

Saltzegber, Barbara Elizabeth

Lancaster?, PA (con't)

Marr: Abt. 1756

Shuetz, George

Marr: Abt. 1740

Lebanon area, PA

Traut, John Wendel George

Res: 1739

Lebanon Co, PA

Faber, Catherine

Birth: January 14, 1810

Lebanon Tp, Lancaster (Lebanon) Co, PA

Kerstetter, Frances

Marr: January 01, 1774

Miller, John

Marr: January 01, 1774

Lebanon, Lancaster (Lebanon) Co, PA

Gieseman, John William

Birth: March 23, 1761

Miller, John

Birth: 1751

Wirth, John Jacob

Birth: February 1763

Lebanon, PA

Schnug, Eva Elizabeth

Res: 1755

Sheetz, John George

Marr: June 30, 1767; Rev. Casper Stoever, Dauphin

Wirth, John Adam

Res: 1755

Wolfkill, Anna Margaret

Marr: June 30, 1767; Rev. Casper Stoever, Dauphin

Little Britain, Lancaster Co, PA

Schrot, John

Census: 1800

Little Britian, Lancaster Co, PA (Sproat)

<No name>

Census: 1790

Schrot, John

Census: 1790

Lower Mahanoy Northumberland Co, PA

Shoop, Catherine

Census: 1860

Wert, David M

Census: 1860

Lower Mahanoy, Northmuberland, PA (Joyn)

Shoop, John

Census: 1850

Lower Mahanoy, Northumberland Co, PA

Lower Mahanoy, Northumberland Co, PA (con't)

Garman, Joanna Catherine
Census: 1850
Census: 1860

Shoop, Catherine
Census: 1850

Shoop, John
Prob: December 23, 1858
Death: December 13, 1858
Census: 1830
Census: 1840

Wert, John Henry
Census: 1860

Wertz, John
Death: May 13, 1861
Census: 1820

Wertz, Sarah
Death: Abt. 1842

Lower Mahanoy, Northumberland Co, PA (Mertz)

Wertz, John
Census: 1850

Lower Mahanoy, Northumberland Co, PA (Wartzs)

Wertz, John
Census: 1860

Lower Mahanoy, Northumberland Co, PA (Wert)

Wertz, John
Census: 1830

Lower Mahanoy, Northumberland Co, PA (Wertz)

Wertz, John
Census: 1840

Loyalton, Dauphin Co, PA

Batdorf, Harvey Clarence
Birth: 1891

Batdorf, Jacob Peter
Burial: 1829

Batdorf, James "Edward"
Birth: February 15, 1885
Res: 1918
Res: 1918

Batdorf, Oscar Newton
Birth: August 15, 1886

Lykens Valley, Lancaster (Dauphin) Co, PA

Wirth, John Adam
Res: Abt. 1765

Lykens, Dauphin Co, PA

Batdorf, George Peter
Census: 1820
Census: 1830

Batdorf, Harry Franklin

Lykens, Dauphin Co, PA (con't)

Death: August 1977

Batdorf, Jacob Peter

Census: 1820

Batdorf, James "Edward"

Census: 1930

Census: 1940

Batdorf, Myrtle Adeline

Census: 1930

Batdorf, Peter

Death: December 05, 1880

Census: 1840

Census: 1850

Census: 1860

Census: 1870

Census: 1880

Batdorf, Romaine

Death: July 1981

Batdorf, Thomas Edward

Census: 1860

Messerschmidt, Maria Elizabeth

Census: 1850

Miller, Anna Sophia

Death: October 22, 1842

Row, Adeline

Res: 1921

Shoop, Catherine

Census: 1870

Steiner, Maria Catherine

Census: 1830

Swartz, Mary Ann

Census: 1870

Welker, Elizabeth

Census: 1850

Census: 1860

Welker, John

Census: 1820

Census: 1830

Census: 1840

Census: 1850

Wert, Beulah Irene

Census: 1930

Census: 1940

Wert, David M

Census: 1870

Wert, Jacob

Birth: July 20, 1804

Wert, John Henry

Census: 1870

Lykens, Lancaster (Dauphin) Co, PA

Frantz, Adam

Birth: 1780

Lykens, Lancaster (Dauphin) Co, PA (con't)

Mahanoy, Northumberland Co, PA

Sheets, Susan
Census: 1810
Wertz, John
Census: 1810

Main St., Elizabethville, Dauphin Co, PA

Peters, Mary Louisa
Res: 1920

Middletown, Lancaster (Dauphin) Co, PA

Welker, Valentine
Res: 1779

Mifflin Tp, Dauphin Co, PA

Gieseman, John William
Will: June 23, 1841
Prob: October 02, 1843

Mifflin, Dauphin Co, PA

Frantz, Adam
Census: 1820
Gieseman, John William
Census: 1820
Census: 1830
Census: 1840
Gieseman, Susan
Death: February 15, 1826; Pilger Fieber u. Kindes Nothen (ie, Pilgrim fever)
Jungblut, Susan
Census: 1820
Miller, Anna Margaret
Census: 1850
Peters, Mary Louisa
Census: 1860
Peters, Samuel
Census: 1860
Schupp, John George
Census: 1850
Swartz, Mary Ann
Census: 1860
Welker, Valentine
Census: 1810

Mifflin, Dauphin Co, PA (Rosie)

Rowe, John William
Census: 1820

Millersburg, Dauphin Co, PA

Deibler, Anna Maria Elizabeth
Death: April 18, 1840
Schupp, John George
Death: August 27, 1839
Welker, Valentine
Census: 1820

Millersburg, Dauphin Co, PA (con't)
Census: 1830
Wirth, John Jacob
Death: January 01, 1833

Millersburg, Lancaster (Dauphin) Co, PA
Deibler, Anna Maria Elizabeth
Birth: January 10, 1760
Miller, Anna Sophia
Birth: August 02, 1776
Welker, John
Birth: August 10, 1783
Wirth, John Adam
Res: 1774

Montgomery Co, PA
Wirth, John Adam
Res: Abt. 1754

mother
Batdorf, Peter
Census: 1830; Lykens, Dauphin Co, PA w
Peters, Samuel
Census: 1840; w

Moutier, Berne, Switzerland
Guerne, Catherine
Marr: August 06, 1743
Joray, Abraham
Baptism: March 20, 1718
Marr: August 06, 1743

Neider-Hilbersheim, Rhineland-Palatinate, Germany
Wolfkill, Anna Margaret
Birth: July 16, 1732
Wolfskiel, John Henry
Birth: November 03, 1706

NJ
Peters, John
Birth: Abt. 1785

Northern Dauphin Co, PA
Welker, John
Census: 1810

Northkill, PA
Gruber, Christian
Res: Bet. 1743–1759

Northumberland (Union) Co, PA
Wertz, Casper
Birth: 1782
Wertz, John
Birth: May 05, 1783

Northumberland Co, PA
Garman, Joanna Catherine

Northumberland Co, PA (con't)

Death: September 23, 1864
Marr: Abt. 1809

Garman, Martin "Marty"
Birth: 1790

Garman, Michael
Birth: 1798

Jury, Susan
Marr: 1783

Kerstetter, Frances
Death: 1818

Miller, Mary
Census: 1790

Shoop, Catherine
Birth: February 24, 1830

Shoop, John
Marr: Abt. 1826

Swartz, Peter
Census: 1790

Welker, Valentine
Marr: 1783

Wert, John Henry
Birth: December 23, 1855

Wertz, Elizabeth
Birth: 1778

Wertz, John
Prob: June 03, 1861
Marr: Abt. 1809

Wertz, John Adam
Birth: 1780

Wertz, John Deitrich
Burial: 1804

Wertz, John Jacob
Birth: 1776

Wertz, Sarah
Birth: Abt. 1811
Marr: Abt. 1826

Northumberland Co, PA (Teterie Vertz)

Wertz, John Deitrich
Census: 1790

Northumberland Co?, PA

Wert, John Henry
Baptism: December 23, 1855

Northumberland?, PA

Miller, Mary
Marr: Abt. 1770

Wertz, John Deitrich
Marr: Abt. 1770

Now Jefferson Tp, Berks Co, PA

Gruber, Christian

Now Jefferson Tp, Berks Co, PA (con't)
Res:

Oakdale Church Circuit, Dauphin Co, PA
Batdorf, James "Edward"
Baptism: June 06, 1886

Oakdale Church, Dauphin Co, PA
Batdorf, James "Edward"
Marr: February 08, 1908
Wert, Beulah Irene
Marr: February 08, 1908

Ofterdingen, Baden-Wurttemberg, Germany
Messerschmidt, Andrew
Birth: October 02, 1708

Ogle, IL
Sheets, Susan
Death: March 23, 1854

OH
Batdorf, George Peter
Death: Bet. 1830–1840; PA
Weiss, Barbara
Death: Aft. 1830; PA
Wert, John
Death: 1829

Old Northkill, Berks Co, PA
Gruber, Anna Margaret
Baptism: April 16, 1759

Old Salem (Werts) Lutheran, Millersburg, Dauphin Co, PA
Deibler, Anna Maria Elizabeth
Burial: 1840
Miller, Anna Sophia
Burial: 1842
Schnug, Eva Elizabeth
Burial: Abt. 1800
Schupp, John George
Burial: 1839
Wirth, John Adam
Burial: 1806
Wirth, John Jacob
Burial: January 03, 1833

Old Salem (Werts) Lutheran, Millersburg, Lancaster (Dauphin) Co, PA
Miller, Anna Sophia
Baptism: Abt. 1776
Welker, John
Baptism: September 22, 1783

PA
<No name>
Birth: Abt. 1800
<No name>

Birth: 1823

<No name>

Birth: 1874

Angelina

Birth: March 1835

Anna

Birth: 1810

Anna

Birth: 1815

Baker, John

Birth: May 19, 1804

Batdorf, Adam Scorvella

Birth: 1882

Batdorf, Alvin Leroy

Birth: 1908

Batdorf, Alvin Thomas

Birth: 1898

Batdorf, Anna

Birth: Abt. 1850

Batdorf, Catherine

Birth: 1818

Batdorf, Catherine

Birth: 1796

Batdorf, Christian

Birth: 1803

Batdorf, Christina

Birth: 1799

Batdorf, Cora Annette

Birth: April 18, 1892

Batdorf, Daniel

Birth: 1824

Batdorf, Elizabeth

Birth: 1839

Batdorf, Elizabeth

Birth: 1828

Batdorf, Esther

Birth: 1836

Batdorf, Eva

Birth: 1802

Batdorf, Frances I

Birth: 1887

Batdorf, George

Birth: 1875

Batdorf, Harry Franklin

Birth: July 21, 1912

Batdorf, Jacob

Birth: 1826

Batdorf, Jacob Peter

Birth: Abt. 1793

Batdorf, John

Birth: 1844

PA (con't)

Batdorf, John
Birth: 1817

Batdorf, John
Birth: 1794

Batdorf, John
Birth: September 07, 1878

Batdorf, John Jacob
Birth: 1805

Batdorf, Jonas
Birth: 1837

Batdorf, Jonathan
Birth: 1822

Batdorf, Kirby
Birth: 1877

Batdorf, Louisa
Birth: 1854

Batdorf, Margaret Irene
Birth: December 05, 1909

Batdorf, Mary Ellen
Birth: 1881

Batdorf, Mildred Catherine
Birth: 1912

Batdorf, Norman
Birth: 1896

Batdorf, Peter S
Birth: 1848

Batdorf, Rebecca
Birth: Abt. 1850

Batdorf, Romaine
Birth: May 24, 1925

Batdorf, Ruth E
Birth: April 29, 1923

Batdorf, Sarah
Birth: 1845

Batdorf, Sarah
Birth: 1815

Batdorf, Stella Louisa
Birth: 1893

Batdorf, Susan
Birth: 1842

Batdorf, Thomas
Birth: 1820

Batdorf, Verna A
Birth: June 02, 1899

Batdorf, William
Birth: 1880

Bellis, Elizabeth
Birth: 1843

Bird?, Sarah
Birth: Abt. 1825

Boyer, Caroline "Carrie" May

Birth: 1884
Carl, Catherine "Kate" M
Birth: 1873
Catherine
Birth: 1833
Catherine
Birth: 1831
Catherine
Birth: 1805
Chubb, Isaac F
Birth: 1849
Elizabeth
Birth: 1854
Elizabeth
Birth: 1812
Elizabeth
Birth: 1806
Elizabeth
Birth: 1813
Elizabeth
Birth: 1806
Elizabeth
Birth: 1816
Emma
Birth: 1870
Faber, Adam
Birth: 1814
Faber, George
Birth: 1815
Faber, Jacob
Birth: 1819
Faber, John
Birth: 1809
Faber, Michael
Birth: 1808
Faber, Sarah Elizabeth
Birth: 1846
Forman, Mary "Polly"
Birth: January 05, 1778
Frantz, Adam
Birth: 1811
Frantz, Catherine
Birth: Abt. 1815
Frantz, Christina
Birth: 1818
Frantz, Jacob
Birth: 1814
Frantz, John
Birth: Abt. 1815
Frantz, John
Birth: 1783

PA (con't)

Frantz, Samuel
Birth: 1824
Frantz, Sarah
Birth: 1821
Frantz, William
Birth: 1812
Frantz, William
Birth: 1785
Garman
Birth: Abt. 1800
Garman, Benjamin
Birth: 1794
Garman, George
Birth: 1796
Garman, Jacob
Birth: March 07, 1792
Garman, Joanna Catherine
Birth: August 02, 1791
Gieseman, Anna Barbara
Birth: 1760
Gieseman, Anna Margaret
Birth: 1749
Gieseman, Anna Maria
Birth: 1800
Gieseman, Catherine
Birth: 1791
Gieseman, Christina
Birth:
Gieseman, George
Birth:
Gieseman, John
Birth:
Gieseman, John
Birth: Abt. 1750
Gieseman, John William
Baptism: May 03, 1761
Gieseman, Magdalena
Birth: 1798
Gieseman, Margaret Elizabeth
Birth:
Gieseman, Susan
Baptism: May 30, 1788
Groetzinge, Susan
Marr: Abt. 1750; Germany
Gruber, Christian
Birth: 1745
Gruber, Christina Elizabeth
Birth: 1745
Gruber, Henry
Birth: Abt. 1750
Gruber, John Adam

PA (con't)

Birth: 1752

Gruber, John Albright

Birth: 1754

Gruber, John George

Birth: 1743

Gruber, Maria Catherine

Birth: 1749

Gruber, Susan

Birth: 1746

Jungblut, Susan

Death: Abt. 1830

Marr: Abt. 1785

Jury, Catherine

Birth: 1755

Jury, Salome "Sarah"

Birth: 1761

Keiper, William Henry

Birth: 1851

Knarr, Elizabeth

Birth: 1810

Kocher, John Adam

Birth: 1872

Maria, Anna

Birth: Abt. 1792

Marlow, Margaret Elizabeth

Birth: 1908

Death: 2004

Mary

Birth: 1848

Matilda

Birth: 1821

Matter, Susan

Birth: 1820

Messerschmidt

Birth:

Messerschmidt, Andrew

Marr: Abt. 1750; Germany

Messerschmidt, Andrew

Birth:

Messerschmidt, Catherine

Birth:

Messerschmidt, George

Birth: 1790

Messerschmidt, Henry

Birth: 1790

Messerschmidt, Jacob

Birth: 1792

Messerschmidt, Julia

Birth:

Messerschmidt, Louis

Birth: 1787

PA (con't)

Miller, Anna Catherine
Birth: 1775
Miller, Anna Magdalena
Birth: 1774
Miller, Christina
Birth: 1782
Miller, Daniel
Birth: 1792
Miller, Elizabeth
Birth: 1787
Miller, John
Birth: 1777
Miller, John Jacob
Birth: 1782
Miller, Mary
Burial: 1804
Miller, Sarah
Birth: 1842
Motter, Mabel Susan Elizabeth
Birth: 1887
Peters, Andrew J
Birth: Abt. 1822
Peters, Elias
Birth: April 1829
Peters, Emma C
Birth: 1846
Peters, Jane R
Birth: March 31, 1858
Peters, John
Birth: 1844
Peters, Jonathan
Birth: 1848
Peters, Jonathan
Birth: Abt. 1825
Peters, Matilda
Birth: Abt. 1837
Peters, Matilda "Tillie"
Birth: 1852
Peters, Matthew
Birth: 1849
Pinkerton, Mary Margaret
Birth: 1841
Rachel
Birth: 1813
Romberger, Daniel George
Birth: 1879
Rosanna
Birth: 1828
Row, Adam Diller
Birth: 1851
Row, Alfred C

PA (con't)

Birth: 1855

Row, Amelia

Birth: 1854

Row, Angelina

Birth: 1843

Row, Elizabeth

Birth: 1819

Row, John

Birth: 1817

Row, Joseph

Birth: 1828

Row, Leah Jane

Birth: 1857

Row, Sarah

Birth: 1820

Row, Sarah Ann

Birth: 1841

Row, Susan

Birth: 1815

Row, Susan

Birth: 1852

Row, Wendel

Birth: 1811

Rowe, Anna M

Birth: Abt. 1780

Rowe, Francis

Birth: Abt. 1778

Rowe, John

Birth: Abt. 1765

Rowe, John George

Birth: 1772

Rowe, Margaret

Birth: Abt. 1767

Rowe, Sarah

Birth: 1791

Rowe, Wendel

Birth: August 07, 1777

Rudy, Jacob

Marr: Abt. 1785

Sarah

Birth: 1805

Schoffstall, Susan

Birth: 1791

Schrot, Eva

Birth: Abt. 1753

Schupp

Birth: Abt. 1800

Sheets, Catherine

Birth: Abt. 1775

Sheets, Catherine

Birth:

PA (con't)

Sheets, Elizabeth
Birth: Abt. 1777
Sheets, Elizabeth
Birth:
Sheets, Jacob
Birth: Abt. 1769
Sheets, Jacob
Birth:
Sheets, John Leonard
Birth: 1749
Sheets, Leonard
Birth: Abt. 1781
Sheets, Mary
Birth:
Sheets, Michael
Birth:
Sheets, Susan
Birth:
Sheetz, John George
Birth: 1746
Shoop, Anna Maria
Birth: Abt. 1808
Shoop, Elizabeth
Birth: Abt. 1808
Shoop, Jacob
Birth: Abt. 1808
Shoop, Joseph
Birth: Abt. 1808
Shoop, Magdalena
Birth: Abt. 1808
Shoop, Michael
Birth: 1806
Shoop, Salome "Sarah"
Birth: 1841
Siegel, Elizabeth
Birth: 1798
Sierer, Mary Elizabeth
Birth: 1853
Susan
Birth: 1823
Swartz, John
Birth: Abt. 1794
Swartz, Peter
Birth: Abt. 1770
Thompson, Eugene Robert
Birth: August 07, 1937
Tschopp, Anna Maria
Birth: 1819
Tschopp, Anna Mary
Birth: 1831
Weiss, Barbara

Birth: Abt. 1772

Welker

Birth: Abt. 1811

Welker, Daniel

Birth: 1801

Welker, Elizabeth

Birth: 1787

Welker, Elizabeth

Birth: 1784

Welker, Peter

Birth: 1788

Welker, William Henry

Birth: 1814

Wert, "Hattie" May

Birth: 1881

Wert, Adam Washington

Birth: 1841

Wert, Amelia Ida

Birth: 1868

Wert, Anna Elizabeth

Birth: 1855

Wert, Caroline "Carrie" Catherine

Birth: 1880

Wert, Catherine

Birth: 1835

Wert, Catherine "Kate" Ann

Birth: 1866

Wert, Daniel Monroe

Birth: 1870

Wert, Elizabeth Jane

Birth: 1853

Wert, Florence Stella

Birth: March 06, 1886

Wert, Isaac Franklin

Birth: 1871

Wert, John Henry

Birth: 1837

Wert, Magdalena

Birth: 1813

Wert, Martha

Birth: 1848

Wert, Martha "Mattie" Valery

Birth: 1864

Wert, Mary Ellen

Birth: 1859

Wert, Matthew

Birth: 1847

Wert, Melinda "Polly"

Birth: 1861

Wert, U

Birth: Abt. 1883; U

PA (con't)

Wertz
Birth: Abt. 1785; U
Wertz, Catherine
Birth: 1831
Wertz, Jacob
Birth: 1816
Wertz, John
Baptism: May 15, 1783
Wertz, John
Birth: 1829
Wertz, John George
Birth: 1828
Wertz, Magdelena
Birth: Abt. 1785
Wertz, Samuel
Birth: 1821
Wirth, John Jacob
Baptism: March 25, 1763
Zerby, Jacob
Birth: 1840
Zimmerman, Christina
Birth: 1826

PA?

Swartz, John
Death: Bet. 1840–1850
Swartz, Peter
Death: Bet. 1810–1820

Paradise, Lancaster Co, PA

Traut, John Wendel George
Death: Bet. February–March 1761
Walter, Maria Magdalena
Death: February 1761

Paradise, Lancaster, PA

Traut, Maria Catherine
Birth: January 24, 1748

parents

Batdorf, Jacob Peter
Census: 1810; w
Forman, Mary "Polly"
Census: 1790; w
Frantz, Susan
Census: 1830; w
Messerschmidt, Maria Elizabeth
Census: 1790; w
Peters, John
Census: 1790; w
Census: 1800; w
Swartz, John
Census: 1800; Greenwood, Mifflin, PA w

parents (con't)

Census: 1810; Greenwood, Mifflin, PA w

Wert, David M

Census: 1840; w

parents)

Heck, Anna Catherine

Immigr: September 28, 1733; Germany to USA (ship Richard & Elizabeth w

Paxtang, Lancaster (Dauphin) Co, PA

Sheets, John George

Birth: Bet. 1773–1774

Shuetz, George

Res: Bet. 1749–1751

Paxton, Lancaster (Dauphin) Co, PA

Sheetz, John George

Res: 1767

Perry Co, PA

Peters, Samuel

Burial: Bet. 1860–1870

Death: Bet. 1860–1870

Philadelphia, PA

Gieseman, George William

Res: 1741

Joray, Abraham

Res: 1754

Messerschmidt, Andrew

Res: 1751

Welker, Valentine

Res: 1772

Wirth, John Adam

Res: 1753

Naturl: September 28, 1753

Wolfskiel, John Henry

Res: 1742

Polyclinic Hospital, Harrisburg, Dauphin Co, PA

Batdorf, Myrtle Adeline

Death: May 08, 1983; Cardiorespiratory arrest w/ASHD w/pacemaker

Thompson, Harper Bruce

Death: July 23, 1981; Cardiorespiratory arrest w/subdural hematoma

Porter, Schuylkill Co, PA

Thompson, Harper Bruce

Census: 1910

Census: 1920

Powells Valley, Dauphin Co, PA

Wert, David M

Birth: April 01, 1829

Reading, Berks Co, PA

Gruber, Christian

Prob: Bet. December 04–14 1781

Reading, Berks Co, PA (con't)
Prob: May 24, 1800

Reiff? Helt?, 523 W. Main St., Lykens, Dauphin Co, PA
Batdorf, James "Edward"
Funrl: 1954

Republican
Thompson, Harper Bruce
PoliticalParty:

Rev. Stoever, Bindagles Lutheran, Palmyra, Lancaster (Lebanon) Co, PA
Schnug, Eva Elizabeth
Marr: August 03, 1755
Wirth, John Adam
Marr: August 03, 1755

Rev. Stoever, Christ (Little Tulpehocken) Lutheran, Bernville, Lancaster (Berks) Co, PA
Gruber, Christian
Marr: January 26, 1742
Stupp, Anna Gunigunda
Marr: January 26, 1742

Rev. Stoever, Trinity Lutheran, New Holland, Lancaster Co, PA
Traut, John Wendel George
Marr: January 23, 1739
Walter, Maria Magdalena
Marr: January 23, 1739

Rev. W.G. Engle, Dauphin Co, PA
Batdorf, Thomas Edward
Marr: December 06, 1874
Peters, Mary Louisa
Marr: December 06, 1874

Rhineland-Palatinate, Germany
Welker, Valentine
Birth: Abt. 1730

Ridgeway, Elk Co, PA
Batdorf, Ruth E
Death: August 16, 2006

Salem Lutheran, Millersburg, Lancaster (Dauphin) Co, PA
Jury, Susan
Baptism: 1759

Sarasota, Sarasota Co, FL
Batdorf, Oscar Newton
Death: August 1981

Schoharie Valley, Schoharie, NY
Stupp, Anna Gunigunda
Birth: December 21, 1721

Schultz Funeral Home, 406 Market St., Lykens, Dauphin Co, PA
Wert, Beulah Irene
Funrl: 1983

Schwaigern, Baden-Wurttemberg, Germany

Wertz, John Deitrich

Birth: June 24, 1740

Schwandorf, Germany

Welker, Valentine

Birth: January 11, 1755

Sheridan, Schuylkill Co, PA

Thompson, Harper Bruce

Birth: September 28, 1907

Sherman Oaks, Los Angeles Co, CA

Batdorf, Verna A

Death: December 1992

Simeon Union Cemetery, Gratz, Dauphin Co, PA

Welker, John

Burial: 1854

Sinzeim, Baden-Wurttemberg, Germany

Gruber, Christian

Birth: October 18, 1712

Slatington, Lehigh Co, PA

Wert, Jacob

Census: 1870

son Jacob

Rudy, Barbara

Census: 1880; Washington, Dauphin Co, PA w

St John Hill (Quittaphilla) Lutheran, Cleona, Lancaster (Lebanon) Co, PA

Kerstetter, Frances

Baptism: April 12, 1752

St John Hill (Quittaphilla) Lutheran, Cleona, Lebanon Co, PA

Rudy, Margaret

Burial: 1825

St. Davids (Salem) Reformed, Millersburg, Dauphin Co, PA

Guerne, Catherine

Burial: 1785

Joray, Abraham

Burial: 1785

Shoop, John

Baptism: August 08, 1805

St. Davids (Salem) Reformed, Millersburg, Lancaster (Dauphin) Co, PA

Jury, Susan

Confir: July 17, 1777

Schupp, John George

Baptism: May 24, 1780

St. Johns (Hill) Lutheran, Berrysburg, Dauphin Co, PA

Frantz, Adam

Baptism: Abt. 1785

Frantz, Susan

Burial: 1861

Gieseman, John William

St. Johns (Hill) Lutheran, Berrysburg, Dauphin Co, PA (con't)

Burial: August 1843

Gieseman, Susan

Burial: February 17, 1826

Gruber, Anna Margaret

Burial: 1837

Row, Adeline

Burial: March 10, 1921

Baptism: March 11, 1860

Row, Daniel

Burial: July 1871

Baptism: August 14, 1813

Rowe, John William

Burial: 1877

Rudy, Barbara

Burial: 1881

Wert, Beulah Irene

Baptism: May 18, 1890

Wert, John Henry

Burial: November 02, 1924

St. Johns (Hill) Lutheran, Lykens, Dauphin Co, PA

Batdorf, Myrtle Adeline

Marr: June 15, 1935

Thompson, Harper Bruce

Marr: June 15, 1935

St. Johns (Oakdale) Cemetery, Loyalton, Dauphin Co, PA

Batdorf, Thomas Edward

Burial: August 16, 1916

Peters, Mary Louisa

Burial: August 06, 1924

Swartz, Mary Ann

Burial: August 12, 1897

St. Johns Union Cemetery, Fredericksburg, Dauphin (Lebanon) Co, PA

Overcash, Anna Barbara

Burial: 1836

Rudy, Jonas

Burial: 1810

St. Johns Union, Fredericksburg, Lancaster (Lebanon) Co, PA

Rudy, Maria "Mollie" Magdalena

Baptism: November 14, 1784

St. Pauls (Bowermans) Lutheran, Enterline, Dauphin Co, PA

Faber, Sarah Elizabeth

Burial: 1902

Rudy, Maria "Mollie" Magdalena

Burial: 1845

Wert, Jacob

Burial:

St. Peters (Fetterhoff) Union, Halifax, Dauphin Co, PA

Faber, Sarah Elizabeth

Burial: 1902

St. Peters (Fetterhoff) Union, Halifax, Dauphin Co, PA (con't)

Wert, Jacob

Burial: 1890

St. Peters (Hoffman) Reformed, Loyalton, Dauphin Co, PA

Batdorf, Peter

Burial: 1880

Baptism: February 27, 1814

Jungblut, Susan

Burial: 1833

Shoop, Catherine

Burial: 1872

Welker, Elizabeth

Burial: 1868

St. Peters (Hoffmans) Church, Lykens, Dauphin Co, PA

Batdorf, Thomas Edward

Baptism: October 12, 1851

State Road 199, Washington Tp., Dauphin Co, PA

Batdorf, James "Edward"

Res: 1920

State Road 199, Washington, Dauphin Co, PA

Wert, John Henry

Res: 1920

Strasburg, Chester (Lancaster) Co, PA

Walter, Maria Magdalena

Birth: January 1717

Strasburg, Lancaster Co, PA

Rowe, Francis "Frank"

Birth: Abt. 1745

Census: 1790

Will: January 08, 1806

Rowe, John William

Birth: June 1785

Marr: 1810

Rudy, Barbara

Birth: April 11, 1796

Marr: 1810

Traut, John Wendel George

Will: February 19, 1760

Strasburg, Lancaster Co, PA (France)

Frantz, John William

Census: 1790

Strasburg, Lancaster Co, PA (Rough)

Rowe, Francis "Frank"

Census: 1800

Strassburg, PA

Walter, Maria Magdalena

Res: 1739

Susquehanna, Dauphin Co, PA

Susquehanna, Dauphin Co, PA (con't)
Sheets, John George
Census: 1820

Swatara Reformed, Fredericksburg, Lancaster (Lebanon) Co, PA
Faber, John
Baptism: April 21, 1777

Swatara, Dauphin Co, PA (Shits)
Sheets, John George
Census: 1810

Swatara, Lancaster (Lebanon) Co, PA
Faber, John
Birth: February 07, 1750
Rudy, Margaret
Birth: December 18, 1753

Swatara, PA
Shuetz, George
Res: 1749

Switzerland
Jury, Abraham
Birth: 1753
Jury, Isaac
Birth: 1745
Jury, Maria Elizabeth
Birth: 1744
Jury, Maria Magdalena
Birth: 1747
Jury, Maria Margaret
Birth: 1749
Jury, Salome
Birth: 1752
Jury, Samuel Frederick
Birth: 1751

Switzerland to USA (ship Nancy)
Guerne, Catherine
Immigr: 1754
Joray, Abraham
Immigr: September 14, 1754

Tower City, Schuylkill Co, PA
Batdorf, Myrtle Adeline
Census: 1940
Thompson, Harper Bruce
Census: 1940

Trinity Lutheran, New Holland, Lancaster Co, PA
Rowe, Francis "Frank"
Marr: January 24, 1764
Schupp, John George
Baptism: September 01, 1759
Traut, Maria Catherine
Marr: January 24, 1764

Trinity Lutheran, New Holland, Lancaster Co, PA (con't)

Tulpehocken, Berks Co, PA

Gieseman, George William
Will: May 1761
Gieseman, John William
Census: 1790
Census: 1800
Gieseman, Susan
Birth: November 10, 1787
Gruber, Christian
Will: July 07, 1780
Stupp, Anna Gunigunda
Prob: Bet. June 04–14 1799
Will: November 09, 1796
Wirth, John Adam
Res: Abt. 1755

Tulpehocken, Chester (Berks) Co, PA

Heck, Anna Catherine
Birth: 1723

Tulpehocken, PA

Stupp, Anna Gunigunda
Res: 1742

Union Co, PA

Maria, Anna
Marr: Abt. 1815
Peters, John
Marr: Abt. 1815
Peters, Samuel
Birth: 1821
Marr: Abt. 1840
Swartz, Mary Ann
Marr: Abt. 1840

Union, Union Co, PA

Peters, Samuel
Census: 1850
Swartz, Mary Ann
Census: 1850

Upper Paxtang Tp, Dauphin Co, PA

Welker, Valentine
Prob: 1831
Will: 1831

Upper Paxtang, Dauphin Co, PA

Jury, Susan
Death: Abt. 1801
Shoop, Catherine
Census: 1850

Upper Paxton, Dauphin Co, PA

Faber, John
Census: 1820

Upper Paxton, Dauphin Co, PA (con't)

Faber, Sarah Elizabeth
Census: 1870
Frantz, Adam
Marr: October 06, 1811
Frantz, John William
Death: 1804
Census: 1800
Gieseman, John William
Census: 1810
Gieseman, Susan
Marr: October 06, 1811
Guerne, Catherine
Death: Bef. February 15, 1785
Joray, Abraham
Will: September 22, 1785
Death: December 1785
Messerschmidt, Andrew
Death: 1801
Census: 1800
Miller, John
Death: 1812
Census: 1800
Census: 1810
Miller, John Peter
Birth: May 17, 1780
Schnug, Eva Elizabeth
Death: 1800
Schupp, John George
Census: 1810
Census: 1820
Census: 1830
Census: 1840
Schupp, John George
Census: 1800
Census: 1810
Census: 1820
Census: 1830
Sheets, John George
Census: 1800
Welker, Valentine
Census: 1800
Wert, David M
Census: 1850
Wirth, John Adam
Death: August 25, 1806
Wirth, John Jacob
Census: 1800
Census: 1810
Census: 1820
Census: 1830

Upper Paxton, Dauphin Co, PA age 45

Washington, Dauphin Co, PA (con't)
Rowe, John William
Census: 1870
Rudy, Barbara
Census: 1870
Swartz, Mary Ann
Death: August 09, 1897; Heart disease
Wert, Beulah Irene
Census: 1900
Census: 1910
Census: 1920
Wert, John Henry
Census: 1880
Census: 1900
Census: 1920

Washington, Dauphin Co, PA (enumerated twice)
Wert, John Henry
Census: 1910

Washington, Dauphin Co, PA (Row)
Swartz, Mary Ann
Census: 1880

Washington, Dauphin Co, PA (West)
Wert, David M
Census: 1900

West Grove Cemetery, Lincoln, Ogle, IL
Sheets, Susan
Burial: 1854

White Deer, Northumberland (Union) Co, PA
Miller, Mary
Death: 1804
Census: 1800
Wertz, John Deitrich
Res: 1775
Death: October 16, 1804
Census: 1800

White Deer, Northumberland (Union), PA
Wertz, John Deitrich
Will: Bet. May 08, 1803–1804

Wiconisco, Dauphin Co, PA
Batdorf, Margaret Irene
Death: December 1990
Row, Adeline
Census: 1870
Row, Daniel
Census: 1840
Census: 1870
Rowe, John William
Census: 1840
Census: 1850

Wiconisco, Dauphin Co, PA (con't)

Census: 1860

Rudy, Barbara

Census: 1850

Census: 1860

Wiconisco, Lancaster (Dauphin) Co, PA

Joray, Abraham

Res: Bet. 1778–1782

with father

Wolfkill, Anna Margaret

Immigr: 1760

Woodlawn Memorial Gardens, Harrisburg, Dauphin Co, PA

Batdorf, Myrtle Adeline

Burial: May 11, 1983

Thompson, Harper Bruce

Burial: 1981

York Co, PA

Garman, Michael

Birth: 1747

Zion (Stone Valley) Lutheran, Dalmatia, Northumberland Co, PA

Garman, Joanna Catherine

Burial: 1864

Kerstetter, Frances

Burial: 1818

Miller, Anna Margaret

Burial: 1857

Miller, John

Burial: 1812

Schupp, John George

Burial: 1854

Shoop, Catherine

Baptism: March 06, 1830

Shoop, John

Burial: 1858

Wertz, John

Burial: 1861

Wertz, Sarah

Burial: Abt. 1842

Zion Lutheran, Jonestown, Lancaster (Lebanon) Co, PA

Faber, John

Marr: February 02, 1774

Rudy, Margaret

Confir: 1774

Marr: February 02, 1774

Zion Lutheran, Manheim, Lancaster Co, PA

Messerschmidt, Andrew

Burial: Abt. 1776

Chapter Four

Our family's kinship.

How we are all related to one another from present to distant past and the outline descendants of Martin Batdorf, our distant ancestor from Darmstadt orgins.

Kinship Report

Name:	Birth Date:	Relationship:
<No name>	1786	Wife of 2nd great grand uncle of husband
<No name>		Wife of grand uncle of husband
<No name>		3rd great grandmother of husband
<No name>		3rd great grandfather of husband
<No name>		3rd great grandfather of husband
<No name>		4th great grandfather of husband
<No name>		Wife of uncle of husband
A, Mary	1836	Wife of grand uncle of husband
A, Mary	1867	Wife of grand uncle of husband
Albert, Jacob	Abt. 1770	Husband of 3rd great grandmother of husband
Angst, Daniel	1786	3rd great grand uncle of husband
Angst, Jacob	Abt. 1790	3rd great grand uncle of husband
Angst, John	1792	3rd great grand uncle of husband
Angst, John Daniel	December 14, 1749	4th great grandfather of husband
Angst, Juliana	1775	3rd great grand aunt of husband
Angst, Maria Elizabeth	November 11, 1776	3rd great grandmother of husband
Angst, William	1794	3rd great grand uncle of husband
Anna	1793	Wife of 2nd great grand uncle of husband
Arrison, Grace	1823	Wife of great grandfather of husband
Artz, Edgar Isaiah	1878	Husband of aunt of husband
Bast, Mary A	1833	Wife of great grandfather of husband
Batdorf, Myrtle Adeline	January 05, 1918	Self
Beedle, Edward	1863	Husband of grand aunt of husband
Bellis, Peter	1800	Husband of 2nd great grand aunt of husband
Benfield, Anna Maria Elizabeth	April 01, 1729	4th great grandmother of husband
Black, George	Abt. 1697	4th great grandfather of husband
Black, John	1735	3rd great grand uncle of husband
Black, Mary	1733	3rd great grand aunt of husband
Black, Mary	1737	3rd great grandmother of husband
Black, William	1739	3rd great grand uncle of husband
Bowman, Margaret	August 20, 1732	4th great grandmother of husband
Boyer, David Alfred	1860	Husband of grand aunt of husband
Braun, John Philip	August 17, 1697	4th great grandfather of husband
Braun, Peter	Abt. 1745	3rd great grandfather of husband
Brown		2nd great grand aunt of husband

Name:	Birth Date:	Relationship:
Brown		2nd great grand aunt of husband
Brown, Anna Maria	February 17, 1815	1st great grand aunt of husband
Brown, Catherine	Abt. 1747	3rd great grandmother of husband
Brown, Elizabeth	1830	1st great grand aunt of husband
Brown, John	1812	1st great grand uncle of husband
Brown, Jonas	Abt. 1790	2nd great grand uncle of husband
Brown, Mary Elizabeth		1st cousin 3x removed of husband
Brown, Mary Magdalena	1816	Great grandmother of husband
Brown, Peter	1775	2nd great grandfather of husband
Brown, Peter	1814	1st great grand uncle of husband
Brown, Philip	Abt. 1788	2nd great grand uncle of husband
Brown, Philip	1821	1st great grand uncle of husband
Brown, Robert	Abt. 1720	4th great grandfather of husband
Brown, William	1815	Husband of 2nd great grand aunt of husband
Brown, William	1818	1st great grand uncle of husband
Brucker, Anna Maria	Abt. 1723	4th great grandmother of husband
Catherine	Abt. 1760	Wife of 3rd great grand uncle of husband
Catherine	Abt. 1760	3rd great grandmother of husband
Catherine	1820	Wife of 1st great grand uncle of husband
Charlesworth, Blanche	1883	Wife of uncle of husband
Cleary, Living		Daughter-in-law
Cochran, Isabelle	February 07, 1699	4th great grandmother of husband
Coleman, Rosanna	1814	Wife of 2nd great grand uncle of husband
Cox, Almeda Ellen	1911	Wife of brother-in-law
Craig, Living		Wife of uncle of husband
Culp, Elizabeth	1842	1st great grand aunt of husband
Culp, Fielta	1848	1st great grand aunt of husband
Culp, Jonas	1839	1st great grand uncle of husband
Culp, Living		1st great grand aunt of husband
Culp, Living		1st great grand aunt of husband
Culp, Living		2nd great grand uncle of husband
Culp, Sarah "Salome" A	June 30, 1844	Great grandmother of husband
Curry, Living		Wife of grandson
Day, Sarah Elizabeth	1859	Wife of grand uncle of husband
Doebler, David S	1816	Husband of 1st great grand aunt of husband
Duncan, Living		Daughter-in-law
Elizabeth	1837	Wife of 1st great grand uncle of husband
Elizabeth	1839	Wife of 1st great grand uncle of husband

Name:	Birth Date:	Relationship:
Esther	1814	Wife of 2nd great grand uncle of husband
Eva, Maria	Abt. 1765	3rd great grandmother of husband
Evans, Margaret "Peggy"	1935	Daughter-in-law
Faust, Agnes A	1855	Wife of grand uncle of husband
Ferree, Margaret Rebecca	1810	Wife of 2nd great grand uncle of husband
Gabriell, Catherine		Wife of 4th great grandfather of husband
Goodman, Anna Maria	1848	Grand aunt of husband
Goodman, Catherine	1846	Grand aunt of husband
Goodman, George H	1853	Grand uncle of husband
Goodman, George?	Abt. 1800	1st great grand uncle of husband
Goodman, Jacob	1849	Grand uncle of husband
Goodman, Jane	1845	Grand aunt of husband
Goodman, John	1841	Grand uncle of husband
Goodman, John?	Abt. 1805	1st great grand uncle of husband
Goodman, Lydia Ann	February 20, 1856	Paternal grandmother of husband
Goodman, Magdalena	1839	Grand aunt of husband
Goodman, Mary	1843	Grand aunt of husband
Goodman, Michael	June 10, 1806	Great grandfather of husband
Goodman, Sarah "Sallie"	1844	Grand aunt of husband
Goodman, Susan	1837	Grand aunt of husband
Goodman, William	1835	Grand uncle of husband
Greene, Living		Husband of granddaughter
Greshammer, Louis A	1835	Husband of 1st great grand aunt of husband
Guise, Abraham?	Abt. 1740	3rd great grand uncle of husband
Guise, John Adam	Bet. 1756–1766	3rd great grandfather of husband
Guise, John?		3rd great grand uncle of husband
Guise, Living		2nd great grand uncle of husband
Guise, Mary A	December 16, 1791	2nd great grandmother of husband
Guise, Peter?		3rd great grand uncle of husband
Guise, Peter?	1795	2nd great grand uncle of husband
Guteman, Jacob	1780	2nd great grandfather of husband
Haas, Anna Sabina		Wife of 4th great grandfather of husband
Hamilton, Jean		4th great grandmother of husband
Hand, Christina "Dinah"	1835	Wife of grand uncle of husband
Harman, Maria Elizabeth	Abt. 1749	4th great grandmother of husband
Hautz?, Catherine		Wife of 1st great grand uncle of husband
Haverstick, Anna Maria		Wife of 1st great grand uncle of husband
Hawk, Elizabeth		Wife of grand uncle of husband
Helen		Wife of grand uncle of husband

Name:	Birth Date:	Relationship:
Hensel, Andrew Guise	February 18, 1831	Great grandfather of husband
Hensel, Andrew W	June 28, 1793	2nd great grandfather of husband
Hensel, Anna Catherine	Abt. 1862	Grand aunt of husband
Hensel, Anna Maria Barbara	1820	1st great grand aunt of husband
Hensel, Anne "Annie" Clarissa Workman	1866	Grand aunt of husband
Hensel, Arthur Preston	1886	Uncle of husband
Hensel, Augusta "Gussie" Mae	February 16, 1885	Mother-in-law
Hensel, Casper	Abt. 1735	4th great grandfather of husband
Hensel, Casper	Abt. 1790	2nd great grand uncle of husband
Hensel, Catherine	1768	3rd great grand aunt of husband
Hensel, Catherine	1792	2nd great grand aunt of husband
Hensel, Edna Boyer	March 30, 1905	Aunt of husband
Hensel, Elmer Elsworth	1891	Uncle of husband
Hensel, Emma	1866	Grand aunt of husband
Hensel, George	1777	3rd great grand uncle of husband
Hensel, George	1796	2nd great grand uncle of husband
Hensel, George	1825	1st great grand uncle of husband
Hensel, Helen Irene	1888	Aunt of husband
Hensel, Howard Andrew Carson	September 02, 1858	Maternal grandfather of husband
Hensel, Ira Sylvester	1856	Grand uncle of husband
Hensel, Jacob	Abt. 1773	3rd great grand uncle of husband
Hensel, Jacob	1795	2nd great grand uncle of husband
Hensel, John	1762	3rd great grand uncle of husband
Hensel, John	1824	1st great grand uncle of husband
Hensel, John Adam	1814	1st great grand uncle of husband
Hensel, John Casper	September 30, 1764	3rd great grandfather of husband
Hensel, John Henry William	1853	Grand uncle of husband
Hensel, Joseph Franklin	1854	Grand uncle of husband
Hensel, Lawrence	1766	3rd great grand uncle of husband
Hensel, Lawrence	Abt. 1791	2nd great grand uncle of husband
Hensel, Lillian "Lillie" Emma Susan	1864	Grand aunt of husband
Hensel, Lillian "Lillie" Verna	1889	Aunt of husband
Hensel, Living		Uncle of husband
Hensel, Living		Aunt of husband
Hensel, Living		Uncle of husband
Hensel, Living		Aunt of husband
Hensel, Living		Aunt of husband
Hensel, Maria Eva	1792	2nd great grand aunt of husband

Name:	Birth Date:	Relationship:
Hensel, Michael	Abt. 1770	3rd great grand uncle of husband
Hensel, Michael	1834	1st great grand uncle of husband
Hensel, Peter	Abt. 1770	3rd great grand uncle of husband
Hensel, Philip	Abt. 1770	3rd great grand uncle of husband
Hensel, Philip	Abt. 1800	2nd great grand uncle of husband
Hockley, Stephanie		Wife of grandson
Hoffman, Elizabeth		Wife of 3rd great grand uncle of husband
Houtz, "Cassie"	1841	Wife of grand uncle of husband
Houtz, Benjamin		Husband of grand aunt of husband
Houtz, Living		Husband of aunt of husband
Juliana	1841	Wife of 1st great grand uncle of husband
Keitchen, Agnes	August 1701	4th great grandmother of husband
Kimmel, Hiram		Husband of grand aunt of husband
King, John		Husband of 1st great grand aunt of husband
Knittle, Living		Husband of aunt of husband
Kulp, Jacob	Abt. 1802	2nd great grandfather of husband
Landis, Living		Wife of grandson
Layman, Elizabeth		3rd great grand aunt of husband
Layman, Henry		3rd great grand uncle of husband
Layman, Jacob		3rd great grand uncle of husband
Layman, John		3rd great grand uncle of husband
Layman, Joseph		3rd great grand uncle of husband
Layman, Martha		3rd great grand aunt of husband
Layman, Mary		3rd great grand aunt of husband
Layman, Rebecca		3rd great grand aunt of husband
Layman, Samuel		3rd great grand uncle of husband
Lehman, Jacob	1744	4th great grandfather of husband
Lehman, Susan	February 19, 1771	3rd great grandmother of husband
Living		Husband of granddaughter
Living		Daughter-in-law
Losch, Elisabeth Magdalena	1699	4th great grandmother of husband
M, Sarah	1810	Wife of 2nd great grandfather of husband
Magdelena, Anna	Abt. 1760	Wife of 3rd great grandfather of husband
Malcolm, Janet	Abt. 1690	4th great grandmother of husband
Maria, Anna	1810	Wife of 1st great grand uncle of husband
Maria?	Abt. 1765	3rd great grandmother of husband
Mary	Abt. 1765	3rd great grandmother of husband
Mary	1826	Wife of 1st great grand uncle of husband
Mason, Elizabeth	May 15, 1709	4th great grandmother of husband
Matter, Elva May	1911	Wife of brother-in-law

Name:	Birth Date:	Relationship:
Matter, John Michael		Husband of 3rd great grand aunt of husband
McCracken, Jordan		Great grandson
McCracken, Kacie Jo		Great granddaughter
McCracken, Kristina		Great granddaughter
McCracken, Mark		Husband of granddaughter
McCracken, Noah James		Great grandson
McCracken, Trista		Great granddaughter
McGough, Charles John	1881	Husband of aunt of husband
McLeran, Margaret	1816	Wife of 1st great grand uncle of husband
Miller, Elizabeth	Abt. 1775	Wife of 3rd great grand uncle of husband
Miller, Martha		Wife of 3rd great grand uncle of husband
Miller, William	1813	Husband of 1st great grand aunt of husband
Moffatt, Agnes	1740	3rd great grand aunt of husband
Moffatt, Agnes	1745	3rd great grand aunt of husband
Moffatt, Allison	1738	3rd great grand aunt of husband
Moffatt, Andrew	1728	3rd great grand uncle of husband
Moffatt, Christina	December 11, 1731	3rd great grandmother of husband
Moffatt, David	September 14, 1700	4th great grandfather of husband
Moffatt, Helen	1729	3rd great grand aunt of husband
Moffatt, Henry	1734	3rd great grand uncle of husband
Moffatt, John	1736	3rd great grand uncle of husband
Moses, Mary Margaret	1850	Wife of paternal grandfather of husband
Moyer, Susan	1833	Wife of 1st great grand uncle of husband
Muckle, Margaret	November 05, 1756	3rd great grandmother of husband
Muckle, Thomas	February 15, 1718/19	4th great grandfather of husband
Penman, Alexander	October 24, 1820	1st great grand uncle of husband
Penman, Anna		Wife of 1st great grand uncle of husband
Penman, Anne	June 13, 1809	1st great grand aunt of husband
Penman, Catherine	July 12, 1802	1st great grand aunt of husband
Penman, David	December 31, 1775	2nd great grandfather of husband
Penman, Elizabeth	February 22, 1807	1st great grand aunt of husband
Penman, Isabelle Stoddart	May 09, 1816	Great grandmother of husband
Penman, James	Abt. 1719	4th great grandfather of husband
Penman, James	October 12, 1811	1st great grand uncle of husband
Penman, John	April 08, 1747	3rd great grandfather of husband

Name:	Birth Date:	Relationship:
Penman, John	April 18, 1798	1st great grand uncle of husband
Penman, Margaret	July 20, 1800	1st great grand aunt of husband
Penman, Miriam		1st great grand aunt of husband
Penman, Robert	December 11, 1824	1st great grand uncle of husband
Pennypacker, Martha	1746	4th great grandmother of husband
Potteiger, Living		Wife of grandson
Powell, George		Husband of grand aunt of husband
Reedy, U	Abt. 1780	Husband of 2nd great grand aunt of husband
Remp, Barbara		Wife of great grandfather of husband
Rendall, Living		2nd great granddaughter
Rendall, Living		Husband of great granddaughter
Rickert, Barbara Ellen	1807	Wife of 2nd great grand uncle of husband
Romano, Living		Wife of grandson
Romberger, Adam	1775	3rd great grand uncle of husband
Romberger, Anna Catherine	1777	3rd great grand aunt of husband
Romberger, Anna Maria	1771	3rd great grand aunt of husband
Romberger, Balthasar	July 05, 1747	3rd great grandfather of husband
Romberger, Henry	1773	3rd great grand uncle of husband
Romberger, Jacob	1806	2nd great grand uncle of husband
Romberger, John Balthaser	May 04, 1716	4th great grandfather of husband
Romberger, Joseph	1811	2nd great grand uncle of husband
Romberger, Salome	1808	2nd great grand aunt of husband
Romberger, Samuel	1803	2nd great grand uncle of husband
Romberger, Susan	April 16, 1799	2nd great grandmother of husband
Russell, James	Abt. 1730	3rd great grand uncle of husband
Russell, Janet	December 21, 1766	2nd great grandmother of husband
Russell, John	Abt. 1690	4th great grandfather of husband
Russell, Living		2nd great grand aunt of husband
Russell, Mary		Wife of 2nd great grand uncle of husband
Russell, Mary	Abt. 1755	2nd great grand aunt of husband
Russell, William		Husband of 2nd great grand aunt of husband
Russell, William	September 28, 1725	3rd great grandfather of husband
Russell, William	Abt. 1755	2nd great grand uncle of husband
Sassaman, Emmanuel	1827	Husband of 1st great grand aunt of husband
Schneck		2nd great grand uncle of husband
Schneck		2nd great grand uncle of husband

Name:	Birth Date:	Relationship:
Schneck, Elizabeth	August 13, 1805	2nd great grandmother of husband
Schneck, Living		2nd great grand uncle of husband
Schneck, Peter	Abt. 1765	3rd great grandfather of husband
Schreckengast?, Anna Maria	June 15, 1795	2nd great grandmother of husband
Semrow, Loretta	1900	Wife of uncle of husband
Shadel, Henry L	1865	Husband of grand aunt of husband
Shannon, Living		Husband of granddaughter
Sidnam	1824	Wife of 1st great grand uncle of husband
Sikora, Living U		Husband of granddaughter
Sikora, Living		Great granddaughter
Sikora, Living		Great granddaughter
Singer, Henry	1825	Husband of 1st great grand aunt of husband
Smink, Isaac	1828	Husband of 1st great grand aunt of husband
Smith, Mary Helen	Abt. 1707	4th great grandmother of husband
Snoke	Abt. 1780	Husband of 2nd great grand aunt of husband
Sophia	1835	Wife of 1st great grand uncle of husband
St. Thompson, Living		Granddaughter
Sterner, Catherine	1890	Wife of uncle of husband
Sterner, Living		Husband of aunt of husband
Stoddart, David	May 19, 1754	3rd great grandfather of husband
Stoddart, Elizabeth	January 05, 1779	2nd great grandmother of husband
Stoddart, James	1767	3rd great grand uncle of husband
Stoddart, John	December 25, 1728	4th great grandfather of husband
Susan	1790	Wife of 2nd great grand uncle of husband
Susan	1838	Wife of 1st great grand uncle of husband
Susan	1882	Wife of uncle of husband
Swab, Catherine "Kate"	1788	Wife of 2nd great grand uncle of husband
Swartz, David	1816	Husband of 1st great grand aunt of husband
Thompson, Abel Franklin	October 19, 1910	Brother-in-law
Thompson, Abel Robert	November 28, 1880	Father-in-law
Thompson, Alexander	October 22, 1805	Great grandfather of husband
Thompson, Alexander F	1845	Grand uncle of husband
Thompson, Anna	1779	2nd great grand aunt of husband
Thompson, Benjamin	1874	Uncle of husband
Thompson, Blanche	1883	Aunt of husband
Thompson, Christina	1792	1st great grand aunt of husband

Name:	Birth Date:	Relationship:
Thompson, David Penman	1837	Grand uncle of husband
Thompson, Elizabeth	1763	2nd great grand aunt of husband
Thompson, Elizabeth	1841	Grand aunt of husband
Thompson, Eugene Robert	August 07, 1937	Son
Thompson, George	1773	2nd great grand uncle of husband
Thompson, George	1835	Grand uncle of husband
Thompson, George W	1802	1st great grand uncle of husband
Thompson, Grissel	1737	3rd great grand aunt of husband
Thompson, Harper Bruce	September 28, 1907	Husband
Thompson, Helen	1761	2nd great grand aunt of husband
Thompson, Helen	1767	2nd great grand aunt of husband
Thompson, Isabelle	1719	3rd great grand aunt of husband
Thompson, Isabelle	1761	2nd great grand aunt of husband
Thompson, Isabelle	1849	Grand aunt of husband
Thompson, Jacobina	1744	3rd great grand aunt of husband
Thompson, James	1725	3rd great grand uncle of husband
Thompson, James C	1851	Grand uncle of husband
Thompson, James Smith	1811	1st great grand uncle of husband
Thompson, Janet "Jennie"	1844	Grand aunt of husband
Thompson, John	1728	3rd great grand uncle of husband
Thompson, John	1804	1st great grand uncle of husband
Thompson, John	1808	1st great grand uncle of husband
Thompson, Living		Granddaughter
Thompson, Living		Uncle of husband
Thompson, Living		Great granddaughter
Thompson, Living		Granddaughter
Thompson, Living		Great granddaughter
Thompson, Living		Grandson
Thompson, Living		Aunt of husband
Thompson, Living		Great granddaughter
Thompson, Living		Great grandson
Thompson, Living		Great granddaughter
Thompson, Living		Granddaughter
Thompson, Living		Son
Thompson, Living		Great grandson
Thompson, Living		Grandson
Thompson, Living		Son
Thompson, Living		Great grandson
Thompson, Living		Great grandson
Thompson, Living		Granddaughter

Name:	Birth Date:	Relationship:
Thompson, Living		Great grandson
Thompson, Lydia Mae	February 07, 1914	Sister-in-law
Thompson, M		Grandson
Thompson, Margaret	1721	3rd great grand aunt of husband
Thompson, Mary	1741	3rd great grand aunt of husband
Thompson, Mary	1764	2nd great grand aunt of husband
Thompson, Mary	1775	2nd great grand aunt of husband
Thompson, Mary	1800	1st great grand aunt of husband
Thompson, Nicole	1777	2nd great grand aunt of husband
Thompson, Oliver Charles	1875	Uncle of husband
Thompson, Robert	June 27, 1771	2nd great grandfather of husband
Thompson, Robert	1795	1st great grand uncle of husband
Thompson, Robert	1836	Grand uncle of husband
Thompson, Robert Bruce	September 24, 1847	Paternal grandfather of husband
Thompson, Virginia D	1905	Sister-in-law
Thompson, Wilbur Clark	1906	Brother-in-law
Thompson, William	1797	1st great grand uncle of husband
Thompson, William W	1839	Grand uncle of husband
Thomson, Robert	October 25, 1695	4th great grandfather of husband
Thomson, Robert	September 13, 1734	3rd great grandfather of husband
Trovinger, Elizabeth	Abt. 1798	2nd great grandmother of husband
Tutto, Nancy	1938	Daughter-in-law
Underkoffler, Living		Husband of aunt of husband
Updegroff, John William	February 24, 1732	4th great grandfather of husband
Updegrove	Abt. 1802	2nd great grand uncle of husband
Updegrove, Anna	1807	2nd great grand aunt of husband
Updegrove, Anna M	1864	Grand aunt of husband
Updegrove, Anna Magdalena	March 09, 1759	3rd great grand aunt of husband
Updegrove, Catherine	1833	1st great grand aunt of husband
Updegrove, Clara Matilda	November 30, 1866	Maternal grandmother of husband
Updegrove, Conrad	November 27, 1771	3rd great grandfather of husband
Updegrove, Daniel	June 28, 1839	Great grandfather of husband
Updegrove, Edward Isaac	November 27, 1771	3rd great grand uncle of husband
Updegrove, Elizabeth	1803	2nd great grand aunt of husband
Updegrove, Ellen	Abt. 1812	Wife of 1st great grand uncle of husband

Name:	Birth Date:	Relationship:
Updegrove, Frances	September 10, 1756	3rd great grand aunt of husband
Updegrove, Jacob	1827	1st great grand uncle of husband
Updegrove, John Adam	1761	3rd great grand uncle of husband
Updegrove, John J	1835	1st great grand uncle of husband
Updegrove, John M	March 23, 1805	2nd great grandfather of husband
Updegrove, Nancy	1838	1st great grand aunt of husband
Updegrove, Nellie	1811	2nd great grand aunt of husband
Updegrove, Nora Jane	1874	Grand aunt of husband
Updegrove, Peter	May 01, 1766	3rd great grand uncle of husband
Updegrove, Rebecca	1847	1st great grand aunt of husband
Updegrove, Sarah	1809	2nd great grand aunt of husband
Updegrove, Solomon	1809	2nd great grand uncle of husband
Updegrove, Solomon	1845	1st great grand uncle of husband
Updegrove, William Henry	1870	Grand uncle of husband
Voller, Catherine	1780	2nd great grandmother of husband
Walter, Maria Salome	Abt. 1730	4th great grandmother of husband
White, Lavinia Eva	1890	Wife of uncle of husband
Wilson, Elizabeth		Wife of 1st great grand uncle of husband
Wilson, Isabelle	Abt. 1720	4th great grandmother of husband
Wilson, James		Husband of 1st great grand aunt of husband
Wittle, Living		Wife of grandson
Workman, ?		1st great grand uncle of husband
Workman, Benjamin	1787	2nd great grand uncle of husband
Workman, Carolina	1831	1st great grand aunt of husband
Workman, Catherine	May 17, 1838	Great grandmother of husband
Workman, Elizabeth	1829	1st great grand aunt of husband
Workman, Jacob		2nd great grand uncle of husband
Workman, Jacob	1819	1st great grand uncle of husband
Workman, James		2nd great grand uncle of husband
Workman, John		2nd great grand uncle of husband
Workman, John	1823	1st great grand uncle of husband
Workman, Joseph	December 03, 1795	2nd great grandfather of husband
Workman, Joseph R	1836	1st great grand uncle of husband
Workman, Nancy	1826	1st great grand aunt of husband
Workman, Susan	1821	1st great grand aunt of husband
Yohe, John F	1887	Husband of aunt of husband
Zimmerman, Peter	1808	Husband of 2nd great grand aunt of husband

Outline Descendant Report for Martin Batdorf

1 Martin Batdorf b: 1726 in Chester Co, PA
... + Barbara Elizabeth Saltzegber b: 1738 in Berks Co., PA, m: Abt. 1756 in Lancaster?, PA
......2 Eva Batdorf b: 1757
...... + Peter Kister
......2 John Michael Batdorf b: 1758
...... + Catherine Emmerich
......2 Maria Elizabeth Batdorf b: 1760
......2 John Adam Batdorf b: 1762
...... + Susan Merkey
......2 Martin Batdorf b: 1763
...... + Wendelina Ebrecht
......2 Maria Barbara Batdorf b: 1766
......2 George Peter Batdorf b: February 11, 1768 in Lancaster Co, PA, d: Bet. 1830–1840 in OH; PA
...... + Barbara Weiss b: Abt. 1772 in PA, m: Abt. 1792 in Dauphin?, PA, d: Aft. 1830 in OH; PA
.........3 Jacob Peter Batdorf b: Abt. 1793 in PA, d: 1829 in Dauphin Co, PA
.... + Maria Catherine Steiner b: Abt. 1790 in Berks Co, PA, m: February 20, 1813 in Christ Lutheran, Stouchsburg, Berks Co, PA, d: Abt. 1840 in Dauphin Co, PA
............4 Peter Batdorf b: January 20, 1814 in Dauphin Co, PA, d: December 05, 1880 in Lykens, Dauphin Co, PA
.... + Elizabeth Welker b: November 23, 1812 in Dauphin Co?, PA, m: Abt. 1831 in Dauphin Co, PA, d: July 07, 1868 in Dauphin Co, PA
...............5 Esther Batdorf b: 1836 in PA
...............5 Jonas Batdorf b: 1837 in PA
.... + Lucetta Rickert b: 1840, d: 1867
..................6 Sarah Batdorf b: 1857 in PA
..................6 John Henry Batdorf b: 1858 in PA
.... + Amelia b: 1858 in PA
.....................7 Harry Batdorf b: 1886 in PA
.....................7 Elsie Batdorf b: 1891 in PA
.....................7 Elizabeth "Bessie" Batdorf b: 1891 in PA
..................6 Edward Franklin Batdorf b: 1859
..................6 Anna Rebecca Batdorf b: 1863
.... + Peter Adam Matter
.....................7 Ralph Matter b: 1886
.... + Caroline McLean
........................8 Living Matter
.....................7 Minnie Eva Matter b: 1887
.... + James Alfred Haas
........................8 Margaret I Haas
........................8 Betty Haas
.....................7 Anne "Annie" Vergie Matter b: 1889
.... + Harper C Hochlander
.....................7 Living Matter
.... + Living Burrell
........................8 Living Matter

........................8 Living Matter
.....................7 Clayton Isiah Matter b: 1891
.....................7 Mary Amelia Matter b: 1892
.... + William Clayton Sauser b: 1889
........................8 Living Sauser
.....................7 Living Matter
.... + Living Klinger
........................8 Living Matter
........................8 Living Matter
........................8 Living Matter
........................8 Living Matter
........................8 Living Matter
........................8 Living Matter
.....................7 Living Matter
.....................7 Living Matter
.....................7 Living Matter
..................6 Amanda Ellen Batdorf b: 1866
...............5 Elizabeth Batdorf b: 1839 in PA
.... + Joseph Russell b: 1836, d: 1901
..................6 James Russell b: 1869
..................6 Frank L Russell b: 1871
.... + <No name> b: 1871
.....................7 Living Russell
.....................7 Living Russell
.....................7 Living Russell
..................6 Henry Russell b: 1872
..................6 "Maggie" Russell b: 1873
..................6 "Katie" Russell b: 1875
..................6 Emma E Russell b: 1877
..................6 Living Russell
...............5 Susan Batdorf b: 1842 in PA
.... + Miller
...............5 John Batdorf b: 1844 in PA
.... + Sarah Miller b: 1842 in PA
..................6 Living Batdorf
..................6 Living Batdorf
..................6 Living Batdorf
..................6 Living Batdorf
..................6 Living Batdorf
..................6 Living Batdorf
..................6 Catherine "Kate" Batdorf b: 1876 in PA
..................6 Mary E Batdorf b: 1879 in PA
...............5 Sarah Batdorf b: 1845 in PA
.... + James H Smith b: 1845, d: 1904
..................6 Daniel Smith b: 1869
..................6 Ida Sevilla Smith b: 1870
..................6 James Harvey Smith b: 1871
..................6 Living Smith
..................6 Living Smith
..................6 Mary Smith b: 1874
..................6 Samuel Smith b: 1876
..................6 Living Smith

..................6 John Smith b: 1879
...............5 Peter S Batdorf b: 1848 in PA
.... + Mary Elizabeth Sierer b: 1853 in PA
..................6 Living Batdorf
..................6 Mary Margaret Batdorf b: 1882 in PA
..................6 Arthur "Ardie" Clayton Batdorf b: 1885 in PA
..................6 Peter Clay Batdorf b: 1887 in PA
.... + Rosalie b: 1892 in PA
.....................7 Living Batdorf
.....................7 Living Batdorf
..................6 Living Batdorf
..................6 Living Batdorf
..................6 Living Batdorf
..................6 Emma Batdorf b: 1875 in PA
..................6 Edmond Batdorf b: 1879
...............5 Anna Batdorf b: Abt. 1850 in PA
...............5 Rebecca Batdorf b: Abt. 1850 in PA
...............5 Thomas Edward Batdorf b: July 02, 1851 in Big Run, Dauphin Co, PA, d: August 13, 1916 in Elizabethville, Dauphin Co, PA; Mitral insufficiency & Bright's disease (ie, Chronic inflammation) of kidneys w/
.... + Mary Louisa Peters b: March 31, 1858 in Dauphin Co, PA, m: December 06, 1874 in Rev. W.G. Engle, Dauphin Co, PA, d: August 03, 1924 in Home, Elizabethville, Dauphin Co, PA; Cerebral hemorrhage
..................6 George Batdorf b: 1875 in PA, d: 1881
..................6 Kirby Batdorf b: 1877 in PA, d: 1881
..................6 John Batdorf b: September 07, 1878 in PA, d: January 1968 in Annville, Lebanon Co, PA
..................6 William Batdorf b: 1880 in PA
.... + <No name> b: 1874 in PA
..................6 Mary Ellen Batdorf b: 1881 in PA, d: 1963
..................6 Adam Scorvella Batdorf b: 1882 in PA, d: 1952
.... + Caroline "Carrie" May Boyer b: 1884 in PA, d: 1973
.....................7 Helen Alotta Batdorf b: 1911 in PA, d: 1973
..................6 James "Edward" Batdorf b: February 15, 1885 in Loyalton, Dauphin Co, PA, d: August 19, 1954 in Home, Lykens, Dauphin Co, PA; Coronary occlusion w/hypertension w/diabetes mellitus
.... + Beulah Irene Wert b: December 31, 1889 in Elizabethville, Dauphin Co, PA, m: February 08, 1908 in Oakdale Church, Dauphin Co, PA, d: June 10, 1983 in Dr. Convalescence Center, Selinsgrove, Snyder Co, PA; Acute congestive cardiac failure w/poss. brain stem CVA & ASCVD
.....................7 Alvin Leroy Batdorf b: 1908 in PA, d: 1972
.... + Margaret Elizabeth Marlow b: 1908 in PA, d: 2004 in PA
........................8 George Batdorf b: Abt. 1930, d: 2008
.... + Cleo d: 1989
........................8 Living Batdorf
.... + Ted Boyer d: Abt. 1990
.....................7 Margaret Irene Batdorf b: December 05, 1909 in PA, d: December 1990 in Wiconisco, Dauphin Co, PA
.... + Albert Forrest Kohler b: 1908, d: 1991
........................8 Living Kohler
.... + Forrest Knorr d: Abt. 1990
........................8 Living Kohler
.... + Living Harmon
.....................7 Mildred Catherine Batdorf b: 1912 in PA, d: June 2010 in Herndon, Dauphin Co., PA

.... + Thomas Randall Moon d: 1960
.........................8 Living Moon
.... + Living Gunderman
............................9 Living Moon
.... + Thomas Posevec
............................9 Living Moon
.... + Jeffery McCurdy
.........................8 Living Moon
.... + Theodore Sawruk d: January 2012
............................9 Living Sawruk
.... + Donna M Golden
.........................8 Thomas L Moon b: Abt. 1940, d: 2008
.... + Phyllis Latshaw
............................9 Rita K Moon
............................9 Thomas A Moon
.........................8 Living Moon
.... + Living Metcalf
............................9 Living Metcalf
............................9 Living Metcalf
.........................8 Living Moon
.... + Living McKee
............................9 Living McKee
.... + Mary Roddy
............................9 Living McKee
.... + Robert Rycrost
............................9 Living McKee
.... + Wendy Goodwin
.... + Amy Snyder
............................9 Living McKee
.... + Scott Schulman
.... + Living Schwalm
.........................8 Living Moon
......................7 Harry Franklin Batdorf b: July 21, 1912 in PA, d: August 1977 in Lykens, Dauphin Co, PA
.... + Grace Naomi Hoy b: 1915, d: 1962
.........................8 Donald Batdorf b: Abt. 1940, d: 1997
.... + Cynthia
.........................8 Living Batdorf
.... + Living Sgrignoli
............................9 Living Sgrignoli
......................7 Myrtle Adeline Batdorf b: January 05, 1918 in Big Run, Dauphin Co, PA, d: May 08, 1983 in Polyclinic Hospital, Harrisburg, Dauphin Co, PA; Cardiorespiratory arrest w/ASHD w/pacemaker
.... + Harper Bruce Thompson b: September 28, 1907 in Sheridan, Schuylkill Co, PA, m: June 15, 1935 in St. Johns (Hill) Lutheran, Lykens, Dauphin Co, PA, d: July 23, 1981 in Polyclinic Hospital, Harrisburg, Dauphin Co, PA; Cardiorespiratory arrest w/subdural hematoma
.........................8 Living Thompson
.... + Living Duncan
............................9 M Thompson
.... + Living Curry
.... + Living Romano
.... + Living Wittle
............................9 Living St. Thompson

.... + Living Shannon
...........................9 Living Thompson
.... + Living
........................8 Eugene Robert Thompson b: August 07, 1937 in PA, d: March 21, 2007 in Harrisburg, Dauphin Co, PA
.... + Margaret "Peggy" Evans b: 1935, d: July 31, 2005
...........................9 Living Thompson
.... + Living Potteiger
.... + Stephanie Hockley
........................8 Living Thompson
.... + Nancy Tutto b: 1938, d: 1988
...........................9 Living Thompson
.... + Living Sikora U
.... + Living Cleary
...........................9 Living Thompson
.... + Mark McCracken
...........................9 Living Thompson
.... + Living Greene
...........................9 Living Thompson
.... + Living Landis
.... + Living
.....................7 Ruth E Batdorf b: April 29, 1923 in PA, d: August 16, 2006 in Ridgeway, Elk Co, PA
.... + Claude M Reed b: 1921, d: 1986
........................8 Linda Reed b: Abt. 1950, d: 1997
.... + Stiely
.....................7 Romaine Batdorf b: May 24, 1925 in PA, d: July 1981 in Lykens, Dauphin Co, PA
.... + Clarence "Bess" D Messner b: 1925, d: 2005
........................8 Living Messner
.... + Living Baker
........................8 Living Messner
........................8 Clarence "Butch" D Messner b: Abt. 1950, d: 1997
..................6 Oscar Newton Batdorf b: August 15, 1886 in Loyalton, Dauphin Co, PA, d: August 1981 in Sarasota, Sarasota Co, FL
.... + Mabel Susan Elizabeth Motter b: 1887 in PA
.....................7 Living Batdorf
.... + Living Coleman
........................8 Living Batdorf
.....................7 Robert L Batdorf b: 1921 in PA, d: 1967
.... + Ruth Webb
........................8 Sandra L Batdorf
........................8 Kay E Batdorf
........................8 Richard P Batdorf
.....................7 Living Batdorf
.... + Living Rudy
........................8 Living Rudy
........................8 Living Rudy
..................6 Frances I Batdorf b: 1887 in PA
.... + Samuel W Lentz b: 1886, d: 1940
.....................7 Galen Leroy Lentz b: 1908, d: 1977
.... + Living Weaver
.....................7 Russell Lentz b: 1912, d: 2003 in PA
.....................7 Mary Emaline Lentz b: 1917, d: 2005 in PA

.... + George Franklin Laudenslager b: 1901, d: 1983 in PA
..................6 Joseph Warren Batdorf b: 1888 in Elizabethtown, Dauphin Co, PA, d: 1928
..................6 Harvey Clarence Batdorf b: 1891 in Loyalton, Dauphin Co, PA, d: 1949
.... + Living Bahney
.....................7 Living Batdorf
.... + Ruth Irene Koppenhaver b: 1914, d: 2007 in PA
.....................7 Living Batdorf
.... + Robert Elmer Hoke b: 1911, d: 1981
.....................7 Living Batdorf
.... + Living Blair
.....................7 Living Batdorf
.....................7 Living Batdorf
..................6 Cora Annette Batdorf b: April 18, 1892 in PA, d: May 1981 in Harrisburg, Dauphin Co, PA
.... + Herbert Eugene Buffington b: 1888, d: 1959
.....................7 Herman Eugene Buffington b: 1912, d: 1981
.....................7 Elwood Franklin Buffington b: 1914, d: 1996 in PA
.....................7 Living Buffington
.....................7 Ernest Edgar Buffington b: 1916, d: 1986
.....................7 Edward Arthur Buffington b: 1919, d: 1991
.....................7 Harold Herbert Buffington b: 1921, d: 1995 in PA
.... + Verna May Schwalm b: 1910, d: 1984 in PA
.....................7 Living Buffington
.....................7 Jay Lester Buffington b: 1924, d: 2001
.... + Grace Naomi Hilbert b: 1928, d: 2007 in PA
.....................7 Living Buffington
.....................7 Living Buffington
.... + Living Harner
.....................7 Living Buffington
.....................7 Living Buffington
.... + Living Uhler
.....................7 Living Buffington
.....................7 Living Buffington
.....................7 Living Buffington
.....................7 Living Buffington
.....................7 Living Buffington
..................6 Stella Louisa Batdorf b: 1893 in PA, d: 1981
.... + Paul
.....................7 Living Paul
.... + Lafayette DeWees b: 1883, d: 1981
.....................7 Donald T DeWees b: 1916 in PA, d: 1984 in PA
.....................7 Living DeWees
.....................7 Living DeWees
.....................7 Living DeWees
.....................7 Lawrence DeWees b: 1929, d: 1972
..................6 Verna A Batdorf b: June 02, 1899 in PA, d: December 1992 in Sherman Oaks, Los Angeles Co, CA
.... + Leon Washington Shultz b: 1890
.....................7 Richard C Shultz b: 1918, d: 1991
.....................7 Living Shultz
.... + Living Dugan
.....................7 Living Shultz
.... + Living Peck

..................6 Living Batdorf
..................6 Norman Batdorf b: 1896 in PA, d: 1896
..................6 Alvin Thomas Batdorf b: 1898 in PA, d: 1898
...............5 Louisa Batdorf b: 1854 in PA
.... + William Frantz b: Abt. 1850
..................6 William Amos Frantz b: 1872
.... + Matilda
.....................7 William Frantz b: 1891
.....................7 Benjamin Frantz b: 1891
.....................7 Living Frantz
.....................7 Living Frantz
.... + Magdalena "Mollie" Lettich b: 1829, d: 1891
...............5 Emma Batdorf b: 1875 in PA
...............5 Edward H Batdorf b: 1877 in PA
............4 Sarah Batdorf b: 1815 in PA
............4 John Batdorf b: 1817 in PA
............4 Catherine Batdorf b: 1818 in PA
............4 Thomas Batdorf b: 1820 in PA
.... + <No name> b: 1823 in PA
...............5 Matilda Batdorf b: 1842
...............5 Amanda Batdorf b: 1846
...............5 Mary Jane Batdorf b: 1846
...............5 Sarah Batdorf b: 1848
............4 Jonathan Batdorf b: 1822 in PA
............4 Daniel Batdorf b: 1824 in PA
.... + Christina Zimmerman b: 1826 in PA
...............5 Alfred E Batdorf b: 1848
.... + Mary Jane Rickett b: 1852, d: 1933
...............5 Sarah Batdorf b: 1850 in PA
...............5 Thomas Batdorf b: 1855 in PA
.... + Emma E b: 1854 in PA
..................6 Charles H Batdorf b: 1879 in PA
...............5 Clara Batdorf b: 1856 in PA
...............5 Christina Batdorf b: 1858 in PA
...............5 Daniel Batdorf b: 1861 in PA
...............5 Elsworth Batdorf b: 1862 in PA
...............5 Alice Batdorf b: 1865 in PA
...............5 Grant Batdorf b: 1868 in PA
...............5 Emma Batdorf b: 1872 in PA
...............5 Elmer E Batdorf b: 1874 in PA
............4 Jacob Batdorf b: 1826 in PA
.... + Rosanna b: 1828 in PA
............4 Elizabeth Batdorf b: 1828 in PA
.........3 John Batdorf b: 1794 in PA
.... + Catherine Daniels b: 1795
............4 Jacob Batdorf b: 1817
............4 John Batdorf b: 1818
............4 William Batdorf b: 1820
............4 Elizabeth Batdorf b: 1822
............4 Jonathan Batdorf b: 1824
............4 Juliana Batdorf b: 1826
............4 Catherine Batdorf b: 1828

............4 Lavinia Batdorf b: 1831
.........3 Catherine Batdorf b: 1796 in PA
.........3 Christina Batdorf b: 1799 in PA
.........3 Eva Batdorf b: 1802 in PA
.........3 Christian Batdorf b: 1803 in PA
.... + Sarah b: 1805 in PA
............4 Peter Batdorf b: 1826 in PA
............4 Christian Batdorf b: 1830 in PA
.... + Sarah Rose b: 1830 in Prussia, Germany
...............5 Mary J Batdorf b: 1853
...............5 Sarah A Batdorf b: 1856
...............5 John Batdorf b: 1866
............4 Amos Batdorf b: 1831 in PA
.... + Susan Stiffler b: 1828 in PA
...............5 Andrew Batdorf b: 1856
...............5 Matilda Batdorf b: 1858
...............5 Anna "Annie" Batdorf b: 1861
...............5 Rose Mary Batdorf b: 1865
.... + William Henry Messner b: 1868
..................6 Living Messner
.... + Living Shomper
.....................7 Living Messner
.....................7 Living Messner
..................6 Maude Pauline Messner b: 1890
.... + James B Keen b: 1880
..................6 Harvey Adam Messner b: 1892 in PA
.... + Verna b: 1885 in PA
.....................7 Living Messner
.....................7 Living Messner
.....................7 Living Messner
.....................7 Kenneth Messner b: 1922 in PA, d: 1992
..................6 Living Messner
.... + Living Kaufman
..................6 Living Messner
.... + Living Clouser
.....................7 Living Messner
..................6 Living Messner
..................6 Living Messner
.... + Living Taylor
...............5 George A Batdorf b: 1871
............4 Henry Batdorf b: 1835 in PA
.... + Lucinda b: 1836 in PA
...............5 Charles L Batdorf b: 1858
...............5 Sidney M Batdorf b: 1860 ; U
...............5 James H Batdorf b: 1863 in PA
...............5 Robert M Batdorf b: 1865 in PA
............4 Elizabeth Batdorf b: 1838 in PA
............4 Amanda Batdorf b: 1841 in PA
............4 Daniel Batdorf b: 1842 in PA
............4 Philip Batdorf b: 1844 in PA
.........3 John Jacob Batdorf b: 1805 in PA
.... + Christina Bush

Chapter Five

Our family's calendar.

Important annual dates of birth, marriage and death.

January 2014

January 2014

S	M	T	W	T	F	S
			1	2	3	4
5	6	7	8	9	10	11
12	13	14	15	16	17	18
19	20	21	22	23	24	25
26	27	28	29	30	31	

February 2014

S	M	T	W	T	F	S
						1
2	3	4	5	6	7	8
9	10	11	12	13	14	15
16	17	18	19	20	21	22
23	24	25	26	27	28	

Sunday	Monday	Tuesday	Wednesday	Thursday	Friday	Saturday
			1 Frances and John Miller John J. Wirth	2 Adeline Row Wert	3	4
5 Myrtle A. Batdorf Thompson Mary A. Swartz Peters	6	7	8 Michael Garman Francis ". Rowe	9	10 Anna M.E. Deibler Schupp	11 Valentine Welker
12	13	14	15	16	17	18
19	20 Peter Batdorf John G. Schupp	21	22	23 Maria M. and John W.G. Traut	24 Maria C. and Francis ". Rowe Maria C. Traut Rowe	25
26 Anna G. and Christian Gruber	27	28	29	30	31	

February 2014

February 2014

S	M	T	W	T	F	S
						1
2	3	4	5	6	7	8
9	10	11	12	13	14	15
16	17	18	19	20	21	22
23	24	25	26	27	28	

March 2014

S	M	T	W	T	F	S
						1
2	3	4	5	6	7	8
9	10	11	12	13	14	15
16	17	18	19	20	21	22
23	24	25	26	27	28	29
30	31					

Sunday	Monday	Tuesday	Wednesday	Thursday	Friday	Saturday
						1
2 Margaret and John Faber	3	4	5	6	7 John Faber	8 Beulah I. and James ". Batdorf
9	10	11 George P. Batdorf	12 Anna M. Miller Schupp	13	14	15 James ". Batdorf Susan Gieseman Frantz Catherine Guerne Joray
16	17	18	19 Anna M. and John W. Gieseman	20 Maria C. and Jacob P. Batdorf	21	22
23	24 Catherine Shoop Wert	25	26	27	28	

March 2014

March 2014

S	M	T	W	T	F	S
						1
2	3	4	5	6	7	8
9	10	11	12	13	14	15
16	17	18	19	20	21	22
23	24	25	26	27	28	29
30	31					

April 2014

S	M	T	W	T	F	S
		1	2	3	4	5
6	7	8	9	10	11	12
13	14	15	16	17	18	19
20	21	22	23	24	25	26
27	28	29	30			

Sunday	Monday	Tuesday	Wednesday	Thursday	Friday	Saturday
						1
2	3 George W. Gieseman	4	5	6 Adeline Row Wert	7	8
9	10	11	12	13	14	15
16	17	18	19 Abraham Joray	20	21 Eugene R. Thompson	22
23 Susan Frantz Row John W. Gieseman Susan Sheets Keck	24	25	26	27	28	29
30 John Faber	31 Mary L. Peters Batdorf					

April 2014

April 2014

S	M	T	W	T	F	S
		1	2	3	4	5
6	7	8	9	10	11	12
13	14	15	16	17	18	19
20	21	22	23	24	25	26
27	28	29	30			

May 2014

S	M	T	W	T	F	S
				1	2	3
4	5	6	7	8	9	10
11	12	13	14	15	16	17
18	19	20	21	22	23	24
25	26	27	28	29	30	31

Sunday	Monday	Tuesday	Wednesday	Thursday	Friday	Saturday
		1 David M. Wert	2	3	4	5 Sarah E. Faber Wert
6	7	8 Anna B. Overcash Rudy	9 Frances Kerstetter Miller	10	11 Barbara Rudy Rowe	12
13	14 Maria ".M. Rudy Faber	15	16	17	18 Anna M.E. Deibler Schupp	19
20	21	22	23	24	25	26
27	28	29	30			

May 2014

May 2014

S	M	T	W	T	F	S
				1	2	3
4	5	6	7	8	9	10
11	12	13	14	15	16	17
18	19	20	21	22	23	24
25	26	27	28	29	30	31

June 2014

S	M	T	W	T	F	S
1	2	3	4	5	6	7
8	9	10	11	12	13	14
15	16	17	18	19	20	21
22	23	24	25	26	27	28
29	30					

Sunday	Monday	Tuesday	Wednesday	Thursday	Friday	Saturday
				1	2	3
4	5 John Wertz	6	7	8 Myrtle A. Batdorf Thompson	9	10
11	12	13 John Wertz	14	15	16	17
18	19	20	21	22	23	24
25 Sarah E. Faber Wert	26	27	28	29	30 Anna G. Stupp Gruber	31

June 2014

June 2014

S	M	T	W	T	F	S
1	2	3	4	5	6	7
8	9	10	11	12	13	14
15	16	17	18	19	20	21
22	23	24	25	26	27	28
29	30					

July 2014

S	M	T	W	T	F	S
		1	2	3	4	5
6	7	8	9	10	11	12
13	14	15	16	17	18	19
20	21	22	23	24	25	26
27	28	29	30	31		

Sunday	Monday	Tuesday	Wednesday	Thursday	Friday	Saturday
1	2	3	4	5	6	7
8 Catherine Shoop Wert	9	10 Beulah I. Wert Batdorf	11	12 Anna M. Gruber Gieseman	13	14
15 Myrtle A. and Harper B. Thompson	16	17 John H. Wolfskiel	18	19	20	21
22	23	24 John D. Wertz	25	26	27	28
29	30 Anna M. and John G. Sheetz					

July 2014

July 2014

S	M	T	W	T	F	S
		1	2	3	4	5
6	7	8	9	10	11	12
13	14	15	16	17	18	19
20	21	22	23	24	25	26
27	28	29	30	31		

August 2014

S	M	T	W	T	F	S
					1	2
3	4	5	6	7	8	9
10	11	12	13	14	15	16
17	18	19	20	21	22	23
24	25	26	27	28	29	30
31						

Sunday	Monday	Tuesday	Wednesday	Thursday	Friday	Saturday
		1	2 Thomas E. Batdorf	3	4	5
6	7 Elizabeth Welker Batdorf	8	9	10 Daniel Row	11	12
13	14	15 John Faber	16 Maria ".M. Rudy Faber Anna M. Wolfkill Sheetz	17	18	19
20 Jacob Wert	21	22	23 Harper B. Thompson	24 Anna M. Miller Schupp	25	26
27	28	29	30	31 Margaret ". Evans Thompson Daniel Row		

August 2014

August 2014						
S	M	T	W	T	F	S
					1	2
3	4	5	6	7	8	9
10	11	12	13	14	15	16
17	18	19	20	21	22	23
24	25	26	27	28	29	30
31						

September 2014						
S	M	T	W	T	F	S
	1	2	3	4	5	6
7	8	9	10	11	12	13
14	15	16	17	18	19	20
21	22	23	24	25	26	27
28	29	30				

Sunday	Monday	Tuesday	Wednesday	Thursday	Friday	Saturday
					1 John Shoop	2 Joanna C. Garman Wertz Anna M. Gruber Gieseman Anna S. Miller Wirth
3 Mary L. Peters Batdorf Eva E. and John A. Wirth	4 John G. Schupp	5	6 Catherine and Abraham Joray	7 Eugene R. Thompson	8	9 Mary A. Swartz Peters
10 John Welker	11	12	13 Thomas E. Batdorf	14	15	16 Susan Sheets Keck
17	18	19 James ". Batdorf	20	21	22	23 John A. Wirth
24	25 John A. Wirth	26 John W. Gieseman	27 John G. Schupp	28	29	30
31						

September 2014

September 2014

S	M	T	W	T	F	S
	1	2	3	4	5	6
7	8	9	10	11	12	13
14	15	16	17	18	19	20
21	22	23	24	25	26	27
28	29	30				

October 2014

S	M	T	W	T	F	S
			1	2	3	4
5	6	7	8	9	10	11
12	13	14	15	16	17	18
19	20	21	22	23	24	25
26	27	28	29	30	31	

Sunday	Monday	Tuesday	Wednesday	Thursday	Friday	Saturday
	1	2	3	4	5	6
7	8	9	10	11	12	13
14	15	16	17	18	19	20
21	22	23 Joanna C. Garman Wertz	24	25	26 Eva and Andrew Messerschmidt	27
28 Anna B. Overcash Rudy Harper B. Thompson	29	30				

October 2014

October 2014						
S	M	T	W	T	F	S
			1	2	3	4
5	6	7	8	9	10	11
12	13	14	15	16	17	18
19	20	21	22	23	24	25
26	27	28	29	30	31	

November 2014						
S	M	T	W	T	F	S
						1
2	3	4	5	6	7	8
9	10	11	12	13	14	15
16	17	18	19	20	21	22
23	24	25	26	27	28	29
30						

Sunday	Monday	Tuesday	Wednesday	Thursday	Friday	Saturday
			1	2 Andrew Messerschmidt	3	4 Margaret Rudy Faber
5	6 Susan and Adam Frantz	7	8	9	10	11
12	13	14	15	16 John D. Wertz	17 Susan Frantz Row	18 Christian Gruber
19	20	21	22 Anna Maria Peters Anna S. Miller Wirth	23	24	25
26	27	28	29	30 John H. Wert	31	

November 2014

November 2014

S	M	T	W	T	F	S
						1
2	3	4	5	6	7	8
9	10	11	12	13	14	15
16	17	18	19	20	21	22
23	24	25	26	27	28	29
30						

December 2014

S	M	T	W	T	F	S
	1	2	3	4	5	6
7	8	9	10	11	12	13
14	15	16	17	18	19	20
21	22	23	24	25	26	27
28	29	30	31			

Sunday	Monday	Tuesday	Wednesday	Thursday	Friday	Saturday
						1
2	3 John H. Wolfskiel	4	5	6	7	8
9	10 Susan Gieseman Frantz	11 John Welker	12	13	14 Christian Gruber	15
16	17	18	19	20	21	22
23 Elizabeth Welker Batdorf	24	25	26	27	28	29
30						

December 2014

December 2014						
S	M	T	W	T	F	S
	1	2	3	4	5	6
7	8	9	10	11	12	13
14	15	16	17	18	19	20
21	22	23	24	25	26	27
28	29	30	31			

January 2015						
S	M	T	W	T	F	S
				1	2	3
4	5	6	7	8	9	10
11	12	13	14	15	16	17
18	19	20	21	22	23	24
25	26	27	28	29	30	31

Sunday	Monday	Tuesday	Wednesday	Thursday	Friday	Saturday
	1	2	3	4	5 Peter Batdorf	6 Mary L. and Thomas E. Batdorf
7	8	9 David M. Wert	10	11	12 Anna C. and George W. Gieseman	13 John Shoop
14	15 Barbara Rudy Rowe	16 Jonas Rudy	17	18 Margaret Rudy Faber	19	20 Jonas Rudy
21 Anna G. Stupp Gruber	22	23 John H. Wert	24	25 Catherine Guerne Joray	26	27
28	29	30	31 Beulah I. Wert Batdorf			

Chapter Six

The Sources Report, Postscript, Afterword and Author's Bio.

Source Report

Source Title: **A Potrait of Our Ancestors**

Citation: A Potrait of Our Ancestors, Jury, vol I, I.P. Baker, 1983, rev. 1986, Selby Publishing, Kokomo, IN, 46902.

Guerne, Catherine
- Marr: August 06, 1743 in Moutier, Berne, Switzerland
- Burial: 1785 in St. Davids (Salem) Reformed, Millersburg, Dauphin Co, PA

Joray, Abraham
- Marr: August 06, 1743 in Moutier, Berne, Switzerland
- Occu: 1784; Constable
- Res: 1771 in Upper Paxton, Lancaster (Dauphin) Co, PA
- Res: Bet. 1778–1782 in Wiconisco, Lancaster (Dauphin) Co, PA
- Birth: March 19, 1718 in Belphrahon, Berne, Switzerland
- Baptism: March 20, 1718 in Moutier, Berne, Switzerland
- Burial: 1785 in St. Davids (Salem) Reformed, Millersburg, Dauphin Co, PA
- Will: September 22, 1785 in Upper Paxton, Dauphin Co, PA
- Occu: 1779; Overseer of Poor

Citation: A Potrait of Our Ancestors, Names of Foreigners Who Took the Oath of Allegiance, 1727-1755, Jury, vol I, I.P. Baker, 1983, rev. 1986, Selby Publishing, Kokomo, IN, 46902.

Joray, Abraham
- Naturl: September 14, 1754

Citation: A Potrait of Our Ancestors.

Batdorf, George Peter
- Birth: February 11, 1768 in Lancaster Co, PA

Source Title: **Abraham Joray**

Citation: Abraham Joray, FHL, Pedigree chart, www.familysearch.org.

Guerne, Catherine
- Marr: August 06, 1743 in Moutier, Berne, Switzerland
- Birth: December 25, 1720 in Eschert, Berne, Switzerland

Joray, Abraham
- Marr: August 06, 1743 in Moutier, Berne, Switzerland
- Birth: March 19, 1718 in Belphrahon, Berne, Switzerland

Citation: Abraham Joray, Passenger and Immigration Lists Index, 1500-1900, myfamily.com, P. William Filby, ancestry.com.

Joray, Abraham
- Immigr: September 14, 1754 in Switzerland to USA (ship Nancy)

Source Title: **Abraham Jury**

Citation: Abraham Jury, Renee Waring, reneelwaring@@aol.com.

Guerne, Catherine
- Marr: August 06, 1743 in Moutier, Berne, Switzerland

Joray, Abraham
- Marr: August 06, 1743 in Moutier, Berne, Switzerland

Source Title: **Abraham Shora**

Citation: Abraham Shora, February 15, 1785, September 22, 1785, Will Abstracts, Dauphin Co, PA, p 22.

Joray, Abraham

Source Title: **Abraham Shora (con't)**

Citation: Abraham Shora, February 15, 1785, September 22, 1785, Will Abstracts, Dauphin Co, PA, p 22.

Joray, Abraham

Will: September 22, 1785 in Upper Paxton, Dauphin Co, PA

Source Title: **Abraham Shorah**

Citation: Abraham Shorah, Probate files, 1785, Bk B, p297, file 3, Dauphin County Courthouse, Reg of Wills, Deborah Hershey, Elizabethtown, PA, Mar 2008.

Joray, Abraham

Occu: 1785; Yeoman

Will: September 22, 1785 in Upper Paxton, Dauphin Co, PA

Source Title: **Abraham Zora**

Citation: Abraham Zora, Renee Waring, reneelwaring@@aol.com.

Joray, Abraham

Immigr: September 14, 1754 in Switzerland to USA (ship Nancy)

Naturl: September 14, 1754

Source Title: **Abram Joray**

Citation: Abram Joray, Comprehensive Hostory of the town of Gratz, PA, p50, Elsie Eaves, EKEaves@@cox.net.

Joray, Abraham

Res: Abt. 1755 in Dauphin Co, PA

Citation: Abram Joray, PA Census, 1772-1890, Philadelphia, PA, www.ancestry.com.

Joray, Abraham

Res: 1754 in Philadelphia, PA

Source Title: **Adam Faber**

Citation: Adam Faber, Baptismal records of Rev. John Casper Stoever, PAGenWeb Lebanon County, PA, Church Records, c/o Mildred Smith.

Faber, John

Baptism: March 18, 1750 in Lancaster (Lebanon) Co?, PA

Source Title: **Adam Frantz**

Citation: Adam Frantz, Dauphin County, Pennnsylavnia, 1800-55, St. Peters (Hoffmans) Church, Lykens, Dauphin Co, PA, www.ancestry.com.

Frantz, Adam

Relgn: Bet. 1816–1819; St. Peters (Hoffmans) Church, Lykens, Dauphin Co, PA

Citation: Adam Frantz, Frantz family, Onetree, ancestry.com.

Frantz, Adam

Birth: 1780 in Lykens, Lancaster (Dauphin) Co, PA

Citation: Adam Frantz, War of 1812 Records, DDC, 1999-, www.ancestry.com.

Frantz, Adam

Miltry: Bet. September 02, 1814–March 05, 1815; War of 1812, Private, 2nd Reg PA Militia (Ritschers), 1st Brig (York, Capt. Philip Fetterhoff)

Source Title: **Adam Wirth**

Citation: Adam Wirth, Baptismal records of Rev. John Casper Stoever, PAGenWeb Lebanon County, PA, Church Records, c/o Mildred Smith.

Wirth, John Adam

Res: Bet. 1755–1763 in Derry, Lancaster (Lebanon) Co, PA

Source Title: **Adeline Row**

Citation: Adeline Row, St. John Evangelical Lutheran Church, Berrysburg, PA, Sara S. Neagley, Elizabethville, PA.

Row, Adeline
- Birth: January 02, 1860 in Dauphin Co, PA
- Baptism: March 11, 1860 in St. Johns (Hill) Lutheran, Berrysburg, Dauphin Co, PA

Source Title: **Ancestors of Richard Alan Lebo**

Citation: Ancestors of Richard Alan Lebo, The Schupp/Shoop Line, Richard A. Lebo, aqua.dev.uga.edu/~lebo.

Deibler, Anna Maria Elizabeth
- Birth: January 10, 1760 in Millersburg, Lancaster (Dauphin) Co, PA
- Burial: 1840 in Old Salem (Werts) Lutheran, Millersburg, Dauphin Co, PA

Miller, Anna Margaret
- Death: July 24, 1857 in Dauphin Co, PA

Schupp, John George
- Census: 1850 in Mifflin, Dauphin Co, PA
- Birth: May 1780 in Upper Paxton, Lancaster (Dauphin) Co, PA
- Res: Abt. 1852 in Alleghenyville, Berks Co, PA

Schupp, John George
- Birth: August 04, 1759 in Upper Paxton, Lancaster (Dauphin) Co, PA
- Death: August 27, 1839 in Millersburg, Dauphin Co, PA
- Baptism: September 01, 1759 in Trinity Lutheran, New Holland, Lancaster Co, PA
- Burial: 1839 in Old Salem (Werts) Lutheran, Millersburg, Dauphin Co, PA
- Res: Abt. 1770 in Earl, Lancaster Co, PA

Source Title: **Andreas Messerschmidt**

Citation: Andreas Messerschmidt, Direct Descendants of Andreas Messerschmidt, Evelyn S. Hartman.

Messerschmidt, Andrew
- Marr: September 26, 1779 in Christ Lutheran, Stouchsburg, Berks Co, PA

Schrot, Eva
- Marr: September 26, 1779 in Christ Lutheran, Stouchsburg, Berks Co, PA

Citation: Andreas Messerschmidt, Immigrants to Pennsylvania, vol 1, ancestry.com.

Messerschmidt, Andrew
- Immigr: September 16, 1751 in Germany to USA (ship Nancy)

Citation: Andreas Messerschmidt, PA Census, 1772-1890, Philadelphia, PA, www.ancestry.com.

Messerschmidt, Andrew
- Res: 1751 in Philadelphia, PA

Citation: Andreas Messerschmidt, Passenger and Immigration Lists Index, 1500-1900, myfamily.com, P. William Filby, ancestry.com.

Messerschmidt, Andrew
- Immigr: September 16, 1751 in Germany to USA (ship Nancy)

Source Title: **Andreas Messersmith**

Citation: Andreas Messersmith, Revolutionary War Military Abstract Card File, PA State Archives, www.digitalarchives.state.pu.us/archive.

Messerschmidt, Andrew
- Miltry: 1776; American Revolution, Private 1st PA Reg, Rifle (Lancaster, Capt. Peter Grubb)

Source Title: **Andrew Messerschmidt**

Citation: Andrew Messerschmidt, Probate files, 1801, Dauphin County Courthouse, Reg of Wills, Deborah Hershey, Elizabethtown, PA, Mar 2008.

Messerschmidt, Andrew

Prob: 1801 in Dauphin Co, PA (listed in index only)

Source Title: **Anna Catherine Heck**

Citation: Anna Catherine Heck, Family Data Collection, Individual Records, www.ancestry.com.

Heck, Anna Catherine

Birth: 1723 in Tulpehocken, Chester (Berks) Co, PA

Source Title: **Anna Guniunda Gubern**

Citation: Anna Guniunda Gubern, Probate file, 1799, unnumbered original papers, 9pp, Berks Co Courthouse, Berks, PA, Norman Nicol, Apr 2008.

Stupp, Anna Gunigunda

Death: May 30, 1799 in Bernville, Tulpehocken, Berks Co, PA

Prob: Bet. June 04–14 1799 in Tulpehocken, Berks Co, PA

Will: November 09, 1796 in Tulpehocken, Berks Co, PA

Source Title: **Anna Kinugonda Stupp**

Citation: Anna Kinugonda Stupp, A Forest of family Trees, www.siteservers.net/family/default.aspx.

Gruber, Christian

Marr: January 26, 1742 in Rev. Stoever, Christ (Little Tulpehocken) Lutheran, Bernville, Lancaster (Berks) Co, PA

Stupp, Anna Gunigunda

Marr: January 26, 1742 in Rev. Stoever, Christ (Little Tulpehocken) Lutheran, Bernville, Lancaster (Berks) Co, PA

Source Title: **Anna Margaretha Gruber**

Citation: Anna Margaretha Gruber, Old Northkill records, c/o Rene, rene@@hurstlandscaping.com.

Gruber, Anna Margaret

Baptism: April 16, 1759 in Old Northkill, Berks Co, PA

Source Title: **Anna Margaretha Miller**

Citation: Anna Margaretha Miller, April 18, 1784, Northumberland Co County, PA 1777-1854, Stone Valley Lutheran, www.ancestry.com.

Miller, Anna Margaret

Birth: February 12, 1784 in Lancaster (Dauphin) Co, PA

Baptism: April 18, 1784 in Dalmatia, Northumberland Co, PA

Source Title: **April's Ancestors**

Citation: April's Ancestors, April Moss, Moss.bunch@@verizon.net, awt.ancestry.com.

Rowe, Francis "Frank"

Marr: January 24, 1764 in Trinity Lutheran, New Holland, Lancaster Co, PA

Birth: Abt. 1745 in Strasburg, Lancaster Co, PA

Traut, Maria Catherine

Marr: January 24, 1764 in Trinity Lutheran, New Holland, Lancaster Co, PA

Birth: January 24, 1748 in Paradise, Lancaster, PA

Source Title: **Baddorf Family**

Citation: Baddorf Family, Gratz History, p 193.

Batdorf, Jacob Peter

Source Title: **Baddorf Family (con't)**

Citation: Baddorf Family, Gratz History, p 193.

Batdorf, Jacob Peter
Death: 1829 in Dauphin Co, PA

Batdorf, Peter
Birth: January 20, 1814 in Dauphin Co, PA
Death: December 05, 1880 in Lykens, Dauphin Co, PA
Burial: 1880 in St. Peters (Hoffman) Reformed, Loyalton, Dauphin Co, PA

Steiner, Maria Catherine
Res: Bet. 1832–1833 in Dauphin Co, PA

Welker, Elizabeth
Birth: November 23, 1812 in Dauphin Co?, PA
Death: July 07, 1868 in Dauphin Co, PA
Burial: 1868 in St. Peters (Hoffman) Reformed, Loyalton, Dauphin Co, PA

Source Title: **Baddorf household**

Citation: Baddorf household, 1810 United States Federal Census, Dauphin Co, PA, ancestry.com & Microfilm, PA State Library, Hbg, PA.

Batdorf, George Peter
Census: 1810 in Heidelberg, Dauphin Co, PA

Citation: Baddorf household, 1820 United States Census, Dauphin Co, PA, PA State library microfilm.

Weiss, Barbara
Census: 1820 in husband; Lykens, Dauphin Co, PA w

Citation: Baddorf household, 1830 United States Census, Dauphin Co, PA, ancestry.com & Microfilm, PA State Library, Hbg, PA.

Steiner, Maria Catherine
Census: 1830 in Lykens, Dauphin Co, PA

Citation: Baddorf household, 1830 United States Census, Dauphin Co, PA, PA State library microfilm.

Batdorf, George Peter
Census: 1830 in Lykens, Dauphin Co, PA

Steiner, Maria Catherine
Census: 1830 in Lykens, Dauphin Co, PA
Census: 1820 in husband; Lykens, Dauphin Co, PA w

Weiss, Barbara
Census: 1830 in husband; Lykens, Dauphin Co, PA w

Citation: Baddorf household, 1870 United States Census, Dauphin Co, PA, ancestry.com & Microfilm, PA State Library, Hbg, PA.

Batdorf, Thomas Edward
Census: 1870 in Berrysburg, Dauphin Co, PA (Wise)
Occu: 1870; Apprentice to Blacksmith

Citation: Baddorf household, 1870 United States Census, Dauphin Co, PA, PA State library microfilm.

Batdorf, Peter
Census: 1870 in Lykens, Dauphin Co, PA

Citation: Baddorf household, 1870 United States Census, Dauphin Co, PA, PA State library microfilm.

Batdorf, Peter
Propty: 1870 in $1000 + $400

Citation: Baddorf household, 1880 United States Census, Dauphin Co, PA, FHL 1255124, Film T9-1124, p 246A, www.familysearch.org.

Source Title: Baddorf household (con't)

Citation: Baddorf household, 1880 United States Census, Dauphin Co, PA, FHL 1255124, Film T9-1124, p 246A, www.familysearch.org.

Batdorf, Thomas Edward
Census: 1880 in Washington, Dauphin Co, PA
Occu: 1880; Laborer

Peters, Mary Louisa
Occu: 1880; Keeping house

Source Title: Badorf Jr household

Citation: Badorf Jr household, 1820 United States Census, Dauphin Co, PA, ancestry.com & Microfilm, PA State Library, Hbg, PA.

Batdorf, Jacob Peter
Census: 1820 in Lykens, Dauphin Co, PA

Citation: Badorf Jr household, 1820 United States Census, Dauphin Co, PA, PA State Library microfilm.

Batdorf, Jacob Peter
Census: 1820 in Lykens, Dauphin Co, PA

Source Title: Badorf Sr household

Citation: Badorf Sr household, 1820 United States Census, Dauphin Co, PA, ancestry.com & Microfilm, PA State Library, Hbg, PA.

Batdorf, George Peter
Census: 1820 in Lykens, Dauphin Co, PA

Source Title: Barbara Rowe

Citation: Barbara Rowe, St. John Evangelical Lutheran Church, Berrysburg, PA, Sara S. Neagley, Elizabethville, PA, 424 6M 24D.

Rudy, Barbara
Burial: 1881 in St. Johns (Hill) Lutheran, Berrysburg, Dauphin Co, PA

Source Title: Barr Genealogy & Related Families

Citation: Barr Genealogy & Related Families, The Gieseman Family, pp 29-67, Rev Ed, Ira R. Barr.

Gieseman, George William
Immigr: October 26, 1741 in Germany to USA (ship Snow Mollie)
Will: May 1761 in Tulpehocken, Berks Co, PA

Source Title: Batdorf data

Citation: Batdorf data, Ancestor Chart for John Batdorf 1812 Vet, Early record sof Batdorf Family, Arthur Batdorf & Associ., YCHS verticle files.

Batdorf, George Peter
Birth: February 11, 1768 in Lancaster Co, PA

Batdorf, Martin
Birth: 1726 in Chester Co, PA

Saltzegber, Barbara Elizabeth
Birth: 1738 in Berks Co., PA

Source Title: Batdorf Family information

Citation: Batdorf Family information, Mildred Moon, Herndon, PA.

Batdorf, James "Edward"
Occu: Abt. 1925; Miner (Lykens Coal Co)

Peters, Mary Louisa
Relgn: Evangelical Church

Source Title: **Batdorf Family information (con't)**

Citation: Batdorf Family information, Mildred Moon, Herndon, PA.

Row, Adeline

Occu: Abt. 1900; Owned farm

Relgn: Lutheran

Citation: Batdorf Family information, Virginia Faust.

Batdorf, Peter

Birth: January 20, 1814 in Dauphin Co, PA

Death: December 05, 1880 in Lykens, Dauphin Co, PA

Baptism: February 27, 1814 in St. Peters (Hoffman) Reformed, Loyalton, Dauphin Co, PA

Burial: 1880 in St. Peters (Hoffman) Reformed, Loyalton, Dauphin Co, PA

Batdorf, Thomas Edward

Birth: July 02, 1851 in Big Run, Dauphin Co, PA

Peters, Mary Louisa

Birth: March 31, 1858 in Dauphin Co, PA

Death: August 03, 1924 in Home, Elizabethville, Dauphin Co, PA; Cerebral hemorrhage

Welker, Elizabeth

Birth: November 23, 1812 in Dauphin Co?, PA

Death: July 07, 1868 in Dauphin Co, PA

Source Title: **Batdorf household**

Citation: Batdorf household, 1820 United States Census, Dauphin Co, PA, ancestry.com & Microfilm, PA State Library, Hbg, PA.

Batdorf, Peter

Census: 1820 in father; Lykens, Dauphin Co, PA w

Citation: Batdorf household, 1830 United States Census, Dauphin Co, PA, ancestry.com & Microfilm, PA State Library, Hbg, PA.

Batdorf, George Peter

Census: 1830 in Lykens, Dauphin Co, PA

Batdorf, Peter

Census: 1830 in mother; Lykens, Dauphin Co, PA w

Citation: Batdorf household, 1840 United States Census, Dauphin Co, PA, ancestry.com & Microfilm, PA State Library, Hbg, PA.

Batdorf, Peter

Census: 1840 in Lykens, Dauphin Co, PA

Citation: Batdorf household, 1840 United States Census, Dauphin Co, PA, PA State library microfilm.

Batdorf, Peter

Census: 1840 in Lykens, Dauphin Co, PA

Citation: Batdorf household, 1880 United States Census, Dauphin Co, PA, Roll T9-1124, p 57A, ED 106, Image 0924, ancestry.com & Microfilm, PA State Library, Hbg, PA.

Batdorf, Peter

Census: 1880 in Lykens, Dauphin Co, PA

Occu: 1880; Farmer

Citation: Batdorf household, 1900 United States Census, Dauphin Co, PA, ancestry.com & Microfilm, PA State Library, Hbg, PA.

Batdorf, James "Edward"

Occu: 1910; Miner (coal miner)

Citation: Batdorf household, 1900 United States Census, Dauphin Co, PA, ancestry.com & Microfilm, PA State Library, Hbg, PA.

Source Title: **Batdorf household (con't)**

Citation: Batdorf household, 1900 United States Census, Dauphin Co, PA, ancestry.com & Microfilm, PA State Library, Hbg, PA.

Batdorf, James "Edward"

Census: 1910 in Washington, Dauphin Co, PA

Citation: Batdorf household, 1910 United States Census, Dauphin Co, PA, ED 120, Sheet 6, ancestry.com & Microfilm, PA State Library, Hbg, PA.

Batdorf, Thomas Edward

Res: 1910 in W. Main St., Elizabethville, Dauphin Co, PA

Citation: Batdorf household, 1910 United States Census, Dauphin Co, PA, ED 120, Sheet 6, ancestry.com & Microfilm, PA State Library, Hbg, PA.

Batdorf, Thomas Edward

Census: 1910 in Elizabethville, Dauphin Co, PA

Occu: 1910; Retired laborer

Citation: Batdorf household, 1920 United States Census, Dauphin Co, PA, Roll T625 1559, p 3A, ED 148, Image 1081, ancestry.com & Microfilm, PA State Library, Hbg, PA.

Batdorf, James "Edward"

Occu: 1920; Miner (Coal mine)

Res: 1920 in State Road 199, Washington Tp., Dauphin Co, PA

Wert, Beulah Irene

Occu: 1920; Dressmaker (at home)

Citation: Batdorf household, 1920 United States Census, Dauphin Co, PA, Roll T625 1559, p 3A, ED 148, Image 1081, ancestry.com & Microfilm, PA State Library, Hbg, PA.

Batdorf, James "Edward"

Census: 1920 in Washington, , PA

Batdorf, Myrtle Adeline

Census: 1920 in Washington, Dauphin Co, PA

Citation: Batdorf household, 1920 United States Census, Dauphin Co, PA, T625 1557, p 10a, ED 53, Image 0812, ancestry.com & Microfilm, PA State Library, Hbg, PA.

Peters, Mary Louisa

Res: 1920 in Main St., Elizabethville, Dauphin Co, PA

Citation: Batdorf household, 1920 United States Census, Dauphin Co, PA, T625 1557, p 10a, ED 53, Image 0812, ancestry.com & Microfilm, PA State Library, Hbg, PA.

Peters, Mary Louisa

Census: 1920 in Elizabethville, Dauphin Co, PA

Citation: Batdorf household, 1930 United States Census, , PA, Roll T626 2027, p 19A, ED 76, Image 0959, ancestry.com & Microfilm, PA State Library, Hbg, PA.

Batdorf, James "Edward"

Census: 1930 in Lykens, Dauphin Co, PA

Citation: Batdorf household, 1930 United States Census, Dauphin Co, PA, Roll T626 2027, p 19A, ED 76, Image 0959, ancestry.com & Microfilm, PA State Library, Hbg, PA.

Batdorf, James "Edward"

Res: 1930 in 480 North St., Lykens, Dauphin Co, PA

Propty: 1930 in $4500

Batdorf, Myrtle Adeline

Educ: 1930; School

Citation: Batdorf household, 1930 United States Census, Dauphin Co, PA, Roll T626 2027, p 19A, ED 76, Image 0959, ancestry.com & Microfilm, PA State Library, Hbg, PA.

Batdorf, James "Edward"

Occu: 1930; Laborer (Coal washery)

Batdorf, Myrtle Adeline

Census: 1930 in Lykens, Dauphin Co, PA

Source Title: **Batdorf household (con't)**

Citation: Batdorf household, 1940 US Federal census, James E Batdorf, Snyder, PA, www.ancestry.com.

Batdorf, James "Edward"

Census: 1940 in Lykens, Dauphin Co, PA

Wert, Beulah Irene

Census: 1940 in Lykens, Dauphin Co, PA

Source Title: **Batdorf-Wert marriage record**

Citation: Batdorf-Wert marriage record, Church record, Rev. O.S. Moyer, Angie Eddy, Maple Grove Cemetery, Elizabethville, PA, p 16.

Batdorf, James "Edward"

Marr: February 08, 1908 in Oakdale Church, Dauphin Co, PA

Occu: 1908; Miner

Wert, Beulah Irene

Marr: February 08, 1908 in Oakdale Church, Dauphin Co, PA

Source Title: **Batrdorf household**

Citation: Batrdorf household, 1830 United States Census, Dauphin Co, PA, ancestry.com & Microfilm, PA State Library, Hbg, PA.

Steiner, Maria Catherine

Census: 1830 in Lykens, Dauphin Co, PA

Source Title: **Beulah Batdorf**

Citation: Beulah Batdorf, June 1983, PA, Social Security Death Index, www.familysearch.org.

Wert, Beulah Irene

Res: 1983 in Big Run, Coaldale, Erdman, Germantown, Loyalton, Lykens, Specktown, all Dauphin Co, PA

Death: June 10, 1983 in Dr. Convalescence Center, Selinsgrove, Snyder Co, PA; Acute congestive cardiac failure w/poss. brain stem CVA & ASCV

SSN: 1983; 162-22-1417

Source Title: **Beulah I Batdorf**

Citation: Beulah I Batdorf, Obituary, Harrisburg Patriot News, 1983.

Wert, Beulah Irene

Death: June 10, 1983 in Dr. Convalescence Center, Selinsgrove, Snyder Co, PA; Acute congestive cardiac failure w/poss. brain stem CVA & ASCV

Funrl: 1983 in Schultz Funeral Home, 406 Market St., Lykens, Dauphin Co, PA

Relgn: 1983; St. Christopher Evangelical Lutheran Church

Citation: Beulah I Batdorf, Social Seurity numident record, application for SS-5, SSA, Nov 2006, Baltimore, MD.

Wert, Beulah Irene

Res: 1956 in Harrisburg, Dauphin Co, PA

Source Title: **Beulah I Batdorf death certificate**

Citation: Beulah I Batdorf death certificate, #0506188, #057537, June 1983, Department of Vital records, New Castle, PA.

Wert, Beulah Irene

Occu: 1983; Seamstress (Clothing)

Res: 1983 in 800 Broad St., Selinsgrove, Snyder Co, PA 17870

Birth: December 31, 1889 in Elizabethville, Dauphin Co, PA

Death: June 10, 1983 in Dr. Convalescence Center, Selinsgrove, Snyder Co, PA; Acute congestive cardiac failure w/poss. brain stem CVA & ASCV

Source Title: **Beulah I Batdorf death certificate (con't)**

Citation: Beulah I Batdorf death certificate, #0506188, #057537, June 1983, Department of Vital records, New Castle, PA.

Wert, Beulah Irene

Burial: June 14, 1983 in Calvary United Methodist, Wiconisco, Dauphin Co, PA

Funrl: 1983 in Schultz Funeral Home, 406 Market St., Lykens, Dauphin Co, PA

SSN: 1983; 162-22-1417

Source Title: **Bodorff household**

Citation: Bodorff household, 1860 United States Census, Dauphin Co, PA, ancestry.com & Microfilm, PA State Library, Hbg, PA.

Batdorf, Peter

Census: 1860 in Lykens, Dauphin Co, PA

Propty: 1860 in $900 + $250

Batdorf, Thomas Edward

Census: 1860 in Lykens, Dauphin Co, PA

Educ: 1860; School

Source Title: **Bordorf household**

Citation: Bordorf household, 1900 United States Census, Dauphin Co, PA, T623 1401, p 76, ED 39, sheet 10B, ancestry.com & Microfilm, PA State Library, Hbg, PA.

Batdorf, James "Edward"

Census: 1900 in Washington, Dauphin Co, PA

Occu: 1900; Day laborer

Batdorf, Thomas Edward

Census: 1900 in Washington, Dauphin Co, PA

Occu: 1900; Coal miner

Source Title: **Bottorff household**

Citation: Bottorff household, 1850 United States Census, Dauphin Co, PA, Roll M432-775, [age 399, Image 363, ancestry.com & Microfilm, PA State Library, Hbg, PA.

Batdorf, Peter

Census: 1850 in Lykens, Dauphin Co, PA

Occu: Bet. 1850–1870; Carpenter

Propty: 1850 in $500

Source Title: **Cather Gissemenen**

Citation: Cather Gissemenen, 1767 Pennsylvania Tax Lists, http://freepages.genealogy.rootsweb.com/~genbel/sept/patowshp1767.htm.

Heck, Anna Catherine

Relgn: 1767; Tulpehocken, Berks Co, PA

Source Title: **Catherine Wert**

Citation: Catherine Wert, Probate files, 1880, A-3, Dauphin County Courthouse, Reg of Wills, Deborah Hershey, Elizabethtown, PA, Mar 2008.

Shoop, Catherine

Prob: June 23, 1880 in Dauphin Co, PA (listed in index only)

Source Title: **Christian Gruber**

Citation: Christian Gruber, 1732, 18th Century Emigrants from German-speaking Lands to North America, A. Kunselman, Birdsboro, PA, Volume 1, 1983, p 461, www.genealogy.com.

Gruber, Christian

Source Title: Christian Gruber (con't)

Citation: Christian Gruber, 1732, 18th Century Emigrants from German-speaking Lands to North America, A. Kunselman, Birdsboro, PA, Volume 1, 1983, p 461, www.genealogy.com.

Gruber, Christian

Immigr: September 30, 1732 in Germany to USA (ship Dragon)

Citation: Christian Gruber, Baptismal records of Rev. John Casper Stoever, PAGenWeb Lebanon County, PA, Church Records, c/o Mildred Smith.

Gruber, Christian

Res: Bet. 1743–1759 in Northkill, PA

Citation: Christian Gruber, Berks County Register of Wills, http://www.berksregofwills.com/Berks_estate_1_search.asp.

Gruber, Christian

Will: July 07, 1780 in Tulpehocken, Berks Co, PA

Citation: Christian Gruber, Biographies from Historical & Biographical Annals, Morton Montgomery, p392, Line of Christian Gruber, www.roostweb.com/~paberks/books/montgomery/g16.html.

Gruber, Christian

Res: Now Jefferson Tp, Berks Co, PA

Burial: 1781 in Christ (Little Tulpehocken) Lutheran, Old Graveyard, Bernville, Berks Co, PA

Naturl: April 10, 1760

Stupp, Anna Gunigunda

Burial: 1799 in Christ (Little Tulpehocken) Lutheran, Old Graveyard, Bernville, Berks Co, PA

Citation: Christian Gruber, Marriage Records of Rev. John Casper Stoever, http://www.chm.davidson.edu/PAGenWeb/records/StoeverMarriages.txt.

Gruber, Christian

Marr: January 26, 1742 in Rev. Stoever, Christ (Little Tulpehocken) Lutheran, Bernville, Lancaster (Berks) Co, PA

Stupp, Anna Gunigunda

Marr: January 26, 1742 in Rev. Stoever, Christ (Little Tulpehocken) Lutheran, Bernville, Lancaster (Berks) Co, PA

Res: 1742 in Tulpehocken, PA

Citation: Christian Gruber, Old Graveyard & Two Cemeteries, Bernville, Berks Co, PA, www.interment.net.

Gruber, Christian

Birth: October 18, 1712 in Sinzeim, Baden-Wurttemberg, Germany

Death: November 14, 1781 in Bernville, Tulpehocken, Berks Co, PA

Burial: 1781 in Christ (Little Tulpehocken) Lutheran, Old Graveyard, Bernville, Berks Co, PA

Stupp, Anna Gunigunda

Name: Stupp, Anna Gunigunda

Burial: 1799 in Christ (Little Tulpehocken) Lutheran, Old Graveyard, Bernville, Berks Co, PA

Citation: Christian Gruber, Passenger and Immigration Lists Index, 1500-1900, myfamily.com, P. William Filby, ancestry.com.

Gruber, Christian

Immigr: September 30, 1732 in Germany to USA (ship Dragon)

Citation: Christian Gruber, Probate file, 1781, unnumbered original papers, 30pp, Berks Co Courthouse, Berks, PA, Norman Nicol, Apr 2008.

Gruber, Christian

Prob: Bet. July 23, 1784–October 31, 1795 in Bern Tp, Berks Co, PA

Prob: May 24, 1800 in Reading, Berks Co, PA

Source Title: **Christian Gruber (con't)**

Citation: Christian Gruber, Probate file, 1781, unnumbered original papers, 30pp, Berks Co Courthouse, Berks, PA, Norman Nicol, Apr 2008.

Gruber, Christian
Prob: Bet. December 04–14 1781 in Reading, Berks Co, PA
Will: July 07, 1780 in Tulpehocken, Berks Co, PA
Occu: 1781; Yeoman

Source Title: **Clay/Klees, Nesbit, etc**

Citation: Clay/Klees, Nesbit, etc, Mike Milliken, MillikenM@@aol.com, rootsweb.com.

Mahr, Maria Magdalena
Burial: January 25, 1767 in Cocalico Reformed Church, Lancaster Co, PA

Sheetz, John George
Marr: June 30, 1767 in Lebanon, PA; Rev. Casper Stoever, Dauphin

Wolfkill, Anna Margaret
Marr: June 30, 1767 in Lebanon, PA; Rev. Casper Stoever, Dauphin
Birth: July 16, 1732 in Neider-Hilbersheim, Rhineland-Palatinate, Germany

Wolfskiel, John Henry
Birth: November 03, 1706 in Neider-Hilbersheim, Rhineland-Palatinate, Germany
Death: June 17, 1787 in Earl, Lancaster Co, PA

Source Title: **Cuniganda Gruber**

Citation: Cuniganda Gruber, November 9, 1796, June 4, 1799, Abstracts of Berks Co, PA Wills, 1785-1800.

Stupp, Anna Gunigunda
Prob: Bet. June 04–14 1799 in Tulpehocken, Berks Co, PA

Source Title: **Daniel Row**

Citation: Daniel Row, Baptismal record, St. John Evangelical Lutheran Church, Dauphin Co, PA, p 64.

Row, Daniel
Birth: July 10, 1813 in Dauphin Co, PA
Baptism: August 14, 1813 in St. Johns (Hill) Lutheran, Berrysburg, Dauphin Co, PA

Citation: Daniel Row, Probate files, 1871, Letter of Admin, Dauphin County Courthouse, Reg of Wills, Deborah Hershey, Elizabethtown, PA, Mar 2008.

Row, Daniel
Prob: August 28, 1871 in Dauphin Co, PA (listed in index only)

Source Title: **Daniel Rowe**

Citation: Daniel Rowe, St. John Evangelical Lutheran Church, Berrysburg, PA, Sara S. Neagley, Elizabethville, PA, 424 6M 24D.

Row, Daniel
Birth: July 10, 1813 in Dauphin Co, PA
Death: July 31, 1871 in Dauphin Co, PA; Bright's disease (ie, Chronic inflammation of kidneys)
Burial: July 1871 in St. Johns (Hill) Lutheran, Berrysburg, Dauphin Co, PA

Source Title: **Dauphin County Names**

Citation: Dauphin County Names, Data p, Robert M Howard, www://genealogy.lv/howard/.

Gieseman, John William
Baptism: May 03, 1761 in PA
Burial: August 1843 in St. Johns (Hill) Lutheran, Berrysburg, Dauphin Co, PA

Source Title: **Dauphin County Names (con't)**

Citation: Dauphin County Names, Data p, Robert M Howard, www://genealogy.lv/howard/.

Rowe, John William

Res: Bet. 1812–1820 in Berrysburg, Dauphin Co, PA

Schrot, Eva

Birth: Abt. 1753 in PA

Schupp, John George

Res: Bet. 1780–1802 in Killinger, Dauphin Co, PA

Welker, John

Birth: August 10, 1783 in Millersburg, Lancaster (Dauphin) Co, PA

Baptism: September 22, 1783 in Old Salem (Werts) Lutheran, Millersburg, Lancaster (Dauphin) Co, PA

Welker, Valentine

Res: Bet. 1784–1801 in Killinger, Dauphin Co, PA

Citation: Dauphin County Names, Data p, www://genealogy.lv/howard/.

Batdorf, Jacob Peter

Res: Bet. 1815–1828 in Berrysburg, Dauphin Co, PA

Source Title: **David Wert**

Citation: David Wert, Dauphin County Register of Wills, bk E, #852, December 20, 1900, , Harrisburg, PA.

Wert, David M

Burial: December 12, 1900 in Calvary United Methodist (aka Union), Wiconisco, Dauphin Co, PA

Citation: David Wert, Wiconisco Calvary Cemetery.

Wert, David M

Burial: December 12, 1900 in Calvary United Methodist (aka Union), Wiconisco, Dauphin Co, PA

Source Title: **David Wert (West) death record**

Citation: David Wert (West) death record, Extract from County Death records, 1893-1906.

Wert, David M

Occu: 1900; Laborer

Death: December 09, 1900 in Dayton, Dauphin Co, PA; Congestion of Lungs

Burial: December 12, 1900 in Calvary United Methodist (aka Union), Wiconisco, Dauphin Co, PA

Source Title: **David Wert death certificate**

Citation: David Wert death certificate, Dauphin County Register of Wills, bk E, #852, December 20, 1900, , Harrisburg, PA.

Wert, David M

Occu: 1900; Laborer

Birth: April 01, 1829 in Powells Valley, Dauphin Co, PA

Death: December 09, 1900 in Dayton, Dauphin Co, PA; Congestion of Lungs

Burial: December 12, 1900 in Calvary United Methodist (aka Union), Wiconisco, Dauphin Co, PA

Source Title: **Deibler family information**

Citation: Deibler family information, Sonny Deibler, sdeibler@@gte.net.

Deibler, Anna Maria Elizabeth

Birth: January 10, 1760 in Millersburg, Lancaster (Dauphin) Co, PA

Death: April 18, 1840 in Millersburg, Dauphin Co, PA

Burial: 1840 in Old Salem (Werts) Lutheran, Millersburg, Dauphin Co, PA

Source Title: **Deibler family information (con't)**

Citation: Deibler family information, Sonny Deibler, sdeibler@@gte.net.

Schupp, John George

Burial: 1839 in Old Salem (Werts) Lutheran, Millersburg, Dauphin Co, PA

Source Title: **Descedants of Martin Stupp**

Citation: Descedants of Martin Stupp, 4 generations, Roger Cramer.

Stupp, Anna Gunigunda

Birth: December 21, 1721 in Schoharie Valley, Schoharie, NY

Source Title: **Descendants of Christian Gruber**

Citation: Descendants of Christian Gruber, WFT 10, Tree 1010, genealogy.com.

Gruber, Christian

Immigr: September 30, 1732 in Germany to USA (ship Dragon)

Source Title: **Descendants of Frederick Adam Faber**

Citation: Descendants of Frederick Adam Faber, Evelyn S Hartman, deanh@@voicenet.com.

Row, Adeline

Birth: January 02, 1860 in Dauphin Co, PA

Source Title: **Descendants of Henry Gruber**

Citation: Descendants of Henry Gruber, WFT 16, Tree 482, www.genealogy.com.

Gruber, Christian

Death: November 14, 1781 in Bernville, Tulpehocken, Berks Co, PA

Stupp, Anna Gunigunda

Death: May 30, 1799 in Bernville, Tulpehocken, Berks Co, PA

Source Title: **Descendants of Michael Garman**

Citation: Descendants of Michael Garman, Evelyn S Hartman, deanh@@voicenet.com.

Garman, Joanna Catherine

Burial: 1864 in Zion (Stone Valley) Lutheran, Dalmatia, Northumberland Co, PA

Garman, Michael

Miltry: Abt. 1782; American Revolution, Sergeant

Citation: Descendants of Michael Garman, Roger Cramer, rogercubs@@aol.com, www.rootsweb.com.

Garman, Michael

Marr: 1785 in Dauphin Co, PA

Birth: 1747 in York Co, PA

Death: January 08, 1800 in IL; PAIllness

Miltry: Abt. 1782; American Revolution, Sergeant

Sheets, Susan

Marr: 1785 in Dauphin Co, PA

Birth: August 16, 1768 in Lancaster Co, PA

Death: March 23, 1854 in Ogle, IL

Burial: 1854 in West Grove Cemetery, Lincoln, Ogle, IL

Source Title: **Deterick Wertz**

Citation: Deterick Wertz, Northumberland Co County Will Index, 1772-1859, http://ftp.rootsweb.com/pub/usgenweb/pa/Northumberland Co/wills/willindx.txt.

Wertz, John Deitrich

Will: Bet. May 08, 1803–1804 in White Deer, Northumberland (Union), PA

Source Title: **Dieter Wurtz**

Citation: Dieter Wurtz, 1767 Pennsylvania Tax Lists, http://freepages.genealogy.rootsweb.com/~genbel/sept/patowshp1767.htm.

Wertz, John Deitrich

Res: 1767 in Heidelberg, Berks Co, PA

Source Title: **Dininni Book**

Citation: Dininni Book, July 10, 1845, August 1, 1845, Dauphin Co, PA, Book E, p 430, The Faber/Fauber/Fawber/Fawver/Farver Family, Chapter XII.

Rudy, Maria "Mollie" Magdalena

Death: January 16, 1845 in Dauphin Co, PA

Citation: Dininni Book, October 1, 1825, October 25, 1825, Lebanon County Will Book, bk A, p 448, The Faber/Fauber/Fawber/Fawver/Farver Family, Chapter XII.

Rudy, Margaret

Prob: October 25, 1825 in Bethel, Lebanon Co, PA

Citation: Dininni Book, The Faber/Fauber/Fawber/Fawver/Farver Family, Chapter XII.

Faber, John

Birth: March 30, 1777 in Lancaster (Lebanon) Co, PA

Faber, John

Marr: February 02, 1774 in Zion Lutheran, Jonestown, Lancaster (Lebanon) Co, PA

Baptism: March 18, 1750 in Lancaster (Lebanon) Co?, PA

Miltry: 1782; American Revolution, Private 2nd PA Reg, 8th Co, 4th class (Lancaster, Capt. Mathias Henning)

Rudy, Margaret

Marr: February 02, 1774 in Zion Lutheran, Jonestown, Lancaster (Lebanon) Co, PA

Birth: December 18, 1753 in Swatara, Lancaster (Lebanon) Co, PA

Death: October 04, 1825 in Bethel, Lebanon Co, PA

Citation: Dininni Book, The Faber/Fauber/Fawber/Fawver/Farver Family, Chapter XII.

Faber, John

Marr: 1805 in Lancaster (Lebanon) Co, PA

Death: July 15, 1828 in Halifax Tp, Dauphin Co, PA

Baptism: April 21, 1777 in Swatara Reformed, Fredericksburg, Lancaster (Lebanon) Co, PA

Burial: 1828 in Hill Cemetery, Halifax, Dauphin Co, PA

Prob: Bet. August 08–13 1828 in Dauphin Co, PA (listed in index only)

Rudy, Maria "Mollie" Magdalena

Marr: 1805 in Lancaster (Lebanon) Co, PA

Death: January 16, 1845 in Dauphin Co, PA

Birth: April 14, 1784 in Bethel, Lancaster (Lebanon) Co, PA

Baptism: November 14, 1784 in St. Johns Union, Fredericksburg, Lancaster (Lebanon) Co, PA

Burial: 1845 in St. Pauls (Bowermans) Lutheran, Enterline, Dauphin Co, PA

Source Title: **Elizabeth Batdorf**

Citation: Elizabeth Batdorf, Hoffmans Reformed Church, Lykens Valley, Dauphin Co, PA, Historical & Genealogical, pp 227-8.

Welker, Elizabeth

Death: July 07, 1868 in Dauphin Co, PA

Source Title: **Elizabeth Wert death record**

Citation: Elizabeth Wert death record, Extract from County Death records, 1893-1906.

Source Title: Elizabeth Wert death record (con't)

Citation: Elizabeth Wert death record, Extract from County Death records, 1893-1906.

Faber, Sarah Elizabeth
Death: April 05, 1902 in Dauphin Co, PA
Burial: 1902 in St. Pauls (Bowermans) Lutheran, Enterline, Dauphin Co, PA

Source Title: Ely household

Citation: Ely household, 1870 United States Census, Dauphin Co, PA, ancestry.com & Microfilm, PA State Library, Hbg, PA.

Row, Adeline
Census: 1870 in Wiconisco, Dauphin Co, PA
Educ: 1870; School

Source Title: Eva Elisabeth Schnug

Citation: Eva Elisabeth Schnug, Passenger and Immigration Lists Index, 1500-1900, myfamily.com, P. William Filby, ancestry.com.

Schnug, Eva Elizabeth
Immigr: 1740 in Germany to USA (ship Samuel Elizabeth)

Source Title: Eva Elizabeth Schnug Wirth

Citation: Eva Elizabeth Schnug Wirth, Wirth's Evangelical Lutheran Church Cemetery, Dauphin Co, PA, www.USGenweb.com, Jonathan Wert.

Schnug, Eva Elizabeth
Birth: 1730 in Baden-Wurttemberg, Germany
Death: 1800 in Upper Paxton, Dauphin Co, PA

Source Title: Faber

Citation: Faber, PA Births, Dauphin County, J. Humphrey.

Faber, John
Relgn: Bet. 1819–1825; Evangelical Reformed Church, Lykens, Upper Paxton, Dauphin Co, PA

Source Title: Faber household

Citation: Faber household, 1800 United States Census, Dauphin, PA, ancestry.com & Microfilm, PA State Library, Hbg, PA.

Rudy, Margaret
Census: 1800 in Bethel, Dauphin Co, PA (listed as head of house)

Citation: Faber household, 1810 United States Census, Dauphin Co, PA, ancestry.com & Microfilm, PA State Library, Hbg, PA.

Faber, Sarah Elizabeth
Census: 1810 in father; Upper Paxton, Dauphin Co, PA w

Citation: Faber household, 1820 United States Census, Dauphin Co, PA, ancestry.com & Microfilm, PA State Library, Hbg, PA.

Faber, Sarah Elizabeth
Census: 1820 in father; Upper Paxton, Dauphin Co, PA w

Source Title: Faver household

Citation: Faver household, 1810 United States Census, Dauphin Co, PA, ancestry.com & Microfilm, PA State Library, Hbg, PA.

Faber, John
Census: 1810 in Upper Paxton, Dauphin Co, PA age 45

Source Title: Fawper household

Source Title: **Fawper household (con't)**

Citation: Fawper household, 1790 United States Census, Dauphin Co, PA, Roll M637 8, p 88, Image 0352, ancestry.com & Microfilm, PA State Library, Hbg, PA.

Faber, John

Census: 1790 in Dauphin Co, PA (Fawper)

Source Title: **Fawver household**

Citation: Fawver household, 1830 United States Census, Northumberland Co, PA, ancestry.com & Microfilm, PA State Library, Hbg, PA.

Rudy, Maria "Mollie" Magdalena

Census: 1830 in Halifax, Dauphin Co, PA

Source Title: **Felty Welker**

Citation: Felty Welker, Greg Welker, gwelker@@chesapeake.net, Dauphin County PA Early Assessment Lists.

Welker, Valentine

Res: 1779 in Middletown, Lancaster (Dauphin) Co, PA

Citation: Felty Welker, Revolutionary War Military Abstract Card File, PA State Archives, www.digitalarchives.state.pu.us/archive.

Welker, Valentine

Miltry: 1778; American Revolution, Private 4th PA Reg, 4th Co, 5th class, (Lancaster, Capt. Jonathan McClure)

Source Title: **Fidler**

Citation: Fidler, Rick Hostetter, PaInfantry@@aol.com, awt.ancestry.com.

Gruber, Anna Margaret

Birth: August 02, 1759 in Berks Co, PA

Gruber, Christian

Death: November 14, 1781 in Bernville, Tulpehocken, Berks Co, PA

Stupp, Anna Gunigunda

Birth: December 21, 1721 in Schoharie Valley, Schoharie, NY

Source Title: **Francis Rou**

Citation: Francis Rou, Probate files, Bk I, vol 1, p403, Lancaster County Archives Division, Lancaster Co Courthouse, Lancaster, PA, Deborah Hershey, Elizabethtown, PA, Mar 2008.

Rowe, Francis "Frank"

Death: Bet. January 08–13 1806 in Lancaster Co, PA

Will: January 08, 1806 in Strasburg, Lancaster Co, PA

Occu: 1806; Wagon maker

Source Title: **Francis Row**

Citation: Francis Row, 1806, Lancaster County, PA Wills, bk I 1-403, Lancaster Co, PA.

Rowe, Francis "Frank"

Prob: January 13, 1806 in Lancaster Co, PA

Citation: Francis Row, Will I-1-403, Estate Inventory 1806, b117, f3, Marge Bardeen, 2006, Lancaster County Historical Society, Lancaster, PA.

Rowe, Francis "Frank"

Prob: January 13, 1806 in Lancaster Co, PA

Source Title: **Francis Rowe**

Citation: Francis Rowe, DAR patriot index, www.dar.org.

Rowe, Francis "Frank"

Death: Bet. January 08–13 1806 in Lancaster Co, PA

Source Title: Francis Rowe (con't)

Citation: Francis Rowe, DAR patriot index, www.dar.org.

Rowe, Francis "Frank"

Miltry: Abt. 1778; American Revolution, Private 1st PA Reg (Lancaster, Capt. Alexander White)

Citation: Francis Rowe, DAR, Application of Janet O N Welty, Wooster, OH, Natl #720047, Aug 2001.

Rowe, Adam

Birth: September 21, 1770 in Lancaster Co, PA

Death: September 05, 1830 in Harrisburg, Dauphin Co, PA

Rowe, Francis "Frank"

Marr: January 24, 1764 in Trinity Lutheran, New Holland, Lancaster Co, PA

Miltry: Abt. 1778; American Revolution, Private 1st PA Reg (Lancaster, Capt. James Brown)

Birth: Abt. 1745 in Strasburg, Lancaster Co, PA

Death: Bet. January 08–13 1806 in Lancaster Co, PA

Miltry: Abt. 1778; American Revolution, Private 1st PA Reg (Lancaster, Capt. Alexander White)

Rowe, Wendel

Birth: August 07, 1777 in PA

Traut, Maria Catherine

Marr: January 24, 1764 in Trinity Lutheran, New Holland, Lancaster Co, PA

Death: 1813 in Lancaster Co, PA

Source Title: Frank Rowe

Citation: Frank Rowe, FHL, Pedigree chart, www.familysearch.org.

Rowe, Francis "Frank"

Birth: Abt. 1745 in Strasburg, Lancaster Co, PA

Rowe, John William

Birth: June 1785 in Strasburg, Lancaster Co, PA

Rudy, Barbara

Birth: April 11, 1796 in Strasburg, Lancaster Co, PA

Death: December 15, 1881 in Berrysburg, Dauphin Co, PA

Citation: Frank Rowe, St. John Evangelical Lutheran Church, Berrysburg, PA, Sara S. Neagley, Elizabethville, PA, 424 6M 24D.

Rowe, Francis "Frank"

Burial: 1806 in Lancaster Co, PA

Source Title: Frantz

Citation: Frantz, PA Births, Dauphin County, J. Humphrey.

Frantz, Adam

Relgn: Bet. 1812–1824; St.John (Hill) Church, Lykens, Upper Paxton, PA

Source Title: Frantz household

Citation: Frantz household, 1790 United States Census, Lancaster Co, PA, ancestry.com & Microfilm, PA State Library, Hbg, PA.

Frantz, Adam

Census: 1790 in father; Strasburg, Lancaster Co, PA w

Citation: Frantz household, 1800 United States Census, Dauphin Co, PA, ancestry.com & Microfilm, PA State Library, Hbg, PA.

Frantz, Adam

Census: 1800 in father; Upper Paxton, Dauphin Co, PA w

Source Title: **Frantz household (con't)**

Citation: Frantz household, 1820 United States Census, Dauphin Co, PA, ancestry.com & Microfilm, PA State Library, Hbg, PA.

Frantz, Susan

Census: 1820 in father; Mifflin, Dauphin Co, PA w

Source Title: **Franz household**

Citation: Franz household, 1800 United States Census, Dauphin Co, PA, Roll M32 40, p 174, Image 7, ancestry.com & Microfilm, PA State Library, Hbg, PA.

Frantz, John William

Census: 1800 in Upper Paxton, Dauphin Co, PA

Source Title: **Franz-Gieseman marriage record**

Citation: Franz-Gieseman marriage record, October 1811, Lykens Valley lower church (David's Reformed) Millersburg, Upper Paxton, Dauphin Co, 1774-1844.

Gieseman, Susan

Birth: November 10, 1787 in Tulpehocken, Berks Co, PA

Death: February 15, 1826 in Mifflin, Dauphin Co, PA; Pilger Fieber u. Kindes Nothen (ie, Pilgrim fever)

Burial: February 17, 1826 in St. Johns (Hill) Lutheran, Berrysburg, Dauphin Co, PA

Citation: Franz-Gieseman marriage record, October 1811, source unknown.

Frantz, Adam

Marr: October 06, 1811 in Upper Paxton, Dauphin Co, PA

Gieseman, Susan

Marr: October 06, 1811 in Upper Paxton, Dauphin Co, PA

Source Title: **Frontz household**

Citation: Frontz household, 1820 United States Census, Dauphin Co, PA, ancestry.com & Microfilm, PA State Library, Hbg, PA.

Frantz, Adam

Occu: 1820; Manufacturing

Citation: Frontz household, 1820 United States Census, Dauphin Co, PA, ancestry.com & Microfilm, PA State Library, Hbg, PA.

Frantz, Adam

Census: 1820 in Mifflin, Dauphin Co, PA

Source Title: **Garman household**

Citation: Garman household, 1850 United States Census, Ogle, IL, p 49, Roll M432-123, ancestry.com.

Sheets, Susan

Census: 1850 in Brookville, Ogle, IL

Source Title: **Garmon household**

Citation: Garmon household, 1790 United States Census, Dauphin Co, PA, ancestry.com & Microfilm, PA State Library, Hbg, PA.

Garman, Michael

Census: 1790 in Dauphin Co, PA

Citation: Garmon household, 1800 United States Census, Northumberland Co, PA, ancestry.com & Microfilm, PA State Library, Hbg, PA.

Garman, Michael

Census: 1800 in Heidelberg, Dauphin (Lebanon) Co, PA

Source Title: **Geeseman household**

Source Title: **Geeseman household (con't)**

Citation: Geeseman household, 1790 United States Census, Berks Co, PA, Roll M637-8, p 8-0145, Image 0145, ancestry.com & Microfilm, PA State Library, Hbg, PA.

Gieseman, John William

Census: 1790 in Tulpehocken, Berks Co, PA

Citation: Geeseman household, 1820 United States Census, Dauphin Co, PA, ancestry.com & Microfilm, PA State Library, Hbg, PA.

Gieseman, John William

Census: 1820 in Mifflin, Dauphin Co, PA

Citation: Geeseman household, 1830 United States Census, Dauphin Co, PA, ancestry.com & Microfilm, PA State Library, Hbg, PA.

Gieseman, John William

Census: 1830 in Mifflin, Dauphin Co, PA

Source Title: **George Schuetz**

Citation: George Schuetz, Baptismal records of Rev. John Casper Stoever, PAGenWeb Lebanon County, PA, Church Records, c/o Mildred Smith.

Shuetz, George

Res: 1749 in Swatara, PA

Source Title: **George Schup**

Citation: George Schup, Wirth's Evangelical Lutheran Church Cemetery, Dauphin Co, PA, www.USGenweb.com, Jonathan Wert.

Schupp, John George

Birth: August 04, 1759 in Upper Paxton, Lancaster (Dauphin) Co, PA

Death: August 27, 1839 in Millersburg, Dauphin Co, PA

Source Title: **George Schupp**

Citation: George Schupp, Stone Valley Cemetery, Robert Straub, Dalmatia, PA, Section A, Row 15, Grave 15.

Schupp, John George

Birth: May 1780 in Upper Paxton, Lancaster (Dauphin) Co, PA

Death: January 20, 1854 in Dauphin Co, PA

Source Title: **George Sheets**

Citation: George Sheets, 1749-1750 Assessment of the Taxables of The South End of Paxtang Township, Lancaster County Taken From Middletown on the Swatara, A. Boyd Hamilton, Harrisburg, PA p 38 Online Transcription by Nancy Piper, http://genealogytrails.com/penn/Dauphin/Census/paxt.

Shuetz, George

Res: Bet. 1749–1751 in Paxtang, Lancaster (Dauphin) Co, PA

Citation: George Sheets, Early Assessment List, South End of Paxtang, 1751, http://maley.net/transcription.

Shuetz, George

Res: Bet. 1749–1751 in Paxtang, Lancaster (Dauphin) Co, PA

Citation: George Sheets, Paxtang Volunteers, Troops sent to Bedford to protect the inhabitants, www.pa-roots.org/data/read.php?51.239165 c/o Sherul Kelso.

Sheetz, John George

Miltry: Abt. 1775; American Revolution, Private 4th PA Reg, ? Co, Paxtang Volunteers (Lancaster, Capt. John Rutherford)

Source Title: **George Sheets Jr**

Citation: George Sheets Jr, FHL, Individual record, www.familysearch.org.

Sheets, John George

Source Title: **George Sheets Jr (con't)**

Citation: George Sheets Jr, FHL, Individual record, www.familysearch.org.

Sheets, John George

Birth: Bet. 1773–1774 in Paxtang, Lancaster (Dauphin) Co, PA

Source Title: **George Shitz**

Citation: George Shitz, Rob Sheetz, Robsheetz32@@wmconnect.com.

Kibler, Elizabeth

Birth: 1720 in Germany?

Shuetz, George

Birth: 1716 in Germany

Citation: George Shitz, Wills: Index to Abstracts, 1721-1819, Lancaster County, PA, http://ftp.rootsweb.com/pub/usgenweb/pa/lancaster/wills/willabsurndxr-z.txt.

Shuetz, George

Will: October 11, 1768 in Lancaster Co, PA

Source Title: **George Shutz**

Citation: George Shutz, Passenger and Immigration Lists Index, 1500-1900, myfamily.com, P. William Filby, ancestry.com.

Shuetz, George

Immigr: Abt. 1737 in Germany to USA (ship Philadelphia)

Source Title: **German household**

Citation: German household, 1810 United States Census, Northumberland Co, PA, ancestry.com & Microfilm, PA State Library, Hbg, PA.

Sheets, Susan

Census: 1810 in Mahanoy, Northumberland Co, PA

Source Title: **Geseman household**

Citation: Geseman household, 1810 United States Census, Dauphin Co, PA, ancestry.com & Microfilm, PA State Library, Hbg, PA.

Gieseman, John William

Census: 1810 in Upper Paxton, Dauphin Co, PA

Gieseman, Susan

Census: 1810 in father; Upper Paxton, Dauphin Co, PA w

Source Title: **Gieseman family information**

Citation: Gieseman family information, Barr Genealogy & related Families: Johns, Gieseman, Replogle, reitz/Wrights and Van Hook, Rev. Ed., Ira R. barr, Abstract, p 29, c/o Mary Ann Booher, LBOOHER6@@woh.rr.com.

Gieseman, George William

Occu: Blacksmith

Citation: Gieseman family information, Geeseaan Cousins Newlsetter, Bernadine N. Geesaman, Quincy, PA.

Gieseman, George William

Marr: December 12, 1749 in Christ (Little Tulpehocken) Lutheran, Bernville, Lancaster (Berks) Co, PA

Death: 1761 in Berks Co, PA

Heck, Anna Catherine

Marr: December 12, 1749 in Christ (Little Tulpehocken) Lutheran, Bernville, Lancaster (Berks) Co, PA

Birth: 1723 in Tulpehocken, Chester (Berks) Co, PA

Citation: Gieseman family information, Geeseman Cousins Newlsetter, Bernadine N. Geesaman, Quincy, PA.

Source Title: **Gieseman family information (con't)**

Citation: Gieseman family information, Geeseman Cousins Newlsetter, Bernadine N. Geesaman, Quincy, PA.

Gieseman, George William

Birth: March 03, 1718 in Darmstadt, Hesse, Germany

Relgn: Evangelical Lutheran Church, Northkill, Berks Co, PA

Gieseman, John William

Marr: February 19, 1782 in Christ (Little Tulpehocken) Lutheran, Bernville, Berks Co, PA

Gruber, Anna Margaret

Marr: February 19, 1782 in Christ (Little Tulpehocken) Lutheran, Bernville, Berks Co, PA

Citation: Gieseman family information, Mary Smith.

Frantz, Adam

Marr: October 06, 1811 in Upper Paxton, Dauphin Co, PA

Gieseman, Susan

Marr: October 06, 1811 in Upper Paxton, Dauphin Co, PA

Birth: November 10, 1787 in Tulpehocken, Berks Co, PA

Death: February 15, 1826 in Mifflin, Dauphin Co, PA; Pilger Fieber u. Kindes Nothen (ie, Pilgrim fever)

Source Title: **Gieseman household**

Citation: Gieseman household, 1790 United States Census, Berks Co, PA, ancestry.com & Microfilm, PA State Library, Hbg, PA.

Gieseman, Susan

Census: 1790 in father; Tulpehocken, Berks Co, PA w

Citation: Gieseman household, 1800 United States Census, Berks Co, PA, ancestry.com & Microfilm, PA State Library, Hbg, PA.

Gieseman, Susan

Census: 1800 in father; Tulpehocken, Berks Co, PA w

Source Title: **Gruber family information**

Citation: Gruber family information, Christina, c_aller@@geocities.com and Gwen, GGDGEN@@aol.com.

Gruber, Christian

Marr: January 26, 1742 in Rev. Stoever, Christ (Little Tulpehocken) Lutheran, Bernville, Lancaster (Berks) Co, PA

Birth: October 18, 1712 in Sinzeim, Baden-Wurttemberg, Germany

Death: November 14, 1781 in Bernville, Tulpehocken, Berks Co, PA

Stupp, Anna Gunigunda

Marr: January 26, 1742 in Rev. Stoever, Christ (Little Tulpehocken) Lutheran, Bernville, Lancaster (Berks) Co, PA

Death: May 30, 1799 in Bernville, Tulpehocken, Berks Co, PA

Citation: Gruber family information, Christina, GGDGEN@@aol.com.

Stupp, Anna Gunigunda

Birth: December 21, 1721 in Schoharie Valley, Schoharie, NY

Citation: Gruber family information, Harry C. Adams Co, Box E, Bedminster, PA 18910.

Gruber, Christian

Birth: October 18, 1712 in Sinzeim, Baden-Wurttemberg, Germany

Source Title: **Gruber-Stulp marriage record**

Citation: Gruber-Stulp marriage record, 1742, Marriage Records of Rev. John Casper Stoever, pa-roots.com.

Source Title: **Gruber-Stulp marriage record (con't)**

Citation: Gruber-Stulp marriage record, 1742, Marriage Records of Rev. John Casper Stoever, pa-roots.com.

Gruber, Christian

Marr: January 26, 1742 in Rev. Stoever, Christ (Little Tulpehocken) Lutheran, Bernville, Lancaster (Berks) Co, PA

Stupp, Anna Gunigunda

Marr: January 26, 1742 in Rev. Stoever, Christ (Little Tulpehocken) Lutheran, Bernville, Lancaster (Berks) Co, PA

Source Title: **GUESMAN-L**

Citation: GUESMAN-L, Geeseman Cousins vol 1, No 3, the Geesman Genealogy, sprocket62@@aol.com,1999.

Heck, Anna Catherine

Immigr: September 28, 1733 in parents); Germany to USA (ship Richard & Elizabeth w

Source Title: **Gusman household**

Citation: Gusman household, 1840 United States Census, Dauphin Co, PA, ancestry.com & Microfilm, PA State Library, Hbg, PA.

Gieseman, John William

Census: 1840 in Mifflin, Dauphin Co, PA

Source Title: **Harman household**

Citation: Harman household, 1870 United States Census, Roll M593 1335, p 649, Image 420, ancestry.com & Microfilm, PA State Library, Hbg, PA.

Faber, Sarah Elizabeth

Occu: 1870; Domestic

Source Title: **Harper B Thompson**

Citation: Harper B Thompson, Obituary, Harrisburg Patriot Newspaper, July 1981.

Thompson, Harper Bruce

Occu: 1981; Retired mail handler (Harrisburg Post Office)

Birth: September 28, 1907 in Sheridan, Schuylkill Co, PA

Death: July 23, 1981 in Polyclinic Hospital, Harrisburg, Dauphin Co, PA; Cardiorespiratory arrest w/subdural hematoma

Burial: 1981 in Woodlawn Memorial Gardens, Harrisburg, Dauphin Co, PA

Funrl: 1981 in Jesse H Geigle, 2100 Linglestown Rd.,Harrisburg, Dauphin Co, PA

Relgn: 1981; Lakeside Lutheran Church

Citation: Harper B Thompson, Social Seurity numident record, application for SS-5, SSA, Nov 2006, Baltimore, MD.

Thompson, Harper Bruce

Res: 1972 in Harrisburg, Dauphin Co, PA

Source Title: **Harper B Thompson death certificate**

Citation: Harper B Thompson death certificate, #2501265, Department of Vital Records, New Castle, PA.

Thompson, Harper Bruce

Res: 1981 in 2600 Green St., Harrisburg, Dauphin Co, PA

Birth: September 28, 1907 in Sheridan, Schuylkill Co, PA

Death: July 23, 1981 in Polyclinic Hospital, Harrisburg, Dauphin Co, PA; Cardiorespiratory arrest w/subdural hematoma

Source Title: **Harper Bruce Thompson birth record**

Citation: Harper Bruce Thompson birth record, #344701, #122649-07, September 1907, Schuylkill Co, PA, Department of Vital Records, New Castle, PA.

Thompson, Harper Bruce

Birth: September 28, 1907 in Sheridan, Schuylkill Co, PA

Source Title: **Harper Thompson**

Citation: Harper Thompson, July 1981, PA, Social Security Death Index, www.familysearch,org.

Thompson, Harper Bruce

Res: 1981 in Beaufort Farms, Camp Curtain, Estherton, Fort Hunter, Harrisburg, Hecktown, Lucknow, Rockville, Uptown, Windsor farms, all Dauphin Co, PA

SSN: 1981; 205-05-3254

Source Title: **Henrich Wolffskehl**

Citation: Henrich Wolffskehl, PA Census, 1772-1890, www.ancestry.com.

Wolfskiel, John Henry

Res: 1742 in Philadelphia, PA

Source Title: **Henry Wolffskeil**

Citation: Henry Wolffskeil, Probate files, 1, Bk F, vol 1, p32, Lancaster County Archives Division, Lancaster Co Courthouse, Lancaster, PA, Deborah Hershey, Elizabethtown, PA, Mar 2008.

Wolfskiel, John Henry

Prob: July 08, 1788 in Earl Tp, Lancaster Co, PA

Will: June 12, 1787 in Earl Tp, Lancaster Co, PA

Occu: June 12, 1787; Yeoman

Citation: Henry Wolffskeil, Wills: Index to Abstracts, 1721-1819, Lancaster County, PA, http://ftp.rootsweb.com/pub/usgenweb/pa/lancaster/wills/willabsurndxr-z.txt.

Wolfskiel, John Henry

Prob: July 08, 1788 in Earl Tp, Lancaster Co, PA

Source Title: **Henry Wolfsiel**

Citation: Henry Wolfsiel, Will F-1-32, Estate Inventory 1788, b128, f9, Marge Bardeen, 2006, Lancaster County Historical Society, Lancaster, PA.

Wolfskiel, John Henry

Prob: July 08, 1788 in Earl Tp, Lancaster Co, PA

Source Title: **Henry Wollfkull**

Citation: Henry Wollfkull, Pennsylvania Naturalizations, 1740-1773, Persons naturalized in the Province of PA, ancestry.com.

Wolfskiel, John Henry

Naturl: September 21, 1760 in Lancaster Co, PA

Source Title: **Henry Woolfkull**

Citation: Henry Woolfkull, Passenger and Immigration Lists Index, 1500-1900, myfamily.com, P. William Filby, ancestry.com.

Wolfskiel, John Henry

Immigr: 1760

Source Title: **Hoover/McHenry family**

Citation: Hoover/McHenry family, Dave Van Doren, dvanore@@neo.rr.com, awt.ancestry.com & Dinini Book.

Faber, John

Source Title: **Hoover/McHenry family (con't)**

Citation: Hoover/McHenry family, Dave Van Doren, dvanore@@neo.rr.com, awt.ancestry.com & Dinini Book.

Faber, John

Death: July 15, 1828 in Halifax Tp, Dauphin Co, PA

Citation: Hoover/McHenry family, Dave Van Doren, dvanore@@neo.rr.com, awt.ancestry.com.

Faber, John

Marr: 1805 in Lancaster (Lebanon) Co, PA

Birth: March 30, 1777 in Lancaster (Lebanon) Co, PA

Faber, John

Birth: February 07, 1750 in Swatara, Lancaster (Lebanon) Co, PA

Burial: 1804 in Bethel Moravian Cemetery, Lebanon, Dauphin (Lebanon) Co, PA

Rudy, Jonas

Birth: December 16, 1751 in Bethel, Lancaster (Lebanon) Co, PA

Death: December 20, 1810 in Bethel, Dauphin (Lebanon) Co, PA

Burial: 1810 in St. Johns Union Cemetery, Fredericksburg, Dauphin (Lebanon) Co, PA

Rudy, Margaret

Birth: December 18, 1753 in Swatara, Lancaster (Lebanon) Co, PA

Death: October 04, 1825 in Bethel, Lebanon Co, PA

Burial: 1825 in St John Hill (Quittaphilla) Lutheran, Cleona, Lebanon Co, PA

Rudy, Maria "Mollie" Magdalena

Marr: 1805 in Lancaster (Lebanon) Co, PA

Birth: April 14, 1784 in Bethel, Lancaster (Lebanon) Co, PA

Source Title: **Hutchinson & Allied Families from East TN**

Citation: Hutchinson & Allied Families from East TN, Terry L Hutchinson, tlhutch_kr@@yahoo.com, awt.ancestry.com.

Traut, John Wendel George

Birth: 1689 in Kleinfischlingen, Rhineland-Palatinate, Germany

Death: Bet. February–March 1761 in Paradise, Lancaster Co, PA

Walter, Maria Magdalena

Birth: January 1717 in Strasburg, Chester (Lancaster) Co, PA

Burial: February 1761 in Cedar Hill (Trout) Cemetery, Strasburg, Lancaster Co, PA

Source Title: **J.M**

Citation: J.M, Stone Valley Cemetery, Robert Straub, Dalmatia, PA, Section A, Row 3, Grave 2.

Miller, John

Burial: 1812 in Zion (Stone Valley) Lutheran, Dalmatia, Northumberland Co, PA

Source Title: **Jacob Rudy**

Citation: Jacob Rudy, Revolutionary War Military Abstract Card File, PA State Archives, www.digitalarchives.state.pu.us/archive.

Rudy, Jacob

Miltry: 1782; American Revolution, Private 3rd PA Reg, 8th Co, 7th class (Lancaster)

Citation: Jacob Rudy, St. John Evangelical Lutheran Church, Berrysburg, PA, Sara S. Neagley, Elizabethville, PA, 424 6M 24D.

Rudy, Jacob

Burial: 1813 in Greensburg Cemetery, Lancaster, Lancaster Co, PA

Source Title: **Jacob Rudy wife**

Citation: Jacob Rudy wife, St. John Evangelical Lutheran Church, Berrysburg, PA, Sara S. Neagley, Elizabethville, PA, 424 6M 24D.

Jungblut, Susan

Burial: 1833 in St. Peters (Hoffman) Reformed, Loyalton, Dauphin Co, PA

Source Title: **Jacob Wert**

Citation: Jacob Wert, HSMUP, Mbg, PA 17061, via mail, not dated or cited.

Wert, Jacob

Burial: St. Pauls (Bowermans) Lutheran, Enterline, Dauphin Co, PA

Citation: Jacob Wert, Wert family, Onetree, ancestry.com.

Wert, Jacob

Death: 1890 in Halifax, Dauphin Co, PA

Source Title: **Jacob Wirt**

Citation: Jacob Wirt, Probate files, 1833, Letter of Admin, A 7/6, Dauphin County Courthouse, Reg of Wills, Deborah Hershey, Elizabethtown, PA, Mar 2008.

Wirth, John Jacob

Prob: January 16, 1833 in Dauphin Co, PA (listed in index only)

Source Title: **Jacob Wirth**

Citation: Jacob Wirth, Wirth's Evangelical Lutheran Church Cemetery, Dauphin Co, PA, www.USGenweb.com, Jonathan Wert.

Wirth, John Jacob

Death: January 01, 1833 in Millersburg, Dauphin Co, PA

Source Title: **James E Batdorf**

Citation: James E Batdorf, Obituary, Harrisburg Patriot news, 1954.

Batdorf, James "Edward"

Res: 1954 in 542 North St., Lykens, Dauphin Co, PA

Burial: August 23, 1954 in Calvary United Methodist, Wiconisco, Dauphin Co, PA

Funrl: 1954 in Reiff? Helt?, 523 W. Main St., Lykens, Dauphin Co, PA

Relgn: 1954; Loyalton EUB Church

Source Title: **James Edward Batdorf**

Citation: James Edward Batdorf, #0506183, #66234-39, August 1954, Department of Vital Records, New Castle, PA.

Batdorf, James "Edward"

Funrl: 1954 in Reiff? Helt?, 523 W. Main St., Lykens, Dauphin Co, PA

Citation: James Edward Batdorf, Church record, Rev. O.S. Moyer, Angie Eddy, Maple Grove Cemetery, Eluzabethville, PA, p 16.

Batdorf, James "Edward"

Baptism: June 06, 1886 in Oakdale Church Circuit, Dauphin Co, PA

Citation: James Edward Batdorf, Church record, Rev. O.S. Moyer, Angie Eddy, Maple Grove Cemetery, Eluzabethville, PA, p 29.

Batdorf, James "Edward"

Birth: February 15, 1885 in Loyalton, Dauphin Co, PA

Citation: James Edward Batdorf, Funeral record copy, John R. Shultz Funeral Home, Lykens, Dauphin Co, PA, 2006, John Shultz, Director.

Batdorf, James "Edward"

Funrl: 1954 in John R. Shultz Funeral Home, 406 Market St., Lykens, Dauphin Co, PA

Source Title: James Edward Batdorf (con't)

Citation: James Edward Batdorf, Social Seurity numident record, application for SS-5, SSA, Nov 2006, Baltimore, MD.

Batdorf, James "Edward"

Birth: February 15, 1885 in Loyalton, Dauphin Co, PA

Citation: James Edward Batdorf, U.S. World War II Draft Registration Cards, 1942, www.ancestry.com.

Batdorf, James "Edward"

Medical: Short height, Medium build, Brown eyes, ? gray hair [1917] Gray eyes, Brown hair, Light complexion, Height 5'6", Weight 143# [1942]

Citation: James Edward Batdorf, United States WW II Draft Reg. Cards, 1942 Record, 2243624, www.ancestry.com.

Batdorf, James "Edward"

Birth: February 15, 1885 in Loyalton, Dauphin Co, PA

Citation: James Edward Batdorf, World War I Draft Registration Cards, 1917-1918 Record, United States WW II Draft Reg. Cards, 1942 Record, 2243624, www.ancestry.com.

Batdorf, James "Edward"

Occu: 1918; Miner (Susquehanna Colliery Co)

Occu: 1942; WPA (Harrisburg, Dauphin Co, PA)

Res: 1918 in Loyalton, Dauphin Co, PA

Res: 1918 in Loyalton, Dauphin Co, PA

Res: 1942 in 542 North Street, Lykens, Dauphin Co, PA

Medical: Short height, Medium build, Brown eyes, ? gray hair [1917] Gray eyes, Brown hair, Light complexion, Height 5'6", Weight 143# [1942]

Source Title: James Edward Batdorf death certificate

Citation: James Edward Batdorf death certificate, #0506183, #66234-39, August 1954, Department of Vital Records, New Castle, PA.

Batdorf, James "Edward"

Occu: 1954; Labor (Lykens Borough)

Res: 1954 in 542 North St., Lykens, Dauphin Co, PA

Birth: February 15, 1885 in Loyalton, Dauphin Co, PA

Death: August 19, 1954 in Home, Lykens, Dauphin Co, PA; Coronary occlusion w/hypertension w/diabetes mellitus

Burial: August 23, 1954 in Calvary United Methodist, Wiconisco, Dauphin Co, PA

SSN: 1954; 205-09-5145

Source Title: Johan Adam Wirth

Citation: Johan Adam Wirth, Immigrants to Pennsylvania, vol 1, ancestry.com.

Wirth, John Adam

Naturl: September 28, 1753 in Philadelphia, PA

Citation: Johan Adam Wirth, Marriage Records of Rev. John Casper Stoever, http://www.chm.davidson.edu/PAGenWeb/records/StoeverMarriages.txt.

Schnug, Eva Elizabeth

Marr: August 03, 1755 in Rev. Stoever, Bindagles Lutheran, Palmyra, Lancaster (Lebanon) Co, PA

Res: 1755 in Lebanon, PA

Wirth, John Adam

Marr: August 03, 1755 in Rev. Stoever, Bindagles Lutheran, Palmyra, Lancaster (Lebanon) Co, PA

Res: 1755 in Lebanon, PA

Citation: Johan Adam Wirth, PA Census, 1772-1890, Philadelphia, PA, www.ancestry.com.

Source Title: **Johan Adam Wirth (con't)**

Citation: Johan Adam Wirth, PA Census, 1772-1890, Philadelphia, PA, www.ancestry.com.

Wirth, John Adam

Res: 1753 in Philadelphia, PA

Source Title: **Johan George Wilhelm Gussemann**

Citation: Johan George Wilhelm Gussemann, Passenger and Immigration Lists Index, 1500-1900, myfamily.com, P. William Filby, ancestry.com.

Gieseman, George William

Immigr: October 26, 1741 in Germany to USA (ship Snow Mollie)

Source Title: **Johann Adam Wirth**

Citation: Johann Adam Wirth, Lykens Valley, Dauphin Co, PA, Wertz Book, Ch 9, pp 221-237, Newsletter 2,3,6,7, Kathleen Odom, knko2@@mci2000.com.

Wirth, John Adam

Res: Abt. 1754 in Montgomery Co, PA

Res: Abt. 1755 in Tulpehocken, Berks Co, PA

Res: Bet. 1755–1763 in Derry, Lancaster (Lebanon) Co, PA

Relgn: Lutheran

Citation: Johann Adam Wirth, Wirth's Evangelical Lutheran Church Cemetery, Dauphin Co, PA, www.USGenweb.com, Jonathan Wert.

Wirth, John Adam

Res: Abt. 1765 in Lykens Valley, Lancaster (Dauphin) Co, PA

Birth: August 23, 1727 in Borod, Rhineland-Palatinate, Germany

Death: August 25, 1806 in Upper Paxton, Dauphin Co, PA

Immigr: September 28, 1753 in Germany to USA (ship Two Brothers)

Source Title: **Johann Dietrich Wertz**

Citation: Johann Dietrich Wertz, One tree, from WFT collection, trees.ancestry.com/owt, www.ancestry.com.

Miller, Mary

Death: 1804 in White Deer, Northumberland (Union) Co, PA

Wertz, John Deitrich

Death: October 16, 1804 in White Deer, Northumberland (Union) Co, PA

Citation: Johann Dietrich Wertz, Property Deed, M503, Northumberland Co, PA, c/o K Poorman, kporrman@@verizon.net.

Wertz, John Deitrich

Will: Bet. May 08, 1803–1804 in White Deer, Northumberland (Union), PA

Citation: Johann Dietrich Wertz, Recorded, M503, Northumberland Co, PA, c/o K Poorman, kporrman@@verizon.net.

Wertz, John Deitrich

Prob: January 30, 1805 in Estate recorded

Source Title: **Johann Dietrich Wuerz**

Citation: Johann Dietrich Wuerz, Bucher family, Onetree, ancestry.com.

Miller, Mary

Birth: 1742 in Germany

Citation: Johann Dietrich Wuerz, Wuerz family, Onetree, ancestry.com.

Wertz, John Deitrich

Death: October 16, 1804 in White Deer, Northumberland (Union) Co, PA

Source Title: **Johann Wendel Traut**

Source Title: **Johann Wendel Traut (con't)**

Citation: Johann Wendel Traut, The Trout Family Hsitorian, Craig Trout, 2006, familytreemaker.genealogy.com/users/t/r/o/Craig-Trout/FILE/0011page.html.

Traut, John Wendel George

Marr: January 23, 1739 in Rev. Stoever, Trinity Lutheran, New Holland, Lancaster Co, PA

Walter, Maria Magdalena

Marr: January 23, 1739 in Rev. Stoever, Trinity Lutheran, New Holland, Lancaster Co, PA

Birth: January 1717 in Strasburg, Chester (Lancaster) Co, PA

Source Title: **Johann Wilhelm Frantz**

Citation: Johann Wilhelm Frantz, Descendants of Johann Wilhelm Frantz, Evelyn S. Hartman.

Frantz, Adam

Birth: 1780 in Lykens, Lancaster (Dauphin) Co, PA

Citation: Johann Wilhelm Frantz, Descendants of JohAnnaWilhelm Frantz, Evelyn S. Hartman.

Frantz, John William

Death: 1804 in Upper Paxton, Dauphin Co, PA

Source Title: **Johannes (John) Faber**

Citation: Johannes (John) Faber, DAR, Application of Mary I Bowerman Dininni, Harrisburg, PA, Natl #596079, May 1981.

Baker, John

Birth: May 19, 1804 in PA

Faber, Elizabeth

Birth: April 10, 1784 in Lancaster Co, PA

Faber, John

Marr: 1805 in Lancaster (Lebanon) Co, PA

Birth: March 30, 1777 in Lancaster (Lebanon) Co, PA

Death: July 15, 1828 in Halifax Tp, Dauphin Co, PA

Faber, John

Birth: February 07, 1750 in Swatara, Lancaster (Lebanon) Co, PA

Death: 1804 in Bethel, Dauphin (Lebanon) Co, PA

Faber, Magdalena

Birth: November 26, 1775 in Lancaster Co, PA

Rudy, Maria "Mollie" Magdalena

Marr: 1805 in Lancaster (Lebanon) Co, PA

Birth: April 14, 1784 in Bethel, Lancaster (Lebanon) Co, PA

Death: July 16, 1845 in Jefferson Tp, Dauphin Co, PA

Source Title: **Johannes Schup**

Citation: Johannes Schup, Stone Valley Cemetery, Robert Straub, Dalmatia, PA, Section A, Row 16, Grave 30.

Shoop, John

Birth: August 01, 1805 in Dauphin Co?, PA

Death: December 13, 1858 in Lower Mahanoy, Northumberland Co, PA

Source Title: **John Faber**

Citation: John Faber, 1777, PA Births, Lebanon County 1714-1800, J.T. Humphreys, 1996, Washington DC.

Faber, John

Birth: March 30, 1777 in Lancaster (Lebanon) Co, PA

Citation: John Faber, FHL, Pedigree chart, www.familysearch.org.

Source Title: **John Faber (con't)**

Citation: John Faber, FHL, Pedigree chart, www.familysearch.org.

Faber, John
Birth: February 07, 1750 in Swatara, Lancaster (Lebanon) Co, PA

Rudy, Margaret
Birth: December 18, 1753 in Swatara, Lancaster (Lebanon) Co, PA
Death: October 04, 1825 in Bethel, Lebanon Co, PA

Citation: John Faber, Probate files, 1828, Letter of Admin., p70, Dauphin County Courthouse, Reg of Wills, Deborah Hershey, Elizabethtown, PA, Mar 2008.

Faber, John
Prob: Bet. August 08–13 1828 in Dauphin Co, PA (listed in index only)

Citation: John Faber, Revolutionary War Military Abstract Card File, PA State Archives, www.digitalarchives.state.pu.us/archive.

Faber, John
Miltry: 1782; American Revolution, Private 2nd PA Reg, 8th Co, 4th class (Lancaster, Capt. Mathias Henning)

Source Title: **John Geo. Schuetz**

Citation: John Geo. Schuetz, Marriage Records of Rev. John Casper Stoever, http://www.chm.davidson.edu/PAGenWeb/records/StoeverMarriages.txt.

Sheetz, John George
Res: 1767 in Paxton, Lancaster (Dauphin) Co, PA

Wolfkill, Anna Margaret
Res: 1767 in Earltown, PA

Source Title: **John Henry Wert**

Citation: John Henry Wert, Probate files, 1938, #988, Letter of Admin, A 213 21/329, Inv 23 N-512, Dauphin County Courthouse, Reg of Wills, Deborah Hershey, Elizabethtown, PA, Mar 2008.

Wert, John Henry
Prob: Bet. November 19, 1924–1938 in Washington Tp, Dauphin Co, PA (listed in index only)

Source Title: **John Jacob Wirth**

Citation: John Jacob Wirth, Adam Wirth (Derry), Baptismal records of Rev. John Casper Stoever, PAGenWeb Lebanon County, PA, Church Records, c/o Mildred Smith.

Wirth, John Jacob
Birth: February 1763 in Lebanon, Lancaster (Lebanon) Co, PA
Baptism: March 25, 1763 in PA

Source Title: **John Mertz (Wertz)**

Citation: John Mertz (Wertz), Probate files, 1862, Northumberland County Courthouse, Reg of Wills, Sunbury, Bk 5, p122, PA, Robyn Jackson, genealogylover@@msn.com, 2008.

Wertz, John
Prob: June 03, 1861 in Northumberland Co, PA

Source Title: **John Miller**

Citation: John Miller, NSSAR, Application of Robert T Coleman, Summerdale, PA, Natl #122061, State #8984, Apr 1996.

Kerstetter, Frances
Marr: January 01, 1774 in Lebanon Tp, Lancaster (Lebanon) Co, PA
Birth: April 09, 1752 in Cleona, Lancaster (Lebanon) Co, PA
Death: 1818 in Northumberland Co, PA

Miller, John

Source Title: John Miller (con't)

Citation: John Miller, NSSAR, Application of Robert T Coleman, Summerdale, PA, Natl #122061, State #8984, Apr 1996.

Miller, John

Marr: January 01, 1774 in Lebanon Tp, Lancaster (Lebanon) Co, PA

Birth: 1751 in Lebanon, Lancaster (Lebanon) Co, PA

Death: 1812 in Upper Paxton, Dauphin Co, PA

Miltry: Bet. 1778–1781; American Revolution, Private 4th PA Reg, 6th Co, 2nd class (Lancaster, Capt. Martin Weaver)

Miller, John Peter

Birth: May 17, 1780 in Upper Paxton, Dauphin Co, PA

Citation: John Miller, Probate files, 1812, Letter of Admin, p97, Dauphin County Courthouse, Reg of Wills, Deborah Hershey, Elizabethtown, PA, Mar 2008.

Miller, John

Prob: April 29, 1812 in Dauphin Co, PA (listed in index only)

Source Title: John Peters

Citation: John Peters, Peters family information, Evelyn S Hartman, deanh@@voicenet.com.

Batdorf, Alvin Leroy

Death: 1972

Batdorf, Cora Annette

Death: May 1981 in Harrisburg, Dauphin Co, PA

Batdorf, Harry Franklin

Death: August 1977 in Lykens, Dauphin Co, PA

Batdorf, Harvey Clarence

Death: 1949

Batdorf, Joseph Warren

Death: 1928

Boyer, Caroline "Carrie" May

Death: 1973

Buffington, Herbert Eugene

Death: 1959

DeWees, Lafayette

Death: 1981

Hoy, Grace Naomi

Death: 1962

Kohler, Albert Forrest

Death: 1991

Lentz, Samuel W

Death: 1940

Reed, Claude M

Death: 1986

Citation: John Peters, Probate files, 1846, Union County Courthouse, Reg of Wills, Union Co, PA, 2008.

Peters, John

Prob: Bet. April 13–27 1846 in East Buffalo Tp, Union Co, PA

Source Title: John Shoop

Citation: John Shoop, Probate files, 1862, Northumberland County Courthouse, Reg of Wills, Sunbury, Bk B, p629, PA, Robyn Jackson, genealogylover@@msn.com, 2008.

Shoop, John

Prob: December 23, 1858 in Lower Mahanoy, Northumberland Co, PA

Source Title: **John Welker**

Citation: John Welker, Barbara Brady O'Keefe, 2120 SW 127 Avenue, Miami, FL & Cindy Maloney, cynwelker8@@rurelated.com.

Welker, John

Occu: 1843; Weaver

Burial: 1854 in Simeon Union Cemetery, Gratz, Dauphin Co, PA

Citation: John Welker, Probate files, 1854, F-413-4, Dauphin County Courthouse, Reg of Wills, Deborah Hershey, Elizabethtown, PA, Mar 2008.

Welker, John

Prob: 1854 in Dauphin Co, PA (listed in index only)

Source Title: **John Wert**

Citation: John Wert, #0042527, #95868-1303, 1924, Department of Vital records, New Castle, PA.

Wert, John Henry

Occu: 1924; Timber laborer (Susquehanna Colliery)

Birth: December 23, 1855 in Northumberland Co, PA

Death: October 30, 1924 in Harrisburg Hospital, Harrisburg, Dauphin Co, PA; Hemorrhage & shock from fractured ribs & other abd. injuries...rolling timber.

Burial: November 02, 1924 in St. Johns (Hill) Lutheran, Berrysburg, Dauphin Co, PA

Funrl: 1924 in Buffington Funeral Home, Elizabethville, Dauphin Co, PA

Source Title: **Jonas Rudy**

Citation: Jonas Rudy, DAR patriot index, www.dar.org.

Rudy, Jonas

Birth: December 16, 1751 in Bethel, Lancaster (Lebanon) Co, PA

Citation: Jonas Rudy, NSSAR, Application of Kimber D Smith, Allentown, PA, Natl #109281, State #8159, Apr 2004.

Baker, John

Birth: May 19, 1804 in PA

Faber, Catherine

Birth: January 14, 1810 in Lebanon Co, PA

Faber, John

Marr: 1805 in Lancaster (Lebanon) Co, PA

Birth: March 30, 1777 in Lancaster (Lebanon) Co, PA

Death: July 15, 1828 in Halifax Tp, Dauphin Co, PA

Overcash, Anna Barbara

Marr: Abt. 1773 in Lancaster (Lebanon) Co, PA

Birth: September 28, 1751 in Bethel, Lancaster (Lebanon) Co, PA

Death: April 08, 1836 in Bethel, Lebanon Co, PA

Rudy, Jonas

Marr: Abt. 1773 in Lancaster (Lebanon) Co, PA

Birth: December 16, 1751 in Bethel, Lancaster (Lebanon) Co, PA

Miltry: 1781; American Revolution, Private 2nd PA Reg, 3rd Co, 8th class (Lancaster, Capt. Casper Stoever)

Rudy, Maria "Mollie" Magdalena

Marr: 1805 in Lancaster (Lebanon) Co, PA

Birth: April 14, 1784 in Bethel, Lancaster (Lebanon) Co, PA

Death: July 16, 1845 in Jefferson Tp, Dauphin Co, PA

Citation: Jonas Rudy, October 15, 1810, February 4, 1811, Abstracts of Wills, Bethel, PA, p 179.

Rudy, Jonas

Source Title: **Jonas Rudy (con't)**

Citation: Jonas Rudy, October 15, 1810, February 4, 1811, Abstracts of Wills, Bethel, PA, p 179.

Rudy, Jonas

Death: December 20, 1810 in Bethel, Dauphin (Lebanon) Co, PA

Citation: Jonas Rudy, Probate files, Bk R-1, roll 37, Lancaster County Archives Division, Lancaster Co Courthouse, Lancaster, PA, Deborah Hershey, Elizabethtown, PA, Mar 2008.

Rudy, Jonas

Prob: Bet. February 04–November 29, 1811 in Bethel Tp, Dauphin (Lebanon) Co, PA

Citation: Jonas Rudy, Revolutionary War Military Abstract Card File, PA State Archives, www.digitalarchives.state.pu.us/archive.

Rudy, Jonas

Miltry: 1781; American Revolution, Private 2nd PA Reg, 3rd Co, 8th class (Lancaster, Capt. Casper Stoever)

Citation: Jonas Rudy, Rudy family, Onetree, ancestry.com.

Rudy, Jonas

Birth: December 16, 1751 in Bethel, Lancaster (Lebanon) Co, PA

Source Title: **Jonas Rudy Sr**

Citation: Jonas Rudy Sr, DAR, Application of Jeanne R Miller, New Harmony, IN, Comp #4-035 IN, Jan 1982.

Rudy, Jonas

Miltry: 1781; American Revolution, Private 2nd PA Reg, 3rd Co, 8th class (Lancaster, Capt. Casper Stoever)

Rudy, Michael

Birth: May 16, 1789 in Dauphin Co, PA

Selzer, Barbara

Birth: 1751

Source Title: **Jury Family**

Citation: Jury Family, A Genealogical Record, 1754-1973, James W. Jury, Wiconisco, PA, rev. 1986.

Jury, Susan

Confir: July 17, 1777 in St. Davids (Salem) Reformed, Millersburg, Lancaster (Dauphin) Co, PA

Source Title: **Knittle household**

Citation: Knittle household, 1930 United States Census, Lehigh Co, PA, ancestry.com & Microfilm, PA State Library, Hbg, PA.

Thompson, Harper Bruce

Census: 1930 in Emmaus, Lehigh Co, PA (Uncle James Knittle)

Occu: 1930; Lineman (Telephone Co)

Res: 1930 in 914 ? St., Emmaus, Lehigh Co, PA

Source Title: **Magdalene Faver**

Citation: Magdalene Faver, Probate files, 1845, Bk E, p430, microfilm file 3, roll 17, Dauphin County Courthouse, Reg of Wills, Deborah Hershey, Elizabethtown, PA, Mar 2008.

Rudy, Maria "Mollie" Magdalena

Prob: August 01, 1845 in Jefferson Tp, Dauphin Co, PA

Will: July 10, 1845 in Jefferson Tp, Dauphin Co, PA

Citation: Magdalene Faver, Probate files, 1845, microfilm file 3, roll 17, Dauphin County Courthouse, Reg of Wills, Deborah Hershey, Elizabethtown, PA, Mar 2008.

Source Title: **Magdalene Faver (con't)**

Citation: Magdalene Faver, Probate files, 1845, microfilm file 3, roll 17, Dauphin County Courthouse, Reg of Wills, Deborah Hershey, Elizabethtown, PA, Mar 2008.

Rudy, Maria "Mollie" Magdalena

Death: July 16, 1845 in Jefferson Tp, Dauphin Co, PA

Source Title: **Magdalene Trout**

Citation: Magdalene Trout, Estate Inventory b124, f6, Marge Bardeen, 2006, Lancaster County Historical Society, Lancaster, PA.

Walter, Maria Magdalena

Prob: 1761 in Lancaster Co, PA

Source Title: **Magdalene Wolffshiel**

Citation: Magdalene Wolffshiel, Lancaster County, PA, Church Records of the 18th Century, vol 1, FE Wright, p 41, Marge Bardeen, 2006, Lancaster County Historical Society, Lancaster, PA.

Mahr, Maria Magdalena

Birth: Abt. 1712 in Germany?

Burial: January 25, 1767 in Cocalico Reformed Church, Lancaster Co, PA

Source Title: **Margaret Faber**

Citation: Margaret Faber, October 1, 1825, October 25, 1825, Lebanon County Will abstracts, Lebanon County, PA, bk A, p 448.

Rudy, Margaret

Prob: October 25, 1825 in Bethel, Lebanon Co, PA

Citation: Margaret Faber, Probate files, 1825, No F-9, 15, Lebanon County Reg of Wills & Clerk of Orphans Court, Lebaonn, PA, Dawn L Resanovich, Register, Dec 2008.

Rudy, Margaret

Prob: October 25, 1825 in Bethel, Lebanon Co, PA

Will: October 01, 1825 in Bethel, Lebanon Co, PA

Source Title: **Margaret Shoop**

Citation: Margaret Shoop, Stone Valley Cemetery, Robert Straub, Dalmatia, PA, Section A, Row 16, Grave 14.

Miller, Anna Margaret

Birth: February 12, 1784 in Lancaster (Dauphin) Co, PA

Death: July 24, 1857 in Dauphin Co, PA

Burial: 1857 in Zion (Stone Valley) Lutheran, Dalmatia, Northumberland Co, PA

Source Title: **Maria Elizabeth Deibler Schup**

Citation: Maria Elizabeth Deibler Schup, Wirth's Evangelical Lutheran Church Cemetery, Dauphin Co, PA, www.USGenweb.com, Jonathan Wert.

Deibler, Anna Maria Elizabeth

Birth: January 10, 1760 in Millersburg, Lancaster (Dauphin) Co, PA

Death: April 18, 1840 in Millersburg, Dauphin Co, PA

Source Title: **Maria Magdalena Walter**

Citation: Maria Magdalena Walter, Family Data Collection, Individual records, ancestry.com.

Walter, Maria Magdalena

Birth: January 1717 in Strasburg, Chester (Lancaster) Co, PA

Source Title: **Maria Magdelena Walter**

Citation: Maria Magdelena Walter, Family Data Collection, Individual Records, www.ancestry.com.

Source Title: **Maria Magdelena Walter (con't)**

Citation: Maria Magdelena Walter, Family Data Collection, Individual Records, www.ancestry.com.

Walter, Maria Magdalena

Death: February 1761 in Paradise, Lancaster Co, PA

Source Title: **Maria Peters**

Citation: Maria Peters, Death notice, Lewisburg Chronicle, Oct. 1852 c/o Union County Historical Society, Maggie Miller, hstorici@@ptd.net.

Maria, Anna

Death: October 22, 1852 in East Buffalo, Union Co, PA

Citation: Maria Peters, Death notice, Lewisburg Chronicle, octo. 1852 c/o Union County Historical Society, Maggie Miller, hstorici@@ptd.net.

Peters, John

Res: Abt. 1830 in East Buffalo, Union Co, PA

Source Title: **Maria Sheetz**

Citation: Maria Sheetz, St. Paul/Bauerman Lutheran & Reformed Church, Enterline, PA, The Perry Historians.

Forman, Mary "Polly"

Birth: January 05, 1778 in PA

Death: June 03, 1848 in Dauphin Co, PA

Source Title: **Mary L Batdorf**

Citation: Mary L Batdorf, #0042526, #7?-23, 1924, Department of Vital records, New Castle, PA.

Peters, Mary Louisa

Occu: 1924; Housekeeper

Birth: March 31, 1858 in Dauphin Co, PA

Burial: August 06, 1924 in St. Johns (Oakdale) Cemetery, Loyalton, Dauphin Co, PA

Funrl: 1924 in Buffington Funeral Home, Elizabethville, Dauphin Co, PA

Source Title: **Mary Peters death certificate**

Citation: Mary Peters death certificate, bk C, #945, 1897, Dauphin County Register of Wills, Harrisburg, PA.

Swartz, Mary Ann

Birth: January 05, 1820 in Juniata, Perry Co, PA

Citation: Mary Peters death certificate, Dauphin County Register of Wills, bk C, #945, 1897, Harrisburg, PA. Source 140, bk C, #945, 1897, Perry County Historians.

Swartz, Mary Ann

Death: August 09, 1897 in Washington, Dauphin Co, PA; Heart disease

Burial: August 12, 1897 in St. Johns (Oakdale) Cemetery, Loyalton, Dauphin Co, PA

Citation: Mary Peters death certificate, Dauphin County Register of Wills, bk C, #945, 1897, Harrisburg, PA.

Swartz, Mary Ann

Death: August 09, 1897 in Washington, Dauphin Co, PA; Heart disease

Citation: Mary Peters death certificate, Mary Peters death record, bk C, #945, 1897, Dauphin County Register of Wills, Harrisburg, PA.

Swartz, Mary Ann

Burial: August 12, 1897 in St. Johns (Oakdale) Cemetery, Loyalton, Dauphin Co, PA

Source Title: **Mary Rowe**

Source Title: **Mary Rowe (con't)**

Citation: Mary Rowe, St. John Evangelical Lutheran Church, Berrysburg, PA, Sara S. Neagley, Elizabethville, PA, 424 6M 24D.

Traut, Maria Catherine

Burial: 1813 in Lancaster Co, PA

Source Title: **Mertz household**

Citation: Mertz household, 1850 United States Census, Northumberland Co, PA, ancestry.com & Microfilm, PA State Library, Hbg, PA.

Wertz, John

Census: 1850 in Lower Mahanoy, Northumberland Co, PA (Mertz)

Occu: 1850; Farmer

Propty: 1850 in $1000

Source Title: **Messerschmidt**

Citation: Messerschmidt, PA Births, Dauphin County, J. Humphrey.

Messerschmidt, Andrew

Relgn: Bet. 1787–1792; Zion Lutheran, Harrisburg, Dauphin Co, PA

Source Title: **Messerschmidt household**

Citation: Messerschmidt household, 1800 United States Census, Dauphin Co, PA, ancestry.com & Microfilm, PA State Library, Hbg, PA.

Messerschmidt, Maria Elizabeth

Census: 1800 in father; Upper Paxton, Dauphin Co, PA w

Source Title: **Messersmith household**

Citation: Messersmith household, 1810 United States Census, Lancaster Co, PA, ancestry.com & Microfilm, PA State Library, Hbg, PA.

Schrot, Eva

Census: 1810 in Lancaster, Lancaster Co, PA (widow)

Source Title: **Michael Garman**

Citation: Michael Garman, DAR patriot index, www.dar.org.

Garman, Michael

Miltry: Abt. 1782; American Revolution, Sergeant

Citation: Michael Garman, DAR, Application of Emma G Krape, A044052, 265635, Nov 1930.

Garman, Michael

Miltry: Bet. March 03–November 25, 1776; American Revolution, Private 2nd PA Reg (Capt. Samuel Watson)

Miltry: Bet. March 01–July 31, 1776; American Revolution, Private 3rd PA Reg (Capt. Thomas Moore)

Miltry: Abt. 1781; American Revolution, Private 4th PA Reg 3rd Co (Lancaster, Capt. George Gantze)

Miltry: Abt. 1782; American Revolution, Sergeant

Citation: Michael Garman, DAR, Application of Kris E Garman, Crystal Lake, IL, Comp #5-065 IL, Aug 2000.

Garman, Jacob

Birth: March 07, 1792 in PA

Garman, Michael

Marr: 1785 in Dauphin Co, PA

Birth: 1747 in York Co, PA

Death: January 08, 1800 in IL; PAIllness

Sheets, Susan

Source Title: **Michael Garman (con't)**

Citation: Michael Garman, DAR, Application of Kris E Garman, Crystal Lake, IL, Comp #5-065 IL, Aug 2000.

Sheets, Susan

Marr: 1785 in Dauphin Co, PA

Birth: August 16, 1768 in Lancaster Co, PA

Citation: Michael Garman, Garman family, Onetree, ancestry.com.

Sheets, Susan

Death: March 23, 1854 in Ogle, IL

Citation: Michael Garman, Potrait & Biographical Album of Ogle County, IL, pub 1886, pp220-221, Cindi Grimm, ggrimm48@@comcast.net.

Garman, Michael

Occu: Blacksmith

Sheets, Susan

Birth: August 16, 1768 in Lancaster Co, PA

Citation: Michael Garman, The Biographical Record of Ogle Co,IL, Published by S.J. Clarke, 1899, Original from the New York Public Library, Digitized Feb 28, 2008, 492 pages.

Garman, Michael

Birth: 1747 in York Co, PA

Miltry: Abt. 1782; American Revolution, Sergeant

Source Title: **Michael Goodman**

Citation: Michael Goodman, Descendants of Michael Goodman, Evelyn S Hartman, deanh@@voicenet.com.

Keiper, William Henry

Death: 1913

Romberger, Daniel George

Death: 1959

Row, Angelina

Death: 1936

Row, Sarah Ann

Death: 1859

Zerby, Jacob

Death: 1913

Source Title: **Miller family information**

Citation: Miller family information, Jim Miller, Halifax, PA.

Deibler, Anna Maria Elizabeth

Birth: January 10, 1760 in Millersburg, Lancaster (Dauphin) Co, PA

Death: April 18, 1840 in Millersburg, Dauphin Co, PA

Kerstetter, Frances

Marr: January 01, 1774 in Lebanon Tp, Lancaster (Lebanon) Co, PA

Burial: 1818 in Zion (Stone Valley) Lutheran, Dalmatia, Northumberland Co, PA

Miller, John

Marr: January 01, 1774 in Lebanon Tp, Lancaster (Lebanon) Co, PA

Birth: 1751 in Lebanon, Lancaster (Lebanon) Co, PA

Death: 1812 in Upper Paxton, Dauphin Co, PA

Burial: 1812 in Zion (Stone Valley) Lutheran, Dalmatia, Northumberland Co, PA

Schupp, John George

Death: January 20, 1854 in Dauphin Co, PA

Source Title: Miller family information (con't)

Citation: Miller family information, Jim Miller, Halifax, PA.

Schupp, John George
Birth: August 04, 1759 in Upper Paxton, Lancaster (Dauphin) Co, PA
Burial: 1839 in Old Salem (Werts) Lutheran, Millersburg, Dauphin Co, PA

Source Title: Miller household

Citation: Miller household, 1790 United States Census, Dauphin Co, PA ancestry.com & Microfilm, PA State Library, Hbg, PA.

Miller, John
Census: 1790 in Dauphin Co, PA

Citation: Miller household, 1810 United States Census, Dauphin Co, PA, ancestry.com & Microfilm, PA State Library, Hbg, PA.

Miller, John
Census: 1810 in Upper Paxton, Dauphin Co, PA

Source Title: Monn & Related Families

Citation: Monn & Related Families, Danni Monn Hopkins, clueless@@clnk.com, awt.ancestry.com.

Faber, John
Marr: 1805 in Lancaster (Lebanon) Co, PA
Birth: March 30, 1777 in Lancaster (Lebanon) Co, PA
Burial: 1828 in Hill Cemetery, Halifax, Dauphin Co, PA

Faber, Sarah Elizabeth
Birth: May 25, 1807 in Lancaster (Lebanon) Co, PA

Miller, Anna Sophia
Birth: August 02, 1776 in Millersburg, Lancaster (Dauphin) Co, PA

Rudy, Maria "Mollie" Magdalena
Marr: 1805 in Lancaster (Lebanon) Co, PA
Death: January 16, 1845 in Dauphin Co, PA
Burial: 1845 in St. Pauls (Bowermans) Lutheran, Enterline, Dauphin Co, PA

Shoop, Catherine
Birth: February 24, 1830 in Northumberland Co, PA
Death: June 08, 1872 in Dauphin Co, PA

Wert, David M
Birth: April 01, 1829 in Powells Valley, Dauphin Co, PA
Death: December 09, 1900 in Dayton, Dauphin Co, PA; Congestion of Lungs

Wert, Jacob
Birth: July 20, 1804 in Lykens, Dauphin Co, PA
Death: 1890 in Halifax, Dauphin Co, PA

Source Title: Mother Faber

Citation: Mother Faber, Zion Evangelical Lutheran Church, Marriages & Burials, 1768-1858, bk 1, p 392, Lebanon County Historical Society.

Faber, John
Marr: February 02, 1774 in Zion Lutheran, Jonestown, Lancaster (Lebanon) Co, PA

Rudy, Margaret
Marr: February 02, 1774 in Zion Lutheran, Jonestown, Lancaster (Lebanon) Co, PA
Birth: December 18, 1753 in Swatara, Lancaster (Lebanon) Co, PA
Death: October 04, 1825 in Bethel, Lebanon Co, PA
Confir: 1774 in Zion Lutheran, Jonestown, Lancaster (Lebanon) Co, PA

Source Title: **Mrs. Adeline Wert death certificate**

Citation: Mrs. Adeline Wert death certificate, #26162, #3457526, March 1921, Department of Vital Records, New Castle, PA.

Frantz, Susan

Birth: March 23, 1819 in Dauphin Co, PA

Row, Adeline

Occu: 1921; Housewife

Birth: January 02, 1860 in Dauphin Co, PA

Death: March 06, 1921 in Harrisburg, Dauphin Co, PA; Sero-fibrinous pleurisy w/myocarditis

Burial: March 10, 1921 in St. Johns (Hill) Lutheran, Berrysburg, Dauphin Co, PA

Funrl: 1921 in Buffington Funeral Home, Elizabethville, Dauphin Co, PA

Res: 1921 in Lykens, Dauphin Co, PA

Row, Daniel

Birth: July 10, 1813 in Dauphin Co, PA

Source Title: **Myrtle A Thompson**

Citation: Myrtle A Thompson, Obituary, Harrisburg Patriot newspaper, 1983.

Batdorf, Myrtle Adeline

Funrl: 1983 in Jesse H Geigle, 2100 Linglestown Rd.,Harrisburg, Dauphin Co, PA

Citation: Myrtle A Thompson, Probate files, 1983, File 424-1983, Dauphin County Courthouse, Reg of Wills, Deborah Hershey, Elizabethtown, PA, Mar 2008.

Batdorf, Myrtle Adeline

Prob: Bet. May 10–19 1983 in Harrisburg, Dauphin Co, PA

Will: March 30, 1979 in Harrisburg, Dauphin Co, PA

Source Title: **Myrtle A Thompson death certificate**

Citation: Myrtle A Thompson death certificate, #3455802, Department of Vital records, New Castle, PA.

Batdorf, Myrtle Adeline

Res: 1983 in 2660A Green St., Harrisburg, Dauphin Co, PA

Death: May 08, 1983 in Polyclinic Hospital, Harrisburg, Dauphin Co, PA; Cardiorespiratory arrest w/ASHD w/pacemaker

Occu: 1983; Housewife

SSN: 1983; 165-26-7303

Source Title: **Myrtle A. Batdorf birth certificate**

Citation: Myrtle A. Batdorf birth certificate, January 1918, Department of Vital records, New Castle, PA.

Batdorf, Myrtle Adeline

Birth: January 05, 1918 in Big Run, Dauphin Co, PA

Source Title: **Myrtle Thompson**

Citation: Myrtle Thompson, Gerald G Thompson.

Batdorf, Myrtle Adeline

Relgn: 1983; Lakeside Lutheran Church

Citation: Myrtle Thompson, May 1983, PA, Social Security Death Index, www.familysearch.org.

Batdorf, Myrtle Adeline

Res: 1983 in Beaufort Farms, Camp Curtain, Estherton, Fort Hunter, Harrisburg, Hecktown, Lucknow, Rockville, Uptown, Windsor farms, all Dauphin Co, PA

Source Title: **Myrtle Thompson (con't)**

Citation: Myrtle Thompson, May 1983, PA, Social Security Death Index, www.familysearch.org.

Batdorf, Myrtle Adeline

SSN: 1983; 165-26-7303

Citation: Myrtle Thompson, Obituary, Harrisburg Patriot newspaper, 1983.

Batdorf, Myrtle Adeline

Res: 1983 in 2660A Green St., Harrisburg, Dauphin Co, PA

Death: May 08, 1983 in Polyclinic Hospital, Harrisburg, Dauphin Co, PA; Cardiorespiratory arrest w/ASHD w/pacemaker

Relgn: 1983; Lakeside Lutheran Church

Source Title: **PA & Other Assorted Data**

Citation: PA & Other Assorted Data, R Howard, rmhoward45@@aol.com, awt.ancestry.com.

Miller, Anna Sophia

Marr: Abt. 1794 in Dauphin Co, PA

Birth: August 02, 1776 in Millersburg, Lancaster (Dauphin) Co, PA

Death: October 22, 1842 in Lykens, Dauphin Co, PA

Burial: 1842 in Old Salem (Werts) Lutheran, Millersburg, Dauphin Co, PA

Wirth, John Jacob

Marr: Abt. 1794 in Dauphin Co, PA

Death: January 01, 1833 in Millersburg, Dauphin Co, PA

Burial: January 03, 1833 in Old Salem (Werts) Lutheran, Millersburg, Dauphin Co, PA

Citation: PA & Other Assorted Data, R Howard, rmhoward45@@aol.com, awt.anecstry.com.

Gieseman, John William

Birth: March 23, 1761 in Lebanon, Lancaster (Lebanon) Co, PA

Death: August 26, 1843 in Dauphin Co, PA

Burial: August 1843 in St. Johns (Hill) Lutheran, Berrysburg, Dauphin Co, PA

Source Title: **Pats Family**

Citation: Pats Family, Pat Scott, pat.scott@@comcast.net, awt.ancestry.com.

Jury, Susan

Birth: 1755 in Upper Paxton, Lancaster (Dauphin) Co, PA

Messerschmidt, Maria Elizabeth

Birth: 1784 in Elizabethville, Lancaster (Dauphin) Co, PA

Death: 1850 in Gratz, Dauphin Co, PA

Welker, Valentine

Death: 1831 in Carsonville, Dauphin Co, PA

Citation: Pats Family, Pat Scott, pat.scott@@comcast.net, awt.anecstry.com.

Welker, Valentine

Birth: January 11, 1755 in Frankenthal, Rhineland-Palatinate, Germany

Source Title: **Peter Batdorf**

Citation: Peter Batdorf, Descendants of Peter Batdorf, Evelyn S Hartman, deanh@@voicenet.com.

Lettich, Magdalena "Mollie"

Death: 1891

Marlow, Margaret Elizabeth

Death: 2004 in PA

Rickert, Lucetta

Death: 1867

Russell, Joseph

Source Title: Peter Batdorf (con't)

Citation: Peter Batdorf, Descendants of Peter Batdorf, Evelyn S Hartman, deanh@@voicenet.com.

Russell, Joseph

Death: 1901

Smith, James H

Death: 1904

Citation: Peter Batdorf, Descendants of Peter Batdorf, Evelyn S. Hartman.

Batdorf, George Peter

Death: Bet. 1830–1840 in OH; PA

Steiner, Maria Catherine

Birth: Abt. 1790 in Berks Co, PA

Citation: Peter Batdorf, Hoffmans Reformed Church, Lykens Valley, Dauphin Co, PA, Historical & Genealogical, pp 227-8.

Batdorf, Peter

Death: December 05, 1880 in Lykens, Dauphin Co, PA

Citation: Peter Batdorf, Probate files, 1829, Letter of Admin, P248 A, Dauphin County Courthouse, Reg of Wills, Deborah Hershey, Elizabethtown, PA, Mar 2008.

Batdorf, Jacob Peter

Prob: 1829 in Dauphin Co, PA (listed in index only)

Citation: Peter Batdorf, Probate files, 1881, Affidavit Rep #5, Dauphin County Courthouse, Reg of Wills, Deborah Hershey, Elizabethtown, PA, Mar 2008.

Batdorf, Peter

Death: December 05, 1880 in Lykens, Dauphin Co, PA

Prob: January 04, 1881 in Dauphin Co, PA

Citation: Peter Batdorf, St. Peters (Hoffmans) Union Church, Burials.

Batdorf, Peter

Birth: January 20, 1814 in Dauphin Co, PA

Death: December 05, 1880 in Lykens, Dauphin Co, PA

Burial: 1880 in St. Peters (Hoffman) Reformed, Loyalton, Dauphin Co, PA

Source Title: Peter Botdorf

Citation: Peter Botdorf, St. Peter's (Hoffman's) Union Church, Lykens, Dauphin Co, PA, Gert Mysliwski, gert@@foothill.net.

Batdorf, Peter

Birth: January 20, 1814 in Dauphin Co, PA

Death: December 05, 1880 in Lykens, Dauphin Co, PA

Source Title: Peters household

Citation: Peters household, 1810 United States Census, Northumberland Co, PA, ancestry.com & Microfilm, PA State Library, Hbg, PA.

Peters, John

Census: 1810

Citation: Peters household, 1820 United States Census, Union Co, PA, ancestry.com & Microfilm, PA State Library, Hbg, PA.

Peters, John

Census: 1820 in Buffalo, Union Co, PA

Citation: Peters household, 1830 United States Census, Union Co, PA, ancestry.com & Microfilm, PA State Library, Hbg, PA.

Peters, John

Census: 1830 in Buffalo, Union Co, PA

Peters, Samuel

Source Title: **Peters household (con't)**

Citation: Peters household, 1830 United States Census, Union Co, PA, ancestry.com & Microfilm, PA State Library, Hbg, PA.

Peters, Samuel

Census: 1830 in Buffalo, Union Co, PA

Citation: Peters household, 1850 United States Census, Dauphin Co, PA, FTM CD305, Disk 10, film 831.

Peters, Samuel

Census: 1850 in Union, Union Co, PA

Occu: 1850; Laborer

Citation: Peters household, 1850 United States Census, Dauphin Co, PA, Pam Patton, poohie@@penn.com.

Peters, Samuel

Census: 1850 in Union, Union Co, PA

Occu: 1850; Laborer

Citation: Peters household, 1850 United States Federal Census, Union, PA, 288, ancestry.com & Microfilm, PA State Library, Hbg, PA.

Maria, Anna

Birth: Abt. 1792 in PA

Census: 1850 in East Buffalo, Union Co, PA

Citation: Peters household, 1860 United States Census, Dauphin Co, PA, Series M653, Roll 1103, p 568, ancestry.com & Microfilm, PA State Library, Hbg, PA.

Peters, Mary Louisa

Census: 1860 in Mifflin, Dauphin Co, PA

Peters, Samuel

Census: 1860 in Mifflin, Dauphin Co, PA

Occu: 1860; Laborer

Propty: 1860 in $150

Citation: Peters household, 1870 United States Census, Dauphin Co, PA, Series M593, Roll 1335 p 538, ancestry.com & Microfilm, PA State Library, Hbg, PA.

Swartz, Mary Ann

Census: 1870 in Lykens, Dauphin Co, PA

Propty: 1870 in $100

Occu: 1870; Keeping house

Source Title: **Peters Research**

Citation: Peters Research, Michael McCormick, Enduring Legacy, Gardners, PA, Feb 2009.

Maria, Anna

Marr: Abt. 1815 in Union Co, PA

Birth: Abt. 1792 in PA

Peters, John

Marr: Abt. 1815 in Union Co, PA

Birth: Abt. 1785 in NJ

Death: Abt. 1846 in Buffalo, Union Co, PA

Source Title: **Phalatien Welcker**

Citation: Phalatien Welcker, Probate files, 1, Bk D, vol 1, p261, Lancaster County Archives Division, Lancaster Co Courthouse, Lancaster, PA, Deborah Hershey, Elizabethtown, PA, Mar 2008.

Welker, Valentine

Prob: October 22, 1782 in Lancaster Co, PA

Will: January 06, 1778 in Donegal Tp, Lancaster Co, PA

Source Title: **Pottorff household**

Citation: Pottorff household, 1800 United States Federal Census, Dauphin Co, PA, ancestry.com & Microfilm, PA State Library, Hbg, PA.

Batdorf, George Peter

Census: 1800 in Heidelberg, Dauphin Co, PA

Batdorf, Jacob Peter

Census: 1800 in father; Heidelberg, Dauphin Co, PA w

Source Title: **Rau/Row**

Citation: Rau/Row, PA Births, Dauphin County, J. Humphrey.

Rowe, John William

Relgn: Bet. 1812–1820; St. Johns (Hill) Lutheran, Lykens, Dauphin Co, PA

Source Title: **Roote household**

Citation: Roote household, 1810 United States Census, Lancaster Co, PA, ancestry.com & Microfilm, PA State Library, Hbg, PA.

Rudy, Jacob

Census: 1810 in Donegal, Lancaster Co, PA

Source Title: **Rosie household**

Citation: Rosie household, 1820 United States Census, Dauphin Co, PA, ancestry.com & Microfilm, PA State Library, Hbg, PA.

Rowe, John William

Occu: 1820; Agriculture

Source Title: **Rough household**

Citation: Rough household, 1800 United States Census, Lancaster Co, PA, ancestry.com & Microfilm, PA State Library, Hbg, PA.

Rowe, Francis "Frank"

Census: 1800 in Strasburg, Lancaster Co, PA (Rough)

Source Title: **Row household**

Citation: Row household, 1820 United States Census, Dauphin Co, PA, ancestry.com & Microfilm, PA State Library, Hbg, PA.

Row, Daniel

Census: 1820 in father; Mifflin, Dauphin Co, PA w

Citation: Row household, 1830 United States Census, Dauphin Co, PA, ancestry.com & Microfilm, PA State Library, Hbg, PA.

Row, Daniel

Census: 1830 in father; Halifax, Dauphin Co, PA w

Citation: Row household, 1840 United States Census, Dauphin Co, PA, ancestry.com & Microfilm, PA State Library, Hbg, PA.

Rowe, John William

Census: 1840 in Wiconisco, Dauphin Co, PA

Citation: Row household, 1850 United States Census, Dauphin Co, PA, ancestry.com & Microfilm, PA State Library, Hbg, PA.

Rowe, John William

Occu: Bet. 1850–1870; Laborer

Propty: 1850 in $150

Citation: Row household, 1850 United States Census, Dauphin Co, PA, ancestry.com & Microfilm, PA State Library, Hbg, PA.

Rowe, John William

Census: 1850 in Wiconisco, Dauphin Co, PA

Source Title: Row household (con't)

Citation: Row household, 1850 United States Census, Dauphin Co, PA, PA State library microfilm.

Row, Daniel

Census: 1850 in Washington, Dauphin Co, PA

Propty: 1850 in $240

Occu: Bet. 1850–1870; Laborer

Citation: Row household, 1860 United States Census, Dauphin Co, PA, ancestry.com & Microfilm, PA State Library, Hbg, PA.

Row, Daniel

Census: 1860 in Washington, Dauphin Co, PA

Propty: 1860 in $9450 + $200

Occu: Bet. 1850–1870; Laborer

Rowe, John William

Census: 1860 in Wiconisco, Dauphin Co, PA

Propty: 1860 in $100

Occu: Bet. 1850–1870; Laborer

Citation: Row household, 1860 United States Census, Dauphin Co, PA, PA State library microfilm.

Row, Adeline

Census: 1860 in Washington, Dauphin Co, PA

Row, Daniel

Census: 1860 in Washington, Dauphin Co, PA

Occu: Bet. 1850–1870; Laborer

Citation: Row household, 1870 United States Census, Dauphin Co, PA, Roll M593-1335, p 710, Image 542, ancestry.com & Microfilm, PA State Library, Hbg, PA.

Rowe, John William

Census: 1870 in Washington, Dauphin Co, PA

Occu: Bet. 1850–1870; Laborer

Rudy, Barbara

Census: 1870 in Washington, Dauphin Co, PA

Occu: 1870; Keeping house

Citation: Row household, 1880 United States Census, Dauphin Co, PA, FHL 1255124, Film T9-1124, p 244A, www.familysearch.org.

Rudy, Barbara

Census: 1880 in son Jacob; Washington, Dauphin Co, PA w

Occu: 1880; Lady

Citation: Row household, 1880 United States Census, Dauphin Co, PA, FHLF 1255124, NA film T9-1124, p 245c, ancestry.com & Microfilm, PA State Library, Hbg, PA.

Swartz, Mary Ann

Census: 1880 in Washington, Dauphin Co, PA (Row)

Occu: 1880; Retired house keeper

Source Title: Rowe family information

Citation: Rowe family information, Howard E Row, Dover, DE.

Frantz, Susan

Birth: March 23, 1819 in Dauphin Co, PA

Death: October 17, 1861 in Berrysburg, Dauphin Co, PA

Jungblut, Susan

Burial: 1833 in St. Peters (Hoffman) Reformed, Loyalton, Dauphin Co, PA

Row, Daniel

Birth: July 10, 1813 in Dauphin Co, PA

Source Title: **Rowe family information (con't)**

Citation: Rowe family information, Howard E Row, Dover, DE.

Row, Daniel

Death: July 31, 1871 in Dauphin Co, PA; Bright's disease (ie, Chronic inflammation of kidneys)

Baptism: August 14, 1813 in St. Johns (Hill) Lutheran, Berrysburg, Dauphin Co, PA

Rowe, Francis "Frank"

Burial: 1806 in Lancaster Co, PA

Rowe, John William

Marr: 1810 in Strasburg, Lancaster Co, PA

Burial: 1877 in St. Johns (Hill) Lutheran, Berrysburg, Dauphin Co, PA

Rudy, Barbara

Marr: 1810 in Strasburg, Lancaster Co, PA

Death: December 15, 1881 in Berrysburg, Dauphin Co, PA

Burial: 1881 in St. Johns (Hill) Lutheran, Berrysburg, Dauphin Co, PA

Rudy, Jacob

Burial: 1813 in Greensburg Cemetery, Lancaster, Lancaster Co, PA

Traut, Maria Catherine

Burial: 1813 in Lancaster Co, PA

Citation: Rowe family information, Janet Welty, JNWelty@@aol.com.

Rowe, Francis "Frank"

Death: Bet. January 08–13 1806 in Lancaster Co, PA

Citation: Rowe family information, Jean Row Romberger, Allentown, PA, jmrrrer@@juno.com.

Rowe, Francis "Frank"

Prob: January 13, 1806 in Lancaster Co, PA

Traut, Maria Catherine

Birth: January 24, 1748 in Paradise, Lancaster, PA

Citation: Rowe family information, St. Michaels Lutheran Church, Strasburg, PA, 1753-1816, Lancaster County Historical Society.

Rowe, Francis "Frank"

Relgn: 1791; St. Michaels Lutheran Church, Strasburg, PA

Citation: Rowe family information, St. Michaels Lutheran Churchyard, Lancaster Co, PA, Lancaster County Historical Society.

Elizabeth, Catherine

Death: 1848

Source Title: **Rowe household**

Citation: Rowe household, 1790 United States Census, Lancaster Co, PA, ancestry.com & Microfilm, PA State Library, Hbg, PA.

Rowe, John William

Census: 1790 in father; Strasburg, Lancaster Co, PA w

Citation: Rowe household, 1800 United States Census, Lancaster Co, PA, ancestry.com & Microfilm, PA State Library, Hbg, PA.

Rowe, John William

Census: 1800 in father age 16; Strasburg, Lancaster Co, PA w

Citation: Rowe household, 1820 United States Census, Dauphin Co, PA, ancestry.com & Microfilm, PA State Library, Hbg, PA.

Jungblut, Susan

Census: 1820 in Mifflin, Dauphin Co, PA

Rowe, John William

Census: 1820 in Mifflin, Dauphin Co, PA (Rosie)

Source Title: **Rowe household (con't)**

Citation: Rowe household, 1820 United States Census, Dauphin Co, PA, PA State library microfilm.

Rowe, John William

Census: 1820 in Mifflin, Dauphin Co, PA (Rosie)

Citation: Rowe household, 1830 United States Census, Dauphin Co, PA, ancestry.com & Microfilm, PA State Library, Hbg, PA.

Rowe, John William

Census: 1830 in Halifax, Dauphin Co, PA

Citation: Rowe household, 1830 United States Census, Dauphin Co, PA, PA State library microfilm.

Rowe, John William

Census: 1830 in Halifax, Dauphin Co, PA

Citation: Rowe household, 1840 United States Census, Dauphin Co, PA, ancestry.com & Microfilm, PA State Library, Hbg, PA.

Row, Daniel

Census: 1840 in Wiconisco, Dauphin Co, PA

Citation: Rowe household, 1840 United States Census, Dauphin Co, PA, PA State library microfilm.

Row, Daniel

Census: 1840 in Wiconisco, Dauphin Co, PA

Source Title: **Rudy household**

Citation: Rudy household, 1790 United States Census, Dauphin Co, PA, Roll M637 8, p 88, Image 0352, ancestry.com & Microfilm, PA State Library, Hbg, PA.

Rudy, Jonas

Census: 1790 in Dauphin Co, PA

Citation: Rudy household, 1800 United States Census, Dauphin Co, PA, Roll M32 40, p 266, Image 54, ancestry.com & Microfilm, PA State Library, Hbg, PA.

Rudy, Jonas

Census: 1800 in Bethel, Dauphin (Lebanon) Co, PA (Jones)

Citation: Rudy household, 1800 United States Census, Lancaster Co, PA, ancestry.com & Microfilm, PA State Library, Hbg, PA.

Rudy, Barbara

Census: 1800 in father; Lancaster Co, PA w

Citation: Rudy household, 1810 United States Census, Dauphin Co, PA, ancestry.com & Microfilm, PA State Library, Hbg, PA.

Rudy, Jonas

Census: 1810 in Hanover, Dauphin (Lebanon) Co, PA

Citation: Rudy household, 1830 United States Census, Lebanon Co, PA, Roll M19 154, p 12, Image 27, ancestry.com & Microfilm, PA State Library, Hbg, PA.

Overcash, Anna Barbara

Census: 1830 in Bethel, Lebanon Co, PA

Source Title: **Samuel Peters**

Citation: Samuel Peters, Descendants of John Peters, Evelyn S. Hartman.

Batdorf, James "Edward"

Marr: February 08, 1908 in Oakdale Church, Dauphin Co, PA

Baptism: June 06, 1886 in Oakdale Church Circuit, Dauphin Co, PA

Batdorf, Myrtle Adeline

Marr: June 15, 1935 in St. Johns (Hill) Lutheran, Lykens, Dauphin Co, PA

Baptism: October 11, 1918 in Evangelical Lutheran Circuit, Lykens, Dauphin Co, PA

Source Title: **Samuel Peters (con't)**

Citation: Samuel Peters, Descendants of John Peters, Evelyn S. Hartman.

Batdorf, Thomas Edward

Marr: December 06, 1874 in Rev. W.G. Engle, Dauphin Co, PA

Baptism: October 12, 1851 in St. Peters (Hoffmans) Church, Lykens, Dauphin Co, PA

Peters, Mary Louisa

Marr: December 06, 1874 in Rev. W.G. Engle, Dauphin Co, PA

Death: August 03, 1924 in Home, Elizabethville, Dauphin Co, PA; Cerebral hemorrhage

Thompson, Harper Bruce

Marr: June 15, 1935 in St. Johns (Hill) Lutheran, Lykens, Dauphin Co, PA

Wert, Beulah Irene

Marr: February 08, 1908 in Oakdale Church, Dauphin Co, PA

Baptism: May 18, 1890 in St. Johns (Hill) Lutheran, Berrysburg, Dauphin Co, PA

Source Title: **Sarah Elizabeth Faber Wert**

Citation: Sarah Elizabeth Faber Wert, HSMUP, Mbg, PA 17061, via mail, not dated or cited.

Faber, Sarah Elizabeth

Burial: 1902 in St. Peters (Fetterhoff) Union, Halifax, Dauphin Co, PA

Source Title: **Schamper?/Buffington household**

Citation: Schamper?/Buffington household, 1850 United States Census, Dauphin Co, PA, PA State library microfilm.

Wert, David M

Occu: 1850; Laborer

Source Title: **Schitz family information**

Citation: Schitz family information, PA Births, Dauphin County, J. Humphrey.

Sheets, John George

Relgn: Bet. 1799–1814; Salem Reformed Church, Harrisburg, Dauphin Co, PA

Source Title: **Schneider-Cornelius (7/2000)**

Citation: Schneider-Cornelius (7/2000), Lynn Schneider, JLynnAS@@aol.com, awt.ancestry.com.

Guerne, Catherine

Birth: December 25, 1720 in Eschert, Berne, Switzerland

Joray, Abraham

Death: December 1785 in Upper Paxton, Dauphin Co, PA

Jury, Susan

Birth: 1755 in Upper Paxton, Lancaster (Dauphin) Co, PA

Welker, Valentine

Death: 1831 in Carsonville, Dauphin Co, PA

Baptism: January 14, 1755 in Germany

Immigr: October 16, 1772 in Germany to USA (ship Crawford)

Naturl: December 28, 1772

Source Title: **Schupp family information**

Citation: Schupp family information, untitled, Jonathan Wert.

Deibler, Anna Maria Elizabeth

Marr: 1779 in Lancaster (Dauphin) Co, PA

Birth: January 10, 1760 in Millersburg, Lancaster (Dauphin) Co, PA

Miller, Anna Margaret

Source Title: **Schupp family information (con't)**

Citation: Schupp family information, untitled, Jonathan Wert.

Miller, Anna Margaret
Death: July 24, 1857 in Dauphin Co, PA
Burial: 1857 in Zion (Stone Valley) Lutheran, Dalmatia, Northumberland Co, PA

Schupp, John George
Birth: May 1780 in Upper Paxton, Lancaster (Dauphin) Co, PA

Schupp, John George
Marr: 1779 in Lancaster (Dauphin) Co, PA
Death: August 27, 1839 in Millersburg, Dauphin Co, PA
Baptism: September 01, 1759 in Trinity Lutheran, New Holland, Lancaster Co, PA

Source Title: **Sheets household**

Citation: Sheets household, 1790 United States Census, Dauphin Co, PA, ancestry.com & Microfilm, PA State Library, Hbg, PA.

Sheetz, John George
Census: 1790 in Dauphin Co, PA

Source Title: **Sheetz family information**

Citation: Sheetz family information, Connie Sheets, clsheets1@@prodigy.net.

Shuetz, George
Death: Abt. 1768 in Lancaster (Dauphin) Co, PA

Citation: Sheetz family information, Rob Sheetz, Robsheetz32@@wmconnect.com.

Forman, Mary "Polly"
Birth: January 05, 1778 in PA
Death: June 03, 1848 in Dauphin Co, PA

Sheets, John George
Birth: Bet. 1773–1774 in Paxtang, Lancaster (Dauphin) Co, PA
Death: 1822 in Dauphin Co, PA

Sheetz, John George
Birth: 1746 in PA

Wolfkill, Anna Margaret
Birth: July 16, 1732 in Neider-Hilbersheim, Rhineland-Palatinate, Germany

Source Title: **Sheetz household**

Citation: Sheetz household, 1810 United States Census, Dauphin Co, PA, Series M252, Roll 54, Part 1, p 99, ancestry.com & Microfilm, PA State Library, Hbg, PA.

Sheets, John George
Census: 1810 in Swatara, Dauphin Co, PA (Shits)

Source Title: **Shetz household**

Citation: Shetz household, 1800 United States Census, Dauphin Co, PA, ancestry.com & Microfilm, PA State Library, Hbg, PA.

Sheets, John George
Census: 1800 in Upper Paxton, Dauphin Co, PA

Citation: Shetz household, 1820 United States Census, Dauphin Co, PA, ancestry.com & Microfilm, PA State Library, Hbg, PA.

Forman, Mary "Polly"
Census: 1820 in husband; Susquehanna, Dauphin Co, PA w

Sheets, John George
Census: 1820 in Susquehanna, Dauphin Co, PA

Source Title: **Shetz household (con't)**

Source Title: **Shoop family information**

Citation: Shoop family information, Are you my cousin, Harold Ward, haroldw1@@juno.com, awt.ancestry.com.

Shoop, John
Birth: August 01, 1805 in Dauphin Co?, PA
Death: December 13, 1858 in Lower Mahanoy, Northumberland Co, PA

Wert, David M
Burial: December 12, 1900 in Calvary United Methodist (aka Union), Wiconisco, Dauphin Co, PA

Wertz, Sarah
Birth: Abt. 1811 in Northumberland Co, PA

Citation: Shoop family information, Are you my cousin, Howard Ward, haroldw1@@juno.com, awt.ancestry.com.

Shoop, Catherine
Birth: February 24, 1830 in Northumberland Co, PA
Death: June 08, 1872 in Dauphin Co, PA
Burial: 1872 in St. Peters (Hoffman) Reformed, Loyalton, Dauphin Co, PA

Wert, David M
Birth: April 01, 1829 in Powells Valley, Dauphin Co, PA
Death: December 09, 1900 in Dayton, Dauphin Co, PA; Congestion of Lungs

Citation: Shoop family information, Northumberland Co County, PA 1777-1865, Stone Valley Lutheran, www.ancestry.com.

Shoop, John
Birth: August 01, 1805 in Dauphin Co?, PA

Source Title: **Shoop household**

Citation: Shoop household, 1800 United States Census, Dauphin Co, PA, ancestry.com & Microfilm, PA State Library, Hbg, PA.

Schupp, John George
Census: 1800 in father; Upper Paxton, Dauphin Co, PA w
Census: 1830 in Upper Paxton, Dauphin Co, PA

Citation: Shoop household, 1810 United States Census, Dauphin Co, PA, ancestry.com & Microfilm, PA State Library, Hbg, PA.

Schupp, John George
Census: 1810 in Upper Paxton, Dauphin Co, PA

Schupp, John George
Census: 1810 in Upper Paxton, Dauphin Co, PA

Shoop, John
Census: 1810 in father; Upper Paxton, Dauphin Co, PA w

Citation: Shoop household, 1820 United States Census, Dauphin Co, PA, ancestry.com & Microfilm, PA State Library, Hbg, PA.

Schupp, John George
Census: 1820 in Upper Paxton, Dauphin Co, PA
Occu: 1820; Agriculture

Schupp, John George
Census: 1820 in Upper Paxton, Dauphin Co, PA

Shoop, John
Census: 1820 in father; Upper Paxton, Dauphin Co, PA w

Citation: Shoop household, 1830 United States Census, Dauphin Co, PA, ancestry.com & Microfilm, PA State Library, Hbg, PA.

Schupp, John George

Source Title: **Shoop household (con't)**

Citation: Shoop household, 1830 United States Census, Dauphin Co, PA, ancestry.com & Microfilm, PA State Library, Hbg, PA.

Schupp, John George

Census: 1830 in Upper Paxton, Dauphin Co, PA

Citation: Shoop household, 1830 United States Census, Northumberland Co, PA, ancestry.com & Microfilm, PA State Library, Hbg, PA.

Shoop, John

Census: 1830 in Lower Mahanoy, Northumberland Co, PA

Citation: Shoop household, 1840 United States Census, Dauphin Co, PA, 344, ancestry.com & Microfilm, PA State Library, Hbg, PA.

Schupp, John George

Census: 1840 in Upper Paxton, Dauphin Co, PA

Citation: Shoop household, 1840 United States Census, Northumberland Co, PA, ancestry.com & Microfilm, PA State Library, Hbg, PA.

Shoop, Catherine

Census: 1840 in father; Lower Mahanoy, Northumberland Co, PA w

Citation: Shoop household, 1850 United States Census, Dauphin Co, PA, ancestry.com & Microfilm, PA State Library, Hbg, PA.

Schupp, John George

Census: 1850 in Mifflin, Dauphin Co, PA

Propty: 1850 in $1100

Shoop, John

Census: 1850 in Lower Mahanoy, Northmuberland, PA (Joyn)

Propty: 1850 in $800

Occu: 1850; Farmer

Citation: Shoop household, 1850 United States Census, Northumberland Co, PA, ancestry.com & Microfilm, PA State Library, Hbg, PA.

Shoop, Catherine

Census: 1850 in Lower Mahanoy, Northumberland Co, PA

Source Title: **Shrott**

Citation: Shrott, PA Births, Lebanon County, J. Humphrey.

Schrot, John

Relgn: 1750; Tabor Reformed, Lebanon, Lebanon,PA

Source Title: **Shup household**

Citation: Shup household, 1800 United States Census, Dauphin Co, PA, ancestry.com & Microfilm, PA State Library, Hbg, PA.

Schupp, John George

Census: 1800 in Upper Paxton, Dauphin Co, PA

Source Title: **Soop household**

Citation: Soop household, 1790 United States Census, Dauphin Co, PA, M637-8, p 92, Iamge 0373, ancestry.com & Microfilm, PA State Library, Hbg, PA.

Schupp, John George

Census: 1790 in Dauphin Co, PA (Soop)

Source Title: **Sophia Miller Wirth**

Citation: Sophia Miller Wirth, Wirth's Evangelical Lutheran Church Cemetery, Dauphin Co, PA, www.USGenweb.com, Jonathan Wert.

Miller, Anna Sophia

Birth: August 02, 1776 in Millersburg, Lancaster (Dauphin) Co, PA

Source Title: **Sophia Miller Wirth (con't)**

Citation: Sophia Miller Wirth, Wirth's Evangelical Lutheran Church Cemetery, Dauphin Co, PA, www.USGenweb.com, Jonathan Wert.

Miller, Anna Sophia

Death: October 22, 1842 in Lykens, Dauphin Co, PA

Source Title: **Sproat household**

Citation: Sproat household, 1790 United States Census, Lancaster Co, PA, Roll M637-8, p 139, Image 0761, ancestry.com.

Schrot, John

Census: 1790 in Little Britian, Lancaster Co, PA (Sproat)

Citation: Sproat household, 1790 United States Census, Lancaster Co, PA, Roll M637-8, p 139, Image 0761, ancestry.com.

<No name>

Census: 1790 in Little Britian, Lancaster Co, PA (Sproat)

Source Title: **Susanna Frantz**

Citation: Susanna Frantz, Dauphin County, Pennnsylavnia, 1800-55, St. Peters (Hoffmans) Church, Lykens, Dauphin Co, PA, www.ancestry.com.

Gieseman, Susan

Res: Bet. 1816–1824 in Dauphin County, PA

Source Title: **Susanna Franz**

Citation: Susanna Franz, St. John's Congr., 17 feb 1826, Mifflin, Dauphin Co, PA, Gert Mysliwski, gert@@foothill.net.

Gieseman, Susan

Death: February 15, 1826 in Mifflin, Dauphin Co, PA; Pilger Fieber u. Kindes Nothen (ie, Pilgrim fever)

Baptism: May 30, 1788 in PA

Burial: February 17, 1826 in St. Johns (Hill) Lutheran, Berrysburg, Dauphin Co, PA

Citation: Susanna Franz, St. John's Congr., 17 feb 1826, Mifflin, Dauphin Co, PA, Gert, gert@@foothill.net.

Frantz, Adam

Marr: October 06, 1811 in Upper Paxton, Dauphin Co, PA

Gieseman, Susan

Marr: October 06, 1811 in Upper Paxton, Dauphin Co, PA

Source Title: **Susanna Jury (Schorah)**

Citation: Susanna Jury (Schorah), 1759, Salem Lutheran Church, Millersburg, Dauphin Co, PA, www.genealogy.com.

Jury, Susan

Baptism: 1759 in Salem Lutheran, Millersburg, Lancaster (Dauphin) Co, PA

Source Title: **Susanna Rowe**

Citation: Susanna Rowe, St. John Evangelical Lutheran Church, Berrysburg, PA, Sara S. Neagley, Elizabethville, PA, 424 6M 24D.

Frantz, Susan

Burial: 1861 in St. Johns (Hill) Lutheran, Berrysburg, Dauphin Co, PA

Citation: Susanna Rowe, St. John Evangelical Lutheran Church, Berrysburg, PA, Sara S. Neagley, Elizabethville, PA.

Frantz, Susan

Birth: March 23, 1819 in Dauphin Co, PA

Death: October 17, 1861 in Berrysburg, Dauphin Co, PA

Source Title: **Susanna Rowe (con't)**

Source Title: **Swartz household**

Citation: Swartz household, 1820 US Federal Census, Juniata, Perry Co, PA, www.ancestry.com.

Swartz, John

Census: 1820 in Juniata, Perry Co, PA

Citation: Swartz household, 1830 United States Census, Perry Co, PA, ancestry.com & Microfilm, PA State Library, Hbg, PA.

Swartz, Mary Ann

Census: 1830 in Juniata, Perry Co, PA; w/parents

Citation: Swartz household, 1840 United States Census, Perry Co, PA, ancestry.com & Microfilm, PA State Library, Hbg, PA.

Swartz, Mary Ann

Census: 1840 in Juniata, Perry Co, PA; w/parents

Source Title: **The Batdorf Family History**

Citation: The Batdorf Family History, Virgina Faust Batdorf, Mennonite Family History, 1990, Elverson, PA.

Batdorf, George Peter

Death: Aft. 1854

Birth: February 11, 1768 in Lancaster Co, PA

Baptism: February 14, 1768

Res: Abt. 1854 in Forreston, IN

Source Title: **The Jury Family**

Citation: The Jury Family, Gratz History, p 151.

Joray, Abraham

Immigr: September 14, 1754 in Switzerland to USA (ship Nancy)

Relgn: St. Davids (Salem) Reformed, Millersburg, Dauphin Co, PA

Source Title: **The Lunnys**

Citation: The Lunnys, William Lunny, rlunny@@msn.com, awt.ancestry.com.

Rowe, Francis "Frank"

Death: Bet. January 08–13 1806 in Lancaster Co, PA

Rowe, John William

Birth: June 1785 in Strasburg, Lancaster Co, PA

Death: 1877 in Berrysburg, Dauphin Co, PA

Source Title: **The Rudys of Gods House & Related Families**

Citation: The Rudys of Gods House & Related Families, Jonas Rudy, Chapter III, p 66.

Rudy, Jonas

Birth: December 16, 1751 in Bethel, Lancaster (Lebanon) Co, PA

Baptism: December 16, 1751 in Bethel, Lancaster (Lebanon) Co, PA

Miltry: 1781; American Revolution, Private 2nd PA Reg, 3rd Co, 8th class (Lancaster, Capt. Casper Stoever)

Citation: The Rudys of Gods House & Related Families, Jonas Rudy, Chapter III, p 80-81.

Faber, John

Death: July 15, 1828 in Halifax Tp, Dauphin Co, PA

Overcash, Anna Barbara

Marr: Abt. 1773 in Lancaster (Lebanon) Co, PA

Birth: September 28, 1751 in Bethel, Lancaster (Lebanon) Co, PA

Death: April 08, 1836 in Bethel, Lebanon Co, PA

Source Title: **The Rudys of Gods House & Related Families (con't)**

Citation: The Rudys of Gods House & Related Families, Jonas Rudy, Chapter III, p 80-81.

Overcash, Anna Barbara

Burial: 1836 in St. Johns Union Cemetery, Fredericksburg, Dauphin (Lebanon) Co, PA

Rudy, Jonas

Marr: Abt. 1773 in Lancaster (Lebanon) Co, PA

Burial: 1810 in St. Johns Union Cemetery, Fredericksburg, Dauphin (Lebanon) Co, PA

Rudy, Maria "Mollie" Magdalena

Death: January 16, 1845 in Dauphin Co, PA

Birth: April 14, 1784 in Bethel, Lancaster (Lebanon) Co, PA

Baptism: November 14, 1784 in St. Johns Union, Fredericksburg, Lancaster (Lebanon) Co, PA

Burial: 1845 in St. Pauls (Bowermans) Lutheran, Enterline, Dauphin Co, PA

Source Title: **Thomas Batdorf**

Citation: Thomas Batdorf, #0102590, #81400-17, 1916, Department of Vital records, New Castle, PA.

Batdorf, Thomas Edward

Occu: 1916; Laborer

Birth: July 02, 1851 in Big Run, Dauphin Co, PA

Death: August 13, 1916 in Elizabethville, Dauphin Co, PA; Mitral insufficiency & Bright's disease (ie, Chronic inflammation) of kidneys w/

Burial: August 16, 1916 in St. Johns (Oakdale) Cemetery, Loyalton, Dauphin Co, PA

Funrl: 1916 in Buffington Funeral Home, Elizabethville, Dauphin Co, PA

Source Title: **Thompson household**

Citation: Thompson household, 1910 United States Census, Schuylkill Co, PA, www.ancestry.com and 1910 United States Census, Schuylkill Co, PA, ED 62, Sheet 32A, PA State Library.

Thompson, Harper Bruce

Census: 1910 in Porter, Schuylkill Co, PA

Citation: Thompson household, 1920 United States Census, Schuylkill Co, PA, PA State library, microfilm image.

Thompson, Harper Bruce

Census: 1920 in Porter, Schuylkill Co, PA

Citation: Thompson household, 1920 United States Census, Schuylkill Co, PA, Roll T625 1651, ED 84, Image 0280, ancestry.com & Microfilm, PA State Library, Hbg, PA.

Thompson, Harper Bruce

Census: 1920 in Porter, Schuylkill Co, PA

Citation: Thompson household, 1920 United States Census, Schuylkill Co, PA, Roll T625 1651, ED 84, Image 0280, www.ancestry.com and 1920 United States Census, Schuylkill Co, PA, PA State library, microfilm image.

Thompson, Harper Bruce

Educ: 1920; School

Citation: Thompson household, 1940 US Federal census, Bruce Thompson, Snyder, PA, www.ancestry.com.

Batdorf, Myrtle Adeline

Census: 1940 in Tower City, Schuylkill Co, PA

Thompson, Harper Bruce

Census: 1940 in Tower City, Schuylkill Co, PA

Source Title: **Thompson household (con't)**

Citation: Thompson household, 1940 US Federal census, Bruce Thompson, Snyder, PA, www.ancestry.com.

Thompson, Harper Bruce
Occu: Lineman (Bell Telephone Co)

Source Title: **Thompson-Batdorf marriage record**

Citation: Thompson-Batdorf marriage record, Register of Wills, Clerk of Orphans Court, Dauphin Co, PA, 1935.

Batdorf, James "Edward"
Occu: 1935; Laborer

Batdorf, Myrtle Adeline
Marr: June 15, 1935 in St. Johns (Hill) Lutheran, Lykens, Dauphin Co, PA
Birth: January 05, 1918 in Big Run, Dauphin Co, PA

Thompson, Harper Bruce
Marr: June 15, 1935 in St. Johns (Hill) Lutheran, Lykens, Dauphin Co, PA

Wert, Beulah Irene
Occu: 1935; Housewife

Source Title: **Traut family information**

Citation: Traut family information, Craig H. Trout, Family Research Site, January 3, 2004, CraigTrout@@aol.com.

Traut, John Wendel George
Birth: 1689 in Kleinfischlingen, Rhineland-Palatinate, Germany

Traut, Maria Catherine
Birth: January 24, 1748 in Paradise, Lancaster, PA

Source Title: **Trout Family Descendancy**

Citation: Trout Family Descendancy, Descendants of Balthasar Troutc1750750, www.jaknouse.athens.oh.us/genealogy/trout1.html.

Traut, John Wendel George
Birth: 1689 in Kleinfischlingen, Rhineland-Palatinate, Germany
Death: Bet. February–March 1761 in Paradise, Lancaster Co, PA

Walter, Maria Magdalena
Birth: January 1717 in Strasburg, Chester (Lancaster) Co, PA
Death: February 1761 in Paradise, Lancaster Co, PA

Source Title: **Valentin Welcker**

Citation: Valentin Welcker, Immigrants into Pennsylvania, vol 1, ancestry.com.

Welker, Valentine
Immigr: October 16, 1772 in Germany to USA (ship Crawford)

Citation: Valentin Welcker, PA Census,1772-1890 Record, Ronald V Jackson, AIS, ancestry.com.

Welker, Valentine
Res: 1772 in Philadelphia, PA

Citation: Valentin Welcker, Passenger and Immigration Lists Index, 1500-1900, myfamily.com, P. William Filby, ancestry.com.

Welker, Valentine
Immigr: October 16, 1772

Citation: Valentin Welcker, Probate files, 1831, W-4, Roll 43, E-85-4, Dauphin County Courthouse, Reg of Wills, Deborah Hershey, Elizabethtown, PA, Mar 2008.

Welker, Valentine
Will: 1831 in Upper Paxtang Tp, Dauphin Co, PA

Source Title: **Valentine Welcker**

Source Title: **Valentine Welcker (con't)**

Citation: Valentine Welcker, Index of Wills and Estates records of Lancaster Co, PA, 1729-1850, 1782, bk D, p 261, Sue suestu@@chartner.net.

Welker, Valentine

Prob: October 22, 1782 in Lancaster Co, PA

Source Title: **Valentine Welker**

Citation: Valentine Welker, Brenda Wallace, February 10, 1997, wallace@@ccia.com.

Welker, Valentine

Death: 1782 in Donegal, Lancaster Co, PA

Citation: Valentine Welker, Direct Descendants of Valentine (Welcher) Welker, Evelyn S. Hartman.

Welker, John

Birth: August 10, 1783 in Millersburg, Lancaster (Dauphin) Co, PA

Welker, Valentine

Birth: January 11, 1755 in Frankenthal, Rhineland-Palatinate, Germany

Immigr: October 16, 1772 in Germany to USA (ship Crawford)

Welker, Valentine

Immigr: October 16, 1772

Citation: Valentine Welker, Greg Welker, gwelker@@chesapeake.net.

Jury, Susan

Marr: 1783 in Northumberland Co, PA

Welker, Valentine

Marr: 1783 in Northumberland Co, PA

Relgn: 1812; St. Davids (Salem) Reformed, Millersburg, Dauphin Co, PA

Welker, Valentine

Immigr: October 16, 1772

Citation: Valentine Welker, Probate files, 1831, W-4, Roll 43, E-85-4, Dauphin County Courthouse, Reg of Wills, Deborah Hershey, Elizabethtown, PA, Mar 2008.

Welker, Valentine

Prob: 1831 in Upper Paxtang Tp, Dauphin Co, PA

Citation: Valentine Welker, Will D-1-261, Estate Inventory 1782, bv148, f5, Marge Bardeen, 2006, Lancaster County Historical Society, Lancaster, PA.

Welker, Valentine

Prob: October 22, 1782 in Lancaster Co, PA

Source Title: **Veronica Kirstetter**

Citation: Veronica Kirstetter, PA Births, Lebanon County, J. Humphrey.

Kerstetter, Frances

Baptism: April 12, 1752 in St John Hill (Quittaphilla) Lutheran, Cleona, Lancaster (Lebanon) Co, PA

Source Title: **Wartzs household**

Citation: Wartzs household, 1860 United States Census, Northumberland Co, PA, ancestry.com & Microfilm, PA State Library, Hbg, PA.

Wertz, John

Census: 1860 in Lower Mahanoy, Northumberland Co, PA (Wartzs)

Propty: 1860 in $2000 + $214

Occu: 1860; Retired farmer

Source Title: **Welcker Data**

Citation: Welcker Data, Roger Cramer, rogercubs@@aol.com.

Welker, Valentine

Source Title: **Welcker Data (con't)**

Citation: Welcker Data, Roger Cramer, rogercubs@@aol.com.

Welker, Valentine

Birth: January 11, 1755 in Schwandorf, Germany

Source Title: **Welker Family**

Citation: Welker Family, Gratz History, p 450-455.

Messerschmidt, Maria Elizabeth

Birth: 1784 in Elizabethville, Lancaster (Dauphin) Co, PA

Welker, John

Occu: 1843; Weaver

Burial: 1854 in Simeon Union Cemetery, Gratz, Dauphin Co, PA

Welker, Valentine

Census: 1800 in Upper Paxton, Dauphin Co, PA

Relgn: 1812; St. Davids (Salem) Reformed, Millersburg, Dauphin Co, PA

Source Title: **Welker family information**

Citation: Welker family information, Roger Cramer, rogercubs@@aol.com.

Welker, John

Death: November 11, 1854 in Dauphin Co, PA; Influenza

Source Title: **Welker household**

Citation: Welker household, 1790 United States Census, Dauphin Co, PA, ancestry.com & Microfilm, PA State Library, Hbg, PA.

Welker, John

Census: 1790 in father; Dauphin Co, PA w

Citation: Welker household, 1800 United States Census, Dauphin Co, PA, ancestry.com & Microfilm, PA State Library, Hbg, PA.

Welker, John

Census: 1800 in father age 16; Upper Paxton, Dauphin Co, PA w

Citation: Welker household, 1810 United States Census, Dauphin Co, PA, ancestry.com & Microfilm, PA State Library, Hbg, PA.

Welker, Valentine

Census: 1810 in Mifflin, Dauphin Co, PA

Citation: Welker household, 1820 United States Census, Dauphin Co, PA, ancestry.com & Microfilm, PA State Library, Hbg, PA.

Welker, Elizabeth

Census: 1820 in father; Lykens, Dauphin Co, PA w

Welker, John

Census: 1820 in Lykens, Dauphin Co, PA

Occu: 1820; Manufacturing

Welker, Valentine

Census: 1820 in Millersburg, Dauphin Co, PA

Citation: Welker household, 1820 United States Census, Dauphin Co, PA, PA State library microfilm.

Welker, John

Census: 1820 in Lykens, Dauphin Co, PA

Welker, Valentine

Census: 1820 in Millersburg, Dauphin Co, PA

Citation: Welker household, 1821 United States Census, Dauphin Co, PA, Roll M252 54m p 538, Image 123, ancestry.com & Microfilm, PA State Library, Hbg, PA.

Welker, John

Source Title: **Welker household (con't)**

Citation: Welker household, 1821 United States Census, Dauphin Co, PA, Roll M252 54m p 538, Image 123, ancestry.com & Microfilm, PA State Library, Hbg, PA.

Welker, John

Census: 1810 in Northern Dauphin Co, PA

Citation: Welker household, 1830 United States Census, Dauphin Co, PA, ancestry.com & Microfilm, PA State Library, Hbg, PA.

Welker, Elizabeth

Census: 1830 in father; Lykens, Dauphin Co, PA w

Welker, John

Census: 1830 in Lykens, Dauphin Co, PA

Welker, Valentine

Census: 1830 in Millersburg, Dauphin Co, PA

Citation: Welker household, 1830 United States Census, Dauphin Co, PA, PA State library microfilm.

Welker, John

Census: 1830 in Lykens, Dauphin Co, PA

Welker, Valentine

Census: 1830 in Millersburg, Dauphin Co, PA

Citation: Welker household, 1840 United States Census, Dauphin Co, PA, ancestry.com & Microfilm, PA State Library, Hbg, PA.

Welker, John

Census: 1840 in Lykens, Dauphin Co, PA

Citation: Welker household, 1840 United States Census, Dauphin Co, PA, PA State library microfilm.

Welker, John

Census: 1840 in Lykens, Dauphin Co, PA

Citation: Welker household, 1850 United States Census, Dauphin Co, PA, ancestry.com & Microfilm, PA State Library, Hbg, PA.

Welker, John

Census: 1850 in Lykens, Dauphin Co, PA

Occu: 1850; Laborer

Propty: 1850 in $200

Source Title: **Welkers in the USA & Nulls from PA**

Citation: Welkers in the USA & Nulls from PA, Greg Welker, gwelker@@chesapeake.net, awt.ancestry.com.

Schupp, John George

Death: January 20, 1854 in Dauphin Co, PA

Citation: Welkers in the USA & Nulls from PA, Greg Welker, gwelker@@chesapeake.net, awt.ancestry.com.

Batdorf, Peter

Birth: January 20, 1814 in Dauphin Co, PA

Death: December 05, 1880 in Lykens, Dauphin Co, PA

Burial: 1880 in St. Peters (Hoffman) Reformed, Loyalton, Dauphin Co, PA

Deibler, Anna Maria Elizabeth

Birth: January 10, 1760 in Millersburg, Lancaster (Dauphin) Co, PA

Death: April 18, 1840 in Millersburg, Dauphin Co, PA

Messerschmidt, Andrew

Birth: Abt. 1751 in Lancaster Co, PA

Death: 1801 in Upper Paxton, Dauphin Co, PA

Schupp, John George

Source Title: **Welkers in the USA & Nulls from PA (con't)**

Citation: Welkers in the USA & Nulls from PA, Greg Welker, gwelker@@chesapeake.net, awt.ancestry.com.

Schupp, John George
Birth: May 1780 in Upper Paxton, Lancaster (Dauphin) Co, PA
Schupp, John George
Death: August 27, 1839 in Millersburg, Dauphin Co, PA
Welker, Elizabeth
Birth: November 23, 1812 in Dauphin Co?, PA
Death: July 07, 1868 in Dauphin Co, PA
Welker, John
Death: November 11, 1854 in Dauphin Co, PA; Influenza
Burial: 1854 in Simeon Union Cemetery, Gratz, Dauphin Co, PA
Welker, Valentine
Birth: January 11, 1755 in Frankenthal, Rhineland-Palatinate, Germany
Death: 1831 in Carsonville, Dauphin Co, PA

Source Title: **Weller Family Search for Roots**

Citation: Weller Family Search for Roots, Brenda Weller, bfw512@@cognigenmail.com, awt.ancestry.com.

Faber, John
Marr: 1805 in Lancaster (Lebanon) Co, PA
Birth: March 30, 1777 in Lancaster (Lebanon) Co, PA
Rudy, Jonas
Birth: December 16, 1751 in Bethel, Lancaster (Lebanon) Co, PA
Death: December 20, 1810 in Bethel, Dauphin (Lebanon) Co, PA
Burial: 1810 in St. Johns Union Cemetery, Fredericksburg, Dauphin (Lebanon) Co, PA
Rudy, Maria "Mollie" Magdalena
Marr: 1805 in Lancaster (Lebanon) Co, PA
Birth: April 14, 1784 in Bethel, Lancaster (Lebanon) Co, PA

Source Title: **Wendel Traut**

Citation: Wendel Traut, Marriage Records of Rev. John Casper Stoever, http://www.chm.davidson.edu/PAGenWeb/records/StoeverMarriages.txt.

Traut, John Wendel George
Marr: January 23, 1739 in Rev. Stoever, Trinity Lutheran, New Holland, Lancaster Co, PA
Res: 1739 in Lebanon area, PA
Walter, Maria Magdalena
Marr: January 23, 1739 in Rev. Stoever, Trinity Lutheran, New Holland, Lancaster Co, PA
Res: 1739 in Strassburg, PA

Source Title: **Wendell Trout**

Citation: Wendell Trout, Estate Inventory 1760, b124, f8, Marge Bardeen, 2006, Lancaster County Historical Society, Lancaster, PA.

Traut, John Wendel George
Will: February 19, 1760 in Strasburg, Lancaster Co, PA

Source Title: **Wendle Trout**

Citation: Wendle Trout, Wills: Index to Abstracts, 1721-1819, Lancaster County, PA, http://ftp.rootsweb.com/pub/usgenweb/pa/lancaster/wills/willabsurndxr-z.txt.

Traut, John Wendel George

Source Title: **Wendle Trout (con't)**

Citation: Wendle Trout, Wills: Index to Abstracts, 1721-1819, Lancaster County, PA, http://ftp.rootsweb.com/pub/usgenweb/pa/lancaster/wills/willabsurndxr-z.txt.

Traut, John Wendel George
Will: February 19, 1760 in Strasburg, Lancaster Co, PA

Source Title: **Wert Family**

Citation: Wert Family, Jonathan Wert, www.mdi-wert.com.

Shoop, John
Death: December 13, 1858 in Lower Mahanoy, Northumberland Co, PA

Citation: Wert Family, Jonathan Wert.

Faber, Sarah Elizabeth
Marr: Abt. 1828 in Dauphin Co, PA
Birth: May 25, 1807 in Lancaster (Lebanon) Co, PA
Death: April 05, 1902 in Dauphin Co, PA

Miller, Anna Sophia
Birth: August 02, 1776 in Millersburg, Lancaster (Dauphin) Co, PA
Death: October 22, 1842 in Lykens, Dauphin Co, PA
Burial: 1842 in Old Salem (Werts) Lutheran, Millersburg, Dauphin Co, PA

Schnug, Eva Elizabeth
Marr: August 03, 1755 in Rev. Stoever, Bindagles Lutheran, Palmyra, Lancaster (Lebanon) Co, PA

Shoop, Catherine
Birth: February 24, 1830 in Northumberland Co, PA
Death: June 08, 1872 in Dauphin Co, PA
Burial: 1872 in St. Peters (Hoffman) Reformed, Loyalton, Dauphin Co, PA

Wert, David M
Birth: April 01, 1829 in Powells Valley, Dauphin Co, PA

Wert, Jacob
Marr: Abt. 1828 in Dauphin Co, PA
Birth: July 20, 1804 in Lykens, Dauphin Co, PA
Burial: 1890 in St. Peters (Fetterhoff) Union, Halifax, Dauphin Co, PA

Wert, John Henry
Burial: November 02, 1924 in St. Johns (Hill) Lutheran, Berrysburg, Dauphin Co, PA

Wirth, John Adam
Marr: August 03, 1755 in Rev. Stoever, Bindagles Lutheran, Palmyra, Lancaster (Lebanon) Co, PA
Res: 1774 in Millersburg, Lancaster (Dauphin) Co, PA
Birth: August 23, 1727 in Borod, Rhineland-Palatinate, Germany
Death: August 25, 1806 in Upper Paxton, Dauphin Co, PA
Burial: 1806 in Old Salem (Werts) Lutheran, Millersburg, Dauphin Co, PA
Immigr: September 28, 1753 in Germany to USA (ship Two Brothers)

Wirth, John Jacob
Death: January 01, 1833 in Millersburg, Dauphin Co, PA
Burial: January 03, 1833 in Old Salem (Werts) Lutheran, Millersburg, Dauphin Co, PA

Citation: Wert Family.

Faber, Sarah Elizabeth
Burial: 1902 in St. Pauls (Bowermans) Lutheran, Enterline, Dauphin Co, PA

Source Title: **Wert Family History**

Source Title: **Wert Family History (con't)**

Citation: Wert Family History, complied genealogy, Jonathan Wert, www.mdi-wert.com, jwert@@mdi-wert.com.

Faber, Sarah Elizabeth
Burial: 1902 in St. Pauls (Bowermans) Lutheran, Enterline, Dauphin Co, PA

Rudy, Maria "Mollie" Magdalena
Death: July 16, 1845 in Jefferson Tp, Dauphin Co, PA
Baptism: November 14, 1784 in St. Johns Union, Fredericksburg, Lancaster (Lebanon) Co, PA

Schnug, Eva Elizabeth
Death: 1800 in Upper Paxton, Dauphin Co, PA
Burial: Abt. 1800 in Old Salem (Werts) Lutheran, Millersburg, Dauphin Co, PA

Wert, Jacob
Death: 1890 in Halifax, Dauphin Co, PA

Wirth, John Jacob
Birth: February 1763 in Lebanon, Lancaster (Lebanon) Co, PA
Baptism: March 25, 1763 in PA
Burial: January 03, 1833 in Old Salem (Werts) Lutheran, Millersburg, Dauphin Co, PA

Citation: Wert Family History, Jonathan Wert.

Schnug, Eva Elizabeth
Birth: 1730 in Baden-Wurttemberg, Germany

Source Title: **Wert family information**

Citation: Wert family information, Dr. Jonathan Wert.

Miller, Anna Margaret
Birth: February 12, 1784 in Lancaster (Dauphin) Co, PA

Source Title: **Wert household**

Citation: Wert household, 1790 United States Census, Northumberland Co, PA, Roll M637-9, p 183, Image 0257, ancestry.com & Microfilm, PA State Library, Hbg, PA.

Wirth, John Jacob
Census: 1790 in father; Dauphin Co, PA w

Citation: Wert household, 1810 United States Census, Dauphin Co, PA, ancestry.com & Microfilm, PA State Library, Hbg, PA.

Wert, Jacob
Census: 1810 in father; Upper Paxton, Dauphin Co, PA w

Citation: Wert household, 1820 United States Census, Dauphin Co, PA, ancestry.com & Microfilm, PA State Library, Hbg, PA.

Wert, Jacob
Census: 1820 in father; Upper Paxton, Dauphin Co, PA w

Citation: Wert household, 1830 United States Census, Dauphin Co, PA ancestry.com & Microfilm, PA State Library, Hbg, PA.

Wert, Jacob
Census: 1830 in Halifax, Dauphin Co, PA

Citation: Wert household, 1830 United States Census, Dauphin Co, PA, ancestry.com & Microfilm, PA State Library, Hbg, PA.

Wert, David M
Census: 1830 in father; Halifax, Dauphin Co, PA w

Citation: Wert household, 1830 United States Census, Dauphin Co, PA, PA State library microfilm.

Wert, Jacob

Source Title: **Wert household (con't)**

Citation: Wert household, 1830 United States Census, Dauphin Co, PA, PA State library microfilm.

Wert, Jacob

Census: 1830 in Halifax, Dauphin Co, PA

Citation: Wert household, 1840 United States Census, Dauphin Co, PA, ancestry.com & Microfilm, PA State Library, Hbg, PA.

Wert, David M

Census: 1840 in parents; w

Wert, Jacob

Census: 1840

Citation: Wert household, 1850 United States Census, Dauphin Co, PA, PA State library microfilm.

Shoop, Catherine

Census: 1850 in Upper Paxtang, Dauphin Co, PA

Wert, David M

Census: 1850 in Upper Paxton, Dauphin Co, PA

Propty: 1850 in $100

Wert, Jacob

Census: 1850 in Jackson, Dauphin Co, PA

Occu: 1850; Farmer

Citation: Wert household, 1870 United States Census, Dauphin Co, PA, PA State library microfilm.

Shoop, Catherine

Name: Shoop, Catherine

Wert, David M

Census: 1870 in Lykens, Dauphin Co, PA

Propty: 1870 in $1000 + $400

Occu: 1870; Laborer

Wert, John Henry

Census: 1870 in Lykens, Dauphin Co, PA

Citation: Wert household, 1870 United States Census, Lehigh Co, PA, ancestry.com.

Faber, Sarah Elizabeth

Occu: 1870; Keeping house

Wert, Jacob

Propty: 1870 in $100

Occu: 1870; Works on RR

Citation: Wert household, 1870 United States Census, Lehigh Co, PA, ancestry.com.

Wert, Jacob

Census: 1870 in Slatington, Lehigh Co, PA

Citation: Wert household, 1880 United States Census, Dauphin Co, PA, FHL 1255124, Film T9-1124, p 251D, www.familysearch.org.

Row, Adeline

Occu: 1880; Keeping house

Wert, John Henry

Census: 1880 in Washington, Dauphin Co, PA

Occu: 1880; Blacksmith

Citation: Wert household, 1900 United States Census, Dauphin Co, PA, www.ancestry.com and 1900 United States Census, Dauphin Co, PA, Pa State Library microfilm image.

Wert, Beulah Irene

Census: 1900 in Washington, Dauphin Co, PA

Educ: 1900; School

Source Title: **Wert household (con't)**

Citation: Wert household, 1900 United States Census, Dauphin Co, PA, www.ancestry.com and 1900 United States Census, Dauphin Co, PA, Pa State Library microfilm image.

Wert, John Henry

Census: 1900 in Washington, Dauphin Co, PA

Occu: 1900; Day laborer

Citation: Wert household, 1910 United States Census, Dauphin Co, PA, ancestry.com & Microfilm, PA State Library, Hbg, PA.

Wert, John Henry

Census: 1910 in Washington, Dauphin Co, PA (enumerated twice)

Occu: 1910; Laborer (?)

Citation: Wert household, 1920 United States Census, Dauphin Co, PA, PA State Library, microfilm image and 1920 United States Census, Dauphin Co, PA, ancestry.com & Microfilm, PA State Library, Hbg, PA.

Wert, John Henry

Census: 1920 in Washington, Dauphin Co, PA

Citation: Wert household, 1920 United States Census, Dauphin Co, PA, PA State Library, microfilm image and 1920 United States Census, Dauphin Co, PA, www.ancestry.com.

Wert, John Henry

Occu: 1920; Laborer (Coal mine)

Res: 1920 in State Road 199, Washington, Dauphin Co, PA

Source Title: **Wert Sr household**

Citation: Wert Sr household, 1830 United States Census, Dauphin Co, PA, PA State library microfilm.

Wirth, John Jacob

Census: 1830 in Upper Paxton, Dauphin Co, PA

Source Title: **Wert Tree**

Citation: Wert Tree, K Shuey, kshuey208@@hotmail.com, awt.ancestry.com.

Miller, Anna Sophia

Death: October 22, 1842 in Lykens, Dauphin Co, PA

Schnug, Eva Elizabeth

Death: 1800 in Upper Paxton, Dauphin Co, PA

Wirth, John Adam

Birth: August 23, 1727 in Borod, Rhineland-Palatinate, Germany

Death: August 25, 1806 in Upper Paxton, Dauphin Co, PA

Source Title: **Wert, Sr. household**

Citation: Wert, Sr. household, 1820 United States Census, Dauphin Co, PA ancestry.com & Microfilm, PA State Library, Hbg, PA.

Wirth, John Jacob

Census: 1830 in Upper Paxton, Dauphin Co, PA

Citation: Wert, Sr. household, 1830 United States Census, Northumberland Co, PA, ancestry.com & Microfilm, PA State Library, Hbg, PA.

Wertz, John

Census: 1830 in Lower Mahanoy, Northumberland Co, PA (Wert)

Citation: Wert, Sr. household, 1860 United States Census, Northumberland Co, PA, ancestry.com & Microfilm, PA State Library, Hbg, PA.

Wert, David M

Census: 1860 in Lower Mahanoy Northumberland Co, PA

Wert, John Henry

Census: 1860 in Lower Mahanoy, Northumberland Co, PA

Source Title: **Wert, Sr. household (con't)**

Citation: Wert, Sr. household, 1870 United States Census, Roll M593 1335, p 649, Image 420, ancestry.com & Microfilm, PA State Library, Hbg, PA.

Faber, Sarah Elizabeth

Census: 1870 in Upper Paxton, Dauphin Co, PA

Source Title: **Werts (Wertz, Wirtz) Notes**

Citation: Werts (Wertz, Wirtz) Notes, Northumberland Co County Historical Society, pp 1-6.

Wertz, John Deitrich

Death: October 16, 1804 in White Deer, Northumberland (Union) Co, PA

Source Title: **Wertz family information**

Citation: Wertz family information, Bob Messerschmidt, Laurel, MD, SusanM4383@@aol.com.

Garman, Joanna Catherine

Burial: 1864 in Zion (Stone Valley) Lutheran, Dalmatia, Northumberland Co, PA

Shoop, Catherine

Birth: February 24, 1830 in Northumberland Co, PA

Death: June 08, 1872 in Dauphin Co, PA

Burial: 1872 in St. Peters (Hoffman) Reformed, Loyalton, Dauphin Co, PA

Wert, David M

Census: 1870 in Lykens, Dauphin Co, PA

Occu: 1870; Laborer

Wertz, John

Burial: 1861 in Zion (Stone Valley) Lutheran, Dalmatia, Northumberland Co, PA

Wertz, John Deitrich

Census: 1800 in White Deer, Northumberland (Union) Co, PA

Birth: June 24, 1740 in Schwaigern, Baden-Wurttemberg, Germany

Wertz, Sarah

Birth: Abt. 1811 in Northumberland Co, PA

Citation: Wertz family information, Carolyn C. Choppin, Puyallup, WA.

Miller, Mary

Marr: Abt. 1770 in Northumberland?, PA

Death: 1804 in White Deer, Northumberland (Union) Co, PA

Wertz, John Deitrich

Marr: Abt. 1770 in Northumberland?, PA

Birth: June 24, 1740 in Schwaigern, Baden-Wurttemberg, Germany

Death: October 16, 1804 in White Deer, Northumberland (Union) Co, PA

Burial: 1804 in Northumberland Co, PA

Census: 1790 in Northumberland Co, PA (Teterie Vertz)

Res: 1775 in White Deer, Northumberland (Union) Co, PA

Citation: Wertz family information, Cindi Grimm, Grimm@@ruralife.net.

Garman, Joanna Catherine

Birth: August 02, 1791 in PA

Death: September 23, 1864 in Northumberland Co, PA

Shoop, Catherine

Birth: February 24, 1830 in Northumberland Co, PA

Baptism: March 06, 1830 in Zion (Stone Valley) Lutheran, Dalmatia, Northumberland Co, PA

Wertz, John

Census: 1850 in Lower Mahanoy, Northumberland Co, PA (Mertz)

Source Title: **Wertz family information (con't)**

Citation: Wertz family information, Cindi Grimm, Grimm@@ruralife.net.

Wertz, John

Birth: May 05, 1783 in Northumberland (Union) Co, PA

Death: May 13, 1861 in Lower Mahanoy, Northumberland Co, PA

Burial: 1861 in Zion (Stone Valley) Lutheran, Dalmatia, Northumberland Co, PA

Citation: Wertz family information, Northumberland Co County, PA 1777-1865, Stone Valley Lutheran, www.ancestry.com.

Wertz, John

Birth: May 05, 1783 in Northumberland (Union) Co, PA

Source Title: **Wertz household**

Citation: Wertz household, 1810 United States Census, Northumberland Co, PA, ancestry.com & Microfilm, PA State Library, Hbg, PA.

Wertz, John

Census: 1810 in Mahanoy, Northumberland Co, PA

Occu: 1810; Far (Farm)

Citation: Wertz household, 1820 United States Census, Northumberland Co, PA, ancestry.com & Microfilm, PA State Library, Hbg, PA.

Wertz, John

Census: 1820 in Lower Mahanoy, Northumberland Co, PA

Occu: 1820; Agriculture

Wertz, Sarah

Census: 1820 in father; Lower Mahanoy, Northumberland Co, PA w

Citation: Wertz household, 1840 United States Census, Northumberland Co, PA, ancestry.com & Microfilm, PA State Library, Hbg, PA.

Wertz, John

Census: 1840 in Lower Mahanoy, Northumberland Co, PA (Wertz)

Source Title: **William Frantz**

Citation: William Frantz, Hoffman's Church, Dauphin County records, Nancy Hendricks, NJHendricks@@earthlink.net.

Frantz, John William

Relgn: Bet. 1774–1785; St. Peters (Hoffmans) Church, Lykens, Dauphin Co, PA

Citation: William Frantz, July 28, 1804, February 11, 1805, Will Abstracts, Dauphin County, PA p 254.

Frantz, John William

Prob: February 11, 1805 in Dauphin Co, PA

Source Title: **William Gieseman**

Citation: William Gieseman, Probate files, 1843, Bk E, p380, file 3, microfilmG-3 (4427), roll 20, Dauphin County Courthouse, Reg of Wills, Deborah Hershey, Elizabethtown, PA, Mar 2008.

Gieseman, John William

Prob: October 02, 1843 in Mifflin Tp, Dauphin Co, PA

Will: June 23, 1841 in Mifflin Tp, Dauphin Co, PA

Source Title: **William Giessman**

Citation: William Giessman, April 23, 1761, May 26, 1761, Abstracts of Berks Co, PA Wills, 1752-1785.

Gieseman, George William

Source Title: **William Giessman (con't)**

Citation: William Giessman, April 23, 1761, May 26, 1761, Abstracts of Berks Co, PA Wills, 1752-1785.

Gieseman, George William

Will: May 1761 in Tulpehocken, Berks Co, PA

Source Title: **William Row**

Citation: William Row, Probate files, 1873, Letter of Admin, Dauphin County Courthouse, Reg of Wills, Deborah Hershey, Elizabethtown, PA, Mar 2008.

Rowe, John William

Will: April 03, 1873 in Dauphin Co, PA (listed in index)

Source Title: **William Rowe**

Citation: William Rowe, Descendants of Frank (Rau) Rowe, Evelyn S. Hartman.

Rowe, John William

Burial: 1877 in St. Johns (Hill) Lutheran, Berrysburg, Dauphin Co, PA

Rudy, Barbara

Birth: April 11, 1796 in Strasburg, Lancaster Co, PA

Death: December 15, 1881 in Berrysburg, Dauphin Co, PA

Citation: William Rowe, Family Data Collection, Individual Records, www.ancestry.com, Edmund West, comp.

Rowe, John William

Marr: 1810 in Strasburg, Lancaster Co, PA

Birth: June 1785 in Strasburg, Lancaster Co, PA

Death: 1877 in Berrysburg, Dauphin Co, PA

Rudy, Barbara

Marr: 1810 in Strasburg, Lancaster Co, PA

Citation: William Rowe, Rowe family, Onetree, ancestry.com.

Rowe, John William

Birth: June 1785 in Strasburg, Lancaster Co, PA

Citation: William Rowe, St. John Evangelical Lutheran Church, Berrysburg, PA, Sara S. Neagley, Elizabethville, PA, 424 6M 24D.

Rowe, John William

Burial: 1877 in St. Johns (Hill) Lutheran, Berrysburg, Dauphin Co, PA

Source Title: **Wirt household**

Citation: Wirt household, 1810 United States Census, Dauphin Co, PA, ancestry.com & Microfilm, PA State Library, Hbg, PA.

Wirth, John Jacob

Census: 1810 in Upper Paxton, Dauphin Co, PA

Citation: Wirt household, 1820 United States Census, Dauphin Co, PA, Roll M33 102, p 276, Image 114, ancestry.com & Microfilm, PA State Library, Hbg, PA.

Wirth, John Jacob

Census: 1820 in Upper Paxton, Dauphin Co, PA

Occu: 1820; Agriculture

Citation: Wirt household, 1860 United States Census, Dauphin Co, PA, PA State library microfilm.

Wert, Jacob

Census: 1860 in Halifax, Dauphin Co, PA (Wist)

Occu: 1860; Laborer

Propty: 1860 in $500 + $100

Source Title: **Wirth family information**

Citation: Wirth family information, WFT 10, Tree 728, genealogy.com.

Source Title: **Wirth family information (con't)**

Citation: Wirth family information, WFT 10, Tree 728, genealogy.com.

Schnug, Eva Elizabeth

Birth: 1730 in Baden-Wurttemberg, Germany

Wirth, John Adam

Occu: Farmer; Weaver

Immigr: September 28, 1753 in Germany to USA (ship Two Brothers)

Prob: 1807 in Harrisburg, Dauphin Co, PA

Source Title: **Wirth household**

Citation: Wirth household, 1790 United States Census, Northumberland Co, PA, ancestry.com & Microfilm, PA State Library, Hbg, PA.

Wirth, John Jacob

Census: 1790 in father; Dauphin Co, PA w

Source Title: **Wurtz/Werts/Wertz Family**

Citation: Wurtz/Werts/Wertz Family, Our Keystone Families, S.C. Brossman, Rehrersburg, PA.

Wertz, John Deitrich

Res: 1775 in White Deer, Northumberland (Union) Co, PA

Source Title: **Yerigh William Geeseman**

Citation: Yerigh William Geeseman, PA Census, 1772-1890, Philadelphia, PA, www.ancestry.com.

Gieseman, George William

Res: 1741 in Philadelphia, PA

Source Title: **Zerber household**

Citation: Zerber household, 1870 United States Census, Dauphin Co, PA, PA State library microfilm.

Row, Daniel

Census: 1870 in Wiconisco, Dauphin Co, PA

Occu: Bet. 1850–1870; Laborer

Postscript

Goals of avid genealogists, like Marc D Thompson, which includes discovering and preserving one's heritage and acknowledging the contributions of their ancestors is a most worthy aspiration. Though it may seem a simple endeavor, it is indeed a most daunting challenge. Marc's research is a testimony to this fact.

For the serious genealogist, researching one's family is very time consuming. I have personally found that I can become so focused on my research that I lose track of time and have no clue as to anything else that is going on around me. It requires not just a few hours or a few days of research, but rather years and maybe a lifetime. Researching family history is an activity that can be built upon with succeeding generations. Blessed are those for whom it is a family activity. As the Pennsylvania Dutch saying goes, "many hands make light work".

We genealogists have many areas available from which they obtain information. For example, an unfathomable amount of time can be spent looking through dusty books of deed and orphan's court records in musty courthouse basements all the while trying to remember to keep your parking meter plugged. Many lazy days are spent strolling through old country cemeteries with child in tow, a weed clipper and camera trying to locate that one particular person or family and praying that if found the stone is readable. For today's researchers, GPS systems make it a bit easier to navigate through unknown towns and cities trying to locate the local historical society. We hope that when found, it is open and that you might get lucky enough to find a new tidbit of family history somewhere amongst all those shelves of books and manuscripts.

Genealogy research is educational. For example, church records are a wealth of information. From them one may learn where the family lived, went to church, baptized their children and were buried. Census records tell us a lot about our relatives. They tell us the names of a particular household, their relationship, ages, marital status, occupations, value of property and even if they owned a radio. The census can give us a hint as to how a relative figured into historical events…whether it is their participation in a war, the opening of new territory. For example, I had never heard of Ogle Co., IL, or Berrien Co., MI before researching my Wertz family. It's fun to see who and how you are related to others…or not related as you may have believed. You might even find an "important" person in your tree. I found President Dwight D. Eisenhower in my maternal tree. Of course Marc is also a relative.

Frustration comes to all. It can come in the form of the inability to locate that one particular relative who has become a 'brick wall." It can present itself as inconsistent spellings whether by the census, church records, legal documents or individuals themselves. For example, generations past, things were spelled just as they sounded. I have a copy of my great grandfather Michael Wertz's carpentry ledger. What a treasure trove! In it, he wrote things just as they sounded to him. For example, "Bett" meant bed. Frustration can come in the form of misinformation and inaccurate assumptions made by other contributors. Also, many online resources once "free" are now are subscription only. When faced with a frustration, fear not for it will only take one tiny discovery to renew enthusiasm.

Genealogy is truly a "labor of love". The researcher gets to meet many of new "cousins" and to make new friends from places never imagined. When my little community of Malta celebrated its 150th birthday in 2000, we wrote a commemoration book. In the course of my research for it, I learned so much about the people who made up the community. I realized as I walked through the cemetery that I could say to many of those buried there, many of whom had been strangers to me just weeks before, I know you now old friend. I know where you lived. I know what you did. I know how you connect to me. Even now, twelve years later, I feel as though I knew some of those travelers thru life more intimately than some of my living relatives and neighbors.

I share Marc's feelings and enthusiasm for discovering our family's heritage and the desire to pass this heritage onto our children. Marc's book is a direct result of decades of research, with the roller coasters of frustrations and joys of discovery along the way. It is his "labor of love."

-- Cindi Wertz Grimm

Afterword

Without my ancestors, I would have been had the chance to experience the wonders of life. Thank you grandma and grandpa, you have allowed me to see beautiful places, do wonderful things and meet amazing people. This is my testament.

About the Author

Marc D. Thompson delved into writing and genealogy at a very early age. He wrote stories, poems, lyrics and family history books. Marc went on to write and research in high school and college, earning a BS degree from Moravian College. He has presented genealogical lectures and authored seven family history volumes and recently published *The Fitness Book of Lists* and *Virtual Personal Training Manual*. His other published works include other genealogical books and a poetry compilation, with poetic appearances in Fighting Chance Magazine, Love's Chance Magazine, Northern Stars Magazine, Offerings, Poetry Motel, Suzerian Enterprises and The Pink Chameleon.

Thompson currently pens a monthly genealogy blog and a fitness blog at ideafit.com. He.is a member of the Association of Professional Genealogists and has founded a PA Genealogy Society. He was the County Coordinator of the Chatham Co, GA USGenweb site and wrote a monthly genealogy column for Atlantic Avenue Magazine. Writing now for over four decades, when he puts pen to paper, eloquent, heat-felt yet real-life truths emerge. He has been influenced by science, art and his relationships, and yet at the samc time marvels at the cosmically-driven direction he receives from energy around him. Thompson believes in what he calls Creatalytical Thinking: The fusion of creativity and analysis to view life more fully and fulfill his place in this world.

MARC D. THOMPSON, VIRTUFIT.NET™

www.VirtuFit.net - marc@VirtuFit.net - skype: VirtuFit

ideafit: www.ideafit.com/profile/marc-d-thompson

Index of Individuals

Index of Individuals

Index of Individuals

Index of Individuals

Index of Individuals

Index of Individuals

Index of Individuals

Index of Individuals

Index of Individuals

Index of Individuals

Index of Individuals

Index of Individuals

Index of Individuals

www.ingramcontent.com/pod-product-compliance
Lightning Source LLC
Chambersburg PA
CBHW081144270326
41930CB00014B/3031

* 9 7 8 0 9 8 8 3 4 4 0 1 3 *